Escape from Custody

Robert Straus

Escape from Custody

A Study of Alcoholism and Institutional
Dependency as Reflected in the
Life Record of a Homeless Man

HARPER & ROW, PUBLISHERS

New York
Evanston
San Francisco
London

Designed by Dorothy Schmiderer

Library of Congress Cataloging in Publication Data

Straus, Robert.
  Escape from custody.
  Includes bibliographical references.
  1. Moore, Frank, 1904–1972.   2. Alcoholism.
I. Moore, Frank, 1904–1972.   II. Title.
[DNLM: 1. Alcoholism. WM274 S912e 1974]
HV5293.M65S76   362.2'92'0924 [B]   73-14066
ISBN 0-06-014149-2

To the memory of the wise and tragic man,
here called Frank Moore,
whose story this book relates

Contents

Acknowledgments

Frank Moore, whose life record is the basis of this book, was the 13th of 203 men whom I interviewed in a 1945 study of alcohol and the homeless man. My initial contact with Frank led to a study of his life history and eventually to an agreement that we would maintain a prospective record of his experiences and observations, especially as they pertained to alcohol use and institutional living. This relationship with Frank was sustained from 1945 until his death in 1972.

Because the preparation of this book has covered a span of twenty-eight years, it would be impossible to acknowledge appropriately everyone who has, in some way, contributed to it. Of special significance has been the influence of four mentors and colleagues begun during my association from 1945 to 1953 with the Yale Center of Alcohol Studies (since 1962 the Rutgers Center of Alcohol Studies). Selden D. Bacon introduced me to the study of drinking behavior and alcohol problems, arranged for my initial research on alcohol and the homeless man, and has been a valued colleague and supportive friend for nearly thirty years. The late E. M. Jellinek first recognized the significance of Frank Moore's life record and encouraged me to prepare his early life history for publication in 1948. The late Raymond G. McCarthy, as collaborator on a 1951 study of problem drinkers on the New York Bowery, contributed to some of the theoretical ideas which are considered in this book. Mark Keller, editor of the *Quarterly Journal of Studies on Alcohol* in which Frank's story was first told, has been a source of constant encouragement and valuable counsel.

The first draft of this manuscript was prepared during a sabbatical leave from the University of Kentucky, spent in the Department of Sociology at Yale University in 1968–69. Partial support for this period was provided by the National Institute of Mental Health through a Special

Research Fellowship, Grant Number MH 039, 103. Yale University provided an office and an ideal balance of privacy and stimulation. Jerome K. Myers arranged for my visiting professorship at Yale and together with August B. Hollingshead generously shared secretarial and research assistance and provided friendly critical insights.

For many years, discussion of Frank Moore's life has been included in my teaching about dependency behavior and alcohol problems at the University of Kentucky Medical Center. Faculty colleagues, especially in the Department of Behavioral Science, and students, too numerous to name individually here, have reacted to Frank's letters, raised questions, made suggestions, and encouraged me in the preparation of this book.

The typing and filing of my correspondence with Frank was no small task. This was begun by Laura Barress, continued by Marilyn Lose, and Martha C. Lancaster completed that task and has devotedly typed the manuscript through its several revisions. Valuable editorial assistance was provided by Janet Turk, Patricia Parkerton, Sylvia Wrobel, and Carolyn Bacdayan. Mrs. Bacdayan's skillful work merits special recognition and appreciation.

Although there were few personal contacts between Frank and my family, my wife, Ruth, and our now grown children Jim, Carol, Peg, and Bill all were a part of my correspondence with him, as if he were one of us. All have lovingly supported the nights and weekends I have devoted to research and writing.

Frank's mother shared much that was painful from her own life. Although Frank encountered many people who were impersonal and cruel, he also met some who were kind and generous. My special gratitude is expressed to the good lady, here called Andrea Bourne, who took Frank in and nursed him through the last months of his life, providing not only escape from institutional living, but the security of a loving family.

Since this is, in so many respects, Frank Moore's book, my great hope is that the knowledge gained from the detailed record of his tragic life will indeed bring respect and a sense of worth to his memory, anonymous as he will remain. May his life also contribute to the understanding of alcoholism and institutional dependency and furnish insights whereby the wasteful course of other lives can be altered.

R.S.

University of Kentucky College of Medicine
Lexington
April, 1973

Escape from Custody

1. The Institutionally Dependent Alcoholic

In this book a detailed sixty-eight-year record of a human life from birth to death is presented and examined with special reference to two distinctive but often related human problems: alcoholism and institutional dependency. Frank Moore, whose life record illustrates both of these problems, has been uniquely qualified through his intelligence, keen powers of observation, wide reading, acute memory, and flair for writing to provide the core material for this study.

Although alcoholism is a far-reaching human problem found in one form or another among most societies and in all social classes within societies, in all occupations and all adult age groups, it is particularly prevalent among that segment of the population often referred to as homeless men. These are the habitués of skid rows, jails, public hospitals, and live-in-type seasonal or transitory jobs. Their lives are often characterized both by frequent intoxication and by a long-term continuing reliance on some form of institutional living where basic necessities are provided, demands on initiative are minimal, and the details of routine living are prescribed. Since most institutional settings forbid drinking, it follows that homeless men generally drink during periods of freedom from custody; at the same time it has become apparent that many such men want to drink primarily when their dependency needs are not being met by institutional living; and when their anxiety and discomfort are aroused and they feel threatened by having to perform even the most basic and rudimentary social amenities or engage in face-to-face relationships with members of the non-institutionally oriented community. For such men alcohol, by reducing anxiety and lowering inhibitions,

1

makes community existence tolerable until they can again retreat to the relative security of another institutional setting. Often intoxication, necessarily in public, provides the means of gaining access to the security of institutional living.

A primary theme of this book, then, is a pattern of life adaptation which I have called the syndrome of institutional dependency. This pattern is manifested in the life records of untold numbers of people in the United States and in other societies who have become so accustomed to having other people provide for their basic needs and prescribe their daily routine that they have lost their initiative and are unable to function effectively without the security afforded by life in formal or informal institutional settings.

Neither the existence of a degree of dependency on another person nor the mere fact of living or working in an institution necessarily indicates the presence of institutional dependency in an individual. To set our discussion in proper perspective, we must first look at dependency and independence as they exist in the normal family and community setting. We must also look briefly at the complex picture of institutions and institutional living in our society. We may then begin to sort out those characteristics of an individual and an institution that often lend themselves to the development of institutional dependency. In this book we are restricting the use of the term "institution" to include both formal organizations such as the hospital or jail, and various other types of working and living arrangements which also involve isolation from normal family and community living.

Dependency and Independence in the Family and Community

"Dependency" is clearly a relative term. At birth the human infant is totally dependent on others for survival, and the first twenty or more years of life in our society are characterized by the gradual inculcation of independent ways of thinking, feeling, acting, and relating to others. Yet the road to independence is lined with a complex system of checks and balances designed to limit the individual, at any particular time and place, to that degree of independence which is deemed appropriate to his chronological age and to his configuration of roles within the family, social class, and the various community systems of which he is a participant. By virtue of the myriad of specialized roles which individuals fulfill in a complex society, all people are constantly dependent to a degree on others whose activities and roles complement their own. Yet, beyond the vague limits of sanctioned, even required, interdependence, society expects its adult members to exhibit certain traits of self-sufficiency associated with their primary family, economic, and community responsibilities; to exert initiative appropriate to major social roles and their inherent responsibilities; to make necessary decisions; and even to demonstrate the example of mature adult behavior for the benefit of a younger generation.

All people, even the most independent, rely to some degree on institutions. Corporations, churches, and fraternal organizations all are engaged in meeting certain dependency needs of their constituents. But the nondependent person is one whose primary patterns of response include the assumption of responsibility for fulfilling obligations to his family, employer, and the community at large, and who manages to meet his own needs and those of his family with a minimum of outside help. He demonstrates a spirit of self-sufficiency and a willingness to make decisions and to be innovative within, of course, the limits of propriety established by society. Within these very general specifications there is a broad scope of acceptable behavior, ranging from imaginative, innovative leadership to the tentative independence of those who squeak by only because their needs are minimal and the support provided by their primary group affiliations is maximum.

Ideally, we conceive of the family as the basic social group in which the development from dependence to independence takes place. In the family procreation occurs, sexual needs are fulfilled, basic needs for food, clothing, and shelter are met, and the young are nurtured, socialized, partially educated, and cared for when ill. While no longer a primary unit for economic production, the family is still the major focal point for economic consumption. Through their families, individuals acquire an identity within the larger society and develop their self-identity. Families provide religious affiliations and values, experiences in the give-and-take of interpersonal relationships, and recreational outlets. It is in the context of the family group that most individuals learn the where, how, what, when, and with whom of social expectations—the do's and dont's, the obligations and responsibilities, the limitations and opportunities. Most families provide for exploration and experimentation in manipulating other people. The family setting provides also an orientation to time and space. As children grow, the community furnishes an extension of many of the functions which are initially experienced within the family. Experiments in interpersonal relations are extended into the neighborhood; values are subjected to peer-group sanctions; education is extended through schools, and religious orientation is formalized in churches; codes of behavior are subject to the law-enforcement system; recreational activities are widened; the horizons of time and space are expanded; and gradually the individual is permitted, then encouraged, and finally forced to take on an independent identity, make independent decisions, assume independent economic responsibilities, and eventually assume an adult role in the cycle of human and societal reproduction and socialization.

Persons who reach adulthood and are unable to meet their own needs, make their own decisions, or deviate from their rigid routines are handicapped. Most of those crippled by dependency manage to get along in society with the help of some compensating person or organization that permits the establishment and maintenance of a dependency relationship. This may be a wife, husband, mother, father, employer, or church. Young people who are unable to relinquish or break away from dependency on a parent have difficulty assuming mature adult roles. Sometimes they cannot achieve normal heterosexual gratification or, if they do, it may be only with someone to whom they can transfer their dependency needs. Sometimes they cannot function satisfactorily in a job situation unless, again, the situation permits them to evade responsibilities, initiative, or decision making.

The above brief and necessarily oversimplified review of family and community living in relation to dependency and independence is offered as a background for a consideration of the characteristics of institutional living, since in many respects institutions comprise the major alternative social organization to the family and to the economic and socializing activities normally found in family, job, and other community ties.

Characteristics of Institutional Living

Various forms of institutional living fulfill four major, partially overlapping, societal functions. First, institutions provide care for persons incapable of caring for themselves, including children who have been cast adrift by the death, divorce, incompatibility, destitution, incompetence, or disinterest of their parents. During the early part of this century society relied heavily on so-called orphan asylums to provide substitute homes in which abandoned children could be nurtured and reared. Similarly, most communities established institutions to provide at least minimal care for aged adults who were disabled, incompetent, unwanted, or indigent. Finally, a vast network of institutions was created to house the victims of physical defects, disabling injury, chronic crippling conditions, or disease such as tuberculosis, mental illness, and retardation.

A second major social function of institutions has been to provide protection for society from persons considered a "threat" to the well-being of others, including violators of social mores or conventions through crime, delinquency, or deviancy; behavioral offenders such as the mentally ill, the drug "addict," the sexual "pervert," and the retarded; and again, victims of certain infectious diseases such as leprosy and tuberculosis.

Third, institutions have provided refuge for persons seeking to withdraw from society. This would include those who seek the sanctuary of religious retreats and also those who find their escape by living in a marginal area such as skid row.

Finally, there have been institutional living arrangements associated with most major societal functions: boarding schools and colleges for education; hospitals and sanitariums for health; county homes and shelters for welfare; jails, prisons, and "reformatories" for public safety, punishment, and "correction"; the military services for defense and war; abbeys, monasteries, and convents for religion; and labor camps and live-in working arrangements for a variety of economic and industrial functions.

Since institutions provide the major alternative to family living, it is important to consider the extent to which they do, in fact, fulfill the functions of the family, and especially the extent to which persons living in institutions are prepared for a return to family and community.

Does institutional living, in fact, provide an adequate alternative to family and community with respect to personality development and socialization? Can persons living in institutions satisfactorily experience the physical, psychological, and social weaning processes which lead from childhood dependence to mature adult roles?

It is characteristic of all forms of institutional living that the basic necessities of life—food, clothing, and shelter—are provided in at least a minimal way, sufficient to sustain life. In most institutions inmates play a totally passive role with respect to these needs; clothing is literally "uniform" and affords little or no opportunity for the expression of individuality. Food is standardized in kind and amount; many institutions economize on labor by providing the conventional three meals a day all within the span of one eight-hour work shift for their food-service employees. In many institutions provisions for the elimination of body wastes are similarly regimented according to organizational convenience rather than human comfort or biological need. Shelter, too, is entirely controlled, often leaving no individual choice regarding spatial limits, heat or cold, fresh air and sunshine, light or darkness, noise or quiet. These characteristics are not limited to punitive institutions or those supported by public funds; they are sometimes reflected also in the experiences of persons paying handsomely for "private" accommodations in prestigious hospitals or those of "advantaged" children in exclusive boarding schools.

Institutional living generally affords limited freedom of movement, and even that freedom which is permitted occurs in isolation from the normal society. Some institutional settings are naturally isolated, such as merchant ships at sea or lumber camps, but most others have been intentionally isolated from the "good society." For many years, it was common social practice to build mental hospitals, sanitariums, and prisons out in the country, far removed from centers of population. Such locations were rarely chosen because of the desire to provide the benefits of a rural setting, which were, in fact, not experienced by inmates or patients. In addition to spatial distance, high walls and barbed-wire fences have served to reinforce society's sense of security and to limit communication and contact between inmates and the outside world. A side effect of the policy of isolating institutions was the need to provide live-in arrangements for many institutional employees, especially those whose rates of remuneration would not permit daily transportation to and from a home in the community. This requirement, in turn, introduced a factor of selection in the characteristics of persons who sought or remained in institutional jobs, many of whom had or developed dependency characteristics akin to those of the patients or inmates they guarded or fed.

Rarely does institutional living afford an individual any opportunity for privacy. Even those isolated in single jail cells or hospital rooms have no control over the presence of others and live constantly in a goldfish bowl, subject to the whims of others who can invade their presence at will. Much institutional living is truly communal, permitting no privacy even for the performance of intimate bodily functions, the public fulfillment of which is considered obscene in the outside world. Most institutions maintain a rigid separation of the sexes and afford only rare opportunities for heterosexual experiences, these usually under difficult, surreptitious, or perfunctory circumstances.

Institutions tend to be characterized by a highly structured, impersonal, uniform routine of living controlled by a caste-type authority system. There are only rare opportunities for the expression of individual initiative and those who experiment with initiative are usually quickly and decisively discouraged. Similarly, opportunities for creative productivity are usually absent or minimal in institutional settings and, until recently, those which existed were rarely related or transferable to the reward systems of the outside society.

Within long-term institutions, there has developed an institutional subculture with its own codes of behavior, sanctions, language, and stratification. Often the subculture derives solidarity from a common antagonism directed at members of the controlling caste. Institutional subcultures tend to reflect a preoccupation with such minor privileges as are available, ritualized routine, and slight variations in basic need fulfillment, such as the quantity of select items of food, the amount of stuffing in a bed mattress, or pitiful scraps of privacy. Additional gratification is sought in homosexual activity, gambling, and a personal fantasy life.[1]

Thus, our review of the characteristics of institutional living shows that it is a process of life adaptation imposed on or assumed by persons who are effectively isolated from the outside society; where inmates play a passive role in acquiring the necessities of life; where movement is highly curtailed and privacy nonexistent; where routine is impersonal and rigid, precluding any individual initiative. One can hardly say that this type of experience even approaches preparing the individual for constructive participation in the real world, especially when compared with the experience of most individuals growing up in a family and within a community where informal but nonetheless effective means exist for inculcating values and encouraging an appropriate degree of independent

---

1. Recognition of the importance of fantasy in the life of persons who have become acclimated to various forms of institutional life is particularly important for research in this field. The sharing of fantasy personal histories is a significant form of recreation, and institutional habitués will generally listen with respect and sympathy to one another's stories and provide appropriate responses even though they know it is all part of a game. Occasionally, observers have been taken in by the fantasy game and have written convincing accounts of the fallen men on skid row or in prisons who typically gave up promising careers in respectable society because of the death or infidelity of a wife or some similar fantasy incident around which they rationalize their present state. While such experiences do occur, the frequency with which they are reported suggest more precipitate downward mobility than has been found in systematic skid-row research. For a more detailed description of this point, see Samuel E. Wallace, *Skid Row as a Way of Life* (Totowa, N.J.: The Bedminster Press, 1965), pp. 198 ff.; and Erving Goffman's discussion of "reciprocally sustained fictions," in *Asylums* (New York: Doubleday, 1961), pp. 150–55.

mature action. The institutionalized individual is often prepared to exist successfully only within the institution with its supports and routine. Further, it should be noted that these characteristics may be true not only for formal or "total" institutions such as hospitals, prisons, and jails, but also of certain occupations such as the military; the Merchant Marine; work camps in the lumber, railroad, construction, and agricultural industries; and "live-in" jobs characteristic of resort areas or of many hospitals and other formal institutions. A kind of institutional living is found even in some rigidly structured families, among the employees of certain very paternalistic corporations, among some of the beneficiaries of our expanding welfare state, and among the virtually ignored derelicts in the skid-row areas of our large cities. Institutional living is widespread in form and deep in its impact on society.

Institutional Dependency

Dependency on institutional living encompasses every aspect of human adaptation; it involves elementary biological functioning, human adaptations to time and space, personality development and status, the socialization of the individual and his adequacy for fulfilling expected social roles. For individuals who become entrapped in the syndrome of institutional dependency, each additional experience seems to reinforce a self-perpetuating condition and to make the possibility of achieving an eventual adjustment to family and community living all the more remote.

Persons who are afflicted with the syndrome of institutional dependency commonly are unable to find an adequate pattern of adaptation to life outside of some form of institution. Many turn to a form of behavior which enables them to avoid the intense insecurity and anxiety which their feelings of inadequacy evoke. Those whose institutional living dates back to childhood or adolescence often appear to be stunted in personality development and to have failed to outgrow some of their childlike responses to people, events, and situations. Others whose institutional living experiences began later in life usually demonstrate regressive behavior; that is, they adopt ways of thinking, acting, feeling, relating to others, and viewing themselves that were appropriate to earlier periods of their life. Regressive behavior is not uncommon in an older person as a concomitant of senility, and it is also frequently seen in persons suffering from a disabling illness which imposes dependency on others to meet intimate bodily needs, comparable to that of the child's dependence on a mother. This same sort of personality regression is a common characteristic, as well, of adults who become well adapted to and dependent on institutional living.

A phenomenon similar to personality regression exists with respect to the socialization process in which most individuals learn the expectations of their particular society: the amenities, the usual ways of sharing, give-and-take, handling of frustrations, engaging in competition, relating to others, and the process by which individuals prepare for and assume adult roles in a family, employment, and the community. Individuals who have lived in institutions during significant periods of their childhood or adolescence, while well socialized to institutional life, are frequently under-socialized[2] for life in the outside world. They have never learned some of the most basic expectations regarding even routine activities in the larger society, such as obtaining and preparing food, selecting clothing, arranging for housing, relating to other people in public places such as restaurants or buses, applying for jobs, or even telling someone else the simplest vital statistics about themselves. Some persons, who once had mastered these activities, after prolonged institutional living tend to lose confidence and are equally unprepared to meet routine demands of community living without experiencing extreme feelings of anxiety or acute panic.

Among the total number of those dependent on some kind of refuge (jail, prison, live-in job, or hospital) are several hundred thousand men and some women in whom institutional dependency is further combined with a form of alcoholism. Although institutionally dependent alcoholics constitute only a fraction of the people who suffer from alcoholism, a very high proportion of institutionally dependent persons use alcohol to help them cope with life in the outside community. Alcohol is often the most accessible and convenient vehicle for a dependent person, cast adrift in an alien society, to find effective and immediate escape from the over-whelming feelings of anxiety and inadequacy with which he is invariably afflicted. The relationship between institutional dependency and alcoholism will be discussed below and documented at some length in later chapters.

We have briefly traced here a picture of the intertwining of personal-

2. The concept of undersocialization became particularly meaningful as a result of the studies which I have reported in "Alcohol and the Homeless Man," *Quarterly Journal of Studies on Alcohol*, 7: 760–804, December, 1946; and in *Medical Care for Seamen* (New Haven: Yale University Press, 1950).

ity regression and undersocialization which supports the dependency status imposed and enforced on inmates, patients, and often even employees by institutional living. It becomes clear that while most forms of institutional living have been created in order to "solve" a social problem, or meet some social need, institutions themselves constitute a social problem of significant magnitude. They are generally maintained at a high cost to society, and when compared with other methods of providing comparable care at the community level, institutions are generally uneconomical. There is reason to believe that many institutions simply do not succeed in fulfilling the functions they were designed for. Reformatories do not generally "reform." Graduates of prisons, whose criminal or antisocial patterns of behavior have often been reinforced by the sanctions and associates of prison life and whose primary social contacts on the outside may have been obtained through contacts on the inside, frequently revert to criminal behavior as soon as they are released. Drug addicts often revert to drug use again, in part because they find themselves accepted only in a society of drug users and in part because drugs may replace the institution in meeting dependency needs. Dependent persons with psychosomatic disorders have often learned how to exacerbate their symptoms in order to regain the protection of the hospital. Former mental patients, whose emotional status may be quite fragile to start with, may not be cured or even treated and revert to their particular form of aberrant behavior. With the exception of some live-in jobs, institutions generally involve the waste of productive manpower. Rates of mortality and of many forms of morbidity are higher in institutional populations than in the community. Virtually every form of institutional living appears to exceed family and community living in its capacity to produce social misfits: persons who are unable to carry their own weight in society and who gravitate back to institutional life.

This is not meant to suggest that institutions cannot be designed to provide socializing experiences and foster personality development so that their "graduates" will be prepared to meet the demands of the larger society. An example of such an attempt is the Israeli kibbutz. In our own society, numerous efforts are underway to perfect institutionally based programs which can prepare persons already crippled (emotionally disturbed children, retardates, prisoners, the mentally ill, and the chronically disabled) to assume a role in the outside society of family and community. In fact the functionality of many traditional forms of institutional living has been subjected to considerable skepticism in recent years. Child-rearing institutions have gradually been giving way to foster homes; probation and parole have partially replaced the use of reformatories for youthful offenders; chemotherapy has made possible the closing of most communicable-disease hospitals and many tuberculosis sanitariums; mental hospitals have instituted intensive treatment units for some kinds of patients, and the concept of community mental health has given hope that the future use of long-term incarceration for mentally ill persons will be drastically reduced; some industries have abandoned the practice of maintaining labor camps; newer institutions are being built closer to population centers, and communities are growing outward toward older institutions so that more and more institutional employees need no longer live in; boarding schools and colleges are becoming less cloistered; the use of faster ships with regular schedules has enabled merchant seamen to maintain families and community ties ashore; military policy has encouraged and facilitated marriage for career personnel; and many voices are being raised to decry the "crime of punishment."

Alcoholism and Institutional Dependency

The tendency to seek alcohol intoxication when not in a custodial setting is a most obvious and consistent behavioral characteristic of the homeless man—an institutionally dependent person. We should look more closely at this behavior and its relationship to the other characteristics of undersocialization and institutional dependency already discussed.

Although institutionally dependent persons comprise no more than a small segment of the total alcoholic population, the men of skid row are probably the most conspicuous excessive drinkers in our society, and because of this their relative contribution to the alcohol problems of society has often been exaggerated. Similarly, because excessive drinking is their most conspicuous trait, there has been a tendency to assume that alcoholism was a cause of their homelessness and dependency. In their fantasy lives many of these men have evolved elaborate tales blaming the evils of alcohol for their fall from imagined respect and prosperity. For most, however, these problems are so interrelated that it is difficult to separate cause and effect.

Most institutionally dependent homeless men turn to alcohol whenever they leave the protection of a custodial environment. To the extent that they are repeatedly using alcohol in ways that cause problems of health or psychological adjustment or interfere with their fulfillment of conventional social expectations regarding family, job, or community responsibilities, they are appropriately classified as alcoholics. But there are numerous forms of alcoholism, and a significant portion of these drinkers manifest a pattern of alcohol use specifically associated with their unfulfilled dependency needs.[3]

Several studies of skid-row drinking have led to the identification of a pattern of alcohol use which is, in some respects, quite different from that found in other segments of society. In my 1946 New Haven study of alcohol and the homeless man it was found that 88 percent of 203 homeless men were excessive drinkers and only 12 percent moderate drinkers or abstainers. Of the 158 homeless excessive drinkers whose patterns of consumption it was possible to identify, three-fourths were "steady excessive" drinkers, who drank whenever possible and who, when drinking, placed greater emphasis on maintaining limited intoxication for as long a duration as possible than on achieving a peak intoxicating effect. Only about a fourth were irregular excessive drinkers who, when drinking, tended to seek the most intensive intoxicating effect possible but who might abstain for varying periods of time between extended sprees. In a follow-up study of 444 men on the Bowery of New York[4] 10 percent were nondrinkers, although half of these reported past difficulties because of drinking; 17 percent were classified as moderate drinkers, of whom about a third reported histories of problem drinking; the rest were classified as heavy drinkers, including 43 percent who were uncontrolled and 28 percent controlled (2 percent were unclassifiable). Although different criteria of classification and labeling were used, the heavy controlled drinkers of the 1951 study corresponded roughly with the steady excessive drinkers of the 1946 study, while the heavy uncontrolled group was roughly comparable to the irregular excessive group.

3. Numerous studies of skid-row populations support the finding that these men are not truly homogeneous with respect to their drinking or life-adjustment patterns. For example, see Joan K. Jackson and Ralph Connor, "The Skid Road Alcoholic," *Quarterly Journal of Studies on Alcohol*, 14: 468–86, 1953; W. J. Peterson and M. A. Maxwell, "The Skid Row 'Wino,'" *Social Problems*, 5: 308–16, 1958; Howard M. Bahr, "Drinking, Interaction, and Identification: Notes on Socialization into Skid Row," *Journal of Health and Social Behavior*, 8, No. 4: 272–85, December, 1967; E. Rubington, "The Chronic Drunkenness Offender," *Annals of the American Academy of Political and Social Science*, 315: 65–72, 1958; Samuel E. Wallace, *Skid Row as a Way of Life* (Totowa, N.J.: The Bedminster Press, 1965); James P. Spradley, *You Owe Yourself a Drunk, An Ethnography of Urban Nomads* (Boston: Little, Brown and Company, 1970).

4. R. Straus and R. G. McCarthy, "Nonaddictive Pathological Drinking Patterns of Homeless Men," *Quarterly Journal of Studies on Alcohol*, 12: 601–11, December, 1951.

On the basis of both studies, McCarthy and I suggested a term—"non-addictive pathological drinkers"—to encompass those heavy or steady users of relatively large amounts of alcohol whose drinking seemed directed, not by a compulsion or irresistible drive to achieve peak intoxication, but rather by the goal of achieving a limited level of intoxication maintained at a plateau for as long a duration as possible. It was noted that these men were attempting to drink a combination of beverages which would enable them to reach a level of alcohol effect, short of the peak impulsively sought by the uncontrolled drinker, and to maintain this level for as long as possible.

In an impressive number of cases the drinking pattern seemed relatively flexible and was determined by the availability of funds and the particular working conditions. Many such men reported that, when they were working for daily wages, they drank each night to the extent of their funds; when they were paid less frequently, they drank less frequently but still with a certain degree of planning and regulation.

The majority of these men spent most of their income on alcohol. They indicated that drinking gave them a feeling of well-being in the midst of poverty and degradation; it provided a form of adjustment, permitting them to overlook their lack of material possessions and status and to forget their loneliness. Drinking gave temporary relief for those suffering from repressed guilt and remorse. The rationalization that drinking was an unfortunate habit helped them defend their sense of personal adequacy and provided release from self-reproach. Among the homeless population, drinking even supplied a certain status. The nondrinker was the exception, often considered queer and avoided by others.

About 70 percent of the men interviewed in the New Haven study stated that they desired no change in their drinking habits. Many of the men said drinking permitted an easy introduction to congenial companions. Only about 10 percent indicated that they usually drank alone, and most drank specifically to solve their loneliness. On the other hand, 90 percent said they usually or always had drinking companions; if they started drinking alone they invariably acquired "friends" in taverns or bars.

Thus, it was concluded that while some homeless men have fallen to their present level as a result of alcoholism and its consequences, for the majority excessive drinking seems to be part of their mode of adaptation to dependency living. It is for this reason that so many of these men can overtly seek incarceration, even knowing that it will deprive them of alcohol, just as they will eventually seek release in part because they crave the psychological and physiological escape into alcoholic euphoria. Alcoholism in institutionally dependent men, therefore, is seen as primarily an associated rather than a causative factor, integrally related to their undersocialization and their inability to provide for their own needs or to express initiative or to relate comfortably to other people.

The view that alcohol use is a form of adjustment to skid row and dependency living rather than as a cause was stressed also by Elmer Bendiner. While observing that "the search for a common denominator among Bowery men always begins—and frequently ends—with the finding that they are all alcoholics," Bendiner concluded that "drinking, while certainly part of the life on the Bowery, is not usually an important reason for being there." Instead, "he drinks to fend off loneliness, or sometimes the lesser chill that the wind sends slashing through his rags. He aspires only to warmth and everlasting 'highness,' rarely to total oblivion." Alcohol makes possible for the Bowery man "a world with rounded, smooth edges—a world of brothers, but not of brotherhood and all the dreary responsibilities which that concept entails."[5]

The major documentation for the present volume is derived from an unusual record of the life story of Frank Moore, which was initiated with a life history in 1945 when Frank was forty-one years of age and continued prospectively until his death in 1972. The relevance of Frank Moore's experiences both to the concept of institutional dependency and to a particular pattern of alcoholism is examined in detail in Chapter 10, which concludes this volume. The life record itself appears in Chapters 3–9. Prior to this, Chapter 2 considers the implications of life-history materials in social-science research and describes the specific research on which the book is based.

5. Elmer Bendiner, *The Bowery Man* (New York: Thomas Nelson and Sons, 1951), p. 92.

2. The Life Record in Social-Science Research

Studies which employ detailed and continuing records of individual human lives are relatively rare in the literature of the behavioral sciences. Yet individual human lives are basic elements of social behavior, and to ignore them seems akin to attempting the study of the structure of matter with only a superficial knowledge of the nature of atoms.

A pioneering example of the use of life history in sociological analysis is the detailed life record of a Polish immigrant by W. I. Thomas and Florian Znaniecki,[1] in which they stressed the fundamental interaction between the individual personality and the social milieu. Although much of their study was based on the observation and analysis of mass phenomena, they concluded that "personal life-records, as complete as possible, constitute the *perfect* type of sociological material, and ... if social science has to use other materials at all it is only because of the practical difficulty of obtaining at the moment a sufficient number of such records to cover the totality of sociological problems, and of the enormous amount of work demanded for an adequate analysis of all the personal materials necessary to characterize the life of a social group."[2] They call the use of mass phenomena without regard to the life histories of the individuals who participate in them "a defect, not an advantage" of sociological method: "A social institution can be fully understood only if we do not limit ourselves to the abstract study of its formal organization, but analyze the way in which it appears in the personal experience of various

1. W. I. Thomas and Florian Znaniecki, *The Polish Peasant in Europe and America* (New York: Alfred A. Knopf, 1927), 2 volumes.
2. *Ibid.*, pp. 1832–33.

members of the group and follow the influence which it has upon their lives. . . . There is no safer and more efficient way of finding among the innumerable antecedents of a social happening the real causes of this happening than to analyze the past of the individuals through whose agency this happening occurred."[3]

Noting that "the ultimate aim of social science, like that of every other science, is to . . . use as few general laws as possible for the explanation of as much concrete social life as possible," Thomas and Znaniecki insist that the social sciences "must reach the actual human experiences and attitudes which constitute the full, live, and active social reality beneath the formal organization of social institutions, or behind the statistically tabulated mass-phenomena which taken in themselves are nothing but symptoms of unknown causal processes and can serve only as provisional ground for sociological hypotheses."[4]

Further consideration of the use of life-history documents has been provided by John Dollard[5] from the perspective of both sociology and psychoanalysis. Dollard viewed the intensive life history as a valuable approach to the exploratory phase of social research, a phase he believed is too often bypassed in favor of intuitive choices of the variables to be studied or measured. By studying the life history of another individual, Dollard claimed that "the familiar and intuitive perceptions of social life can be made clear and external."[6] In stipulating criteria for utilizing the life history in social research Dollard stressed that the individual subject must be viewed as a specimen in a cultural series; the organic basis of behavior must be viewed in a context of its social relevance; the peculiar role of the family in transmitting culture must be recognized; the continuity of experiences from childhood through adulthood must be stressed; the impact of the social milieu must carefully and continuously be considered; and the life-history material must be organized and viewed in a meaningful conceptual frame of reference.

In the sociological literature, several significant attempts to utilize life-history materials appeared shortly after Thomas and Znaniecki charted the course. Notable examples are Clifford Shaw's effective use of the

3. *Ibid.*, p. 1833.
4. *Ibid.*, p. 1834.
5. John Dollard, *Criteria for the Life History* (New Haven: Yale University Press, 1935); and "The Life History in Community Studies," *American Sociological Review*, 3: 724–37, 1938.
6. Dollard, 1938, p. 724.

life-history technique in his studies of juvenile delinquency;[7] Edwin
Sutherland's presentation and interpretation of the personal story of a
professional thief;[8] and Allison Davis and John Dollard's use of several
life-history sketches as a basis for their consideration of the effects of
caste and class on personality development.[9]

Although the use of life-record documents is more compatible in a
general way with anthropological than with sociological methodological
style, the anthropological literature also has relatively few examples of
detailed life records continuing over significant periods of time. Only
two anthropologists, Clyde Kluckhohn[10] in 1945 and L. L. Langness[11]
in 1965, appear to have seriously promoted life-history taking as a major
form of anthropological methodology. Langness documents and attempts
to explain the sparsity of significant detailed biographical materials in
anthropology. Among the notable exceptions is the autobiography of
Don Talayesva, a Hopi chief, in *Sun Chief*, compiled, edited, and ana-
lyzed by Leo W. Simmons.[12] More recently, the use of life-history material has been made prominent as a major methodological style by an-
thropologist Oscar Lewis in his studies of the culture of peasant families
in Mexico and Puerto Rico.[13] Lewis has employed as the primary basis
for his descriptions of the culture of poverty in Mexico and Puerto Rico
both autobiographical life histories recorded on tape by his subjects and
minutely detailed descriptions of the ordinary events in the lives of his
subjects on ordinary days.

In the psychological literature, despite the model provided by Freud

7. Clifford R. Shaw, *The Jack-Roller. A Delinquent Boy's Own Story* (Chicago: University of Chicago Press, 1930).

8. Edwin H. Sutherland, *The Professional Thief* (Chicago: University of Chicago Press, 1937).

9. Allison Davis and John Dollard, *Children of Bondage* (Washington, D.C.: American Council of Education, 1940).

10. Clyde Kluckhohn, "The Personal Document in Anthropological Science," in *The Use of Personal Documents in History, Anthropology and Sociology*, Louis Gotts-chalk, Clyde Kluckhohn, and Robert Angell (eds.) (New York: Social Science Research Council, Bulletin 53, 1945), pp. 78–173.

11. L. L. Langness, *The Life History in Anthropological Science*, Studies in Anthropological Method (New York: Holt, Rinehart and Winston, 1965). Includes a twenty-four-page selected bibliography of biographical and methodological works.

12. Leo W. Simmons, *Sun Chief, the Autobiography of a Hopi Indian* (New Haven: Yale University Press, 1942).

13. Oscar Lewis, *Five Families* (New York: Basic Books, 1959); *Children of Sanchez* (New York: Random House, 1961); *Pedro Martinez* (New York: Random House, 1964); and *La Vida, a Puerto Rican Family in the Culture of Poverty* (New York: Random House, 1966).

for the intensive study of individual lives, relatively few intensive examinations of life records over long spans of time are available. A very pertinent intensive examination of personal records is provided by Gordon Allport. In discussing the use of personal documents in the study of theories on personality, Allport[14] identifies four criteria for the use of such documents: the establishment of their representativeness with respect to some universe, their internal adequacy for the use made of them, their reliability as checked by independent sources, and the ability to demonstrate the validity of any interpretations made from them. For many years Allport employed in his teaching a series of some three hundred letters written over a period of eleven and a half years by a woman to a college friend of her son and his wife. He then published a selection from the letters along with several suggested approaches to their interpretation.[15] In the preface of the volume, Allport notes that intimate letters are "often better than fiction or biography, even than autobiography, [for] they tell us what a particular concrete human life is like." He notes that the value is enhanced "if the letters are written over a considerable period of time, presenting consecutively the inner narrative of a life as it unfolds."[16]

Of more recent note is the use of family-history data compiled over a span of several years by Senn and Hartford in their study of child health and childbearing.[17] Here the authors have relied primarily on in-depth family histories in order to illustrate effectively basic premises regarding the importance of "the family climate preceding the firstborn, the 'personality' of the neonate as he enters the family orbit, the action of the environment on the infant, the infant's impact on his milieu—the beginnings of child-parent family integration."[18]

Biographical material on individuals who lack stable home or community ties is particularly difficult to obtain, in part because such individuals seldom have the capacity or motivation for engaging in a continuing literary effort, in part because they are seldom in one place long enough. An exception, which has significant relevance to the present volume, is a series of forty letters written over a thirteen-month period by "William

14. Gordon W. Allport, *The Use of Personal Documents in Psychological Science* (New York: Social Science Research Council, Bulletin 49, 1942).
15. Gordon W. Allport, *Letters from Jenny* (New York: Harcourt, Brace and World, 1965).
16. *Ibid.*, p. v.
17. Milton J. E. Senn and Claire Hartford, *The Firstborn: Experiences of Eight American Families* (Cambridge: Harvard University Press, 1968).
18. *Ibid.*, p. 1.

R. Tanner" to James P. Spradley and included in Spradley's *You Owe Yourself a Drunk: An Ethnography of Urban Nomads.*[19]

An unusual opportunity occurred in 1945 for me to study the life history of a homeless man in whom were clustered numerous forms of pathology, including alcoholism, a persistent pattern of dependency on living in various institutional settings, and the inability to achieve an adequate adaptation to life outside of a protected environment.

At the time, I was a graduate student in sociology at Yale University and was employed by the Department of Applied Physiology, home base of Yale's Center of Alcohol Studies, to look at the drinking patterns of homeless men. Two research ("Yale Plan") clinics had been established for the study and treatment of alcoholism, but since homeless men were conspicuously absent from the clientele of these clinics, an attempt was being made to help fill a knowledge gap. The study was considered exploratory, and I was instructed explicitly to liken myself to the bear going over the mountain "to see what he could see."

It was arranged that I should interview each man who came to live and work at the Men's Social Service Center of the Salvation Army in New Haven. The Salvation Army contributed to the study by facilitating an initial contact with each man admitted to the center and by providing a place where I could talk with each man privately. Like similar programs throughout the country, this center provided dormitory housing and meals in exchange for work in collecting and salvaging for sale discarded newspapers, magazines, clothing, and furniture donated by people in the community.

In many respects, the opportunities for meaningful research proved much greater than had been anticipated. Experience revealed that the majority of homeless alcoholics had developed a set of pat responses which they were accustomed to giving in the countless situations when they were interviewed at various jails, missions, shelters, and employment agencies. Most also had fantasy life histories which they exchanged with each other as a way of putting some spice into their dull, routine existence. Somewhere between the safe pat responses and the fantasy life lay the true histories and experiences of these men. I appealed for their help in providing, from their own past, information which only they could provide and which someday might be useful in helping others. For most, the simple suggestion that their true experiences and opinions

19. James P. Spradley, *You Owe Yourself a Drunk, An Ethnography of Urban Nomads* (Boston: Little, Brown and Company, 1970).

were respected and could be of value was sufficient to elicit a consistent story.

The study of homeless men was continued for a year. It included interviews with 203 men who comprised consecutive admissions to the Social Service Center of the Salvation Army during that time. The project soon assumed some specific goals and a focus and eventually led to two publications: "Alcohol and the Homeless Man,"[20] and "Some Sociological Concomitants of Excessive Drinking as Revealed in the Life History of an Itinerant Inebriate."[21]

The second article related in some detail the story of Frank Moore as it was recorded during the summer of 1945 and through subsequent contacts and correspondence continuing through March, 1948.

After the publication of Frank's life story in 1948, he continued to provide a record of his life as it unfolded. Thus, from the time of our first meeting in July, 1945, until Frank's death in September, 1972, a developing life record of more than twenty-seven years was maintained. This was recorded primarily through 324 letters written by Frank to me and by personal visits with Frank, which were most numerous during the period 1945–53 when I was living in New Haven. After I moved to Syracuse, I rarely saw Frank, although he was often in the upper New York State area. Then, after I moved to Lexington, Kentucky, in 1956, there were no contacts except through correspondence until 1966, when I made the first of several trips to New England in order to locate and visit with Frank.

Although Frank's record was maintained until his death in September, 1972, it is not entirely complete. There are some unexplained periods of silence. There are references to occasional letters which Frank wrote but which I never received and which most probably were censored by the institution in which they were written. There were some lapses when Frank was highly mobile and failed to hear from me. Some institutions restricted the number and length of letters which could be sent; many restricted the kinds of items inmates could receive. I tried to encourage Frank by replying to most of his letters and as far as possible by providing him with things he needed or could not otherwise obtain. Most of my letters contained from one to five dollars wrapped in plain paper to escape detection. A high percentage of these were received. At other

20. R. Straus, "Alcohol and the Homeless Man," *Quarterly Journal of Studies on Alcohol*, 7: 360–404, 1946.

21. R. Straus, "Some Sociological Concomitants of Excessive Drinking as Revealed in the Life History of an Itinerant Inebriate," *Quarterly Journal of Studies on Alcohol*, 9: 1–52, 1948.

times I sent tobacco, clothing, writing materials, books, candy, copies of articles on alcohol or other subjects of mutual interest, and copies of my own publications or descriptions of other professional activities with which I was currently involved.

In the present volume the life history of Frank Moore serves to document the concept of institutional dependency and the experiences of an alcoholic homeless man. Frank Moore's story also provides insights into a number of subjects of interest to behavioral scientists and others who are concerned with personality development, life-adaptation patterns, socialization, and various forms of human pathology. His life was dominated by several problems interrelated with his alcoholism and institutional dependency. There was alienation from his family and community. In particular, his ambivalent feelings toward his mother and his turbulent relationship with her profoundly affected his personality and lifelong pattern of adaptation. While rejection of and by his family and community led Frank to his first institutional experience, there developed a growing dependency on institutional custody of one form or another which perpetuated his feelings of rejection by society and his inability to make an adequate adjustment to society. This is especially evident through numerous descriptions of his brief interludes of failure between episodes of institutional living.

Discussions of Frank's reasons for drinking and descriptions of his use of alcohol contribute to an understanding of a particular form of alcoholism which is characteristic of persons who are institutionally dependent. As the years went by, alcohol served several functions: it permitted Frank to "punish" the mother and society which he held responsible for his failure, it helped alleviate his discomfort when thrown on his own resources, and it assured him re-entry into the system of institutional custody.

Finally, from the viewpoint of methodology in the study of human behavior, this is an unusual document distinguished particularly by the fact that for twenty-seven of the sixty-eight years of Frank Moore's life it has been recorded prospectively. The variety of materials incorporated in this volume includes a life history recorded retrospectively through personal interviews covering the years from his birth in 1904 to 1945; a contemporary record found in 322 letters written by Frank to me from 1946 until shortly before his death in 1972; a brief but revealing record of Frank's life provided in letters from his mother; and my personal notes recording events related to me by Frank during our sporadic meetings since 1945. Together, these materials cover an entire life span, beginning with some events that occurred during his mother's pregnancy and extending to his death. Although they are uneven in their depth and leave some gaps in detail, the materials encompass most of the significant events in Frank's life. They provide sufficient detail on the family, community, and other social environments to meet the criteria of social and cultural relevance set down by Allport and Dollard. They meet Allport's requirements that reliability be checked by an independent source (the correspondence with Frank's mother and my few contacts with other significant persons in Frank's life), and they are "adequate" in Allport's terms to illustrate clearly several distinct behavioral phenomena (alcoholism, homelessness, dependency, family instability, institutional living, undersocialization, and others), which provide a framework for organization, conceptualization, and analysis.

Like Wladek, the Polish peasant, and Don Talayesva, the Hopi chief, Frank Moore had both literary interests and interest in his own life story. He was also a philosopher of the social scene. For all three individuals, their inner satisfactions seemed to provide their most significant motivation for providing a life story. Like Allport's Jenny Masterson, whose letters were written for very personal reasons, Frank Moore, Wladek, and Don Talayesva were very intelligent human beings, and all had a fluency of expression that makes their stories of more than passing interest.

Howard S. Becker has noted that "the most persistent difficulty in the scientific study of deviant behavior is a lack of solid data, a paucity of facts and information on which to base our theories . . . there are simply not enough studies that provide us with facts about the lives of deviants as they live them. . . . Just as we need precise anatomical descriptions of animals before we can begin to theorize about them and experiment with their physiological and biochemical functioning, just so we need precise and detailed descriptions of social anatomy before we know just what phenomena are present to be theorized about."[22]

The detailed descriptions of Frank Moore's life as he lived it are presented here in the hope that they can help fill the void so clearly identified by Becker as it applies to a better understanding of the syndrome of institutional dependency and the forms of alcoholism so often associated with this way of life.

In this volume, pseudonyms have been used to identify nearly all per-

22. Howard S. Becker, *Outsiders, Studies in the Sociology of Deviance* (New York: The Free Press of Glencoe, 1964), pp. 165–66.

sons and places. Exceptions are some famous persons to whom Frank alludes in his letters: some of the staff at the Yale Center of Alcohol Studies whose prominence in research on alcohol problems makes their identity pertinent; the three communities in which I have lived since the study was initiated in 1945 (New Haven, Connecticut; Syracuse, New York; and Lexington, Kentucky); such distinctive organizations as the federal penitentiary at Alcatraz, the Salvation Army, the Seaman's Church Institute, Bellevue Hospital, and Alcoholics Anonymous; and such large cities as New York, Philadelphia, Chicago, and Boston, when their identification in no way compromises the anonymity of organizations or persons. This respect for anonymity has even led to the elimination of most references to the specific states through which Frank's story unfolds. It can be said simply that most of his experiences took place in the area covered by New York, Connecticut, Massachusetts, and Rhode Island. There were occasional journeys into New Jersey, Pennsylvania, and northern New England. Only Frank's military and federal-prison episodes took him beyond this territory, and the identity of such places has not been concealed. In addition to the names of persons, such identifying data as occupations and some specific family relationships also have been altered to protect anonymity while preserving their significant general identity.

In the pages which follow, Chapter 3 presents the life history of Frank Moore from his birth in 1904 to our meeting in 1945. Chapter 4 describes Frank's life from the time of our initial meeting in 1945 through 1948, along with a discussion of my numerous unsuccessful attempts to guide Frank into some form of rehabilitation. In Chapter 5 Frank's mother tells the story of his life and of her own experiences preceding and following his birth through a correspondence with her which I initiated in 1948. The continuation of Frank's story is told primarily through the letters which he wrote to me: Chapter 6 (1949-55) documents the entrenchment of dependency on total institutions;[23] Chapter 7 (1956-62) details his continuing institutional dependency back within home New England territory; Chapter 8 (1963-66) reveals a deepened and acute evaluation of himself and of society and a deliberate attempt to become a noninstitutionalized resident of his home town, Calvinville;

---

23. Goffman in *Asylums* uses the term "total institutions" to include formal establishments like hospitals, prisons, or jails as differentiated from an institutional-like setting such as would be found in a lumber work camp, the Merchant Marine, or skid-row shelter programs.

and Chapter 9 (1967–72) reports the periodic stability and relative respectability he achieved although increasingly beset by deteriorating health up to the time of his death. In keeping with our goal of presenting as complete a life record as possible, Chapters 6 through 9 include a substantial proportion of Frank's correspondence. Only those letters or portions of letters which are redundant or deal with matters considered irrelevant to the understanding of Frank, the illustration of behavioral principles, or the major themes of this book have been omitted.

Chapter 10 draws on the events of Frank's life story as well as his observations and interpretations for a more detailed consideration of alcoholism and the syndrome of institutional dependency.

3. Frank Moore's Life History; 1904-45

My first meeting with Frank Moore took place on July 25, 1945, the day after his arrival at the Salvation Army Men's Social Service Center in New Haven. He was the thirteenth man whom I interviewed at the center and it was quickly apparent that there was something which set him apart. He was intelligent and had an avid interest in many subjects. He gave the impression, and this accorded with his self-description, of being a thinking man: "I've read everything—thought about it all." A good rapport developed between us rapidly.

He quoted Schopenhauer on pleasure and pain. He mentioned several articles on alcohol or alcoholism and said that he had read a good deal about Alcoholics Anonymous but did not see how they could possibly be successful. He took with him some pamphlets on alcohol, promising to read and discuss them with me, and said that he would like to have more.

Frank was five feet, nine inches tall, weighing a well-distributed 175 pounds. His complexion was ruddy, his skin weatherbeaten, his hair thin and light brown. Sunken blue eyes contributed to a facial expression which appeared both unhealthy and unhappy. Polite and respectful, he seemed to feel he ought to talk about himself, that it could do no harm. At the same time, it was as though he had given up on himself.

After a discussion of the natural and social sciences, Frank said that it might be possible for the social sciences to work out laws for governing behavior. He said, however, that many of the men who stay at shelters scoff at the "ologists" trying to study alcoholics. Frank disagreed with them, feeling those "ologists" were making a real beginning in the study of the problem. The fact that "alcoholics are helpless to rehabilitate themselves" was proof to Frank that they do not know nearly as much as they think they know about their own problem.

My initial visit with Frank was concerned with obtaining basic data for my study of alcohol use among homeless men. During our second visit, I asked Frank if he would be interested in a program such as that of the Yale Plan Clinic. He wanted to know more about it. Was their approach psychological or biological? What were their methods? What practical aid was offered?

I also suggested recording a fairly detailed and complete life history which might be very helpful to those who were trying to learn more about the diagnosis and treatment of alcoholics. No reference was made to the possibility of such a life history's helping Frank. He agreed to co-operate, saying one never knew what such a project might yield. We established that anonymity would be preserved by altering names of identifiable persons and places and that he would have the opportunity to read over the recorded material and make corrections and additions. Without further ado, he began a formal recitation of his life history, which appears here as recorded from the notes I made while Frank talked.

The life history as Frank told it in seven interview sessions was obviously subject to the great limitations of memory, time, his knowledge about some events, selective recall, and a few examples of intentional omission or modification. Many aspects of the story seem bizarre, yet it was told with an internal consistency and an air of sincerity. The life history from 1904 to 1945 which follows is Frank's story as I reconstructed it from the detailed notes I made while he talked. Since no electronic recording devices were available, it was not possible to record Frank's exact phraseology. However, the events and chronology were checked with Frank and as many of Frank's own expressions as possible were retained.[1]

The Life History

I was born in 1904, and shortly after that my father committed suicide. It was one of those things that was hushed up and never

1. In a somewhat different form, Frank's life history from 1904 to 1945 as related here was originally published in an article entitled "Some Sociological Concomitants of Excessive Drinking as Revealed in the Life History of an Itinerant Inebriate," in the *Quarterly Journal of Studies on Alcohol*, 9: 1–52, 1948.

talked about. I never understood the real story. I know there was some sort of disgrace connected with it and my father's family never had anything to do with my mother after that. My mother was only eighteen at the time. The only things I know about my father are from what my mother said at various times and what I learned from some personal papers of his that I once saw. Once in a while my mother would make an indirect reference to him such as in speaking about a person she would say, "He was a friend of your father." His name was George Moore and he was born in Maine about 1882, an only son. He was good at athletics and had a knack for sketching and drawing. After serving in the Navy during the Spanish-American War, he became a silversmith and designer. From a tintype picture of him, I think I look like him.

I don't know anything about how he met my mother or about their relationship. I know that my mother was living in her father's home when I was born. I don't even know if my father was living with them. As far back as I can remember I was aware that something was "wrong," something that made me different from the other kids. I thought about it because I guessed it was something they didn't want me to talk about.

My mother was Roberta Eaton. She was born in Calvinville in 1886. Her family was very respected in the town. They had been living there for over a hundred years. Her father, my grandfather, was the town's first sanitation inspector and a highly respected citizen. She had two sisters. One died in childhood and the other married and went to live with her husband in New Hampshire.

My mother was at the head of her class in high school, but soon after she graduated she married my father when she was only sixteen. After my father committed suicide she left me with my grandfather and went off to study nursing. She must have thought I was a burden to her. She may have come back to see me when I was young, but I don't really remember. She led her own life and never bothered too much with me. We never could understand each other.

I remember being raised by my grandfather and an odd assortment of housekeepers. They all felt that I was just an obligation to them and nobody treated me as if I was their own. Only one stands out in my memory as being interested in me as a person. She was a Miss Keller, an English lady. She seemed disillusioned and disappointed. After all, she was a housekeeper in a neighborhood where all the neighbors were husband and wife. She was an alien in a small Yankee town and being a housekeeper in a small town is an enigma anyway. Most of the other housekeepers had only artificial affection for me and treated me well for my grandfather's sake.

I knew all the time that something was wrong, but I didn't understand it. I thought it had something to do with my not having a father and mother, and my playmates made fun of it in a way I didn't understand. All the other kids had mothers and fathers. When they called me by my last name I resented it and I realized that that was their purpose.

My grandfather never mentioned my father or mother, and I didn't question him. I just knew intuitively that there were things not to be talked about. My grandfather was very formal and always introduced me on the street as his grandson. He acted proud of me generally and talked as if he expected good things of me.

My grandfather was very reputable in town, honest, hard-working, clean-spoken. He was not affiliated with any religious sect or lodge, something about a blackball, some reason he didn't care to identify himself with a group. He had been to sea as a young man—insisted on my being punctual at meals and bedtime. There were some things that I could do when I got older, such as drinking coffee. I never remember him giving me a whipping; just the manner in which he talked to me would make me feel hurt or ashamed. There was a great deal of affection but he told me that if I ever got licked, don't come crying to him about it.

He was a hard man, hard-hearted physically. I don't think he had any close friends, but he was the only person I ever had any real affection for. I've always been glad that he died before I hit the skids. He often referred to walking the straight and narrow.

When I was about ten, my mother got married again. When I was twelve, she came back to Calvinville with her new husband. He was forty and my mother only twenty-eight when they got married. His name was Edward Greene, a Vermonter. He was a hard-working man with a variety of occupations, but I guess mostly a cabinetmaker. He was very successful and a good provider but uneducated.

I had two great uncles, my grandfather's brothers. One lived with my grandfather. He was the town's truant officer until he retired. He was always at a rolltop desk and he kept scrapbooks. He was very kindly. I remember when he died they told me he had just gone away, but later I sort of sensed that it was permanent.

There was another brother who operated a grocery store a few blocks from my grandfather's house. He was alderman of the ward. I used to go to the store to buy candy but he never treated me as a relative. He never visited our house and we never went there. I often wondered about this situation and once I asked my mother about it. She told me that my grandfather and great uncle had had a money dispute long ago.

There was another relative, my mother's sister. She was my favorite. She knew how to appeal to children with candy and affection. I used to see this aunt two or three times a year. I remember everybody liked her.

I remember some of the teachers I had in grade school. My first-grade teacher was a childish type. I guess you might say she had the right mentality to deal with first-grade children. There were a couple of children in that class who were antisocial, not adapted to school at all, couldn't even learn to write. I don't remember any particular friends in that year. I can remember a few vague things about the other teachers.

In the seventh grade I had a teacher who was the Lady Bountiful type. We used to go to her home and walk to school with her. She played Victrola records and taught folk dancing. She was a graduate of a good teachers' training school and later became a state parole officer, but in those days that was considered pretty radical procedure. I guess that was the first time I was in contact with the opposite sex. I had my first crush on a girl. I adored her from afar. I think it was her curls that attracted me because later she cut them off and I didn't seem to care about her any more.

About this time, I first learned about sex by listening to smutty talk from the older boys at school. I always had been taught that babies came in a sugar barrel or a paper bag, but I gradually came to realize that boys were different from girls. Then I knew somehow that men had some sort of sexual relations with women to produce babies. In high school I noticed some of the girls developing breasts and I remember thinking this was immodest and too early.

Most of the time I got along all right with the other kids. I was never a leader because there was always someone bigger and tougher. But sometimes they would pick on me. The boys would run after me, yelling, "Moorey, Moorey, Moorey!" I didn't understand why, but I always felt that they meant something derogatory. I thought they were referring to my father and the fact that he committed suicide.

It was in the seventh grade that my mother came back to Calvinville. She came to school to visit. I don't think she was ever interested in any one thing I was doing, just in my general progress. I didn't like that because that was unusual in those days. The kids thought it was sissy when a parent displayed too much interest in a child. I remember one family in town with a lot of money. They had an electric auto and the mother used to call for her children and drive them home from school. We all called them sissies.

My mother was a woman whose life was finished very young. She wouldn't stand for it so she left me in the care of my grandfather and tried to make life over again. Then she remarried and tried to adapt herself to a pattern and settle down with security. As far back as I remember there was criticism about my mother because she wasn't there to look out for me. My earliest memory of her was standing one day waiting for a street car. Someone came up and referred to me as her brother, and she said, "Oh, he's not my brother, he's my son." She was a tired woman and worried. She never understood me, but she worried. She was a hypochondriac. I'm not accusing her of that. It's a fact and I understand it.

I don't know if I resent the fact that she went off and left me. She was very young. I'm not sure she was wrong, but at the same time she didn't play ball with what the world thinks. I suppose there's a parallel to the Hindu wife who is supposed to cast herself on her husband's funeral pyre.

In the eighth grade I had a teacher, Miss Priscilla Scott, as Puritan as her name suggests. She had been my mother's teacher also. She was fair and had a sense of honor, but she was dry and sarcastic. I can't imagine anyone being more virgin or ever having anything to do with a man.

It was in the eighth grade also that my grandfather gave me a membership in the Y.M.C.A. as a Christmas present. After that I practically lived there. I took part in all the activities. My stepfather didn't like my belonging there. Although all classes of boys in Calvinville belonged, he thought it was a rich man's son's club. He had had no advantages as a boy, and he thought I was having it too easy. I would place him in the lower middle class socioeconomically. He owned his own home and made improvements on it and also bought some adjoining land.

My relationship with my stepfather was a sort of armed truce. I was an unwanted obligation to him. I remember a book, *Sorrell and*

Son, that was about an ideal relationship between a father and his son. My relationship with my stepfather was just the opposite. I never took any questions or problems to him, never talked to him about my school work, never took any moral problems to him. I just knew he didn't understand me.

In high school I took a college preparatory or Latin course. I never had any real expectation of going to college. There were no plans ever made for it; that was just the course I took. I had Latin, English, algebra, and ancient history. It was one of the few times that they let me select things for myself. I liked ancient history—it included mythology, Galley's *Classic Myths,* and Bulfinch's *Age of Fables.* I liked the literature we read in English. I can still remember the algebra rules without ever applying them. Today, I couldn't even figure out the cost of a pound of peaches although I remember all the rules by heart.

I remember the Latin teacher best. I began to stammer about that time. I had trouble pronouncing the sound *w.* I'd start a recitation and sit down when I saw the sound coming. She talked to me to try to determine whether I knew my studies or just had an inability to pronounce it. She was a young teacher just out of normal school. I didn't have much confidence in her. I think the other kids in the class were happy to see me have a problem over pronunciation.

During that year I played a lot of basketball at the Y, but toward the middle of December I got influenza and missed about six weeks of school. When I got back all the other kids were six or seven lessons ahead of me. I made a half-hearted effort to catch up but I was too far behind and never did. The rest of the year I stumbled through everything except ancient history because I was interested in that and I read up on it. By June, I had flunked Latin, English and algebra.

When I started my freshman year over again, my schoolmates had all progressed, and instead of feeling one term behind, I felt ten terms behind. When I seemed bright at the start of the second year they all said that I'd been through it before and should know it. I'd done a lot of studying but I never volunteered because I figured that I'd been in class before and knew it already. I made high marks but I began to think that this was the end of school. I had no prospect of going to college and I wasn't mechanically inclined—small industries didn't interest me. Besides, I was being girl conscious, long trousers and clothes conscious, and I wanted money.

Before I got sick, freshman year, there had never been any question of my passing all the classes, but my mother and grandfather realized that I had missed a lot of work and took my failing as a matter of fact. By May of that second year I quit school. I told my mother I was no longer interested and she said that there was no need for me to go to school if I didn't want to. My grandfather wanted me to continue, but he was advising me to do something against my whim, and at the time I saw a chance to have my own way.

After I left school I got a job in a brass foundry in a nearby town working a drill press. I wasn't interested in the technical part of the work. What I was doing was just a small operation in a big plant. The work didn't require finesse or knowledge. There was a die mark on the auto frames and I had to place the drill precisely, press down a lever, and stock them. It was purely mechanical. I lived at home and commuted to work by trolley. I was earning $22 a week, big money for a sixteen-year-old. I paid $8 a week for board. My stepfather had always worked and paid his own way, so I had to, too. I spent about $10 a week on clothing. This was 1920 and clothing was very high. Out of the remaining $4 I used to pay the carfare, buy a cheap novel, and gorge myself on ice-cream sodas over the weekend. My stepfather thought this was quite a sum for me to fritter away every weekend. I only worked there for about two months although there was nothing wrong with the job.

One weekend I went to Harrison to visit my aunt. Harrison was the big town in the area, about four times the size of Calvinville, and I saw the Navy recruiting station there. I knew my father had been in the Navy and I had always intended to join the Navy when I was old enough and big enough. I had seen signs in the post office with age limits and all that, and I knew that I was big enough but not old enough. I went upstairs to the sub-recruiting office and I was met by a chief petty officer. He said, "Come in and sit down and have a cigarette." I had never smoked in my life and told him that I didn't smoke. I said that I'd come to join the Navy. He asked how old I was and I told him sixteen. I got on the scales and I weighed 130. At that time I was five feet six. He said, "You're supposed to be eighteen to get in the Navy," and the gist of his words was "Do you think you could remember that you are eighteen?" He asked about home and where I was born. Then he said there were several small towns in the state where they didn't start to record births till about 1910. He said, "We'll put your birthplace down as one of these small towns—you remember you're eighteen—if you don't remember they won't let you stay in."

That was my first experience that all rules and regulations are not to be followed literally. Later this brought me into conflict with powers that be. There I was, leaving a small town, and this was escape right there and then.

At that time it was possible to select your branch of service, and due to the fact that I'd just left school, the chief petty officer thought I'd be adapted to the Navy hospital corps. You are immediately sent to school there and they feel that if you have just been to school you are mentally more pliable; they felt they could teach you more things. He told me I'd leave the next day for Boston.

I went home and told my mother that I'd joined the Navy. She said that she didn't know whether she'd let me. I gave her to understand that I was already in and nothing could be done about it. My grandfather thought it was a good thing; he approved of it. My stepfather probably thought that some barrier had been removed. Of course, I had the feeling too that some barrier had been removed. I never felt that my stepfather, mother, and I were ever happy as the three of us. I felt that the problem could be me, but I doubted that she could be happy with him.

You understand I really knew my mother for only a short time. For the first two years in the Navy I only saw her once and then there was a ten-year interval. I was very sympathetic toward her. She used to mention the fact that I was getting older, that I should settle down, that I should accomplish something. I think she meant more material success. She never understood me. We have never understood each other because she measures success in material things. When a man seeks happiness he doesn't need money, property, social standing, leadership in public affairs. He can find it through work, fair labor for pay, honesty, assuming one's obligations, not tying oneself to any particular group or ideas of a particular group, self-sufficiency in an economic sense, congenial occupation, good health. A man can be a good man without being a successful man. My mother believed that you've got to have material things. She had no interest in honesty and fair play, just in how much money you could make and what plans you had for security. Women are twice as practical as men.

I went to Boston to the main recruiting office. It was the first time I had ever been as far as Boston, but I didn't have any trouble finding my way. For the physical examination they put me in a room with fifteen or twenty other men, all stripped. I didn't feel any embarrassment, I guess because I was used to this from the Y.

One of the pharmacist's mates asked me whether I had ever had the clap and I didn't know what he was talking about. From Boston, they sent me to Newport and I had a feeling that I was leaving everything I knew behind and starting out all over again.

In Newport, we had a period of quarantine. We slept in hammocks. Men came from different parts of the country. I met southerners for the first time. I learned to smoke—everyone else smoked. I remember one fellow from Tennessee. At night he'd get down on the floor under his hammock and pray. The other men thought it was peculiar but respected his moral courage. I met a fellow named Marks—a Jewish fellow. It was the first contact I ever had with a Hebrew. Of course, I found the Jew just the same as any other human being. We took basic recruit training for about a month. I didn't mind the Navy discipline because the truth of it is I joined the Navy for my own selfish ends. Later when I was taking an exam for a higher grade in the Navy I was asked why I had joined and I gave the stock answer that I had joined to help my country, but I really joined in order to get out of an unpleasant situation and to start life over again.

After a month of basic training, I started a nine-month course at the Hospital Corps Training School. It was strictly class work with no practical application. The instructors were doctors and warrant officers in the Navy. Some of the subjects such as laboratory work and compounding appealed to me, while others like dietetics I did not like. I found it easy to grasp the work, but some of the older men did not. Many of the men in that school would later be serving on independent medical duty in small ships where they would be the only medical personnel. When you graduated from the course they gave you a certificate from the Bureau of Medicine and Surgery in Washington and men with those certificates were always in demand as corpsmen in civilian hospitals.

After six weeks in the Navy, they gave me a forty-two-hour leave. I went home that time, but although I was only a four- or five-hour bus ride away most of the time I didn't go home again for two years. The usual conception of military life is discipline and restrictions, but in my own case discipline and restrictions seemed to have been removed; that is, I could smoke and swear.

My mother used to write to me about twice a month, and my grandfather also wrote and came to see me once at Newport. I used to spend a lot of my free time at Newport Beach, at the Navy Y, or go to the movies at the post. I went through one class after another and had no trouble with the school work. The things I learned I've never forgotten. When I enlisted they listed me as a hospital apprentice second class. I took to the stuff as a duck to water. I've always figured that if it had been something else, I'd probably have done just the same as with hospital work.

After nine months they made me a hospital apprentice first class, and they sent me to the Norfolk Navy Yard Hospital. That was the longest trip I had ever taken. There we began to do practical work. I was assigned to a forty-bed surgical ward and I worked a twelve-hour day. That was the first time I saw someone die, but then I saw so much of it. I watched people die without a groan or murmur, and I realized that it is a lot easier to die than people think. There were three venereal wards at the hospital, and the corpsmen who worked in those wards told big tales of vicious diseases they were dealing with. I kept away from those patients as though they had leprosy.

There was one nurse in particular. I remember her name was Miss Grace Darn. She was very beautiful. She used to say to me, "Why do you look at the floor when you talk to me?" I was very bashful and I wanted to keep the lovelight from my eyes.

One morning after I had been there for about four months, I missed a roll call. I was court-martialed as an example because the practice of missing roll call was widespread, and I was given three days on bread and water. However, there were fifteen of us sentenced that day and there were only two cells in the brig so we had to take turns. The brig was right next to a store and my friends saw to it that I was well nourished. I thought the whole thing was a big joke.

At about that time I ran across a man carrying a bottle of corn whiskey. It was a very common thing in those days for people from downtown to approach the servicemen. The price was $3. Also about that time I went ashore with a young Italian boy about my own age. We went to a house of prostitution and we shared a room. The women were very businesslike and professional, and for my part I wasn't sure what was expected of me. He was in a bed on the other side of the room and we began to laugh at each other. The women were in a hurry to get it over with and on to the next customer, and it wasn't consummated. We just laughed and the women became impatient and mad. They got their money anyway.

In 1921 I was transferred to the Navy Yard Dispensary in Ports-

mouth where I worked with civilian cases, employees at the yard. I
served under a senior nurse in the Navy. She used hair dye and everything. After a while I requested an examination for promotion to pharmacist's mate, third class, and I hadn't even begun to shave at that
time.

I remember right about that time I took my first drink; it was
corn whiskey and I became violently ill from it. I didn't have another
drink for at least a year. In Portsmouth I met the first homosexual I
had ever met. I had heard a lot of talk about those people without
ever having met one. I wouldn't know one if I met one. There were
two men who talked a lot about their friend Doc Swade of Washington. One day in the mess hall one of these sailors introduced me to a
civilian as his friend Doc Swade from Washington. A few weeks later
this fellow came up to me one day and stuck out his hand and asked if
I'd seen the other two men. I said no and he said, "Let's go down to
Ocean View"—that's a summer resort. I told him no, I was going on
watch in the morning. He insisted. Then I told him that I was financially embarrassed. He convinced me that I would be doing him a
favor, so I went with him. He wanted to spend money on different
amusements. I couldn't figure him out. I had no idea there was anything wrong with him. Then he wanted to go and stay at the hotel
overnight. I told him that I had watch. I didn't want to risk it. He kept
pleading, and then the first glimmer struck me—could he be one of
those? When I got the idea, I certainly was not going to stay down
there. I rode back in a taxi with him to Norfolk. I jumped out and
left him as if getting away from a mad dog—scared to death at that.
After that he wrote me a couple of letters—he worked for the Bureau
of Printing and Engraving in Washington—about what a delightful
night it was to sleep—"perfumed breeze, summer air." After that, when
I saw the other two fellows, I thought what I knew about them.

That same year, I had my first real sexual experience. There was a
place in St. Helena across from the Navy Yard. I went over there with
some of the other fellows, and this waitress worked in the restaurant.
I think these other men put her up to it. I don't know whether they
said or just suspected that I was a virgin but they were going to undo
it. It was a joke for them. She would hug me and put her arms around
me. She was probably five or six years older than I was but I thought
she loved me. I found that she was for hire and thought a good deal
about it. It probably took me a month before I paid her and had re-

lations with her. It seemed that those women would inspect the men to see if they had venereal disease. I thought I was very matter of fact. I found out something then that became more and more apparent to me as I grew older—that you just can't accept and have relations with any woman without affection. In later life, for a woman to attract me sexually, I'd have to be in proximity to her for a length of time and know her, like her, and all that. Well, we got paid twice a month and usually about every payday after that I'd patronize some house of prostitution. I never took any protective measures against venereal disease. I guess I was just taking a chance, but I never contracted any.

In 1921 I was transferred to the Marine Barracks in Norfolk. This was a receiving station for men returning from service in the tropics. Many of them needed treatment for venereal disease. Half of them had malaria. Their skin was yellow and the men were "tropical." To me they brought vivid tales of the banana republics, along with monkeys, parrots, and mongrel dogs, and tales of bandits. It was regular Richard Harding Davis stuff and I swallowed it hook, line, and sinker. They told me about the Navy corpsmen who were serving there who were their own boss. The following year, I requested transfer to Haiti.

They sent me to the Dominican Republic. In those days they had water, electricity, and sewage only in the few big cities. I was immediately taken with the tropics. It seemed to me that all were living for the day when they could get back to the States. One American dollar was worth five of their dollars and one could buy a horse for $20. I bought a horse. When I was off duty I would practice medicine on the natives. I found every type of skin disease and venereal disease. I visited two leper colonies. Elephantiasis was prevalent. Ninety percent of the Marines had malaria and dengue fever. I had dengue. Syphilis was as common as a headache. There would be long lines waiting at the hospital each week for treatment—all outpatient stuff.

I was a kid—a third class pharmacist's mate with a rating equal to a sergeant in the marines. They have to work six years to get that far and I'd only been in for a couple of years. The medics were looked up to by the natives—they were respected. They had a common faith that the medics could cure anything. I wanted a lot of experience. Ninety percent of the natives were black. The servicemen referred to them as *gooks*. After a man had been there two months he was said to be color blind. I believe that most of the men tried to get drunk before they went out and had relations with the native women. I was discriminating and tried to find one as white as possible. I underwent a big conflict there the first time I ever saw a woman manhandled by a man. It was a big Marine and he really threw this native woman around.

I stayed in the Dominican Republic eighteen months. During that time I learned to gamble so women and booze didn't interest me much. However, drinking was almost a social compulsion. I'd go where a gang was celebrating and they'd offer me a drink. I'd get out of it if there was a way to get out of it.

I was sent back to the States and spent three months in Hampton Roads, Virginia, and then was discharged at the expiration of my enlistment.[2] I visited two or three cities in Virginia, but after a few weeks of civilian life I decided I missed the gang. Also I liked the idea of not having responsibility. I decided it would be easier to be wild in the Army, so I threw over my training and enlisted in the Army.

They sent me to Fort Eustis in the Coast Artillery. I found a lot of difference between the Marines and the Army. In the Army it was a case of getting in one place and staying there. I was promoted to private first class and made a fifth-class gun mechanic, but there were a few old noncommissioned officers and little chance for further promotion at Eustis. I discovered that in the Army you can be smart and still not get anywhere. Life there consisted of infantry drill, maneuvers, maintenance of equipment, and basketball. I joined the battery team and before long had worked myself up to the regiment team and finally the post team.

One of my best friends was a company clerk. This man had once had extensive business experience but he had been forced out of Mexico in connection with some sort of oil fraud. He got me interested in literature—to be interested in some sort of mental outlook—philosophy. I matured late. There was a sort of separation between the mental outlook and my environment. I was just a dumb private in the Army but I found that the better things weren't altogether isolated from me. Among the works I read during that period were those of Shelley, Rabelais, Byron, Swinburne, Aristophanes, and a great deal of other satire. Garrison life in peacetime was a humdrum monotony. I supplemented my pay with a little successful gambling. I felt adjusted and was considered a good soldier. I drank very little—occasionally

---

2. This episode was later identified as a dishonorable discharge. Hence the switch to the Army.

some corn whiskey. It was during Prohibition. I would become very nauseated and never became habituated. The officers had little contact with the men. I got the impression from Kipling that the best army officers are gentlemen and the most successful soldiers are blackguards.

I had no future outlook at that time—no occupational plans, no economic plans. I was just taking life as it came, just as if there was always to be an Army. I had no permanent attachments with any women, no affection because I had always realized that it was transitory. The good women I was in contact with seemed to be inaccessible, and I never became acquainted with them.

After three years at Fort Eustis my enlistment expired and I reenlisted. By my own choice I was sent to a different station, Fort Moultrie, South Carolina. This was a great financial success for me. The battery commander would tolerate no drinking on the post, but he never objected to gambling. I had always played poker for percentage, not luck. I don't believe in luck, so I quit gambling and ran a poker game in my quarters. I sold chips, supplied cards, and cut the deck. I got 25 cents on every $5 played, and since there were no operating expenses I realized profit of about $200 a month. I never held on to the money, though. I never had any desire to own a car and I never gave a thought to future security. I was a good-time Charlie. I gave it away or threw it away.

Aside from the poker games, I spent most of my time reading but not airing my views. The men were old soldiers and most of them were married. At this post I sometimes thought of getting married myself. Drinking never became a habit there. I had an occasional drink of corn whiskey, but it usually made me sick and then I wouldn't want any more for months afterwards.

Later on, they sent me to Fort Benning, Georgia, as a machine gunner in the infantry. It was a very rigorous outfit. I was just a typical doughfoot there, carrying a tripod. It was strictly a camp life. We slept four in pyramidal tents. I had been in Virginia and the Carolinas but down in Georgia I became conscious, for the first time, of the fact that I was a Yankee. We were accepted, but there was never a close comradeship with those fellows who were in their own back yard. There was a lot of gathering in cliques, with the New Englanders together. This was the first big Army post I was in. There were more regulations, strict rules, M.P.'s in town, restricted districts. The whole code was not what you do but what you can get away with.

In 1932 my enlistment terminated again. I began to think that I was
getting middle-aged—I was then twenty-eight—and I decided I should
make a change because if I waited until later it would only be harder.
I left Fort Benning and went to Boston. That was in the middle of the
Depression so I signed up for a trip with the Army Transport Service
to San Francisco. I was on the West Coast for a few months. While I
was there I got a letter from my mother telling me that my grandfather had died. He was in his seventies. The letter had taken some
time to reach me. I felt bad; he was the only person I ever really
loved. I'm glad he never knew what became of me. I returned to New
York and from New York went home.[3]

I hadn't been home in ten years. I suppose they tried to make me
feel at home. I was very shy about meeting people. There was unemployment. My stepfather was working and I wasn't. I felt out of
place. I had never realized the necessity of having a job. My grandfather had left his property to my mother. It was a small town and I
had lost the contacts with my schoolmates. I thought that people were
overcurious about people they didn't recognize. I was dissatisfied and
unhappy. About that time there didn't seem to be any opportunity
there and I said that I was going to Boston. There were a couple of
insurance policies that my grandfather had been paying on since I was
small, and I cashed them in and went to Boston.

In Boston, it seemed that I had just to stand on a street corner and
a man offered me a job. It was as caretaker of an apartment house.
There was a bootlegger on the first floor, bookies on the second floor, and
prostitution on the third floor. It was right there in the West End of
Boston. The place was noisy and I went where it was more quiet to
live. Prior to getting this job I'd stayed at a rooming house and one
of the men there told me how two men could get an apartment cheap.
So he and I got a place with two bedrooms and a kitchen. My working hours were short. It was a regular janitor's job. The owner of the
place got me another job in a respectable place. Between the two
jobs I managed to have a radio, I halfway furnished the place, bought

3. As later revealed by Frank's mother, and still later by Frank himself, his formal
military career was terminated in 1928 with a prison sentence for an escapade which
included stealing an officer's car and striking a civilian police officer when apprehended. Frank did take a trip with the Army Transport Service to the West Coast,
where he was imprisoned at Alcatraz, but he was there for five years—not just for
a few months. This is one of the two major life events which Frank omitted from
his original life history, which it should be remembered was provided within the
first few weeks of our acquaintance.

new things—clothing. What I'm trying to get at is that this only took a few months. Then I was comfortably situated with nothing else to aspire to. This other man I was living with—he was quite a bit older —made me acquainted with others. An evening's entertainment would be bridge and listening to the radio. Through him I met a professional choir singer. He was a regular bohemian type—lived easily, got along comfortably. Through him I began to go into a speakeasy in the North End of Boston. I'd go in there and drink.

This particular place made quite an impression on me. I'd been living very comfortably. I met different people, nurses from Massachusetts General Hospital, a couple of students from Harvard, a few men who were probably criminals. There was singing, dancing, drinking of home-brew beer. Probably it was the atmosphere more than the booze that attracted me. After two months of beer I began drinking Italian wine. In a short period I seemed to develop a tolerance. I found I could drink a little more and a little more. This was when I really developed the drinking.[4] I found I could tolerate as much as some of the people who were drinking regularly. After a period of a few weeks I began to drink grain alcohol and ginger ale. I'd always stay till midnight or one o'clock, when they closed. Occasionally this singer would stop over and stay at my apartment. He'd always drink in the morning—start right in where he had left off. I saw that he would not suffer any ill effects, so I began to try a small one in the morning. A small one grew into a big one. A few months of this—and that's the first time it ever crossed my head that the world could be a pretty dull place without something to drink. Before I had this apartment I was living in, another man had lived there for a long time. When he became drunk he thought he still lived there—he'd be up there trying to fit his key into my lock. My attitude was, How could a man ever get that low? It was my idea that a person could drink and even get drunk and still maintain a moderate respectability.

Through working in the apartment house I became acquainted with an Italian girl from a large family. She was only seventeen. She'd never been out with anybody—not innocent but strictly a virgin. She visited

4. Frank's description here of developing an alcoholic drinking pattern within a few months after he discovered that he could retain alcohol is contrary to the more common route to alcoholism through ten to fifteen years of increasingly extensive drinking. However, it is not uncommon for individuals like Frank, who initially have experienced hypersensitivity to alcohol, to become alcoholics quite quickly if and when they develop an ability to tolerate alcohol at all.

my apartment a good many times. She brought some of her father's Italian wine. There were never any sexual relations. I probably felt some affection for her but she was the first decent girl I'd ever come into contact with. I realized the seriousness of the situation. I thought I'd better get out of there. So I bought a ticket to New York and then on to Philadelphia.

I was able to get a job in a private tuberculosis sanitarium for women in New Jersey. That place was really isolated. There I used to go on periodic drinking sprees with another attendant. I stayed there for about four months, but the pay was small and the work was only that of a porter. It required no skill, so I finally left and went back to Boston, where I got a job in a veterans' mental hospital.

That made quite an impression on me. I was locked in a ward with forty or fifty madmen. A good many impressions I received there revolutionized my thinking. There were different manifestations of insanity—some homicide, some suicide. There were a couple of patients with Korsakoff's psychosis. One of the nurses said to me, "You seem to be paying particular attention to this patient" (one of the Korsakoff psychosis patients), and I said, "Yeah, I'm going to end up like that myself." The men were vets of World War I and I had spent much time in the service. I was sympathetic. I had the desire to render service—it was not altogether a matter of compensation. Although drinking was strictly taboo I had my pint or fifth every day. I'm not bragging. I developed a sort of professional curiosity, read textbooks on alcoholism, tried to understand it. I met doctors, lawyers, epileptics, a few prize fighters. I discovered it is possible for people with brains to go crazy. I was there for seven months on night duty. Then one day I went to Boston to buy a pair of shoes. I got drunk and when I woke up the time for returning was past. I called up the superintendent to say that I was sick and would be in later. Then I thought it over and felt disgusted with lies and excuses, and I never went back. I left my belongings and mailed in the keys. This was the first job I ever lost through drinking.

The next few years were marked by progression, habituation, tolerance for booze. I never seriously tried to stop until about 1938. At one time I got particularly depressed about the drinking and went to see a psychoanalyst in Cambridge. A friend thought it might help me and he thought the psychoanalyst might be interested in me. This psychoanalyst was a pretty smart guy from Harvard. Both he and his wife were doctors. His method was to start with heredity, education, and environment. I was pretty sure he was trying to see whether I was a paranoid, whether I had an Oedipus complex, or this or that. He'd ask me a particular question and say, "Did that make you mad?" I'd say, "No, I realize why you asked me." From the bad prognosis this doctor found, I assumed that I was more or less psychologically pre-determined to remain an alcoholic.

At about that time I had been reading some literature by Tolstoy, and I decided that some people should work with their brains and others with their hands, so I took a job in the Maine woods as a lumber hand. I spent four months there. It was twenty miles from the highway; there were no lights, no telephone, no radio. It was like going back a hundred years. There was no place to get a drink there so I stayed sober the whole time. I became physically rejuvenated, toughened up, but I was working with Finlanders, French Canadians, Poles, and Russians; they didn't satisfy me intellectually, so I quit.

I went from there to Boston and then to New Hampshire, where I enrolled in a veterans' CCC camp. After six weeks I was promoted to assistant leader. We were allowed $2 a week in a canteen fund and this was enough to buy twenty bottles of beer, with which I got drunk every weekend. After about four months I headed back to Boston. They had withheld over $100 from my pay at the CCC, so when I got to Boston I went on a big binge. Then I went over to Albany and got a temporary job in a recreation center. After a while I enrolled in a veterans' CCC for the Second Corps Area, and they sent me to Fort Dix, New Jersey, and from there to another camp. The men in this camp were all veterans and 90 percent of them drank as much as possible every weekend. After about three weeks, I woke up one Sunday morning and found they were looking for one of them. I said I didn't know where he was. Then I found out I had had a fight with him the night before and he was in the hospital. I didn't remember anything about it. They brought me up before some local justice of the peace. He said he understood that it was a drunken brawl—that we were both at fault—but that he couldn't release me while the other man was in the hospital. So he gave me thirty days in jail.

That was the first time I was ever in jail for any length of time. Before that I had been detained only overnight. I was very much upset over the fact that I didn't remember anything about the fight. Well, I had a lot of time to think it over in the thirty days. I didn't know how badly he was hurt, but he recovered and I was released and discharged from the vets' CCC. I went to the nearest large town, Philadelphia. Remember, I had just got thirty days for half killing a man. I made a lot of resolutions about keeping my hands in my pockets, but I got drunk that night in Philadelphia and woke up the next morning in jail with a broken thumb. I'd never been arrested there before, so they released me the next morning. I went to one of those medical colleges in Philadelphia to get the hand fixed up. I had no funds. This doctor was good—he put on a smooth dressing and took lots of care. I hitched through New York—stayed overnight in a municipal lodging house there and had the dressing changed in Bellevue Hospital in New York. Then I got a ride to Manchester, New Hampshire. I removed the dressing from my hand and passed a physical and re-enrolled in the vets' CCC. This time I went to Vermont. It was the summertime and I played baseball in the afternoon and worked in the morning. I stayed there long enough to play on the South District championship team and be awarded a little gold baseball. I came out of there—some of the men had got jobs in a state hospital. I secured a job through an application and through a doctor on the staff there who had been one of my patients at the veterans hospital.

The plant there was divided into different buildings. There was a woman supervisor in charge of my building—two nurses in my ward, five attendants, and only forty-five patients. They were bedridden, helpless, incurable; they were sent there to die. Drinking was verboten, but I drank a quart of gin a day—was never drunk. There was a state liquor store where one could buy a quart for only $1.24. I found an excuse to leave the ward and go to my quarters for a drink at different times of the day. That sort of sustained me while working—at night I'd drink beer in a tavern.

The other attendants weren't trained—it was just a job for them. I'd had experience in this work. I took steps toward compensation for my drinking. I had eleven uniforms. I was always immaculate while stiff as a boot. I was sympathetic toward the patients. I took pride in their appearance—saw to it that they were properly nourished. My work wasn't open to criticism. It didn't affect my efficiency—I was sort of stimulated, but some mornings I would be feeding a patient and I would think to myself, "I ought to be in there and you ought to be feeding me." I was maintaining the appearance and doing the work but I was often sick from the effect of the booze I had been drinking the night before. About this time I found I could escape a lot of the bad effects of a binge by using hypnotic medicines—amytal and the like. That is, I could sleep and I wouldn't suffer any of the nervousness. It's a very effective drug, not habit-forming or anything like that.

Association between attendants and nurses was frowned upon. Many of the nurses there graduated as student nurses at that hospital. We fraternized in town. It was nothing serious, just convivial, that we could work together in the daytime and make whoopee at night. I left there on an impulse. I worked till noontime one day and I looked back in the ward and said, "This doesn't make sense."

Then I went on a spree for three or four days in nearby towns. Then I decided to go home. I came into the house and sat down in a rocker. My mother began to talk and talk. I told her I'd been on a bender. I said I was very sick and nervous and did she mind if I retired. She said she hadn't realized there was anything wrong with me. It was the first time I ever had any suffering or bad nervousness after drinking.

The next day I went to a doctor in Calvinville. He didn't know me and hadn't heard anything about me. I went to his place in the evening after office hours. I explained that I was an alcoholic and was suffering from withdrawal effects of alcohol—that the symptoms were nervousness, couldn't sleep, tremor in the hands, feeling of apprehension. Well, I don't believe that the man had ever had an alcoholic up before him in a professional capacity. I told him I was familiar with the nature of the disease and its usual treatment. He told me what he'd read and heard about—what little experience he'd had. He gave me a shot of Vitamin B_1 in the arm and a few drops of sedative. That was the death of my hopes for treatment from a general practitioner. I didn't think I could go to a doctor to be treated for booze. I decided it was more or less impossible.

After that I took off for Boston. There, through a friend, I got a job with a country doctor in New Hampshire who had just finished his internship in Boston. I worked for him for three months as general medical assistant. We got drunk together. He knew all the standard recuperators from getting drunk—amytal, adrenalin in the eye, a clean white jacket. It was a nice life, country town, country people—good standing in the community—small pay. I told him my intentions of quitting. I quit with a recommendation as conscientious, courteous, knowledge of asepsis, ethics. He told me that when the world got too tough there would always be a place for me there. I never took him up on it. One time he told me that I should think about going to medical school. I told him that I was too old and no money.

Then in 1939 the war started. I wrote to the British Consul in Boston and volunteered my service in the Canadian Army. I had thought I would get in on the ground floor. They declined because I was an American citizen, but they hinted that if I went to Canada they would find a way around the regulations. However, that took a bit of initiative so I never got there.

Then I went to Providence, where I got a job in a foundry. After a couple of weeks I went on to New Haven and found a job as a stoker fireman in a large laundry. I earned $40 to $50 a week. I was pleased with the work and thought that I was there for a long time. Most of the men were old employees. I lived in a private home—a rooming house kept by the widow of a Navy man. She was one of those busybodies. The job was all right. I was drinking at off hours. Probably half my pay went for booze. I can't give any good reason for my quitting. They knew that I drank but it was under control. After I gave them notice I even went downtown to pick up another fireman for them. I had probably $100 and I came down and worked in the Hotel Swift as a fireman.

Well, about this time I saw the Yale students parading around the Green so I began to think of getting into the service myself. I realized I was too old for military, so I enrolled in the Maritime Service. I was sent to Brooklyn, New York, Sheepshead Bay. It was very rugged training—they tried to cram in months what it usually takes years to learn. I was sent to Milwaukee to try out on one of those new diesel ocean tugs built up there. There was very little drinking during training. The first few weeks we were not allowed ashore at all. I felt excellent. They had boxing and I had more than one kid say to me, "I'll go easy on you, Pop." In Milwaukee, there was subsistence money and plenty of drinking.

On a leave in Chicago I became acquainted with a woman. She had a brother in the Navy. We became acquainted through that medium. I supposed that whatever interest she had in me was only because of her brother in the Navy. So the first time we went out and got drunk together I found out her feelings were not so platonic. In fact we

lived more or less like we were married for a few months. Sometimes
we registered as man and wife in hotels—sometimes without baggage.
That was probably my longest attachment. We disagreed about everything. She acted like a lady and I could go out in public with her—
sexual outlet too. I had the feeling that it couldn't go on forever. I
was dissatisfied with being on the lakes during the war, so I left one
night on the last passenger train after we'd been drinking all day. She
saw me off and all that business.[5]

I came down to New York and worked for a steamship company
till April, 1944. During this time I sailed out to the tropics and there
was drinking in the ports. I'd just spent $400 for booze. I was sick
and I had been sick the last few days before we got to port. I went
to a Marine hospital in Massachusetts for six weeks. I had gastro-
enteritis. It could have been the booze or it could have been the water
in foreign ports. I was getting sick of making money and then going
on a drunk. I suspected periods of ten to twelve days without any
drinking was what was causing the big benders. I figured I'd stay on
shore where I could get the booze and I'd be more content. I signed
up with an employment agent in Boston and shipped down to New
Haven to work in the yards as a freight hand. There were long hours.
I wasn't working for any particular reason, just money. When I became tired and wanted a drink I could get it. I shipped into New York
City and shipped out on the Pennsylvania Railroad to Trenton, worked
four months there for the railroad. I used to get drunk in Philadelphia.
I had a lot of money, I'd get drunk, didn't feel like working. On the
way back to Boston I stopped in Fieldcrest. I was accosted on Main
Street—a man offered me a job. I worked for seven months for a
carloading company as a freight handler and loader. I was offered a
job as a checker, but I wouldn't take it because I would get paid
every week instead of every night. After deductions I got $6 to $9 a
day. About $2.50 went for living expenses; the rest for rum. So in
February of this year (1945) I woke up in a third-rate hotel, sick, no
money, just the prospect of going back to work and doing the whole
thing over again. It didn't make sense.

I knew of people in town who had received aid from the Salvation
Army. I went to the local branch, was frank, explained myself, told

5. As later revealed by Frank's mother, this is actually a description of Frank's
marriage. His wife was an employee in a public infirmary where Frank was being
treated for alcoholism.

them what my mode of living had been. I could go back but I didn't want to. He sent me to the Salvation Army hotel. I went to work in the baling room. We were paid on commission. The pay was small, good living quarters. I usually had a room to myself; there were other beds but they were usually empty. In the first few weeks I was dissatisfied about the financial returns. Then I adopted a more reasonable attitude. I figured that probably money wouldn't do me any good. I got drunk once a week down there, privately in my room, no interference. I did the work. I did meet a good friend down there. He was a successful businessman, hobbies, bookcollecting, stampcollecting, antiques. I became acquainted with him through his purchases of salvage from the Salvation Army. I stayed down there till July.

Then I figured I'd try to earn money again. I went to work for a carloading company for a week. I gave my money to the foreman to keep for me every night. But I got up one morning and one of the men in the hotel said, "Wait a minute, I got some beer coming." I said I had to go work, but he said, "Wait a minute, it'll be right up." Had some beer, a little more beer; at ten o'clock I went out and got a quart of rum. I worked three weeks in all and went back to the Salvation Army. I had worked there; they were glad to see me and they gave me back my old job. I stayed there till I came to New Haven. I said I'd been in Fieldcrest for about a year and what did I have for it—no money, no prospects. I knew a lot of people who were always drinking. Maybe if I go where I'm not known I can stay sober if I want to. I came here (New Haven Salvation Army Center) and got the same job. The first thing I did in the morning was to load the same truck that I usually loaded the first thing in the morning in Fieldcrest. I said to the fellow, "I didn't have to come here to load you up." Well, there you have it. My whole life history.[6]

6. A table listing the major events in Frank's life from his birth in 1904 through 1944 is found in Appendix I.

4. A Transitional Period, 1945-48

In the process of recording Frank's life history we embarked on a relationship involving numerous informal discussions of his current life situation, several attempts to bring him some professional help through the Yale Plan Clinic and other resources, some provisions for his immediate needs for food, clothing, shelter, and transportation, and an emerging friendship. This chapter, which covers the years 1945–48, recounts the shift from formal interviews to informal and diverse encounters and begins a prospective record of Frank's life told in part through selections from his letters.

This chapter also covers a significant transitional period for Frank. In 1945 and 1946 Frank's life-adjustment pattern revolved around semiformal institutional settings such as skid row, live-in jobs, and other institutions of transiency. In 1947, however, he spent half of the year in a public infirmary, a rehabilitation home for alcoholics, and a mental hospital. By 1948, a pattern of dependency on formal institutional settings including jails, mental hospitals, and public infirmaries was more firmly established and this pattern continued with only a few interludes of major variation for the next seventeen years.[1]

Unlike many alcoholics, who tend to deny or de-emphasize the significance of alcoholism in their life problems, Frank was not reluctant to think of himself and have others view him as an alcoholic. Frank began our second interview just two days after we first met with a reference to his alcohol problem. He felt that the problem of alcohol could prob-

1. See Table on page 349, Chapter 10.

ably be handled in about a hundred years. He compared it with tuberculosis, untreatable for so long, but with which doctors were now getting good results. He had read the book *Alcoholics Anonymous* and said he had enjoyed reading his own experiences into the case histories but he still did not think the organization could be of much help to alcoholics.

Frank had taken his first drink when he was seventeen, but had not had another for some time. Heavy drinking started in 1933 at the age of twenty-nine. He said he drank to escape reality. Although he disliked people who always say they are different, he felt that he was different because he had none of the usual aftereffects, such as a big head or a disgusted feeling. The only effect he felt was a nervousness, indescribable but entirely abnormal in its intensity. He didn't worry about anything in particular, he just got jittery. He blamed his heavy drinking on a feeling of inferiority and worthlessness which had increased with time so now he felt he was too far gone for rehabilitation. He said that alcohol has a destructive effect on the mind and body about which nothing can be done.

After impatiently reading a typed copy of the first day's material, he said, "You haven't asked me yet how my face got all scratched up." He then related the following:

"I was sitting on my bunk Saturday afternoon after getting paid and I said to the man in the next bunk that it was a week since I'd had a drink. I haven't been able to go more than seventeen days this year without getting drunk. I went up to a place on the main street and bought a fifth of rum. I had about $5 to start with and I took the rest of it and the rum and went into one of the saloons. I had about fifteen beers and got to talking with the bartender. Then I decided to drink some of the rum, so I left and the next thing I knew it was night and I woke up swimming in the river among a bunch of old ties—no idea how I got there. I had only a nickel left and no rum. I've reached the final stage. I can't remember a thing about it, don't know how I got there. I feel resentful that I can't remember because I'd hate to think of some guy throwing me in and my not knowing it."

After telling his story, Frank said he really felt he had reached the final stage because of his loss of memory and because he felt neither disgusted nor worried but just nervous. He added that every time he had a little money he got to thinking that it would never get him anywhere so he might as well spend it and get drunk. I suggested that he could arrange to have his wages withheld, and he replied, "If I did that they'd think I'm crazy." He said that about the only other thing he really liked well was candy, but he also liked a good meal—not what you get "in these hash joints"—but in an air-conditioned Chinese restaurant. I then mentioned the program offered by the Yale Plan Clinic[2] and he answered that he would like to know more about it.

Frank appeared for the third session in a clean white shirt and freshly bathed. He was planning to leave the Social Service Center within a few days and wanted to know how I would handle the rest of the life history. He had no plans but felt restless and found the living conditions uncomfortable. It was hard to live in a room filled with drinkers and not drink. We agreed on an interview later in the week. On Saturday Frank planned to spend the afternoon looking around for a job in New Haven.

When I again suggested the possibility of his visiting the Yale Plan Clinic, he said that he had once seen a psychoanalyst in Cambridge—"this man must have known his business since he had gone to Harvard" —and he had told him his case was pretty hopeless. Frank told me about one of Freud's cases he had read about—a man saw a pair of women's boots under a bed the first time he witnessed sexual intercourse; later this man was arrested and sent to an institution because he had been masturbating in front of a store window filled with women's shoes. He thought the case and Freud's interpretation of a connection between the two incidents were "disgusting and ridiculous."

Frank asked me what I thought of behaviorism and explained his understanding of the term—that certain acts become firmly set in the behavior of an individual and nothing can be done to change these acts. He believed he knew what would eventually happen to him. He would go along just as he was, gradually getting worse, and finally if he could stand the strain physically he would end up in an asylum or at least as a public charge. He had several times put himself in a position where he couldn't get alcohol but it had never worked.

He had not written to his mother for two years except to send Mother's Day cards, and she had no idea where he was or what condition he was in. She had told him many times that he shouldn't stay in

2. The Yale Plan Clinics in New Haven and Hartford were established in 1944 by the Yale Center of Alcohol Studies. At that time, these clinics represented an initial experiment in trying to provide effective medical, psychological and social work treatment specifically for alcoholics on an outpatient basis. These clinics served as a model for similar programs established during the late 1940's throughout the country. In 1949 the Yale Plan Clinics became units of the publicly supported Connecticut Commission on Alcoholism.

Calvinville because there are no opportunities in a small town. He remarked that the trouble with coming from a small town like that was that everything was either all black or all white. When one goes back all the people one meets ask, "Where have you been?" "What have you been doing?" "What line are you in now?" It appeared to be painful for him to talk about his own life and his low spirits were very apparent.

To the fourth interview Frank brought a book of Kipling's writings. He said while he appreciated my interest in obtaining a life history which could be used as a measuring stick in helping others, recalling some events made him pretty unhappy. He then opened Kipling to "An Interview with Mark Twain," and located a section about the autobiographical aspects of Twain's works. He quoted Twain as saying that no man can give a really true picture of himself for one is bound to color any autobiographical story. The reader unconsciously reads the truth into autobiographical writing so while the words may not be true literally they are accurate as the reader unconsciously interprets them. Frank seemed comforted with Mark Twain's assurance that it would not be too serious if parts of his own story were not quite accurate.

Frank was in fine spirits. The depression of the previous interview had disappeared and he talked freely and easily about himself. He had seen an advertisement by a large local laundry for workers. After calling the laundry and asking for the foreman, whom he had known, he reminded the foreman that he had worked as a fireman for him a few years before and asked if there was a job he could have. The foreman told him to come out on Monday, that he would have something for him. They started talking about some of the men whom Frank had known at the laundry and suddenly the foreman said, "Oh, now I remember you. Don't bother coming out here. You drink too much." The working conditions at this laundry were excellent; they had done everything to make it nice for the employees; and laundries in other cities had sent men to study these working conditions. He added that most of the workers stayed there for a long time—a form of permanent employment. He realized, he said, that his present experience might be some form of punishment that is bound to come to drinkers; that he was being punished for drinking by being kept from a permanent type of job with fine working conditions. As he told me this, Frank grinned in a way that suggested this was just what he had expected, that his case was hopeless.

When I again proposed a visit to the Yale Plan Clinic, he answered that although he felt it was hopeless to expect any help he wasn't getting anywhere by himself and had nothing to lose.

The following Monday Frank appeared with a red face and, slightly embarrassed, reported the events of his weekend. He had first had his hair cut, then read quite a bit in *Alcohol Explored*,[3] had dinner, bought some candy bars, and "hung around." He had gone through Saturday evening without drinking, but on Sunday morning to avoid religious service he and one of the other men had gone to the "dugout" (illegal saloon) and had a few beers topped off with a pint of rum. Frank said the drinks had not affected him much physically but he had become mentally depressed. He reminded me that *Alcohol Explored* discusses some cases of alcoholics who could not be cured and noted that he was not able to find much encouragement for himself.

Following the life-history session on Wednesday, I told Frank that he had an appointment at the Yale Plan Clinic on Friday. His only comment was that if it had been for Saturday he would have had time to get his suit pressed.

On Thursday, Frank said he was not sure he would go to the clinic as he knew they could not help him and he was tired of all this sympathy. He knew what would eventually become of him, and he did not see why he should bother going through all this business. "Besides," he said, "you have my life history and you can do whatever you want with it." I told him that appointments at the clinic were difficult to obtain and I hoped he would change his mind.

On Friday, I called for Frank as prearranged, but he said he had definitely decided not to go to the clinic. He spoke of trying unsuccessfully to telephone me and added that he had taken his suit to the cleaner's "as a sort of insurance so I can't go." He was very apologetic about the inconvenience he had caused.

After completion of the life-history recording in early August and my abortive attempt to interest Frank in the Yale Plan Clinic, I maintained contact with him on a casual basis for several weeks. Frank's life followed a regular pattern: he worked hard at the center all week—doing the work ordinarily assigned to three or four men—and he used his wages of about $10 for weekend drinking.

During this period Frank made few friends and was in many respects quite antisocial. When sober he spent much free time reading, and was considered by the other men to be an intellectual snob. When he drank it was alone or with one other person. While drunk he was mean, sometimes vicious, and the other men stayed out of his way. Perhaps his most

3. H. W. Haggard and E. M. Jellinek, *Alcohol Explored* (Garden City, N.Y.: Doubleday, 1942).

outstanding trait at the center was his compulsive striving for neatness and cleanliness. His person and belongings were usually immaculate; he was precise in making his bed; and he devoted odd moments of the working day to sweeping up the yard and generally straightening things out.

Early in October a representative of the Yale Plan Clinic visited the center and Frank was one of several men I invited to meet him. Frank asked several questions on the findings of physiological research and on the physical and chemical effects of alcohol. He remarked that he could drink over two quarts of whiskey a day and that he had no difficulty in abstaining during the week. He questioned whether he could be considered an alcoholic. The visitor later commented on Frank's "flattened emotional tone." Frank was invited to come to the clinic and see how it operated but he was not pressed to do so.

About a week later, Frank visited the clinic on a social basis in my company. I left after introducing him. During this visit no attempt was made to question him; the conversation centered on the physiological aspects of drinking. Frank boasted of his physical capacity as a workman and of his capacity to drink. He left in a friendly manner but gave no indication that his defensive resistance to the understanding of alcoholism as a personal problem had been influenced.

About two weeks after his social visit to the Yale Plan Clinic, Frank was on the losing end of a drunken brawl with two other men at the center. According to several reports the argument started over some money spent on rum and ended when Frank was hit by a brass ornament, sustained a deep three-inch gash on his head above the left ear, and was knocked unconscious.

Frank worked as usual on Monday, wearing a cap over his wound. He made no mention of the fight until I asked him what had happened. Then he just said he did not remember much of it. Toward the middle of the week, the cut became infected and, after a great deal of suffering, Frank became delirious and was taken to the hospital. Previously he had told the foreman that he wanted to wait until his "friend Straus" came down before doing anything about his wound. I visited Frank twice while he was in the hospital.[4] The first time he greeted me with: "Well, I guess you're laughing because you know I can't get any rum this week-

4. Frank was visited also by my mother, who was serving as a diversional therapist at the same hospital. This expression of interest in him made quite an impression and he later referred to the visit several times in his letters.

end." On the second visit he said he had had a weekend "candy binge instead of a rum binge." When Frank returned to the center after eight days he looked well and said he felt fine. He reported that the hospital people had wanted him to stay a few more days but he had insisted on leaving. A social service worker had visited him and offered to get city aid in paying for his hospital bill. He had asked why the city should pay for him and declined the offer. He promised the hospital authorities that he would pay his $75 bill in weekly installments of $5 or $10.

Frank repeated several times that he had not felt as well in years and had no desire to drink. He proudly displayed several candy bars and said that they were a "substitute." He added that if he felt as well in a week or so he would think about going to the Yale Plan Clinic. He spoke also of looking for a better-paying job but thought he would wait until he was confident that he would not go back to the bottle. He appeared to be in a state of mild elation.

The following Monday Frank reported that he had gone to a movie on Friday evening, to another movie on Saturday evening, and that on Sunday he had eaten two turkey dinners and taken a five-mile walk. He admitted that it had been somewhat difficult to pass the time over the weekend and he realized more than ever that, with nowhere else to go, the bar is the poor man's clubroom. He mentioned also that he had hardly noticed the Monday work, whereas on other Mondays it had been most difficult.

A week later Frank reported another weekend of sobriety during which he had seen another movie, a sandlot football game, and had again consumed two dinners on Sunday. He spoke again of looking for another job and said he was interested in an advertisement he had seen for workers at a state institution for the feeble-minded. A three-way conversation between Frank, the foreman, and myself turned to the subject of women. The foreman stressed the necessity of keeping women in their place, and Frank said his feeling toward women was based on two books which he had read, *Aphrodite* and Schopenhauer's *Essay on Women*. He felt women were always setting a trap with their physical voluptuousness.

On the subject of alcohol, Frank said he didn't have to drink because he had a lot of other things to interest him. He added that he was beginning to feel very intolerant of the other men at the center "who can't do anything but go out and get drunk."

The following Monday Frank reported another weekend without drinking, but several other men at the center said he had slipped. There were no outward signs of this. Frank said he had paid an installment on his hospital bill and produced a receipt. He mentioned also visiting one of the patients he had met there and taking him some candy. When I asked if he had seen any movies he said that there hadn't been any good ones to see and that he had spent much of his time reading a rather technical history of medicine.

On Friday of the same week Frank stormed through his work in a vicious mood, complaining the work had become too heavy and he was being taken advantage of. He threw things around and cursed as he gave his orders to the other men. On Monday he greeted me with the news that he had gotten "good and drunk" over the weekend. He had started out to get a haircut on Saturday but had stopped at a bar. He had continued drinking and Sunday he felt "pretty awful." He pointed out that he had not even made a payment on his hospital bill.

About two weeks before Christmas Frank wrote to his mother. Within ten days there were three letters in reply. He said the letters contained "general news" and that his mother was urging him to settle down with a steady job. After reading to me from one letter which advised him not to return to Calvinville because the town was too small for "opportunity," he said he really did not feel this would handicap him. He thought many people living there were much happier than people in big cities who were striving to outdo their neighbors. He found something ideal about the noncompetitive nature of life in a small town and said he would return to Calvinville if he felt he would be welcome.

Frank wanted to get a steady job which would pay enough for him to set up a decent little apartment and allow him to cultivate some of his interests—books, plays, movies. He recalled his nice three-room apartment in a good neighborhood in Boston in 1933, which he had furnished himself and for which he had also been able to buy a radio and many convenient appliances. Beyond that point, however, he had nothing else to do with his money and felt this to be one of the reasons he had started to drink heavily. He then brought up the clinic and asked me several questions on specific methods of treatment. I told him these questions could be answered by someone there, but nothing was said about an appointment.

In the middle of January, 1946, Frank informed me that he had asked for an increase in his salary, which was then $12 a week. He had been turned down and was leaving the center the next morning to look for another job. A few days later I heard that Frank and another man had left, obtained jobs as laborers at a local manufacturing firm, and taken a room together in town, but that the other man had returned to the center saying he could not live with Frank.

The next Monday, Frank called me to say that he was at a downtown hotel and asked me to stop and see him. I found him in a thin suit and a crew-neck cotton shirt—in late January. I greeted him with: "I hear you've been working." Frank replied, "I was." He related that he had been paid on the previous Friday and had been drinking ever since. "I want to be put in an institution. I'm crazy and I ought to be in a mad-house." He told me he had known on Friday that he would go out on a bender and had hardly been able to wait for his pay. After drinking about twenty beers and a quart of rum Friday night, he asked at the hotel to be called at six in the morning, but slept through the call. When he awoke he called the factory and said that he would be in to work on Sunday,[5] but he then drank the rest of the day and evening and slept through the call again. He continued drinking until Monday afternoon. We sat for an hour or so over black coffee in a nearby lunchroom while Frank asked numerous questions concerning his future. He finally agreed to visit the Yale Plan Clinic. I gave him $3 to pay for his room and for food when he felt like eating and told him to expect me the next day.

When I called for Frank the next afternoon, I found him barely able to navigate. He had spent the $3 on more beer and rum. After another session with black coffee, he was able to walk the few blocks to the clinic. There a physician examined him and made arrangements to send him to a rest farm operated by members of Alcoholics Anonymous.

At the rest farm, Frank recovered rapidly from the effects of his bender. While he was not talkative the first two or three days, he soon became active in preparing coffee and assisting in the kitchen. He made himself at home and toward the end of his seven-day stay exhibited some elements of sociability. While there, he wrote his first letter to me.

Hope Hollow
Wednesday
January 31, 1946

Dear Bob:

There is no other house for miles as far as one can see. A nice bleak landscape, bare trees, and rugged hills. A splended sense of isolation

5. Frank's job as a stationary fireman required working on Sundays in order to keep the furnaces operating.

far from the crowd's madding strife. A black horse with his back covered with fine snow standing stolidly in the pasture and reminding one
of Walt Whitman's "Me Imperturbe."

Unable as yet to assume my social duties in regard to conversations
and persiflage, it is very apparent to me that I am living with very fine
people. Nice cuisine.

It appears that I recuperate quickly and that I must consider plans
to find my way back (the way back to the same old things or into
metamorphosis). It is a strange commentary on human affairs that I
can feel myself so full of hope after absorbing more than my fair share
of the slings and arrows.

The treatment so far is physiological and is doing much good. One
can not help realizing the insecurity of my present condition. All this
present circumstance would be quite enjoyable could I envision a
future economic independence and rehabilitation. To be fair I don't
suppose I will achieve in a matter of days the security that other men
spend a lifetime fighting for.

Mr. McCarthy[6] called about an hour ago and he feels that I should
drop in on him Friday. I suppose my immediate needs are employment, a place to live. I believe my limited wardrobe of working clothes
was irretrievably lost when I checked out of the hotel. I suppose with
all my good intentions it is going to be tough to regain my solvent
situation of a week ago.

Hope to see you soon,

Moorey

On the morning of February 5, Frank returned to the clinic. The car
which was to have brought him had broken down so he had hitchhiked.
He appeared relaxed and rested upon arrival although he still evidenced
a lack of emotional depth. He spoke of the need to establish himself
economically and of a desire to go to A.A. meetings. He left and returned in the afternoon, having regained his former job firing a furnace.
After retrieving his clothing and obtaining a hotel room, he requested a
loan to pay for his room and food until he would be paid so I gave him
$3.50.

On February 6 and 10 Frank visited the clinic briefly, and on February
8 was seen at an A.A. meeting. He complained of the heat in the boiler

6. The late Raymond G. McCarthy, staff member of the Yale Plan Clinic.

room where he worked. He accounted for the money lent to him and was given an additional $10.

On Monday, February 12, Frank visited the clinic again. He reported that he had remained sober over the weekend. This was contrary to the report that he had appeared at an A.A. meeting on Saturday while under the influence. Frank said little about A.A. and spoke mostly about his immediate economic needs. Some of his enthusiasm seemed to have waned. On February 14, Frank attended a group meeting at the clinic. He said he had had a difficult weekend but had not been drinking and was getting along financially. He left immediately after the meeting without talking to anyone.

In the meantime, we had had three telephone conversations and I had invited him to my home for dinner on the 18th. He failed to appear that night, and we later learned that he had lost his job because of drinking, had gone to an A.A. meeting, and been taken back to the rest farm. He left without notice and shortly afterward spent five days in the Fieldcrest Jail for drunkenness. In Fieldcrest, a member of A.A. to whom Frank mentioned his former service in the Merchant Marine gave him a bus ticket to New York and suggested that he contact someone at the Seamen's A.A. Club. The person whom Frank was to see was out of town when he arrived in New York; he was sent to a seamen's church home for free room and board to await the return of this man. "I went crazy sitting around in a big room with nothing to drink while everyone around me was drunk." He left and signed up with an employment recruitment organization which assigned him to work at the railroad yards near New Haven. After working for two weeks Frank collected his pay and went into New Haven, where, on the morning of April 10, he telephoned my office and left a number where he could be reached. When I called the number (that of a bar) at 2:30, I was told that Frank had waited for a call but had left about ten minutes before.

On April 22, I received the following letter, written on the 18th:

Fieldcrest County Jail

Mon. Nite from F. G. Moore
Dear Bob:

Tried to reach you by phone last week and waited hours for a return call. Things could have been much different had I succeeded.

Am sentenced to ten days' confinement here.

Lost my job and lost my glasses; can't half read what I am writing.

Not a cent for smokes, and sweet charity was responsible for the purchase of this writing paper.

Things are difficult and I hope you will find it worthwhile and possible to get in touch with me.

After all, I did cut my drunks from weekly to fortnitely affairs.

If it appeared that I was probing for rock bottom, this is it.

Went into the "shakes" last Saturday P.M. while waiting transfer up here. Not feeling well enough to think straight or write that way now.

I hope to hear from you.

Moorey

I sent Frank a short note suggesting that if he wanted to take up where he had left off with the Yale Plan Clinic, he should return to New Haven and it might be possible for him to obtain room, board, and work again at the Salvation Army Center.

On April 30, Frank telephoned me from a local bar. He seemed to be in bad shape and said several times that it was "very difficult," that he had money but he wanted me to come and get him. When I suggested the Salvation Army he said, "Yes, but don't you think you have the wrong angle there? I am in no condition to go back there." When I assured him that arrangements had been made for him to be taken in at the center despite his condition, he expressed some doubt as to his ability to get there but he said he would try.

He didn't appear at the center until the next morning but was quite sober. He said that he didn't know what had happened when he left the tavern but that he must have passed out in the street because the first thing he remembered was waking up in the police lockup. He vaguely remembered pleading guilty and being given a suspended sentence and then had come to the center. Frank was very depressed and pessimistic about any possibility of tackling the alcohol problem successfully. His thinking was not clear and he showed definite signs of his recent bender.

This time he remained at the center for two months. He settled back into his previous pattern of hard work during the week and hard drinking on each weekend. Whenever the clinic was mentioned, he said that he wanted to wait. He described one weekend on which he went into a blackout Saturday afternoon and woke up on Sunday morning in a downtown hotel, the dirtiest place he had ever seen. He also went through a two-week period of considerable elation during which he joked freely with the other men, sang, danced, and even jumped rope in his free moments. He told the foreman jokingly that it would be better if they paid him in smokes but gave no evidence of being bothered by his drinking problem.

Early in July, Frank was asked to leave the center after he objected rather vociferously to the presence of another man, who, he claimed, was a faker. He was not heard from for nearly six months until a member of Alcoholics Anonymous, whom Frank had met at the rest farm and for whom he apparently had considerable respect, received the following letter:

Davenport State Infirmary
December 20, 1946

Dear Tom:

Some wiseacre has postulated that a goodly portion of human enjoyment consists of viewing our own happy state as compared to miseries of others. If such is the case, this letter should give you a belly laugh.

I was admitted to this institution on October 29 with a broken hand sustained in an imbroglio, the details of which are lost in the limbo of alcoholic blackout. The doctors have applied the "laying on of the hands," nature has taken charge, and the hand is well. However, I have stayed on in the role of sweeper, general factotum, and boy scout.

For six years prior to my arrival here I was unable to maintain a sober interlude for more than two weeks. It has been eight weeks this time. Now the fact is I can leave here whenever I wish (to go thru the same thing all over again) or stay here sober.

I deeply regret that I can not ascribe the true cause of this self-imposed sobriety. The disinterested logician would say "the broken hand"; and the more fervent brothers would ascribe some supernal intercession. However, it is unlikely that a broken hand or for that matter a broken head, would account for such a divergence in my behavior. And I cannot bring myself to such presumptuousness as to believe that my particular fate concerns Deity. Conscience? atrophied a long time! Sense of responsibility? de good Lawd forbid!

Believe me, Tom, when I affirm I am not giving you the metaphorical "needle." I don't know the cause of this sudden turnabout. Maybe this affliction will run its course; my antibodies, phagocytes, and natural powers of resistance will certainly overcome this virus.

Just consider the fact that if I had not been a drunk, I would have been denied meeting J.B., J.M., E.M., and J. and a host of others, really princes of fellows. It is a God-given privilege of alcoholics to converse with their fellows with frankness and sincerity.

Pity the God-forsaken teetotaler who must cushion every speech with understatement and who fears self-revelation.

I can see nothing incongruous in saying that we drunks indulge in as much self-satisfaction after a week's sobriety as a teetotaler would feel after he had stepped on someone's neck in his climb up the ladder of success.

I suppose what really got me started on this letter to you was the fact that I got to wondering how you feel when your kind interest and best efforts have been to no avail. Do you feel so certain your methods are infallible that when you fail you ascribe unworthiness of the individual as the cause of failure?

A few months ago, I came in contact with a person who felt he had the power to form judgment. Fragmentary information relayed to him caused him to state that "I had not had my nose rubbed enough in the dirt."

During my stay in New Haven, I became acquainted with a Robert Straus. I have never worn my heart on my sleeve, but Straus so insinuated himself into my affection that I confided a personal history which would be told to a close friend (not delivered from a rostrum in competition with other declaimers of the God-awful).

I think Straus could set you right in regard to whether I have had my nose rubbed in the dirt enough.

Recently I have been mentally reviewing the progressive disintegration which has taken place down thru the years: lesser responsibilities, lesser pay, the estrangement of relatives & friends, financial insolvency, necrosis of interests & ambitions, & thru it all, the lack of intellectuality or spirituality to cope with the situation.

Unfortunately, I do not possess that fine sensibility that causes men to find refuge in insanity. An inherited strong physical condition obviates early death. Possibly I will survive five thousand hangovers.

It's going to be a long, hard grind, Tom. Too bad I have the intelligence to realize this.

You should be splitting yourself with laughing.

Honestly yours,
Frank Moore

Could you obtain Straus' address for me—if this long dry spell lasts much longer I will write to McCarthy.

Toward the end of January, 1947, on a Sunday evening, I received a telephone call from Frank in New Haven. He was at the local A.A. rooms. I met him there, and we spent some hours talking in a nearby restaurant. Frank said that he had thumbed his way to New Haven from the Davenport infirmary, where he had spent three months with an injured hand. After leaving New Haven in July he had done railroad work until injured and hospitalized. He told of writing for a number of credentials so that he could get another job with the Merchant Marine. He produced a birth certificate and a certificate of his training in the Navy medical corps. He also had a letter from an official of the Seamen's Church Institute in New York telling him that it would require a week to obtain certain necessary seaman's papers and that he could board and work for that period if he came to the institute. I put Frank up at a local hotel for the night and gave him a railroad ticket to New York. I also wrote a letter of introduction to an acquaintance at the Alcoholics Anonymous Seamen's Club. A few days later I received an answer which read in part:

> Your letter received, but as you will see by the enclosed note, I was out at the time that Moore stopped in. I am very sorry that I could not be of any help. I called Jim Miller at the Seamen's Church Institute, and he said that Moore had stopped in to see him and that he gave him meal tickets and a place to stay for two days. He also gave him enough money to get his seaman's papers and offered him a job.
>
> However, our friend Moore has not been heard from since January 28. I would have liked to meet him and at least speak to him, but that I was not given a chance to do.

The following note from Frank was enclosed. It was scrawled in red crayon on yellow paper:

Dear Jack:

Saw a Mr. Miller at Institute. Gave me bed tickets for two nights and meal tickets.

Shoving off tomorrow. Can't see my way clear hanging around New York City bumming Seamen's A.A. or Church Institute.

Moore

Frank was next heard from on March 18 when he telephoned me again from the New Haven clubrooms of Alcoholics Anonymous, drunk. He said he had $3 and a bottle of rum. He told of leaving New York on the railroad, of working in a labor camp for a few weeks, going on a bender, and landing in Bellevue Hospital for two days. After leaving the hospital he had visited the Seamen's A.A. Club, where he was "offered no help." He then shipped out again for railroad work and had been at Warehouse Point for three weeks before going on another bender and coming to New Haven. It was impossible for me to see Frank that evening and I suggested that he contact the Yale Plan Clinic in the morning, offering to call the clinic in advance to explain. Frank called again later in the evening and reported that they were having a "revival" at A.A. and he had not been able to stomach it. He said that he was "in pretty bad shape" but not bad enough for a policeman to pay any attention to him. Referring to his earlier trip to New York, Frank said I muffed that one by sending him down to the biggest city in the world with only twenty cents in his pockets. Frank said he didn't want to appear ungrateful; he remembered other loans of several dollars and all the money which the clinic had spent on his account. He added, "That is my trouble—too much conscience."

Frank telephoned the clinic the next morning for an appointment, spoke of one beer to give him courage to make the phone call. He appeared at the clinic depressed and confused, and had difficulty sustaining a consecutive thought process. He showed wage receipts from Warehouse Point and said he had five days' wages coming to him there. He also mentioned the Davenport Infirmary, saying he had had pneumonia and had stayed on for three months as an unpaid attendant. He said he'd gotten satisfaction from helping people who were worse off than he but had left the infirmary because it was located too near Calvinville, where his mother still lived, and it reflected on her that he should be without status.

Frank thought his case was hopeless and wondered whether anyone could tell if he were a mental case or if it were completely hopeless. He asked if they thought he should be turned over to the police and punished. He spoke of his father's suicide and said he was considering a similar act: "When I think about it I wonder if I've got the nerve. I don't own a gun. I don't think I could get one. A knife is pretty messy because I'd be all over blood. There's a bridge down here in New Haven about thirty-five feet high, but I suppose if I jump off that I'd only break

my leg. It all looks hopeless to me." Later that same day Frank stated
that he would like to go to a state hospital to work since it might satisfy
him to work with sick people who were worse off than he. He said that
during the day he had had only three beers because a bartender had
refused to serve him more, saying he had had enough. "I must have been
in bad shape."

Frank gave some evidence that his resistance to receiving help might
be weakening: "If I should get out of this and come back with $1,000
in my pocket, I wouldn't tell you anything. Now I feel that everything is
so hopeless that I might as well talk about myself." Two or three times
he offered to answer questions which might determine whether or not
he was sane.

The clinic arranged for temporary board and gave Frank railroad fare
to go to Warehouse Point to collect his wages. He was to return to New
Haven to work and visit the clinic. Frank did not return.

The next news of Frank came about four months later when I received
a telephone call from a young lady who said that Frank had asked her to
call. For about six weeks he had been at her mother's rest home for alcoholics, where he had joined A.A. and had "good results." She reported that
Frank had made himself a general handyman around the place and that
"he never lets Mother do the dishes any more." Her conversation indicated that Frank had made a good impression. She told me, "Frank is
really a fine person. It is so wonderful that he has been able to overcome
this. You wouldn't recognize him; he has changed so. He looked so disreputable when he first came to Mother's and now he is so well adjusted."
For the past two weeks Frank had had a job with a trucking firm in a
nearby city and was living in town during the week and at the rest farm
on weekends. At the suggestion of the young lady, I wrote to Frank in care
of her mother. Apparently Frank did not receive this letter. He was not
heard from until several months later when the following letter arrived:

Northway State Hospital
December 3, 1947

Dear Bob:

It is probable that many neurotic persons seek sanctuary in cloistered abbeys and monasteries from worldly responsibility and cares.
The churches would be the first to deny this. However, the personality
and character of some of these persons seem to bear out this theory.

Such a rationalization I find to be wholly adaptable to my present situation. I am altogether the beneficiary and neither produce nor am held accountable for contribution to the individual nor society.

This helter-skelter preamble and beginning in the "middle of things" seems to set the purpose of this letter all awry. However, I know you will be glad to hear from me for the same reason that a pathologist follows the course of an interesting case of small pox.

Late last year I was fortunate enough to excite the interest of a Dr. Kaltzman at the Davenport Infirmary. Thru his friendship and kindly attitude I was able to tread the "straight and narrow" for a period of three months. When I left him I regressed to my former ways. There had been progress and without too much stimulus. It was quite a "let-down" to find out I was the same old leopard.

A series of binges from January thru April describes the first part of this year. During the aftermath of one of these carouses, I saw our mutual acquaintance, Tom Wynn, who gave me a dollar and said I looked like a *dire*lect (this is what he said) and I probably looked like a dire something-or-other.

I write not to disprove what Tom did speak, but a week later I secured a job in Fieldcrest and received higher wages than I had ever earned before. As long as I was in immediate debt, it was easy to stay sober, but when I had discharged my obligations to all persons with whom I was in near contact, I reverted to type.

In spite of telephone calls and messages to return to work for a week after I left, I wound up on the Bowery. I came on to Indigo and contacted A.A., as Tom advised me to do when I expressed the intention of deserting the big city.

At Indigo I found the usual idealists, screwballs, levelers, and frauds that are usually found in a human organization. At the invitation of one of its members I went to his home which had been adapted to a convalescent resort for the more provident drunkard. I stayed a short time as an attendant and wet-nurse to the maudlin drunk. The situation that I found here substantiated my theory that the "bottom" of a drunkard depends more on his friends and relatives than on his individual merit.

Thru contact with people I met here I secured a job. My sense of obligation to these people sufficed to make it obligatory on my part to remain sober again for three months. Note that this is the second occasion where I did achieve sobriety which was, for me, a protracted period.

This last occasion I lay to the fact that I had become more acquainted with the private lives of some of these members, and the shock of finding their code was not a hell of a lot superior to my own made drinking reasonable.

I greatly fear that I shall never dramatize my sobriety from the rostrum. My commitment to this institution was voluntary but the duration of my stay is not on this basis.

It is unlikely that I shall write home of this unfortunate circumstance, and I would be glad to hear from you. Never read your article on alcoholic seamen and am interested. Best wishes to Mrs. Straus and the children.

Frank

The year 1947 ended with Frank committed as a patient at the Wideway State Hospital after a bender and hospitalization at Bellevue.

Frank's letters of 1948 from several institutions include his first reflections on the idea of recording his life's experiences as a contribution to science. He also speculated about the validity of his evaluations and conclusions, and on the effectiveness of hospitals, sanitariums, and especially jails, in dealing with his problem. These letters also include his reflections on his role as observer, reporter, confidant, and friend to the author.

Wideway State Hospital
January 24, 1948

Dear Bob:

. . . . .

I left Northway on December 12th with ten dollars and the admonition to go and sin no more. I purchased a ticket to N.Y.C. but while on the train and before reaching Riverpoint, I made a decision that it was a difficult task to begin anew at my age, with my limitations of earning power, and revolted at the forthcoming associations on what would become my social level.

And so I disembarked at Riverpoint, purchased the ambrosia that makes kings out of paupers, that dispels the fears and sorrows that infest the human soul. It was only a temporary anodyne, as it always was. Some few days later, I was admitted to Bellevue with a case of incipient "DT's."

The undeserving sick (read alcoholics) at Bellevue are attended by interns. The one who attended me was youthful and his innocence invigorating. His questions were all prepared verbatim from the textbook. I succumbed to the temptation to tell him the truth in answer to his questions regarding my personal attitude toward life and existing social order. The truth was enough to insure my removal to this bastion of society.

Sometimes, Bob, I think my letters to you savor of that beseeching look of a mendicant on New York's Bowery. One must confide in somebody of course and I suppose that is reason enough for writing. You are my metaphorical Wailing Wall and Confessional.

You know that I am cognizant of the practical methods used by the moralists for the amelioration (read exploitation) of drunkards. And now I seem to have embarked upon a personal survey of measures practiced by the state.

I admit all of this without aim and will probably produce no tangible benefits. However it does lead to that true knowledge of conditions, which one never arrives at thru theorizing.

. . . . .

Wideway State Hospital
Mar. 15, 1948

Dear Bob:

Correspondence ritual decrees that a person acknowledge receipt of a letter by stating that he is glad to hear from "so and so."

To hell with formula, I was *very* glad to hear from you.

If you have tears, prepare to shed them now. Since my last writing to you, I have appeared before what is known as "initial staff." The function of this euphemistically named conclave is that of a diagnostic board. Assembled data adduced from relatives, employers, the patient, et al., the physical appearance, the bearing and attitude of the patient, tend toward a proper evaluation of a case—the diagnosis, disposition and treatment (if any).

The inquisitions (apologies to Torquemada), are slated for particular days of the week. The great number of patients, the brief time allotted to each patient, has caused the procedure to be referred to, among the patients, as Willow Run psychiatry.

I would like to regard this process with detached tolerance and merely assume it is only a preview of what socialized medicine would be like. Because it is my funeral, I fear that I miss this purely objective view.

The patients sit on benches, along a corridor outside the consulting room, and formulate answers to a series of questions which they believe will be asked them in the star chamber.

Hollywood does very well in the portrayal of wary appearing psychiatrists, however in reality, there is a dearth of mentally sparring around.

The high-light of my short interview was reached with the opening question by a doctor who has dramatic flair and stage presence. He asked me if I wanted a drink. I couldn't resist the temptation to tell him the truth. Indeed the idols I have loved so long, have done my credit in this world much wrong.

Some few days later, the doctor, who is assigned to my case, informed me that it had been decided that I should stay here for a period of six months or a year.

I don't believe that I am of an unreasonably suspicious nature, but I couldn't help but recall earlier questionings, which seemed directed toward finding out whether I had relatives or friends with money or influence who would be interested in my case. Obviously I had been weighed and found wanting.

Before my advent to this particular Laughing Academy, I had been examined by sundry doctors, sixty days at Northway, and by your own Dr. Remonda at the clinic who assured me: "You got br-r-rains." What has brought about this startling denouement? Why this turn-about policy and decision that I must stay in durance vile? Truly this is a question for the Quiz Kids.

The long range program plotted for me, is that after a long period of incarceration, I shall be referred to the tender mercy of a state employed social worker, (professional "do-gooder") for rehabilitation and my next "binge." Such is the bleak picture, Bob. I can't imagine a more unwilling and unlikely prospect than myself.

Of course there is always the alternative of appealing to the offices of the Attorney General, such correspondence is not legally censorable, and request my discharge on the grounds that I am not truly psychotic and that this restriction and restraint are unlikely to produce beneficial results. The tax-payers, of course, don't count.

There is no likelihood of my following such a course. I don't know anything in particular I would like to do if I were released from here. Verily an impasse. A cul-de-sac.

In reference to your compiling data of case histories, I regard my own as drab and without particular merit. I believe my greatest single contribution to the study of alcoholism occurred one day in a hotel lobby. On the previous day you had loaned me three dollars, (still unrepaid), to take care of the day's "living expenses." You asked me the next day if I had continued to drink after leaving you. I answered: yes, that I had used the three dollars to purchase another fifth of rum.

Looking at this matter in a superficial way, it would appear that I had, not only betrayed the confidence and trust that had been placed in me, but also that I had permanently injured the altruism of another.

Yet there is another angle, it could have been my high regard of you as a person, a wish that you would really understand a problem with which you were trying to deal, and the desire to hold fast to a remaining shred of integrity, that incited my truthfulness.

Marcus Aurelius Moore is talking, Bob. We must do the best we can to the extent of our ability but the world is surely a pediculous place.

I hope that you may find it convenient to send me an inexpensive note book. I might have the inclination to write a journal of sorts (de profundis rumblings). You know I incline toward the belief of the mechanistic philosophers that a person is the result of his total experience. I might write a series of events which I feel have influenced my present condition. A likely sounding title would be, "Yesterday, this day's madness did prepare." No literary worth but for more accurate self appraisal.

Writing this letter has helped pass a Sunday, when many of the other patients have visitors. If I had my life to live over I would surely grasp my friends "with hoops of steel."

The Seamens Institute of New York City has sent me books and I have taught a number of fellow screw-balls to play chess and bridge. For purely selfish reasons. Helps to ameliorate my own lot.

Give my regards to your mother who was so kind to me while in the New Haven Hospital. It seems as if I had lived ninety years.

Frank

Wideway State Hospital
April 20th, 1948

Dear Bob:

I received your letter and also the notebook, for which many thanks.

My efforts toward writing the "Memories of Custody" have neither been consistent nor self-satisfying. My feeble attempts to irony would cause the shades of Swift and Cervantes to rise up in wrath. I fear my feeble darts directed toward the juggernaut of existent order will never cause a stir among the demi-gods of satire. My efforts approximate that of a figurative terado (?) worm, gnawing at the pilings of status quo.

I suppose almost every person, at some time, has considered the idea of writing their experiences and so we are buried beneath a welter of memories from the pen of the least consequential. Fortunately, upon reconsideration, most of us realize that we have no new ideas to express nor a novel way of stating an old idea.

The field of letters is so overcrowded with dipsomaniacs and libertines that it almost seems that respectability militates against literary fame. Any disertation of the sordid and morbid is assured an audience and Tennyson gathers dust on library shelves.

What do I think is worth writing about?

I sit at a dining room table with three other men. On my left is a person who believes all his food is medicated. Across, sits a gentleman, who rants of a pencil-shaped electrical device with a convex attachment to fit over the human eye. The electrical current will vibrate over the conjunctivae, increase the orbital secretions and so improve eye sight. (That's as clear as he can describe the matter to me.) The other gentleman is under the delusion that having sewed patches on his trousers, every day, that some leprechaun removes the patches every night. His Sisyphus exertions are without end.

These same persons carried bread, day after day, from the dining room to cast thru their iron grilled windows to scavenger birds during those past months when snow covered the ground. The deference they show toward the aged and infirm would shame the man of the street. It is amazing how, as a matter of fact, they assume the obligation of making beds of the lame and ministering to the requirements of persons less able than themselves. When one of these patients receives a food package from a visitor, he shares with the others as if he could not enjoy these things while others were in want. Is this the manifestation of some inherent goodness that transcends their insanity? Or is this the remaining vestige of some formerly acquired behavior pattern?

My status here remains unchanged. In the past month, the doctor who is assigned to my case expended an uneasy ten minutes toward my correction and cure.

In a sense, I am referred to as being sick. It is fashionable now-a-days to say a criminal is "sick," a drunkard is "sick," a sexual psychopath is "sick," etc. It seems to me that the word "sick" has ceased to be definitive. If I am "sick," where is the treatment?

I have come to the conclusion that there is a line of demarcation between the deserving sick and the undeserving sick.

Some of these patients have relatives who are concerned toward these patients being returned to social responsibilities and economic productivity. I can very well see why a doctor would direct his efforts toward the recovery of such patients rather than toward some waif with whom no one is interested.

To the contrary every patient's progress or disintegration reflects upon the person in whose care he is entrusted. And then again, it is no skin off the doctor's chin whether he cures or maims.

As you know it is my peculiar delusion that my pathological drinking is as much the concern of society as it is my own. Hence these last two episodes in state hospitals.

I waived a sanity hearing thru advice of the doctors at Bellevue with the hope something might be done here. After being here three months it is with regret rather than defiance that I feel I will be essentially the same person when I am discharged as at the time of arrival. A God-damned unwilling martyr, as it were.

I shall be glad to hear from you and look forward to your next letter.

Sincerely
Frank

Wideway State Hospital
May 1, 1948

Dear Bob:

. . . . .

As near as I can reason things out, my case has been disposed of in the following manner.

I have been transferred to a building which houses cases of prolonged custodial care. The evidence in support of this measure, is previous hospitalization, many arrests, economic instability, and no definite tendencies toward any worth-while aim.

My own efforts to effect a change would receive a minimum of attention. This is one of those wards where a patient never is regarded other than casually unless he refuses to work, assaults another patient, etc. Patients that I talk with, preface their conversations with "When I came here six weeks ago" and "When I came here three years ago," etc. It is interesting to conjecture what I would be like after staying here as long as some of them.

Some of them are sociable, all of them harmless, deterioration is plainly evident. One of them with whom I play chess, states that he could play much better six years ago when he first came here. I don't regard his statement as an alibi for losing. I believe him. A person would necessarily need be an egotist in an absolute sense, not to have been influenced by his associates and surroundings of six years.

It appears to me, Bob, that a person of my years is pretty indelibly stamped with the habit of years. Occasionally, some cataclysmic change comes over an individual, he gets religion, suffers some physical impairment, etc. that changes the course of his life. I see no immediate prospect of these things.

I do not look forward with pleasure to the prospect of forever eating from battered tin cups, the constant and prolonged association with misfits, social casualties, and erratic personalities.

I would feel deeply obligated to an individual who directed efforts toward my social rehabilitation.

Whether that sense of obligation would keep me "in line" for any protracted length of time, is, I admit, problematical. On the other hand, do you think I should stay here permanently?

I hope you may give the matter some consideration. I don't know, but as near as I can figure out, there are certain legal requirements to be met, a temporary place of residence, prospects of employment, etc. I don't believe a sponsor would commit himself to some permanent responsibility of any kind.

I can't find out these things because of some unexplainable policy in these places of keeping such information remote and obscure. My doctor's name is Dr. Schwartz. Would you care to approach him via correspondence.

Enough wailing and wincing for today.

Frank

Wideway State Hospital
May 22, 1948

Dear Bob:

You commended my previous letters which will make future writing more difficult. Cyrano de Bergerac wrote a "whale" of a letter altogether contrary to that ungodly nose and truculent manner. Fortunately for me, I realize the inevitable errors of the self-educated, as I go on my bumbling way, mangling the metaphor and scrambling the syntax.

It appears to me that prolixity is my chief weakness, viz,—

"When in disgrace with fortune and men's eyes, I, all alone, beweep my outcast state," it is fine to have a friend journey many parasangs, forego his own work and pleasure, to assuage the plight of another.

In other words, Bob, I was very glad to see you the other day. The Anglo-Saxon heritage is undemonstrative and too apt to conceal the emotions. Just another liability that I have accrued with passing years, that has its bases in experience.

During the past fracas, I served on one of the first Liberty ships, which rolled with every wave, never missing any of them. We carried a number of British aviators as passengers. I saw one of these men, stripped to the waist, sitting on a stool, heeding the "call of nature," when a ton of sea water came down the ventilator and over his head. When the deluge abated, I waited with sadistic glee, his reaction. Brushing the salt from his eyes, he offered the following comment: "This is quite difficult."

It was very kind of you to come down here and I hope to merit your interest.

What opinion did you form? You came, you saw, and you wondered. If I were the seventh son of the seventh son, I would divine your thoughts as follows: He is physically well, well nourished, sober, not too unhappy, with no arduous work beyond his capabilities; yet persists in the opinion that he has a soul, welcomes risk, and conflict and the resultant "blood sweat and tears."

I received a shave and wore my own clothes for the occasion of your visit. The every day habilaments are furnished by the state. Did you ever read Carlyle's "Sartor Resartus?" One finds the degree to which he wrote the truth under these circumstances. I venture that if you take Albert Einstein, let him go without a shave for a few days, rig him in regalia furnished by the state, turn him loose in a room with forty other screwballs—and I defy you to pick him out.

Thru association over a period of time, he would give indication of knowledge and training, but on further consideration, if he had been sent here by competent alienists, you would still persist that he might be in the proper place. If the professor persisted that he was in the wrong place and desired to go home, that would mark him as no different from the lunatics. Phantasy? Whimsey? I know!

Today I had an interview with Dr. Schwartz; He said, "what do you desire me to do." I said, "discharge me, in that I am not insane, and there is no benefit to be derived by staying." He said my history did not indicate returning me to the same conditions which I left before coming here. I asked him if the alternative was: to stay in an insane hospital.

He said that unless there was a radical change in the conditions under which I have lived, it is best for me to "stay awhile longer." That phrase has been used as a soothing syrup for the most hopeless cases.

Just how in hell am I to effect this radical change? I neither created the social or economic systems and they have been in practice too long, for me to attempt tampering. He does not think that I am insane but if he were to recommend release, and I were to bounce back again, it would reflect on his professional reputation.

It's a rotten medicine to take, that a person must continue to live under these conditions rather than jeopardize another's business standing. In common with bums and bankers, lout and genius, I probably have a wrong sense of values.

Do not feel called upon to answer all this persiflage. This is my confessional.

Frank

Wideway State Hospital
Sunday, June 7, 1948

Dear Bob:

To continue the jeremiad, lest I lapse into the limbo of lost souls. (About stereotypes)—Following your line of reason that no one would wish to keep me in an insane asylum without reason to believe that benefits would be derived and that there are too many people on the street awaiting admittance, I requested an interview with my doctor relative to the possibility of my being discharged.—Did you ever deal with a stereotype? The stereotype adopts a mode of behavior or speech that is applicable to certain conditions, and produces foreordained results (disposing of a situation). The stereotype's plan of action is decided upon before the situation arises. The stereotype seldom realizes that he is dealing out stereotypes. The stereotype usually can be detected thru his use of certain words and phrases. During an interview with a stereotype, you feel that you are being talked to in a classroom, and that the same speech has been used many times over for the same occasion, your ears are jarred with such phrases as "in the light of psychiatric experience" and "in such cases we have found," etc. etc.

As near as I can apprehend, thru prolonged abstinence I am supposed to accumulate a confidence that I can live without the damned stuff. To the contrary, I fear I will go out of here with more "kinks" than I arrived with.

For one thing, I apprehend the dire consequences of my complete cure. Suppose the word got around. I imagine five thousand toss-pots descending on Wideway like locusts for the magic panacea—doctors of alcohology injecting antibodies into the blood stream and immunizing against the effects of alcohol (these anti-bodies would alter the composition of alcohol so that when it was absorbed into the blood stream, the alcohol would cause the subject to break out in purple spots in lieu of getting gloriously drunk). Lest he seek psychic effect thru the use of some other narcotic, he would be psychologically indoctrinated to the extent that he leaves this abode of wrath and tears, feeling that everybody loves him, and that God is in Heaven, and that all's well below.

.   .   .   .   .

In my own case, I can't for the life of me absorb the idea that these doctors have the kindest feelings toward me by closely immuring me with gibbering idiots. Whatever compassion I have felt toward the demented has flown out the window. I attribute this fact to the necessity of sleeping in a bed fourteen inches removed from a loon who lulls me to sleep every night with a constant flow of gibberish directed to neither man or God. These doctors and attendants have a day off once a week, but I am sweating this out on a twenty-four hour basis every day. As the politicians say, let us examine the record—we are weighed periodically, I have lost fourteen pounds in the last three months.

It is an unlikely fact, but if you know anyone who contemplates appealing to science, as it is administered in a state hospital, tell them first to write me for a detailed prospectus.

A carton of Bull Durham tobacco would last me a month.

Frank

Wideway State Hospital
Sat. Night, June 13, 1948

Dear Bob:

A librarian comes over here on Monday evenings and I expressed the desire to read Thornton Wilders' "Ides of March." During the middle of the week, a messenger brought me over the book. Trivia? Hell, everything assumes major importance in this sphere, and things that are accepted so casually "outside," here are regarded as major beneficiencies.

In recalling your latest letter, I find myself "hard put" to explain your kindly interest in my affairs.

There has certainly been nothing in my nature to merit your solicitude. Our relationship has been a rather one-sided affair. So far it has been imposition and infringement on my part. Yet I have come to depend on you as the only favorable means by which I can change myself and my present state of affairs.

Frank

Wideway State Hospital
June 22, 1948

Dear Bob:

Let the joy be unconfined, at long last, etc. & etc. I was interviewed by my doctor today & he spoke most encouragingly.

He wants to know my destination upon discharge. Of course, there is a legal restriction against shipping discharged lunatics over state borders.

To meet such restrictions & to convenience my discharge, I told him I would stay in the state.

He was concerned as to my ability to establish myself. I told him that I had been "lone-wolfing it" since I was sixteen.

I did not confide to him such heroics that once I took on a job firing a high pressure boiler & slept in a park after my first day's work, nor another instance when coming off a binge I had unloaded a carload of bagged cement although I had not eaten for two days.

However I think he is convinced of my ability to get started after a fashion.

To effect a discharge from the hospital entails a bit of routine mummery consisting of going before what is known as "home staff" where it will probably have been decided that I am to go "home" (bitter stuff), or excuses will have been formulated for keeping me here, even before I face that august body.

I expect that if the omens are favorable, I will be discharged in from ten days to a month. On the other hand, he may have just been letting me play with the bird (Pandora's).

However, it seems a good time to let you know I would have fared much worse without your bolstering & I mean this.

I will be furnished transportation to the city, & my only solution is to hire out on the railroad which will not necessitate any holdover expense, as would be necessary under any other condition of employment. Alack my shrinking biceps, triceps, deltoids, et al.

My suit which is in fair condition & low cut shoes will be the "new look" in laboring clothing. I would be better off if I was dressed in a tough suit of coveralls & heavy gloves.

Instinct is a hell of thing & I suppose I will keep bruising my tender shins against insurmountable obstacles.

The way I see it, it would only take a mere thousand dollars to get started on the right foot. Know anybody who is about to die intestate?

Seriously, I dread the recurrence of my past experience & the thousand cumulative causes that lead to drinking.

As I look back on some of those situations, it seems to me that I had used *all* my initiative & energy to effect a temporary security, & therefore had none of these qualities left, to hold on to what I had attained.

Sounds clear as mud, but I am in hurry to get this in the mail, so it will go out in the morning.

I received tobacco last week, for which many thanks. It is a damn shame that I go on expecting someone else to alleviate these god-awful predicaments with which I become enmeshed.

Sincerely,

Frank

One binge and jail sentence later, and at the beginning of an intensified pattern of drinking after long hospital stays, I received the following:

November 2, 1948
Riverpoint County Jail

Dear Bob:

Received your kind letter about ten days ago.

Every school boy remembers the fable where the traveler was lost for want of a horse, the horse was lost thru want of a shoe, the shoe was lost thru want of a nail, etc. & etc.

The present circumstance should be regarded in the light of a sequence of events that led up to this circumstance. Shuffle the whole thing together & append to my chronicles.

I was released on Saturday, Oct. 30. My assets were thirty-eight cents. It was near noon when I was delivered out of custody.

I followed your counsel & after a foot-some trek arrived at the shelter offices.

They supplied me with a written visa for one meal, said that I might stay at their dormitory on Sat. & Sun. night & that the dormitory clerk would be on duty from 4 p.m. until midnite.

That afternoon I walked a few miles out to the Riverpoint Hospital & applied for work. I was told to apply to the Personnel Dept. on Mon. morning. (Footsore & love's labor lost). Came the night. The struggling pangs of appetite were aroused. I applied to some Bowling alleys & earned $5.63 setting up pins. Ah, my aching back, & that youth's sweet scented manuscript should close! It was quarter of twelve at night & too late to go to the dormitory. I rented a room for the night down in Riverpoint's far-flung tenderloin at the rate of one dollar. Sunday until noon was spent traipsing around with my own loneliness. My good intentions were becoming threadbare. Began drinking beer at noon to stifle "the spurns that patient merit of the unworthy takes." Tried, unsuccessfully, to contact an A.A. via telephone. Applied at the dormitory, & was to be expected, met with the usual officious clerk with that always present intolerance for his own kind, who castigated me for not showing up the previous night & that I could not stay there this night. Called police & their attention that I had been drinking. Pled Not Guilty in court. Will be tried Nov. 15. I am so incensed at this cock-eyed world that I am considering returning to my previous form of servitude.

Frank

December 28, 1948
Davenport State Infirmary

Dear Bob:

. . . . .

I was released from the Bastile shortly after writing you the last time. I had defended & pleaded my own case to the magistrate of the Riverpoint court. Shades of Portia & Gladstone! I bedecked myself for the occasion with a Meritorious Service Medal, campaign ribbons & called to the court's attention the fact that I was an extraordinary drunk rather than the every day genus. Truly the last refuge of a scoundrel is patriotism.

I cited the fact that sending me to jail was an evasion rather than a solution, & that a thousand other men would stand in my place in the prisoner's docket, & would continue to do so until constructive means were employed to alleviate this perennial headache. Like Johnny Appleseed, I have left a germ of an idea, in some places. I was released with the sympathy & condolences of the court.

That same evening I attended an A.A. meeting in Riverpoint. I sat in a rear seat like a skeleton at the feast. My unprepossessing appearance deterred zealous members from contriving an acquaintance, & I spoke to no one. I left the meeting feeling how aptly Hamlet stated, "Words! Words! Words!"

And so out of the meeting, into the night, across the bridge and onto the open highway.

It is surprising to discover, the trend of one's thoughts under the stars, & how big a blister will grow on one's foot, before it finally bursts.

And so thru the night & I arrived at Westtop, the next day at 3:00 P.M. Back to my native state,—"Breathes there the man with breath so alcoholic, who never to himself hath said, etc."

I solicited that Red Cross Chapter for alms & met a Miss Kerry, who is field secretary. I have long since sensed a coterie of the mind which apprehend each other after the preliminary fiddle-faddle. Here, I thought, is another one of those rare individuals to whom one can be truthful.

After my letting down of the hair, Miss Kerry made long distance calls & was authorized to extend veteran's temporary aid. What price glory! She was a bright red rose in a world of thorns. Brains & attractive. Alack my long departed youth.

She arranged for my meals at an excellent cafeteria (supper, breakfast, & lunch to carry) & a lodging at the Salvation Army.

And so the next day over the highway & into Perkinsville.

Walt Whitman or John Masefield surely never had corns on their feet when they wrote the rhapsodies of the open road.

Upon arrival I called at the local A.A. & was greeted by a member who desired to know specifically just what I wanted. I weighed this person & found him wanting & stated that I would not care to bother him. . . . I looked at him too long & searchingly. Just between you and I, Bob, I wanted someone to talk to, & I hereby swear "at" this fraternity for the duration to my existence.

As a comparison, I was provided a supper by the Traveler's Aid Society & referred to the Bethel Mission for lodging. I was confronted in the front hall by an inebriate who had passed out on the floor, the walls were studded with framings around him which stated: Jesus Saves, God is Love, etc. After removing my shoe & sock in the sitting room, some nameless derelict tendered me a Band-Aid from his eyeglass case. (Shades of Abou ben Adhem! may he lay with the houris in Paradise, & drink mead with the heroes in Valhalla, when he greets his uncertain hereafter!)

The next day was Saturday which brought into being the "weekend" which is a bane to all knights of the road & I decided to stay in Perkinsville until Monday. I viewed with alarm the prospect of being eaten by pediculi at the Bethel (while in a sober state). Aside from the asthetic slant, I was too cognizant, at one time, on the Biological Transmission of Disease.

That forenoon, the Red Cross arranged for me to stay at the Y.M.C.A. over the weekend & to eat at the Waldorf. Note: I regard these solicitations of the Red Cross as the ultimate disintegration of all principles. When I feel it is necessary to point out the very few honorable accomplishments of an entire lifetime, I have broke faith with myself.

My safari eastward was leading me to sanctuary in Davenport, surcease from the slings & arrows of outrageous fortune, & in lieu of panhandling the individual, I now prey on the Commonwealth in its entirety.

On my second day here, I selected as my assignment a ward which is generally considered "impossible."—Ten incorrigibles, boys about ten years, morons, imbeciles, untidy cases, & congenitally deformed.

So far, my ward has been commended as the cleanest in the buildings, I feed them individually with a spoon, comb their hair (an untoward procedure here) & play God in general, as I am given a free hand. As I watch them jump on their Christmas toys & destroy them, I thank something or other that I *do* know my own limitations & I am not going to let it "get me down."

You have probably heard about a lot of people who consecrate themselves to work of this nature. Strictly between you and I, Bob, consecration is a bunch of crap. Only by hard work, dirty work, self control, & patience, is any real improvement made in the lives of other people.

An embryo Florence Nightingale asked me today when I was going to get on the payroll, & that I should get on the payroll. I am frankly bored with telling people, that I am all "washed-up" at forty-four, all opportunities are behind me, & that I would surely flunk any chance to pursue a normal life, that henceforth I seek to become known as an indigent homeless, & that I have awakened only the desultory interest of the legal & medical profession.

It will be interesting to note how long I last at this labor of love, before lack of recognition drives me out of here onto another drunk.

Frank

Send along the saga of Moore[7] & your copy of alcoholism among seamen.[8]

As noted at the beginning of this chapter, the events of Frank's life from 1945 to 1948 mark a transition from semi-informal to more formal institutional living, and clearly demonstrate his interrelated problems of alcohol dependency and institutional dependency. This is evident from the following summary review of major events.

As 1945 began, Frank was working as a freight handler in Fieldcrest, living in a cheap hotel and drinking daily. From February to June he lived and worked at the Fieldcrest Salvation Army Men's Social Service Center. In July he returned to his job as a freight handler for three weeks, went back to the Salvation Army, stayed there briefly, and then went to the Salvation Army's Center in New Haven, where I met him and we had the first interview, the substance of which is in Chapter 3. Frank remained at the New Haven center until January of 1946 except for an eight-day hospitalization in October for an injury incurred while drunk.

The first five months of 1946 included several episodes of working as a laborer in New Haven, visits to the Yale Plan Clinic, refuge in an A.A. rest farm, at least two arrests for drunkenness, an excursion to New York City and the Seamen's Church Institute, and work on a railroad labor gang. In May and June he was back in the New Haven Salvation Army. The summer months were spent on live-in jobs, including a railroad labor gang, and in November Frank was hospitalized at the Davenport State Infirmary, where he ended the year as a live-in employee.

Early in 1947, Frank paid a brief visit to New Haven en route to New

7. Straus (1948), op. cit.
8. This is a reference to my book *Medical Care for Seamen* (New Haven: Yale University Press, 1950), which was then in manuscript form. Actually it contained only minor references to alcoholism among seamen.

York City, where he stayed at the Seamen's Church Institute, worked on the railroad, and was hospitalized at Bellevue for acute intoxication. In March he visited the Yale Plan Clinic in New Haven briefly and embarked on another bender. In April he worked for a week in Fieldcrest and again went on a bender. From May through July he lived at an A.A. rest home in Udingo; from August through September he held several laboring jobs; from October to December he was a patient at the Northway State Hospital; and the year ended with a bender in New York City, hospitalization at Bellevue, and commitment to the Wideway State Hospital.

During the first seven months of 1948 Frank continued as a patient in the Wideway State Hospital, a large institution with accommodations for several thousand. Shortly after he left Wideway he was arrested for drunkenness and sentenced to sixty days in the Riverpoint County Jail. Just a day after his release from jail, he was rearrested. In November he undertook a cross-country trek toward refuge at the Davenport State Infirmary, where he spent the last weeks of the year as a live-in employee.

5. Frank's Mother's Story

During the first three years of my contacts with Frank I made no effort to seek more information about his mother than he seemed ready or willing to provide. He occasionally referred to his mother and once read aloud part of a letter from her in which she advised him not to come back to Calvinville because there were no opportunities for him in such a small town. Therefore, it came as a totally unanticipated opportunity when I received the following letter from Frank's mother, Roberta C. Greene, in December, 1948:

Calvinville
December 13, 1948

Dear Mr. Straus:

Your name has been given to an correspondent as one who might know the whereabouts of my son Frank Moore. He was in a hospital and released as convalescent on July 29. I have not heard from him for a year.

His wife has died and a letter from one of her daughters states that expenses are paid but money (just what I don't know) was supposed to be divided between two daughters and is held up amount of 1/3 (as I believe he is entitled to by law). She wanted proof of his death or whereabouts. I answered & said that he was alive & would try for address.

Can you help? If you know or hear I will send her address, the daughter who wrote.

Thanking you and trusting you will take a minute to answer. It is his business but he might as well have it as it is his.

Very truly yours,
Mrs. E. T. Greene
(Frank's mother)

I answered Mrs. Greene's request for information by explaining the nature of my acquaintance with Frank, including the life record I was keeping and the unsuccessful efforts I had made to work with him through the Yale Plan Clinic. I wrote that any information which she might provide about his life would be appreciated, although I indicated that I realized this might be painful for her. Mrs. Greene replied almost immediately, not only in considerable detail about events and circumstances surrounding Frank's childhood and early adult life, but also about the attitudes and feelings she had toward Frank, with a revealing candidness that continued to characterize her correspondence.

Calvinville
Dec. 20, 1948

Robert Straus, Ph.D.
My dear Sir: Subject Frank G. Moore
Yours of Dec. 17 at hand. First, thank you for what you have tried to do for my son.

He was born May 9, 1904 at C.ville. I was 18 years of age. Just how his delivery was accomplished I do not know and doctors (2) asked my aunt not to tell, reason being that sometimes people thought things should not be done that way. He could not be born and the cervix would not let him thru. I was either cut or torn completely thru rectal wall, etc. I was married at 16 unbeknown to my mother and was pregnant at the time. Two weeks later she took me to a surgeon without my husband's consent and an operation (abortion) performed. I took medicine for the first month when F. was coming along. My mother had an unhappy life, six children (3 miscarriages) one an abortion and did not want us to have any. We lived here and my husband was resented for having married me & getting me with child. The fact was overlooked that I had a part. My husband was an x navy man discharged for neurasthenia. A congressman got the fact for us. He was quite temperamental—hobby of revolvers and he and my mother hated each other. My mother worked & when she was at home he did not want me to go downstairs & she did not want me up. His old maid cousin came here to do the house work and she hated him too and made trouble. All thru my pregnancy was the theme "Perhaps it will die." I was very unhappy and disturbed. They had a row (mother & husband) I was not up (2 wks. before birth) and he was ordered from house. He came down and was not allowed in. When time came and nothing accomplished the 2 doctors gave me medicine and child born as stated. I was very ill. They did not send for my husband & not until he had a note from doctor was he allowed in. He committed suicide (shot himself) May 24, 1904 at 5 A.M. after his one visit the night before my mother stayed in the room & when he threatened to jump off wharf before morning—told him to go ahead. After my recovery I was around about seven months—my sister was 16 my aunt to keep house mother working—I had to go to work. I did not have the training of my child. My sister had the most. He had *everything* he wanted. I trained to be a nurse in a State Hospital for two years but was of an extremely nervous temperament and gave it up. I liked the studies, clinics etc and could do for the people—no matter what. I was first acquainted with what I called faulty reasoning in Frank when at 15 yrs. I asked him to get a certain article in store & he insisted on getting another. I had to go with quiet insistence step by step to store to have him change it. He did. When it was over I explained to him and when we got there said, "Who is right." He said, "I am." When he left High School I found several books stamped with High School that were so many (reference) that they could not all have been borrowed and had to return them. His principal said as his grades went up his conduct in school—down. He never made any direct statement on just what he did. Frank was never expelled. While I was away working Frank went into Navy at 16 giving his age as 18 and a false birth place. He was a Pharmacist Mate 3rd class at end of first enlistment age 18. He had re-enlisted before he came home. I wanted him to wait because I thought he might be more contented as it was more harmonious than when he left. When he went back he was sent to San Domingo (his request) attached to Marines—plenty of time on hands. Told me later he was *never homesick* on his 1st enlistment but was on second. Sent home large allotment placed in his own name and could only be drawn out only on his signature. When he got back into States he kept sending for 50-60 etc. until used up. He was dishonorably discharged from that term of enlistment—never would have known only wrote to Chaplain. Was allowed to rehabilitate & got into trouble again. *I did not see him from 18 years old until he was 29.* He and a few others were in guard house got out & jumped into Colonels machine & got caught 17 miles away. Frank was sentenced to 7 years some others 5 years sent to N.Y. and thence to *Alcatraz* where he stayed 5 years. A disciplinary barracks where they were not allowed to *speak*. Had 2 years off for good behavior & thru a friend here had the Sec. of Navy transfer him to East Coast for discharge. Frank was sore about it but there was a depression and I felt he ought not to be cast adrift. He came home—could not speak a full sentence without hesitation and trouble. Worked when somebody handed it to him—would not look for it. He was very erratic and it would take nothing for him to go to pieces even if he was doing something for himself. He commenced to drink more and one day (this is a small place 13,000) met a man in a saloon told him who he was and the man who lived in this section of city said that he knew me. I did not know him but of him & family. Frank called me a slut and said he was ashamed to be seen on street with me. I put him out. His stepfather got him a room & board and Frank had an insurance policy (we paid for) he was cashing in. He left Mr. G. to pay it all & went. Back again—the last policy $173 and spent most of it and back in a week. I told him I was sorry—he would have to look for work. One night before Christmas he sent me a special delivery that he was in a town farm. He had gone in and out of different State Hospitals as a voluntary patient—different poor farms one right here in our city when I was considered not much for not—allowing him to get drunk, abuse (with lips) me, take rings (that belonged to me) and his step father could support him. He took the rings because I was willing to buy his ticket to Boston but would not give him cash. He was in Merchant Marine during war—got drunk & landed in St. Hospital Chicago. They are under the system when if you have no money you go there—a county affair. They let him go. He came home stayed 4 days and if any one ever had Hell I did—because I wanted him to try to get his sea mans papers lost while drunk. He could not ship without them. That was in 1943.

Marriage

He married a woman about 60 who was cook at the poor farm here. She had 2 children one who is an invalid. When she was to get thru then he hung around here and I think he expected us to take them in. I said that he had a responsibility to establish a home and he said that only one who wanted a meal ticket would look at it that way. I told him his father might be alive today if we had not been living here. I told him they were like babies in the wood and asked him what he was thinking of. His answer was, *"I thought she would be good for a few years yet."* He got a nurses job at a S. Hospital got considerable small cases from her and sent numerous telegrams for her to pay for and while he was sent up for drunkenness she became ill and left town. She came to see me and told me how she had blamed me but he had done the same to her. He tried to get in touch with her but her sister would not tell where she was. I heard around Christmas two years ago but no address. She was a simple soul but very good hearted a native of Ireland. One daughter is an invalid the other in a T.B. Sanitorium.

If you hear from him it would be advisable to tell him why I want him to write—about his wife money etc otherwise he would not write as I blasted him out after he landed in Bellevue last Christmas and I had gone without to send a gift to Northway. I suppose (?) he told you he had been at Wideway St. Hospital from Xmas to Sept.? They also probably tried to help him (not the Supt.) but also tried to get my shirt(?) to support him. I have a small cottage taxed for $1,000 built by my great grandmother. I am 63 had one bad coronary attack & a slight shock that affected the pous area (balance of body) in January right after I heard the psychiatrist report at Alcatraz.

moderate drink

Very unstable—faulty reasoning

a nomad

This is hard to write and if I have told you things he hasn't, just use the information to help understand the problem. It is not written to expose or hurt him.

He says he has nothing to work for. I looked at his teeth and mentioned other things but no go.

I honestly feel and have felt since his last visit I could do no more. I pray God every night to enlighten his mind & strengthen his will but wonder what his father and I passed down to build up.

Again thank you

(Mrs. E. T.) Roberta Greene

Enclosed is his last letter to me (Dec. 9, 1947) written with pencil because I could not do it all in ink.

The summary of Frank's life provided by his mother was remarkable in a number of respects. First, it corroborated with even more lurid details the events surrounding Frank's birth. It told of the intense hatred between Frank's father and his grandmother, of the grandmother's opposition to the pregnancy, and the hope that the pregnancy would be interrupted. It provided details about the instability and suicide of Frank's father and of his mother's own need to leave his upbringing to the care of others.

Regarding Frank's childhood, his mother mentioned that her sister and an aunt helped care for him, while Frank's story included only a series of housekeepers, and made no mention whatsoever of his maternal grandmother. Both Frank and his mother indicated that his material needs were well provided for, and Frank gave great credit to his grandfather's parental role.

Both Frank's story and Mrs. Greene's indicated increasing stress with the onset of adolescence. She did not mention reclaiming her role as mother but neither did she discuss the circumstances surrounding her leaving him. There is consistency in the details both provide about his delinquency problems, his quitting school, enlisting in the Navy, and the first few years of military service. Mrs. Greene mentioned a dishonorable discharge, an event Frank omitted. She evidently was confused about subsequent events. The episode, whatever it was, leading to imprisonment in Alcatraz apparently took place in 1928 shortly after a second enlistment in the Army. Mrs. Greene seemed under the impression he had remained in the Navy, and also thought he had been in constant solitary confinement while in Alcatraz, although she reported that his sentence was reduced from seven years to five for good behavior.

Frank's omissions in the story are in keeping with the discussion he introduced quite early in my recording of the life history when he quoted Mark Twain and warned that his story would not be a "really true picture" of himself. He did allude to one aspect of the Alcatraz episode when he told of shipping out with the Army Transport Service to the West Coast. There are also numerous references in later correspondence to experiences he had while in San Francisco or on the West Coast which could conceivably have taken place in the context of the penitentiary's recreational program.

Nothing in Mrs. Greene's story of the period 1933 through 1944 seems essentially inconsistent with the story Frank told, but she recounts different events and details until his marriage and there are obviously many gaps and no clear chronology. The marriage apparently took place in 1943 and lasted only a few months. Frank had altered the location and the relationship when he told of his living at that time with a woman as if they were man and wife.

With her letter of December 20, 1948, Mrs. Greene enclosed the letter she received from Frank written from Northway on December 9, 1947.

Northway
December 9, 1947

Dear Mother:

Received your letter this noon. It was unexpected, as I did not intend to let you know of the situation. . . . I suppose it was necessary to complete their records that impelled the authorities here to let you know.

"Coronary thrombosis shall not defer these zealots from their duty," would be a fitting inscription to any commemoration of their efforts. The poet has also immortalized this "clumsy plunging of fingertips among heart-strings."

You see I am my old sardonic self. . . . I wondered what I might write that may cause your lot to be easier. Always I have wanted to heed Gramp's admonition not to come home crying when I was licked. I had intended it so in the present condition.

There have been occasions when I might have been rewarded, had I subscribed to ideas and tenets, which I knew to be wrong. There are penalties for being honest.

If I could have been complacent and smug, self-sufficient, and trampling on all and sundry who obstructed my route to a particular goal, I would have been the normal man. My goals changed or vanished when I found the sacrifices necessary, in myself and others, to the attainment of such goals.

My philosophy never aroused great sympathy from you, but for myself, it has been a panacea for broken head, and bones, and situations, as at the present.

I came here October 16 on a voluntary commitment. I had remained sober on two occasions for three months and failed again. I was greatly depressed and believed it possible that I would have committed some act more antisocial than getting drunk.

I had affiliated myself with an organization known as Alcoholics Anonymous and had considerable faith. To make everything brief, I made the mistake of associating too closely with a Fundamentalist and his daily coercing was altogether unpalatable.

It would have been altogether to my best interest to jump on the bandwagon but the remaining scruples of a drunkard came to the fore. And so the end of another experiment.

I hoped for a particular treatment when I came to this hospital, known as the Conditioned Reflex Treatment. It consists of administering small quantities of alcohol by mouth, and then the subcutaneous injection of emetics. The Theory is: to provide emesis by alcohol without emetic. I have heard of good reports. . . . I have requested this treatment, but so far have met only the air of profundity and mumbo-jumbo that the profession reserves for the layman.

The shock treatments by insulin and electricity are administered here, and I see the possibility of being operated on for mastoid for the treatment of flat feet. Hope this is clear to you.

Sometimes the patient is credited with an insight into his own case and so I hope there is an unlikelihood of becoming a sacrificial lamb on the altar of pseudoscience.

There will be one of two dispositions of my case, viz.: I will be discharged from here as having "no psychosis." Secondly, the cost of my maintenance here will be charged to my home state, and after a short interim here I will be transferred to a hospital there to become a workable subject for their host of clinicians and that veritable horde of social workers who were lucky enough to secure jobs before the advent of civil service.

Physical condition excellent. Outlook unfavorable. Your efforts—negligible.

I would be glad to receive letters from you encouraging a lost cause. Hope you will refrain from recriminations which are probably deserved but of doubtful value. It seems I am altogether unable to make you, ever, happy. I deplore this incapacity. With all the love that I am capable of feeling.

Frank

This letter and subsequent letters to and about Frank's mother demonstrate the sense of abandonment first noted in references to her in the life history. Frank contrasts what he perceives to be social expectations of a mother's responsibility to a son and a son's devotion to a mother with his own mother's desertion of him as an infant and rejection of him as an adult and his inability to feel toward his mother the affection expected by social conventions.

I had written to Mrs. Greene that Frank was in the Riverpoint Jail, and then after receiving his letter of December 28, 1948, from Davenport, I wrote to her again. Her reply of January 4, 1949, continues her story of Frank's life and marriage. A later letter from Mrs. Greene identified Frank's inheritance from his wife as $450, which was sent to Frank before he left Davenport in 1949.

In May, 1949, Mrs. Green summarized her despair in a letter addressed to Frank at Davenport. The letter was returned unclaimed, and Mrs. Greene sent it on to me almost a year later.

Calvinville
Jan 4, 1949

Mr. Robert Straus, Ph.D.
My dear Dr. Straus:

Thank you for your letters. I wrote to Frank at Riverpoint and sent a copy of the letter from his step-daughter. I also told him that I had been unable to get further information. I asked Mrs. Creighton when her mother died, and how but simply received a Christmas card and she said that she would write later. I also told Frank that I was far from well and said that I was thinking and hoping for him. That was all. Perhaps your letter has been returned. I am looking for a return of mine.

He has been at Davenport several times and the last time about two years ago did attendant's work and as he graduated from Newport R.I. Hospital school and Norfolk, Va. was put on a ward with an opportunity to do a great deal and a clergyman wrote to me that he did much to help. As you know, these places are under staffed and no nurse or attendant can give full attention to one patient. This clergyman also said that if it were his own brother he would rather that he would be there than outside as he was. He went out on leave after a few months and did not return.

He seemed to think any one was on top of the world if they were on welfare. During the depression I was on it for two weeks and that was his attitude. It is all Greek to me. I had a great grandfather that drank heavily but no one has since on either side. One remark he made was that he was afraid to go to sleep. It shows a fear.

It just seems to me the fact that he can't meet the problems. Most

of us do even if it takes a toll in health etc. I blame myself because
tho I was just I haven't much love (as it is supposed to be) in my nature. I had it knocked out of me from the beginning. I feel that I
have failed him and yet I could not do differently. If anyone is to be
helped they have to really want it. He always said that he could "handle it." I said "yes, it looks so." There isn't much he does not know
about—told of trying the weed, can't spell it marijunan (canabis indick)
used to stay in his room and sulk—would not eat.

   Well, to sum it up, he is not hungry or cold and I trust not drinking. Thank you much.

Roberta C. Greene

A post card addressed to Mrs. Roberta Catherine Greene was sent to
me by Mrs. Greene with her letter of February 25, 1950:

Jan. 25, 1949

Dear Roberta:
   Got in touch with Frank at Davenport: Told him to go for his share
of estate. He is very bitter toward you. How can one be toward a
Mother? He must be very unhappy: It seemed so from the very long
and bitter letter. Perhaps this money will give Frank a incentive to
do better. I'm still with my Mother in law. Not feeling very well this
past two weeks. Just dread to think R[1] may go back to Sanatorium.
Will write letter later to you. All thanks for locating Frank.

Sincerely,
Nancy Sullivan Creighton

A letter from Mrs. Greene to Frank Moore addressed to Davenport State
Infirmary and returned unclaimed was sent to me on February 25, 1950:

May 17, 1949

Son:
   For a long time I have wanted to write to you but could not. You
might be interested to know that right after you went into Belleview
in N. Y. I had a shock. You have known for a long time my health.
For months I was no good. They tried to make me pay your board and
it was a mess. I gradually got around & had a dizzy spell the follow-

---

1. Nancy Creighton's sister, Frank's other stepdaughter.

ing July & fell & broke the fence down in yard and arm black as
coal. By that time I did not get out any. Last January another fall with
concussion—lost taste and sight for a few days and broke a vein in the
forearm so I can't do much with it can't write much hurt my back.
So much for me. Suppose when I die they will say oh she was sick.
No work here all winter just enough to get by one petticoat a coat for
6 yrs. etc. Well, I suppose you have had your trouble too. I was well
woman until the West Coast it finished me. I am not going to preach
to you. Lots have tried to help you but you lay it on to others, never
yourself. No one can help unless you want to be helped. See enclosed.
I finally managed to find you. One letter came back from Riverpoint
County Jail. I write blind. It was a hard day on Mothers day & your
birthday. There isn't any thing I can do about you or for you but at
least you can get around. If there is anything I can do let me know.
I worry about you & dream & pray. Nancy in spite of my asking her
would not tell me when your wife died or how. I only asked that.
Barbara was a nice woman. If you feel you would like to write to me
without recriminations—we both made big mistakes, do so.

Your still living Mother

Including this correspondence with Frank's mother in 1948 and 1949,
a total of thirteen letters were received from her, the last written on
August 10, 1956. She also sent me three letters to be forwarded to Frank,
and he sent four letters to his mother through me. Since most of these
letters refer to current events they will be found in Chapter 6 arranged
chronologically along with Frank's letters to me.

Further discussion of the complex relationship between Frank and his
mother and its impact on his life pattern will be found in Chapter 10.

6. *Total Institutional Dependency,* 1949-55

The beginning of 1949 found Frank living in the Davenport State Infirmary as a working inmate. For the next several years, Frank demonstrated a pattern of almost total institutional dependency. He lived for the greater part of each year in a patchwork of punitive and rehabilitative institutions, punctuated with only brief periods of wandering or benders. The years 1949 through 1955 include the peaks of his institutional living, with more than fifty weeks out of each of the years 1949, 1951, and 1954 spent in hospitals, rehabilitation programs, prisons, or jails.

During this period, Frank wandered primarily through New York and New England, with some brief penetrations into Pennsylvania. But in 1956 he returned to New England and his narrower circle of "home territory." There began a gradual but marked settling-down process detailed later in Chapters 7, 8, and 9.

After 1948 my personal contacts with Frank became much less frequent. Thus, the continuing story of Frank's life in this and subsequent chapters is told primarily through the letters he wrote to me from the wide variety of institutions and situations which enabled him to sustain life.

Overall, the letters for the years 1949 through 1955 are rich in detail, be they of his last bender and "Sybaritic" wanderings, his intellectual diversions, his complaints about communal life, his mother, or his encounters with staff, patients, jailers, or inmates. Narrative episodic descriptions of his personal experiences during these years serve as a rich source of data which he himself drew on in later years, beginning about

95

1956, in broadening his generalizations and deepening his analyses of himself and his life pattern and of society's handling of the alcoholic and the institutionally dependent.

Frank's letters and those comprising the three-way correspondence with his mother, Mrs. Greene, and me are excerpted and presented in chronological order. Explanatory notes are provided to fill in details and to clarify or highlight some aspects of the correspondence, but the story is essentially told by Frank himself. There is included at the beginning of each year's correspondence a listing of Frank's living arrangements for that year. Appendix III provides a list by date of all of the letters received from Frank.

1949

January–April	Davenport State Infirmary
May	Bender on the banks of the Mercy River
May–December	Stonycreek Prison Farm

Early in January, 1949, I wrote to Frank at the Davenport Infirmary telling him that I had heard from his mother and had given her his address. I decided to make brief mention but no great issue of his mother's additions to his life story. I hoped to avoid the possibility that the initiation of communication with his mother might block communication with Frank.

In this letter, I also proposed another attempt to work with Frank in New Haven. I told him we would make arrangements for an intensive program for him so that there would be no waiting for appointments and no wasted time. I offered to write an official letter, if necessary, to provide a train ticket, and to meet him on arrival.

Six weeks later I received a letter from a social worker at the Davenport State Infirmary stating that Frank Moore would like to return to the Yale Plan Clinic and that she would be glad to make arrangements for him to come to New Haven.

Unfortunately, although my offer had been made with the best of intentions, it could not be fulfilled. By the time I received a reply, the clinic was about to move to a different location and become part of a newly established public agency. Although my colleagues at the clinic did not completely withdraw their earlier offer to do what they could for Frank, their pending move and my own travel schedule, in connection with a different research project, made it impossible to plan for his visit until late in April. The clinic staff were also concerned about the implications of inviting an out-of-state resident to come for treatment in what was now a publicly supported facility. Faced with this new problem, which had not been a factor in earlier efforts to work with him, the clinic staff decided to re-evaluate Frank's prognosis. Their decision was that little hope could be held out for making any impact on his problems on a strictly outpatient basis. Since Frank had already demonstrated on several occasions an inability to maintain sobriety while working and living on his own in the community, they felt that significant therapy could occur only in a controlled inpatient environment where he might experience a long enough period of sobriety, combined with other therapeutic measures, to help him gain confidence, and begin to focus on realistic long-term goals. They realized that a return to stable community living without alcohol would require fairly long and gradual socializing experiences to compensate for his deep-seated feelings of social and psychological inadequacy, which had been reinforced by so many of his life experiences. In short, the clinic staff decided that the task of providing rehabilitation for Frank Moore, if achievable at all, was beyond their manpower and facility resources. I tried to convey this evaluation in my reply to the social worker and in a separate letter to Frank, stressing the absence of resources at the clinic for meeting his needs for living arrangements while undergoing study or treatment.

A few months later, in August, 1949, the question of rehabilitation for Frank was raised again in a letter from the superintendent of Stonycreek State Farm. In my reply, I was again unable to offer encouragement, and I wrote to Frank:

This week we received a letter from Superintendent Williams inquiring about the possibilities of our taking you off his hands. I went over the subject with Dr. Remonda who reiterated his previous stand that further attempts to work with you on an outpatient basis are contraindicated and that since inpatient facilities are just not now available here, it would be unwise to raise false hopes by attempting treatment under circumstances even more limited than those which have proved inadequate in the past. . . . I have sought the best advice available,

Frank, and I do feel that the best thing is not to bring you here until such time as we are set up so that we feel we really have a fighting chance of helping you.

In the period which followed, Frank both recognized and tried to reject his growing pattern of institutionalization. He looked back to his early success as a teen-aged pharmacist's mate in the Navy, began reading medical texts, and asked if any hospital school of nursing would accept him as a student. His search for an occupational goal was seasoned with a realistic lack of self-confidence and by an awareness that he belonged to an "untouchable" caste in the eyes of society and of most potential employers.

Stonycreek State Farm
August 24, 1949

Dear Bob:

. . . . .

It is very true I do not wish to return to the same conditions which would lead to the inevitable upsurge & violent down-swing. In the selfish desire to drag myself from this alcoholic morass, I would be among the first to agree that nothing would be accomplished, except under regulated guidance.

The next goal (perhaps unattainable) is to convince someone that I would be worthy of the time, trouble, & expense, if & when, such facilities are available. I would wait patiently if I knew such facilities would be available. . . .

For the past few months I have been strenuously reading anatomy, materia medica, pharmacology, hematology, etc., as a means of mental occupation, with a somewhat hazy notion that one day I will be a valued member of a hospital staff. There is, as usual, the ever present lack of guidance & correction that is the inescapable plight of the self-educated, no matter how determined & energetic he might be.

Frank

Stonycreek State Farm
September 16, 1949

Dear Bob:

. . . . .

I have, for a long time, felt the necessity of developing an all-consuming interest that would lead toward constructive living. At an age, when it appears that ambition should be defunct, & enthusiasm shrouded in a sepulchre, I believe that I have found that interest. Whether it shall die aborning, for lack of attention, I don't know.

For the past few months I have become engrossed in a study that will pay dividends in the event that I can enroll in a school of nursing at the hoary old age of forty-five. Regardless of this learned lore, it will be useless unless I am certified as a graduate of a hospital school of nursing. Pardon the braggadoçia which submits that I know more materia medica, pharmacy, anatomy & physiology, symptomology, than the usual registered nurse is required to know.

It is important for me to know, Bob, if any such schools exist where my age would not be a detriment to enrollment. N.B. (I have thrust the booze to the background, pro-tem, & there is a great possibility that it may cease to play its tragic part). Can you get such information for me.

Elatedly—
Frank

In replying to Frank's letter of September 16, I confirmed the difficulties which he already knew would make certification as a nurse a remote possibility, yet tried to encourage him to continue his studies, and suggested that he try to realign his ambitions to a somewhat more realistic level.

1950

January	Released from Stonycreek to a live-in job
February	Hillhouse State Hospital
March	Visit at mother's home in Calvinville, job as caretaker, bender
April–May	Franklyn Jail, 60-day sentence for larceny
May–December	Self-commitment to Liberty State Hospital
December	Davenport State Infirmary

Frank began 1950 with a new lease on life, having just been released from Stonycreek to a live-in job. The ensuing months brought him an entire spectrum of experiences, some offering hope and "decency," and some only physical and psychological bruises. He persisted nonetheless with what he finally called "the false belief that [one] can start anew at whatever age."

Oceanside
January 11, 1950

Dear Bob:

This is a strange and unwieldy pen. Am sending just a brief note at this time. Must tell somebody how glad I am.

Was released about a week ago thru the intercession of a local clergyman. I had attended thirty consecutive Sunday church services & A.A. meetings which follow those services. The minister was one of those hard-headed & logical types who do not dispense the evangelism & emotional fervorino. The best possible person to impress me.

I am living in a small town on the seashore. There are three other fellows here taking care of pedigreed collies, love birds, canaries, cats, etc., also a summer camp which operates from June thru the summer, for children from eight to twelve years of age. . . . I have a room of my own in this fine old mansion (Georgian) a radio & piano in my room. We have a colored lady cook & wonderful food. It seems nice to have a box of cigars. I wonder if this decency is going to bore me. . . . Every morning I ride into the city with the boss in Packard (whoops!), get to work about ten o'clock, which consists of restoring to a habitable state an immense run down sandstone manse which will be used to house pensioners.

When I see you again I will be an expert wall washer, white-washer, painter & paperhanger & what else have you. I came back here at 6 P.M. via the Packard (home! James!). No understanding has been reached in regard to wages. The second day the boss handed me five bucks for cigarettes! Decency is quite a novelty, & I know that you will be glad to know I am on the right side of the tracks for a change. Write.

Frank

This arrangement about which Frank was so euphoric was short-lived. On January 30 I received a letter from the superintendent of the Hillhouse State Hospital, informing me that Frank had been admitted for "care and treatment" and enclosing a questionnaire to provide information for diagnosis and therapy. I replied, and heard again from the superintendent that Frank would be there only a month. I wrote to Mrs. Greene telling her of Frank's whereabouts and asking if I should share with the hospital any of the information about Frank she had confided to me. Her reply of February 25 asked that I keep the information to myself. It was followed three days later by a letter from Frank from Calvinville which summarized some of the dilemma faced by the discharged, institutionally dependent individual.

Calvinville
February 28, 1950

Dear Bob:

I was discharged from the hospital Thursday of the past week. My period of legal incarceration had expired. The hospital authorities were not too anxious to release me because of humane reasons—Zero weather, no funds, insufficiently dressed (no hat), no prospect of employment, etc. However, their legal responsibilities were consumated, & a medical staff had reached a finding of "no psychosis." And so Frank Moore was no longer their headache & I was discharged forthwith.

As a matter of my personal experience, it appears that sitting at a table three times a day & sleeping in a bed every night, for a comparatively brief period, restores the individual to the false belief that he can start anew at whatever age, that he can secure employment if he is willing to work harder, for less wages, & to live under marginal conditions. The physiologists are familiar with the storing up of the body sugar, & in conjunction with salutary effects of hygienic living even for a short period of time in an institution, the individual's morale is stimulated—all of which accounts for the aforementioned "masquerade" & his willingness to return to an indigent & derelict condition that resulted in his hospitalization.—I mean that he is willing to hazard the possibility (which becomes reality).

Upon leaving the institution, I had considered in a hazy manner, going to New Haven. After considering my past failures, my accumulation of indebtedness (various forms) to you, your justification in believing that I was "beyond the pale," it became more acceptable to travel an uncertain way toward an unpredictable result, preferably among strangers who must needs arrive at their conclusions only by what was visibly apparent.

The first day I arrived at Carlyle & after a preview of possible lodgings for the night, I entered a combination tavern & saloon. I made a concise & brief statement to the proprietor to the effect that I had one dollar, that the one dollar was all the money I had, that there was no possibility of paying more. He gave me the register to sign, told me to hold on to the dollar, & personally conducted me to a decent room. Another humane act of another person & another one of those bitter debts that pile like Ossa on Pelion in the memory of a man who feels he is not justified in believing that he will ever repay the kindness.

The next day was raw with high winds when I emerged from the hotel. Walking or thumbing was a physical impossibility. I huddled in various saloons & the railroad station all that day (summer underwear & no head gear). The morale was shrinking & stamina was ebbing thru my scanty coverings.

That night I applied, at the police station, with the bald statement that I requested a night's lodging. The captain directed the turnkey to heat me a can of soup before placing me in a cell. I have found that sometimes it is unnecessary to state your needs. They become too damned apparent without the need to say anything. Sunday morning I was released at 6 A.M.

While walking the highway along the frozen Polywog in the direction of Carlyle, I considered the possibility of going to my mother's home.

Now, all the aforementioned sordid saga is written with the object in mind of showing the causes & events that lead toward decisions.

I probably walked half the distance to Calvinville & yet reached the city by noon. I waited around the railroad station for an hour getting warm & trying to make up my mind to go home or not. I went to the Church Rectory (my mother is a converted Catholic), & stated that I had not communicated with my mother for a couple of years, & requested the priest's advice as to the advisability of going to my mother's. It was unnecessary to acquaint him with my condition or past life. Such things are readily apparent to those psychologists without portfolio.

He stated that my mother was alive & the decision to go there was one that I had to make for myself.

No one can project himself fully into the other man's boots. To summarize, it was a decision that I would not foist on any man.

My mother welcomed me affectionately & my step-father in a friendly manner. Up to the moment of writing (noon, Tuesday), they have done everything to make me feel comfortable. Nothing could be asked in regard to the manner in which they have received me.

They have learned indirectly, thru the institutions, of my vicissitudes. In the forthright & realistic manner of people, they are desirous of doing something that is neither evasive nor inconclusive,—& realize their inability.

Consider my predicament, forty-six years of age, employment possibilities (almost nil) in this small town, an illogical burden on a man twice my age. Can you see why it is out of the question to accept this decent hospitality for even a short time?

Can you not offer slight encouragement toward my making a start at however low level (social agency or otherwise) in New Haven? Or must this be another retreat of the Grand Army from Moscow with all its scenic & atmospheric effects? I hope I may hear from you real soon.

Frank

In answer to Frank's letter of February 28 from his mother's home, I wrote suggesting that he seek work as a live-in employee at Davenport or in some other setting where his basic living needs could be met while he might experience some satisfaction and personal gratification that comes from being of service to others. Frank followed this advice, finding employment as an aide to a crippled musician. This led to his next bout with the law and incarceration, which I heard about through a letter from his mother (April 28, 1950) with an enclosed clipping dated March 9.

LOCAL MAN MUST SERVE 60 DAYS ON CHECK CHARGE—March 9, 1950

Frank Moore, age 45, Calvinville, appeared in district court this morning on a charge of larceny of checks and cash amounting to $338.35.

According to police, Moore was given the money by Jonathan C. Daily, age 65, a crippled musician, to deposit in the bank Monday. The money was not deposited and Moore disappeared.

A warrant was issued yesterday for Moore's arrest and he was picked up in Westville last night by the police of that city. In his possession were found checks for $300, $10.85 and $2.50. He said he had spent the $25 in cash. The defendant was brought back to Calvinville.

Moore pleaded guilty and in his statement before the court today claimed liquor was the cause of his downfall and asked to be committed. Judge Franklyn T. Donahue obliged by sentencing him to serve 60 days in the house of correction.

Calvinville
April 28, 1950

Dear Dr. Straus:

· · · · ·

He is an alcoholic and I sometimes think they use it as an excuse. I cried for days. It seemed so awful to steal from that cripple for liquor. I can't understand it. I don't believe he wants to stop.

He may be out any day now if he has behaved himself and I had no money or anything. I am not the only person with a son like this but would you believe it some of these *fools* in this city won't speak to me since it happened and the irony of it is that they have short memories of themselves and their sons.

· · · · ·

Gratefully yours,
Roberta C. Greene

The jail sentence for larceny kept Frank confined until early May. His period of freedom was obviously brief, for his next letter from the Liberty State Hospital, written in mid-June, indicated that he had already been there for about a month, having voluntarily committed himself for treatment. His next letters describe a course of Antabuse "treatment" and reflect the mixture of hope and cynicism that pervaded Frank's communications at this time. He remained at Liberty State Hospital until sometime in December, and before the year was over he found his way back to the Davenport Infirmary.

Liberty State Hospital
Alcoholic Ward
June 17, 1950

Dear Bob:

Far be it for me to jump from my tiled bath shouting, "Eureka." But, hearken! About a month ago I was admitted here on a voluntary basis without too much to do in re my predecessors, past condition of servitude, etc. I volunteered to be treated by "Antabuse" (free). After the usual preliminary tests, electrocardiograms, blood pressure, etc., I was given my first "work out" last Tuesday. On Saturday previous I took four tablets of "Antabuse," three tablets on Sunday, two tablets on Monday, & one & one-half on Tuesday morning. Tuesday afternoon I was wheeled to the treatment room for metabolism test & then forthwith handed the ordinary beaker of bourbon whiskey (Old Stag). The treatment is administered by couplets. Two patients at the same time in the same room. My partner was well soaked with Slav. After a five minute interval I felt the bulk of my blood fly to my head. Breathing became difficult, somewhat symptomatic of asthma. In ten or fifteen minutes more the heart began to accelerate to the extent of trying to jump clear from the chest. No nausea as yet. After twenty minutes had elapsed from the first drink, the second drink is given to the patient; the respiratory & cardiac symptoms grow more exaggerated, breathlessness, feeling of smothering or drowning, the second drink made me as weak & limp as a rag. Blood pressure continues to drop from the beginning of the operation. No nausea after second drink.

After an interval of twenty minutes after the second drink the doctor informed me how much my blood pressure had dropped and asked me if I desired a third drink of whiskey. I countered by asking him what he thought was best. He reiterated my blood pressure readings. I then stated that I would like the third drink because I wanted the treatment "to work." After the third drink there was a copious emesis & stupor. I was wheeled to my room & kept in bed for twenty-four hours. Bad effects for about one day—gastric discomfort.

Since that time I have taken one tablet a day & at week intervals I will be returned to a treatment room & administered a half an ounce of whiskey only, from which I will suffer the torments of the damned.

The most moronic product of the jungle must needs apprehend that it is impossible to imbibe even fractional amounts of alcohol while antabuse is in the system. The whole system of success in the use of this drug stems upon the fact that there must be a person or a group who will see to it that the individual will take the daily tablet of antabuse.

The state will furnish & supply me with these tablets for a year after I leave here. Who in hell is going to see to it that I take them?

Here is the most liberal, farseeing & intelligent attitude that I have ever experienced in my alcohol odyssey. After I was here for three days I was granted a parole of the grounds. The doctor is young & smart as a whip. We think he knows our faults & foibles, without the recourse to professional pomposity, beard tuggings, etc.

He points out to me that I can stay as long as I wish. That in the course of a couple of months I may be able to get on the patients pay roll ($20 a month on a probationary basis) & thence as a psychiatric aide at $140 per month.

As usual I anticipate all the difficulties that go along with this rosy picture. There are about a dozen patients who are in the same status as I. However they can send their shirts home to the laundry, their suits to the cleaners, etc., engage in social activities, Journeys to A.A. groups thru this little state.

When I succeed in getting on the patients pay-roll, I will have this one damn shirt that I wash every night, my run down at the heel shoes, & clothing that will permit me to go no where.

Six weeks sobriety leads up to some unpleasant stock-taking. I only wish some sequence of circumstances might tend to make the opportunity here more attainable. Ex-patients here have shown that they can fill responsible positions at very good pay. If I am an alcoholic, it is possible for me to do likewise. If to the contrary I am psycho-neurotic, neurotic, psychopathic, etc., what follows will bear that fact out.

This antabuse treatment, to my own mind, affords the first real test in regards any constructive treatment. I hope I shall be worthy the opportunities which this place seems to afford.

For the time being I shall not communicate with my mother. There seems to be an irremediable twist in that relationship & if I can once, & for all, cause myself to believe that I can live without the relationships which other men have, I can take care of Frank Moore in such a manner that he is self-sustaining & an asset to the community.

I have not given the usual thought or legibility to this letter. Am trying to cultivate a slogging stamina in lieu of brilliance.

Sincerely,
Frank G. Moore

Liberty State Hospital
August 27, 1950

Dear Bob:

I am behind with my correspondence. Things are coming fast, miracles are happening, & etc.

My doctor saw his superior, & fifteen minutes later I was in the supervisor's office receiving my keys as a "patient employee." This is undoubtedly some form of retribution, in that others have had the job of locking me in & caring for me, & now it is my turn to manipulate the lock by the way of a change.

The material benefits of this status are: 20 dollars a month pay & the promise that if I remain sober 90 days I will be placed on 140 dollars a month basis: I eat in the nurses & attendants cafeteria; & I could have a room of my own. I have chosen to remain in my same quarters for the time being. It could be that there is a beneficial deterrent influence in so doing, because I have the opportunity to view new arrivals in their various states of screaming meemies, et al. After three months I may have sufficient confidence to take up private quarters.

The difficulties that I have encountered in my first few weeks are minor. I started work with a fifty cent operating capital & I am still smoking institution tobacco. My wardrobe is so scant it is necessary for me to wash my own clothes each night after completing twelve hours duty. I do not have even a cheap dollar watch with which to take a patient's pulse which necessitates the borrowing of someone else's each time I perform this duty. My first pay will be along about the 3rd or 5th of next month.

Believe me Bob, when I say I am happy for this opportunity which has been extended to me & that I am grateful to all those concerned (my doctor, the hospital superintendent, & the liberal policy of this State).

Two half days of my work week are spent on the Antabuse team, in which I am concerned in the taking of blood and urine specimens, five specimens of blood & three urine for each patient. I am the liaison between the alcoholic ward & the doctor. Being of those who are initiated to the inner shrine I answer the cautious questions of those who are inclined to volunteer, & so far have felt instrumental in having a number give it a trial. Only one who has taken it since my coming here has had a relapse. There have been others previously.

One of the first volunteers found out that if he stopped taking the tablets for four days (he had taken one tablet daily for a short time) that he could drink without getting a reaction. And he passed the good word down the line.

The way I look at it is this way, if a man is what I called a premeditated drunk & can plan his bender four days ahead of time, there is no sense in giving him antabuse.

On the other hand, if the drinker is impulsive & gives way to the urge of the moment (for a million different reasons) & starts his drinking in that manner, Antabuse is indicated. The way I see it, is that he has a four day margin to rid himself of the particular "ants in the pants" that are bothering him. This is crude but I hope you see what I mean.

Do you remember one time, Bob, that I said, come the millenium, the scientists would discover some drug that would cause a man to break out in bright purple spots after taking a drink? Well get a load of this:

After taking one tablet daily for two & one-half months, Dr. Bray called me over for the grand experiment. He gave me one-half ounce of whiskey (15 cc's) & in fifteen minutes (Brotherrr!) I was breathing like a windbroken horse, my eyes were watering & the outside corners of my eyes were drawn down in the direction of the corners of my mouth; combined with my alopecia (baldness to you) & sunken cheeks, I was the saddest looking so & so you ever saw. I feel safe in saying that no bartender in the country would serve me a second drink after seeing what one drink would do to me.

We work 60 hours a week here, 5 days of 12 hours, & I have every Fri. & Sat. off. Because I worked on V.J. day which is celebrated here, I have this Sunday off duty also. Three days off in a row & I have come out here a mile from the hospital, under the shade of an old apple tree across from the private graveyard (6 graves) of pioneers, to write this letter & so excuse writing which is performed on the back of book. Sounds buccolic, Thomas Gray & all that.

There is a red-hot union of hospital employees here & they are yammering for a 40 hour week. This could turn out to be a hell of a good break for

Frank   Moore

1951

| January–November | Davenport State Infirmary |
| December | Liberty State Hospital |

From August, 1950, to March, 1951, I heard nothing from Frank. Then, in a brief note from the Davenport State Infirmary on March 18, he wrote:

It is five or six months since I last wrote you. No need to go into details. Perhaps in my hoary sixties I will compile the "Drunkard's Odyssey" of an impossible person in an incomprehensible world. . . . Each licking is harder to take.

The only other letter for the entire year was written in December. In this he dismissed briefly his year at Davenport State Infirmary, where he was able to maintain a rhythmical encounter with alcohol while enjoying the security of institutional living. In December he left this situation to commit himself again voluntarily to Liberty State Hospital, where he had had a satisfying experience the year before, moving from the status of patient to live-in employee. He described his commitment as his "last chance" for treatment. "I know I cannot expect anything after this."

Liberty State Hospital
December 8, 1951

Dear Bob:

Note the above address. I stayed at the Davenport State Infirmary for one year. It seemed a proper place to "round out" my declining years. But I reckoned without the "inner man." I'll leave it to the philosophers to isolate that factor which makes fools jump out of the frying pan into the fire.

On the evening of five days of the week, during that year, I spent reiterating the fundamental theorems of Euclid, the mastering of the mysterious logarithm, & the use of trigonometric tables. The other two evenings were spent in alcoholic vapor which was made possible thru small gratuities from grateful state employees for work performed.

Whatever it is that occasions an ancient courtesan to attempt another assignation, or makes retired fire horses fret in their stalls, prompted me to give this place one more fling. I arrived here two weeks ago today on a "voluntary commitment," giving a nebulous residence, & stating for the official records, that I had undergone the antabuse treatment here before & that under that treatment I had remained sober for seven months, & that I wished to repeat the treatment.

I found a new incumbent here in lieu of Dr. Bray. His name is Dr. Long. So far my opinion coincides with that of the other patients here, viz, that he has enough of the crusader spirit, & that he is interested in the job he is paid to perform.

I am on antabuse treatment again. In view of my last experience with it, I know that I myself, wish to take the tablets 99% of the time, but who in hell is going to see to it that I take the tablets the other 1% of the time, if I leave here.

It is the only weakness I see in the whole "set-up." So far I haven't found anyone unduly worried about whether I drink or not. With some it might be a wife or a parish priest, but I lack any such person to "ride herd" on Frank Moore.

I could leave here at any time without clothing or money, & somehow or other manage to exist, but the chances are against my "making good" because I inevitably return to booze sometime during the depressing struggle.

I believe my chances here at the hospital are better than elsewhere, & the experiment has a feeling of finality about it. This is about my last chance. I know I can not expect anything after this.

Fortified as I was, upon my arrival here, I demanded of the doctor that he either kill or cure me. I am sober now but I still feel the same way about it.

One of the minor difficulties that beset me at the moment is one in which you might be able to advise. When a patient comes to work as an employee, he must necessarily be distinguished by his garb from that of other patients, i.e., he needs clothing. White shirts & black bow ties are compulsory here. I have neither suit nor shoes to match the job requirements. This is one of those jobs where truly "the apparel oft proclaims the man" (Polonius in Hamlet.)

Now, National Committees may rise & fall, Research Foundations ply the functions, et al, but where in hell am I going to get these clothes, before I can avail myself of this opportunity.

Don't you think I deserve one other crack to redemption. Can you think of any way I could be aided? I hope to hear.

Sincerely,
Frank

1952[1]

January–March	Liberty State Hospital (commitment)
March–April	Liberty State Hospital (live-in employee), bender, Riverpoint Jail
May–June	Hospital in New Jersey, jail in New Jersey
July	Visit in New Haven, live-in job in resort area
Mid-August	Easton Heights Men's Shelter
November	Indigo County Jail

1. Only about twenty-five weeks of this year are accounted for through Frank's two letters and our one meeting during the year.

The first word I had from or about Frank in 1952 came on May 19 when I received a telephone call from the local Red Cross Home Service with the information that Frank had been hospitalized in New Jersey following a two-month bender and asking if I would be responsible for him if he were to come to New Haven. I explained the clinic's inability to assume responsibility for out-of-state alcoholics and also their lack of residence facilities, but I expressed my personal interest in Frank and offered to meet his immediate needs were he to come. Ten days later I received a letter from a probation officer in New Jersey seeking informa-tion about Frank's "character, habits, attitude, intelligence, and conduct." On July 11, the Travelers Aid Society called, seeking and obtaining my guarantee of Frank's transportation costs to New Haven. He had been given twenty-four hours to leave a town in New Jersey or be jailed there, and he had told the Travelers Aid people that he could get a job in New Haven.

On July 18, Frank arrived in New Haven, late in the afternoon, and called me. He said he had walked from New Jersey and had not eaten in two days. I never learned why he had not come by train or bus a week earlier. I met him downtown and took him to a restaurant, where he related his most recent experiences while he ate. He had achieved a civil service rating on his job at Liberty State Hospital. He found it good pay, good working conditions, and interesting work, but one weekend he took off to see a burlesque show, started drinking, and, when he came to, found himself in jail in Riverpoint (about two hundred miles away). From Riverpoint, he drifted into New Jersey. Most recently, he had been on the road for seven or eight days, walking much of the way during a record-breaking heat wave.

At this time a new possibility had developed for trying to help Frank —a rehabilitation program for alcoholics at Heaven Hill in the New York metropolitan area. This project was established with the express intent of exploring ways of providing rehabilitation for men who had become institutionally dependent, were undersocialized, were often chronic users of alcohol, and were unemployable in their present state. The program was designed to provide, through good food, medical care, a hygienic environment, and prosthetic devices when indicated, an oppor-tunity for homeless men to attain physical health in an isolated environ-ment protected from society and themselves. As their health improved, the men were expected to take on work responsibilities and engage in oc-cupational training. A number of socializing experiences were gradually worked into the program, and the men were expected to assume specific responsibilities, first in groups and later as individuals. Eventually, they were sent back into the community on simple errands or for recreation, then to work while still living at Heaven Hill, and finally to try their wings at "living out" with a gradually reduced tie to their "home on the hill."

From its beginning Heaven Hill was conceived as an experimental project. I had been asked to evaluate its long-term impact and had begun this task when Frank appeared in New Haven. I told him briefly of the Heaven Hill development, suggested he go there, and offered to write a letter of introduction, which I felt sure would gain him admittance. I suggested a night's lodging at a local "mission-type" shelter or a local hotel, or transportation by air-conditioned train toward Heaven Hill. Frank chose the last, and I bought him a train ticket, some food, and cigarettes, and gave him some change. Then, as on other occasions, the desirability of providing him with enough cash to meet some basic needs raised the dilemma that it would probably merely facilitate his getting drunk. This time, I gave Frank only enough change for carfare despite the fact that he had earlier admonished me for sending him into the "big city" with only twenty cents in his pocket. In any event, Frank did not reach Heaven Hill on this occasion. He was faced with having to wait a few days for group transportation and chose, instead, to move on. The rest of the year was spent in odd jobs, drinking, and jail. On November 23, from Indigo County Jail, he wrote:

I will be released from here a few days before Christmas . . . no job, no clothes, and retaining all the drawbacks which have contributed toward my being a successful failure.

1953

January–June	Unaccounted for
July	Chesterfield County Penitentiary
September–December	Heaven Hill Rehabilitation Program

The first word about Frank in 1953 came in May from Mrs. Greene, who had received a Mother's Day card from him. He did not write to me until July, and then he told only of wandering through the upper New York State region. Frank's affinity for upstate New York during the early part of 1953 may have been his way of "casing" the territory, since my impending change of job and residence to Syracuse, New York, in June, 1953, was planned a year in advance and was known to Frank. During much of the time between 1953 and 1956, while I was in Syracuse, Frank was wandering through the upper New York State region. Another move in 1956 seemed similarly to affect the territory in which Frank chose to live, at least temporarily.

In my reply to Frank's letter in July, I urged him again to seek the sanctuary and rehabilitation opportunities at Heaven Hill, and this time he made it. From there he appreciatively confided, "I am happier now than I have been for a long time."

> Heaven Hill
> October 26, 1953

Dear Bob:

Too often have I written to you when I was in a "spot." Well I am in a "spot" now, but it is a good one.

I have been here almost two months, & have postponed writing because I felt unable to tell you my impressions of the place (and do it justice).

The many tangible & intangible benefits that have come during my short stay here are worthy of a more profound exposition than I am able to portray at this time.

Sufficient to say that if anyone, as damned analytical (fault-finding?) as I, can find nothing wrong with this place, it must be all right. No other possibility exists, reductis ad absurdem etc.

As you advised, I contacted Mr. Edwards & Mr. Dietz upon my arrival here. Their many kindnesses in interview, in re clothing, employment, & general friendliness reflect the high regard they feel toward you. I find both these men singularly adapted for the job at hand—no sentiment but humane, decent & fair dealing.

I have noticed that the men here who appear the best integrated, recognize the advantage of staying here. Without looking at the clothing, it is almost possible to recognize the new-comer by his wild talk. The men who have stayed here for quite some time, on the other hand, do not have that attitude of the whole solar system passing in elliptical orbits around the seat of their pants.

God grant that I have the native sense, animal cunning, instinct of self preservation, to stay here & that thru the course of time I might rediscover beauty, intelligence, & goodness, & have the clear head to recognize them.

I'll stop now before I really let my hair down. However appropriate it is to write these things, they really look like hell in the gray dawn.

Being sincere is new & rather uncomfortable. Thanks for the "good steer," Bob, & as they say at commencement day, I will watch your career with etc. etc.

I hope to write you the more formal critique at some later day. I am happier now than I have been for a long time.

F.

1954

January–July	Heaven Hill Rehabilitation Program
August–September	Riverpoint County Jail
September–October	Oldtown County Jail
October	Silver Hill Shelter (2 weeks)
October–December	Riverpoint County Jail (10 weeks)

Frank remained at Heaven Hill from his arrival in the late summer of 1953 until the program terminated and he was turned away eleven months later. Preliminary study of the Heaven Hill program suggested that it was having an effective impact on a small but significant number of its residents, and that a workable formula for the successful rehabilitation of a certain segment of homeless men was indeed being evolved. Tragically, the program was caught up in a jurisdictional dispute between governmental agencies. A different agency won the facilities and, quite precipitately, in August, 1954, the program was terminated. Ironically, many of the residents soon returned to the Hill, but this time as prisoners and for incarceration rather than for rehabilitation.

Frank's interest in his mother's well-being was stimulated by several letters which she apparently wrote to him at Heaven Hill. He responded from there while he was still savoring the security and dignity of its rehabilitative program. But later on, from jail, he could not bring himself to communicate directly with her. At his request, I wrote to Mrs. Greene on November 1, and in responding to my letter she enclosed a warm, supporting note for Frank (November 6, 1954).

While still at Heaven Hill, on June 18, Frank expressed to his mother some feelings of self-satisfaction, but after he was turned out of Heaven Hill in July he stepped right back into the familiar cycle of alcohol, trouble with the law, and jail. Frank's five periods of institutional care during the last half of 1954 were interspersed with four episodes of drinking and wandering which, although together they covered only two weeks of the year, were sufficient to secure his institutionalization for the remaining time.

He wrote (September 1, 1954) from the Riverpoint County Jail:

Is it inevitable that I return to periodic employment and a Baedeker tour of the country's jails? Can you suggest a milieu where I can't get the stuff?

For the rest of 1954, Frank made just such a tour; from Riverpoint County Jail, to Oldtown County Jail, to a religious shelter for homeless men at Silver Hill Shelter, and back to Riverpoint.

Heaven Hill
June 18, 1954

Dear Mother:

Received yours a few days ago & glad to hear. No, I am not restricted in my writing but, time goes by so fast, & the little non-essential things claim so much of one's time.

The fact is, I am not restricted in any way, & could leave here tomorrow if I wished. The past spring was a trying time for me. It seems that every spring I have been lured by new places & new faces. So now I have got by the spring of the year.

There were many things held out to me as being the possible rewards if I stopped drinking.

One person said I would have my pick of jobs, another said that I would acquire money, etc. Each one held out some particular reward, & each according to his own aims.

However, it has been 10 months now since I have had a drink, & during that time I have never had over fifty dollars in my pocket at one time. And in the way of jobs, many people have tried to influence me to leave here, get bigger money, bigger headaches, bigger dissatisfaction, etc. . . . Man does not live by bread alone, but, toward what end or purpose, are they anxious to acquire money & material possessions at whatever cost. For nearly a year now, I have slept on a foam rubber mattress every night, sat down to eat three times a day, have earned what I have received, am beholden to none, & however suspicious & reserved a person may be, I have found that they exhibit a real liking for me when they know me better.

As I say, I am not acquiring anything, but I am well founded in the belief that I am "wanted," that I am "necessary" & what I am doing is worthwhile.

Frank

Riverpoint County Jail
October 24, 1954

Dear Bob:

"Eternal spirit of the chainless mind! Brightest in dungeons! etc. & Etc." Nothing but such poetry may compensate such an aimless existence. . . . Arrived here today . . . 90 days . . . district court . . . Put my head thru thirty dollars worth of glass window. . . . Minor abrasion of forehead . . . Two weeks from now it will not even show.

I wish that I were able to collate the existent material for a tome entitled "Survival," which I believe, would make Captain Bligh's feat of seamanship a pecadillo by comparison.

Is it possible for you to weave some sort of fabrication to my mother to account for my absence of writing to her? This concern is repeatedly recurrent & I wish that I was adequate of some sort of plausability.

It would be of benefit to hear from you & to feel that someone, somewhere is concerned about me.

Sincerely,
Frank

The following note was enclosed in a letter from Mrs. Green dated November 6, 1954, with a request that I send it on to Frank.

Dear Son

I love you dearly. You have made a misstep after doing so well. No one is perfect. My last letter came back. I shall continue to pray for your enlightenment stability and for the help you need so much. Dr. Straus wrote me. Do not give up now. You showed what you could do for 11 months. When you come out try again tho God knows I don't know where you would get in. *Try*, dear son, *try*.

Mother

1955

January	Riverpoint County Jail
January–February	Sageville County Jail, wandering southeast 180 miles
February–March	Anchorport County Jail, wandering northwest 150 miles
March–May	Amsterdam County Jail
May–mid-September	Riverpoint County Jail
Mid-September–mid-October	Chippewa County Jail
Mid-October	Westtown's Men's Service Center
Mid-October–December	Sageville County Jail

This was a prolific year in letter writing for Frank. His forty-eight weeks in sundry jails interspersed with benders brought forth a total of thirty letters. There was some attempt on his part to take a larger look at his own problems and at how they were shared by many other "displaced personalities" in society (February 6, 1955). His letters were still highly personal in their recounting of the details of periodic wanderings or rehabilitation attempts, in the contemplation of a personal release through suicide, or in discussion of his own inadequacies and antipathies toward various aspects of conventional society which he felt he should be able to cope with. Throughout the year, however, there is evidence of continuing hope for his own eventual rehabilitation:

I have long since embarked on an intellectual pilgrimage aimed toward the modification of my own character. . . .

Consider the possibility that I may yet be able to exist without being at loggerheads with the aims & purposes of people about me (July 25, 1955).

January–March. The first part of 1955 brought a continuation of the pattern of 1954, as Frank noted with vivid detail in his letter of March 27. Earlier, from the Sageville Jail, he evaluated his "field study" of the Heaven Hill program and suggested criteria for other rehabilitation efforts (February 6, 1955).

Sageville County Jail
January 25, 1955

Dear Bob:

Forwarded herewith is a resume of my latest caper: The locale is near a little town on the east bank of the Hudson, the time—last Friday, and the temperature at 0° F. According to the State Trooper, I was curled up sleeping on the shoulder of the road (infantile regression). The next day I was taken before a justice of peace and sentenced to 30 days. All of which is "old hat" and scarcely noteworthy. However, who knows but that I may yet establish some sort of record for stamina or determine the boundary of judicial patience.

Incidently, I didn't even catch a cold from my al fresco siesta. It appears that I am going to survive for something. Do you remember the fellow you met down in New Haven who wrote that series "Skid Row" U.S.A.? If he could wangle his way into about forty different precinct stations and county jails, he would gather some rather readable material, if only from the dissimilar manner in which different communities deal with an endemic problem. However this may savor of brazen guffaw; I'm really sick of it. In another twenty-five days another derelict will be set adrift to repeat the process in a new milieu. If the money is appropriated for the Coast Guard to permanently remove wrecks which endanger navigation, I, for one, can see nothing incongruous if the state should appropriate the money to salvage wrecks which are still seaworthy. In your ministrations to the younger generation (their education), you could bring out this fact. A letter from you would be a pleasant surcease from days which are monotonously dull.

Sincerely,
Frank

Sageville County Jail
February 6, 1955

Dear Bob:

Your last letter was coming down the river while mine was going up (Evangeline & Gabriel without the pathos). In regard the resumption of a Heaven Hill program, let us begin with three axioms (1) politicians control the purse strings, (2) public opinion sways the politician, (3) public opinion is molded by the press. . . . Jack Alexander in the Saturday Evening Post of ten years ago brought an intelligible view of alcoholism to the public at large, which is yet reflected in the kindlier attitude of police, courts, & back doors where I have begged for something to eat. Any resumption of the Hill program will be the result of the prodding of the press, rather than the murmurings from the towers of ivory. This is not a panegyric to journalism & my own sympathies incline toward science rather than penny-a-line hack writers.

There is no doubt, however, that scientific fact is negligible to the public ear, & the so called "objectivity" is repellant to the masses as truth always has been. I venture that any man who tells the truth on every occasion is a damned unpleasant person, that he stands accused of "psychopathic baldness of statement" & that he is described as "emotionally blunted." So much for the shortcoming of "fair science."

Now, if you will agree that the press should be utilized toward the return of the Hill program, it follows that in order to be effective the best journalist must be induced to accept the task. Whoever undertakes to perform the work must be practical (but not too practical), religious (but not too religious), sympathetic without being maudlin, & an altruist without being a dreamer. He must season his product with a sprinkling of pathos, with just a dash of statistics. Possibly he should be humane & cynical too. A good "end product" will be the result of skillful blending rather than a richness of ingredients. If you find such a journalist, put him to work.

Though I am unqualified for such a mission myself, my long "field study" in alcoholism has resulted in the accumulation of cogent facts which may be of service to the journalistic investigator. I am presenting herewith a fragmentary outline of the subjects which should be embodied in such a work.

1. That a type of alcoholic exists, who, in his relentless pursuit of failure is not amenable to counsel or treatment (either chemotherapy, psychology or psychiatry). Menninger called this "negativism" which is, after all, another generalization.

2. That in any given community there exists a great number of individuals, who, because of the presence or absence of indefinable unit characteristics (Mendel) resort to alcohol & become, permanently, habitues of county jails & poorhouses.

3. That such disposition of such "displaced personalities," is unsound from a judicial, fiscal, & moral point of view.

4. That the Heaven Hill program be inaugurated in other states.

5. That *no* deviation from particular sections of that program be permitted; these sections are:

(a) Absolute isolation from the community & inaccessibility of alcohol.

(b) Admission & discharge should be voluntary. If a person decided to leave, he shall be considered ineligible to readmission until six months have elapsed. (This will eliminate the man who would use the facility as a recuperative hostel).

(c) No police whatsoever. The only measure of discipline for infraction of necessary regulations would be that of being told to leave.

(d) That a laundry, farm, or shoe shop be incorporated in the set up & if the (value) goods produced exceed the cost of hill maintenance, the individuals should be paid $1 or $2 a day. Not more than $2 (Only one type of work program) in order to reduce cost of skilled supervision.

You take it from here Bob, & be sure the program is administered by men like Dietz & Edwards & not by some political hack reaping his reward. A salient factor of the old program was, that out of the thousands who were processed in the era of Heaven, & over a period of years, there was no racial incident or the commission of a single felony. Significant?

Frank

Amsterdam County Jail
March 27, 1955

Dear Bob:

Received your last letter telling of your virus infection, food poisoning, & the trick patella. You might derive some satisfaction in the knowledge that, some day, you will be, at least, mourned. When I cross the river Styx, I expect to bum a cigarette from Charon & do my own rowing. In re the immunities, & antibodies of a St. Bernard existence, I confess that I would prefer the frailty, accomplishment, & short life of a Keats, in lieu of stamina to endure & prolong a life of futility & repeated failure. . . . Space will allow but a brief exposition of the annuals of an inebriate, viz: I left Anchorport a week ago Friday in a snow storm, flakes as big as your hand. Got as far as Chesterfield. Met a professional pool hustler, a man of 65, drunken, & bewhiskered, & yet so good that he manages to stage a perennial (?) drunk. . . . In brief we made a tour of the pool parlours & wine shops. Slept in the R.R. station that night. For my "cut" I had enough to get grogged up & went out to the beach & slept on that stone jetty that day in the sun, & got my bald head so sun-burned that it is still peeling like an onion. Crawled into a car on a parking lot that night, but couldn't close the window entirely & damned near froze to death. Next day, Sunday, made my way to Silver Hill by night fall. All filled up & slept on a table, about 40″ long that night & hit the highway in a driving rain & walked a good way up to here. Fellow that did pick me up finally & gave me a ride, passed me a dollar without solicitation & so I managed to get two pints of wine, to keep out the winter chill. And so now I have 60 days of assured & continued existence. I can understand a soldier in his forced marches, hunger, privation etc., & his ideals & his leadership, but fail to apprehend what keeps a tramp going, without these same ideals & leadership. Would like to hear from you. . . .

F.

April–August, 1955. Frank was always probing for an explanation, as well as a palliative, to his condition. His letters in this period covered ruminations on genetics and his own heredity, the strings of the "injustices" he had suffered, the potential release of suicide, and his mental diversions, which in this case took the form of self-tutoring in trigonometry.

During this period he also made several clear references to his growing recognition of his alienation and "exile" from society and from conventional behavior. Perhaps in response to a study I sent him, he also took a hard look at his own institutional dependency and his inadequacies in social interaction. And yet, in all seriousness, he offered another constructive attempt to plan some sort of rehabilitation for himself, "Moore's Utopia," where the demands and conventions of society would not impinge on the individual's life style or integrity, and would offer to the individual "the opportunity to collate his own experience in life" (July 25, 1955).

Amsterdam County Jail
April 17, 1955

Dear Bob:

If a person were to write of his accomplishments during a lifetime, it could be written on a cigarette paper. If he were to write of his opinions, prejudices, & the vagaries of his mind, the world could not supply a single individual with sufficient paper. . . . Having dispensed with my diurnal quota of cracker-barrel philosophy, we will proceed to the journal, which I have variously labeled: Inanities of an Inebriate, Asininities of an Alcoholic, & the Dissertations of a Drunkard. . . . I am continuously impressed when I hear people say of another: "He hasn't got it in him," or "I knew he had it in him." It seems to me that the untutored & simple man intuitively grasps a bit of knowledge, which is revealed to a scientist thru tortuous processes. A quaint Austrian monk crossing tall & dwarf varieties of sweet peas, the hybrids & their descendants with dominant & recessive characteristics, following infallible & predictable mathematical laws, are unfamiliar facts to the layman, yet, he would be quick to admit that a colt from a Texas mustang & sired by a percheron stallion could not win in a race with "Boston Doge." The farmer of Canada would not plant wheat seed from the Nile River section, or if he did, he would not fix the blame on the wheat seed when it failed to mature in the short Canadian summer. He would readily admit that no other results were to be expected. Quick to apply & reap the benefits of knowledge in all other spheres, man is a laggard in accepting the same laws as applying to himself. . . . The opponents of such a schism would say of a man whom they dislike, "He blames his ancestors for his own misbehavior," or "If we accept such an idea, everyone will do as he damn well pleases, & no man will be held accountable for his vice, crime, et al." On the other hand, the proponents of such a schism would say of a man whom they *did* like, "It is not his fault, look at his genealogical tree." It appears to me, that we have an argumentum ad hominem in both cases. Both opinions refer to the man rather than to the idea; in one case we *like* the man, & in the other we *dislike* the man. The acceptance or rejection of hereditary influences, then, depends on whether we are lovers or haters of mankind. . . . One thing I have noticed about getting an opinion down on paper, the opinion becomes more indelibly impressed in the writer's mind, which is unfortunate if I am wrong in the denial of free will, criminality, & responsibility for innate & congenital characteristics.

Sincerely,

F.

Amsterdam County Jail
April 24, 1955

Dear Bob:

The present regurgitation concerns the pathogenesis of suicide. . . . While at Sageville, I wrote you of the man who strangled himself with his shirt. One should not be indicted of undue morbidity. Should he exhibit passing interest in the manner with which drunkards, figuratively, thumb their noses to the various purgatories, paradises, Nirvanas, & Valhallas. Indeed, John Donne's "For Whom the Bell Tolls" has lived in literature for hundreds of years, in which he enjoins us, "No man is an island entire of himself," & "Every man's death diminishes me because I am involved in mankind."

I suppose anyone would grant that no happy man ever committed suicide. While at Anchorport, I read a treatise "What Makes Men Unhappy" by the antique English writer, Hazlitt. He finds that men live under the most adverse circumstances & yet find compensatory joy in a continued existence, & that the only intolerable condition is "injustice." Here we have the abstract, not the concrete. What did he mean? The injustice of friends & family? The injustice of his employers? The injustice of his social system? The clue probably would be found in the history of the time in which he wrote. . . . Again, in the novel "Lord Jim," Joseph Conrad swerves from the main theme to tell of a master mariner at the peak of his profession, stopping his watch, hanging it on the rail, before he stepped over the stern into the night, while the ship was under way. Conrad gives us the faintest of hints, in stating that under given circumstances, certain men find life unacceptable. Here we have "given circumstances" & "certain men," which are, surely both variable. . . . I have evolved in my idle brain (?) a novel method to dissuade these potential bloaters on the surface of our harbors & those who would stretch with elongated necks & pendulous tongues. Suppose the individual could be induced to postpone his act of finality until he could evoke the following conditions: (1) a lavish chamber, (2) a luxuriant bed, (3) manuscripts of Schopenhauer's "Denial of the Will to Live," Bryant's "Thanatopsis" (who would not like to lay down with the saints & seers of the ages?), & Socrates "Address to the Athenians," (4) aged whiskey laced with a lethal dose of the Papaver Somniferum, & (5) a repeating record player with an album of Rachmaninoff's concertos. Thus a transition could be effected with grandeur which is seldom attained in life. One, so considerate of the esthetic sensibilities of his fellow travelers, would surely merit the title of "neat gentleman." Consider the time & trouble necessary to unsnarl a corpse from the wheels of a subway train. . . . So endeth another footnote on the facets of alcoholism. Swift had a solution of the Irish question.

Sincerely,

F.

On April 29, 1955, Frank sent me an envelope containing several newspaper clippings about the suicide of a prisoner at the Amsterdam Jail.

Amsterdam County Jail
May 8, 1955

Dear Bob:

. . . . .

Sometimes, when I review the sentiments expressed in my letters to you, I wonder if you believe these places of confinement are musty libraries where all that is best in human thought is available to the incarcerated. I assure you of the contrary. The mental diversions of the past few months (offered) are the daily papers & the horror comic books. . . . To return to the adjustments—I remember that I was arrested in Schenectady for drunkenness on a Saturday & stayed in the city jail 'til Monday morning. Over the week end I worked out with a stubby pencil & a roll of toilet paper, the manner by which Archimedes determined the numerical value of pi. Of course I had the hazy idea to begin with, but only under those circumstances, could I work it out to my thorough comprehension. It has been a long time since I read John Stuart Mill's "Triumph or Truth" & during the past week I have consumed much time thinking of how, when a man has lived a considerable time & arrived at a few incontrovertible truths, he can see it trampled, ignored & discounted. By usual standards this ill-spent time, must have been what Byron meant when he wrote: "Eternal spirit of the chainless mind, Brightest in dungeons, etc." Hell, we all dramatize ourselves & live the "strange lives of Walter Mitty."

Sincerely,

F.

Amsterdam County Jail
May 23, 1955

Dear Bob:

. . . . .

Can you get me a copy of Wentworth & Smith's "Plane Trigonometry" (second hand). It is a standard text in most schools & I wish to familiarize myself with every problem in *detail*. When I am 60, I will begin to be useful again. This six months could be preparatory to that end.

I bought a nice slide rule while I was at Heaven Hill. Of course I could not keep it for long after leaving there. What I received for it, financed a one day drunk. The pertinent fact is, that for about 7 months at Heaven, I devoted one hour each night, (eye strain) to practice manipulation = square roots, cube roots, logarithms, sines, tangents, division, & multiplication.

I am sending you a sample of my latest investigation. I think it is pretty dry stuff & tho I understand it, I will go no farther with it.[2]

All of which is to support my latest request of you for the "trigonometry." I can solve any right triangle, other triangle, regular polygon, make a table of the natural functions; convert common logs to natural logs.

Would you like to send me a problem to support the above? I claim also that I can solve a quadratic equation by four different methods.

You were certainly right in your phraseology re (doing things under my own conditions). What a "screwed-up" man I am!

Sincerely,

F.

Riverpoint County Jail
June 14, 1955

Dear Bob:

. . . . .

I have no doubts but what a vagrant idealizes home to a greater extent than his stable brother. Recalling your article in the Quarterly, "Alcohol & the Homeless Man," I wonder if you considered that in many cases, these men are not homeless *in a majority of cases*, but rather, they are exiles, even if self imposed.

I recall your studies of jurisprudence. Do you remember, that among Greeks of their golden age, that the work-house & penitentiary were unknown. Also the supreme penalty, other than death, was exile. That the exile had no protector, no standing in the courts of a foreign city, no government to avenge an outrage on him. That he could be starved, stripped & even murdered with impunity. That if he died abroad he would not be assured of a decent funeral pyre.

My letters to you indicate the modern concomitants of exile.

. . . . .

Sincerely,

F.

2. Several pages of mathematical equations were written on the back of this letter and the one sent on July 25, 1955.

Riverpoint County Jail
July 3, 1955

Dear Bob:

I received the book, clipping & a copy of your latest work.[3]

The following statement was most significant: "the basic problem for a large segment of these men is one of dependency, not alcohol," also "out of this are now developing suggestions for rehabilitation which aim to meet dependency needs as a prerequisite to any shift in drinking pattern." If, as you state, there are so many variables & intangibles that each patient must be approached as an individual, so it follows with the corrective environment to reduce this dependency & feelings of inadequacy.

The word "dependency" would here need clarification. I am sure many of these men could & would produce useful work, performed by themselves, removed from the necessity of collaboration with others. Indeed, any favorable prognosis is dependent on this condition. Yet, you will surely agree that this is not the usual conception of "dependency." The usual interpretation implies laziness, sloth, inertia, lack of interest, depleted energies & lack of inner drives. Admitting the dependency pattern, we are confronted by a paradox, the dependent who is a social rebel & prides himself on the fact that he is an "independent man," independent in his tastes, opinions, etc.

His "independence" will continue to prevent social interaction & any worthwhile accomplishment is contingent on his removal from the scramble for high priced cars, deep-freezes, & easy winnings at the nearest track, & other various & sundry "normal" endeavor. Like W. T. Sherman, he does not choose to run.

In general, I have never read a single piece of literature on this subject so direct & unbiased, honest. P. 22 was most delectable, concerning the man who stopped drinking altogether & became so difficult to live with that his wife divorced him.

Especially worthy was the fact that most men do not wish to change themselves. They would, however, like to reap the benefits of persons, who are unlike themselves. Here is an interlocking of psychiatry and philosophy.

F.

3. A chapter entitled "Alcoholism," published in Arnold M. Rose (ed.), *Mental Health and Mental Disorder* (New York: W. W. Norton & Co., 1955).

Riverpoint County Jail
July 25, 1955

Dear Bob:

Received your note & clipping today.

Thoreau in his treatise on "Civil Disobedience" stated that under certain conditions, jail is the only refuge for an honest man. To brief you on this damned radical: he was a New Englander who refused to pay taxes to a government to support a war with Mexico (with whom he had no quarrel) & a government which tolerated slavery. If he was around today, he would probably be averse to warring with the Volga boatmen (in spite of the coercion of the press & radio).

You see I do have a kind of social interaction (or thought anyhow). All of which leads to the question of what in hell are we going to do with this man who gets out of here the first part of September & has no aspirations toward "social interaction."

Is there no milieu for a person who is constitutionally, congenitally, temperamentally, et al, unsuited for this social interaction. Is there no place where a man might live & work alone, to have the opportunity to collate his own experience in life, to avail himself of the legacy of history (social & scientific) bequeathed by the men who lived before him? Hell, I desire nothing new. I wish the opportunity to avail myself of what is already here. Let's get specific:

Consider Moore's Utopia: a shack in the Adirondacks, Maine woods, an island (geography is not important); plain subsistence, a token service where I would be custodian of a property, clearing land, improving the value of the property; a token salary (a dollar a day would suffice for clothes, tobacco, books); & the opportunity to investigate a single phase of human art & science.

Is this exorbitant, if viewed in contrast to the desires of most individuals? I am over fifty. Why make further social demands of me? What psychic trauma, environmental factor, or hereditary influence would cause me to turn to the bottle, under the conditions listed above?

I am not indicating a treatment for drunkards, in general, (the transporting of these incorrigibles to a Botany Bay) but you know it is altogether possible for a person to gain insight into his own particular problems. I have long since embarked on an intellectual pilgrimage aimed toward the modification of my own character. The discipline of any study should alter the feeblest of minds.

This Utopia has been present in my mind for a long time. I have been backward about expressing such an idea, lest it be considered that I am trying to establish a private & solitary "bug-house." I am quite serious about this, & if your social contacts could lead to any such opportunity, you may be able to present the case in a manner more palatable to the normal intelligence.

I am sick of analysis & would try the path of integration for awhile. I hope you will not disregard what may seem to be the miasma from a malarial swamp & that you will comment on this in your next letter.

Forget for awhile, how I might be useful to others & consider the possibility that I may yet be able to exist without being at loggerheads with the aims & purposes of people about me.

Sincerely,

F.

September–December, 1955. When Frank was discharged from the Riverpoint Jail in mid-September he headed westward, following my urging that he seek the services of a program for homeless alcoholics which had been established in Westtown. I had written to him about my good friend Carl Thomas, who was directing the Westtown program, and I also wrote to Thomas introducing Frank.

Unfortunately, Frank was arrested en route to Westtown and jailed at Chippewa. On his release he finally made it to Westtown and spent about a week there before heading east again. At about 2 A.M. on Sunday morning, October 15, I received a phone call from Frank. He was in a high state of elation and apparent inebriation. He said that he was at the bus station en route from Westtown to Riverpoint and was just phoning to say hello during a brief bus stop. As things turned out, he was really on his way to being charged with second-degree burglary while intoxicated and to being incarcerated at Sageville.

In two later letters from the Sageville County Jail, he again reminisced about the Heaven Hill program. In one he sent a critique of the rehabilitative program at Westtown, which he thought fell far short of its intent, especially in comparison to Heaven Hill, and he admonished me as a professional, "You had Heaven Hill & you let it get away from you" (November 4, 1955). In another letter he described the blatant maneuvers of political personalities in charge of various public institutions and intimately involved in the demise of Heaven Hill (November 23, 1955).

Sageville County Jail
October 24, 1955

Dear Bob:

It was possible to earn 15 dollars a day in Westtown during week days but when Sat. nite came around, I could not countenance the vicissitudes of Water St. Rather than involve myself with drinking around there, & especially after Carl had befriended me, I bought some booze & embarked on the night bus to Riverpoint. Drinking all day in Riverpoint. Never remember leaving the town.

About 4 A.M. Monday morning I am picked up by the State Police, in possession of about $20 dollars worth of cigarette & cigars, and they assure me that I broke a plate glass window in a grocery store. Because there were people living on the second floor of this place, the charge is *not* breaking and entering. When I was arraigned before the justice of peace, the next day, I was charged with 2nd degree burglary. . . . I am held for action of the grand jury, trial & possibly prison. It is sometimes months, in cases of this kind, before the outcome is known. . . . If you desire I will terminate my correspondence, but it might be interesting to know if an inebriate, without money for counsel can be convicted of a criminality of which he has no recollection. . . . In retrospect I might write you from prison a clearer concept of "criminality & the inebriate." These people know little of me & will follow the line of least resistance. I suppose my mother will find out about this in some way (tho surely not thru me). A carton of Bull Durham costs only a dollar at a tobacco store, & will do much to assuage the next few weeks, when I really have a problem. Haven't given me back my eye-glasses yet.

Frank

Sageville County Jail
November 4, 1955

Dear Bob:

Submitted herewith is a brief report of the Westtown set-up. Impressions among different persons are variable, & these are mine.

"Critique of Social Service Center, Westtown, N.Y."

I arrived at the Center at night-fall & the man on duty at the desk was a policeman dressed in mufti. He asked me to specifically state what it was that I desired. Having very long entertained definite aspirations, I stated that I hoped to begin at a most humble job, & if continued sobriety was maintained, I hoped to graduate toward increased responsibility & reward, with an end view in the direction of total abstinence. He gave the impression of being capable & of having insight of the problem to which he was assigned. He directed me to lodging & arranged for an interview for the next day with Carl Thomas.

I found Carl Thomas a warm, normal man of practical compassion, using every possible means to deal with an insurmountable problem, handicapped by the locale of his plant. The following existing conditions are important:

(1) Dormitories—clean & comfortable, individual lockers & adequate bed covering.

(2) Hygienic facilities—showers, toilets, washrooms, mirrors adequate & clean.

(3) Washing machines for soiled clothes, shoe-shining & shaving equipment, available at the desk, to be returned after use.

(4) Recreation-room with television, books, periodicals & magazines.

(5) In this large room of a hundred chairs, a man may gather strength thru the realization that he is not the only one in the world with troubles, or, he may be overcome by the defeatism which is characteristic to his social order. (According to his temperament).

(6) A minimum of surreptitious drinking. An easy disposal of empty bottles by means of windows overhanging the river.

(7) An absence of "informers." Few men have the malice necessary to indict another, for the faults of which they are themselves guilty.

(8) The Center affords a labor pool to the city, of casual & migrant workers necessary to that area.

(9) Considered judicially, economically & financially, the Center is beyond criticism.

Summary: Any set-up which does not strictly isolate him from the accessibility of alcohol is a foregone failure, in spite of the best laid plans of mice & men. You had Heaven Hill & you let it get away from you.

Very Sincerely,
Frank

Sageville County Jail
November 15, 1955

Dear Bob:

I received the carton of tobacco about a week ago, for which, many thanks; & yesterday the letter telling me of my mother's broken pelvis. I most certainly would like to write to her, but feel altogether inadequate towards writing the sort of letter the occasion calls for. If you knew her as I do, you would realize the anguish that she felt, on learning of my present condition. There is just nothing that I could write to her to condone myself or to alleviate her distress. I am as impotent toward fulfilling her present needs, as I have been in the past.

It is five years since I have visited her & over a year since I have written.

As I had long expected, I find myself in a negative position when the emergency arises. If you do write to her, mitigate my offences to my mother's eyes.

Sincerely,
Frank

Sageville County Jail
November 23, 1955

Dear Bob:

Relative to your conversations with Judge Gleason concerning Heaven Hill under its present auspices: I have met a few of your acquaintances, Edwards, Drs. Long & Poray, who thru accident or design assumed certain duties which engaged their interest, sympathies, & best efforts. If such men ever become eminent, they will retain the same good qualities as they possessed in their "salad years." It is unfortunate that people of this caliber, in public service, are the exception rather than the rule. It has been a practice of the most virtuous public figures to reward their constituents. Oftimes the constituents are as far removed from their patrons, as the poles. And so I believe it is in the case of Judge Gleason & the incumbent rajah on Heaven Hill. Gleason is progressive, & the rajah is a residium of the Old Stone Age. We bow to the inevitable.

Lincoln, the greatest moral force in American politics had Stanton & Salmon Chase, & in my time I have seen a haberdasher elected president of the greatest nation on earth; a bucket shop operator on Wall St. appointed a police commissioner; a wholesale grocer appointed the superintendent of a state hospital; & a street car conductor named the head of a penal institution, & so on, ad nauseam. Is there no gauge to the fitness, temperament, & training of a man to fill a particular job?? And is it impossible for a good man to attain high office, except that he rise to the crest on the coat-tails of the Hagues,

Pendergasts, & their rear echelons? It is not my purpose to engage in a tirade against the powers that be, but rather to point out that nothing decent is to be expected of these rewarded loyal political hacks.

While I was at Heaven Hill, we were visited by the commissioner & the incumbent warden. One of the habitues with whom I had become acquainted, & whose statements, I had every reason to believe, who had dwelt on the hill thru its various administrations (narcotic, penal, & welfare), pointed out this warden, & informed me of him rather extensively. This wise old "lag" prognosticated (accurately, as it turned out), that the warden sought to regain control of Heaven Hill & to have it placed under his jurisdiction. Further, that during his previous tenure, Heaven Hill was referred to, by the inhabitants of Village Peak across the bay, as "The Warden's Hill" as to distinguish it from the main purgatory at Village. This "Warden's Hill" label is more than a little symbolic, if one considers the fine residence, garage, bus service, free gardeners, mechanics, & servants at his disposal. Considering the physical aspect of this hulking relict of the "Boss Tweed era," one suspects he would not neglect the opportunities to a gourmet, or forego the culinary possibilities.

As a matter of history, he replaced Martin, a most humane man, on the pretext of crowded conditions at Village. I am sure Martin & Chandler (his executive) would agree with me, that it was for the things he wanted for himself, rather than any desire to make life more desirable for others, that prompted his successful efforts to regain jurisdiction. Last week I saw a picture in one of the New York tabloids showing the warden standing in front of a pile of broken toys which were to be repaired at Heaven Hill for distribution by the Police Athletic League. This is a fine example of not "hiding your light beneath a bushel." Even if one heeds the political axiom of keeping your name & face in the public news, is nothing too mawkish & sentimental to be politically expedient? Another picture on the same page, showed a man of advanced age with corrugated brow repainting these toys on Heaven Hill. Perhaps this man hopes that by assiduous application to this task, he may obtain a partial remission of sentence, in order that he might return to the mainland & get drunk on schedule for Christmas, all the time never suspecting that he is playing a minor role, in elevating the commissioner, eventually, to the Supreme Court of New York. In a few years, I will say to you, "I told you so."

· · · · ·

Is there really anything to this formalized training & thinking? I venture that a man who thinks, in an environment where his associates do not think, & who chooses to be moral when his associates are amoral, is a damned schizophrenic. No trial, nothing to read, nothing to do, unlimited time to recapitulate my past transgressions & resurrect my ancient grudges, affords the excuse of writing this letter. Have you published anything further, regarding Frank, other than that "homeless man" study?

Sincerely
Frank

7. Continuing Institutional Dependency, 1956-62

After a short venture toward the Middle West in the late summer of 1956, Frank returned to the Northeast and became somewhat less of a wanderer, although he continued to depend on institutional living in jails and in various hospitals and other custodial settings.

Beginning also in 1956, there was a change in the quality of Frank's correspondence. While up to this time his letters were primarily narrative and episodic, they now dealt with a broader range of topics, often in some depth. They were still highly personal and relevant to Frank's problems, but also included more penetrating observations and analyses. His relations with a specific individual were projected to all of society; his convictions and legal embroilments were viewed from the perspective of the total class of indigent inebriates; his court trials were held up against the background of the entire legal profession and system. His own personal lack of success in being rehabilitated now called forth criticism of and disbelief in the public's misunderstanding, ignorance, inefficiency, and outright hypocrisy in coping with social ills, instead of his earlier emphasis on his own personal inadequacies.

These more global observations were still amply and vividly interspersed with descriptions of Frank's continuing adventures in leaping from moving freight trains, euphorically sleeping in snowbanks, and stoically enduring "the life of a wharf rat."

1956

January–August	Sageville County Jail
August	Central City Men's Shelter
September–October	Sacred Heights Home, Staunton
October–December	Unaccounted for

The twenty-nine letters received from Frank in 1956 contained an excellent cross-section of his feelings and observations on the myriad problems that he, as an alcoholic and institutionally dependent individual, had to cope with. These included his alienation from family and society; the travesty of legal counsel and "justice" for the chronic indigent alcoholic; society's classification of the alcoholic as a criminal and an incurable "leech" without rights; and the revolving door through jails, hospitals, and "rehabilitation" programs. He found this life not without compensations—"And believe me the experiences of this sort of life do have an extrinsic & intrinsic value" (April 13, 1956), among them the freedom of a life unencumbered by any material needs or possessions.

The first eight months of 1956 were spent in the Sageville Jail. From there, Frank's correspondence with his mother brought out the intensity of their mutual ambivalence and distrust; each yearning for a reconciliatory relationship with the other that their lifelong hostility toward each other would not permit. In the summer of 1956, I made a sudden decision to move from Syracuse to Lexington, Kentucky. When he was released from the Sageville Jail (in upper New York State), Frank apparently began to follow my tracks. His journey was interrupted when he broke his leg while leaping from a freight train.

Perhaps Frank learned that the jails and other refuges of the middle South are less hospitable to strangers and less commodious than those of the Northeast. In any event, when he was able, he headed back to more familiar territory.

Sageville County Jail
January 10, 1956

Dear Bob:

. . . . .

Today I was brought before the court here; notified of my right to have counsel; & when I stated that I had no funds, a counsel was appointed by the court, to appear with me when I am arraigned on this coming Friday the 13th. On the old Roman calendar, this was called the Ides of January. It is amusing to reflect, that when Rome was the greatest city on the face of the earth, that no act of city administration, however trivial & picayune, could be acted upon until all formalities had been complied with, & the multitudinous Roman officialdom had conducted their investigations, surveys, & reports. This method was adhered to, not only in the acts of public beneficence, but also in the squandering of public moneys & atrocious judgments.

Where were we? Oh yes, it seems it is illegal to arraign, try, & sentence a man in this state of criminal charges, unless he is represented by legal counsel. Of course, the law does not stipulate that his counsel shall be properly recompensed, that he shall be interested, that his defense shall be adequate, that he must be a counsel in fact, as well as in name. It appears to me to be an unhappy cross & necessary evil to be borne by the practitioners of the law, who must take their turn at this noisesome task. The closest approximation that comes to my mind, is that on merchant vessels, the ordinary seamen take their turn at a tripping line that empties the garbage barrel.

. . . . .

If a man is so improvident as to have no money, should he complain that he languishes in jail, while his better-heeled criminal brothers romp the streets on bail? (This is quite a factor, in that, after I am arraigned, I may not be brought to trial until June). Shall he indulge in heart-burnings & recriminations because his counsel & the prosecutor belong to the same political party, the same clubs, the same church & have the same professional & social interests? Who would pardon the puerile faith of this "nobody" from "nowhere" who squawks "Fiat Justitia ruat Coelum": (that's the gag I couldn't remember in my last letter). Consider the upheaval in the attorney's hierarchy, should his counsel battle "all out" & secure an acquittal.

. . . . .

F.

Sageville County Jail
January 18, 1956

Dear Bob:

It is impossible here to mail a letter in a plain envelope. Will you send this enclosure to my mother in such a wrapper?

Dear Mother:

Dr. Straus informed me sometime ago, that you had learned thru your local newspapers of my latest trouble. I would never have volunteered any information concerning my antecedents or previous address which led to this publication and would have done anything to spare you the pain and embarrassment, which it must have caused. . . . It seems that police authorities are most cooperative in their business and I carried social security cards and other data, which led to my identification with your city. . . . It appears as another example that no one lives for self alone and how our deeds set up a chain action either for good or evil.

For that concern which you may have in regard to the present incident, this letter is to inform you that I was tried today in the county court. I was sentenced to one year in this county jail. I wish that I might tell you of things connected with this incident which would alleviate the shame you feel. The best that I can offer at this time is that the judge realized unofficially that there was no malice, also that the injured party must be redressed. In a case of this kind, other people's feelings must be considered beside my own and in the present instance I do not feel that I have been unduly imposed upon.

It has been a year and a half since I last wrote you. I feel incapable of making you understand my reasons for not writing. Call it what you will, I have felt that one who elects my manner of living (voluntarily or otherwise) must necessarily forfeit the affection and regard which reward the more stable majority. I assure you it is most unpleasant to be a lone wolf, and to be regarded well only by those persons whose interests I have served to their profit. It is not my intention to convey any bitterness in that statement, and there might even be some virtue in merely enduring such an existence.

. . . Do you remember the time that you and my grandfather went down to Boston to see me off on the boat to Norfolk when I was in the Navy? When I went aboard he embraced me and there were tears in his eyes and he told you that he felt that he would never see me again. Others can call it premonition but you and I know how right he was. I am very grateful that he did not live to view my ultimate failure and disgrace. I know he expected so much of me. . . . Quite a while back while I was in the town of Riverpoint I had some kindred premonition. I was particularly unsuccessful and beaten at that time and felt that it was necessary then to visit you and that we might somehow be reconciled to one another and that never again would such an event be possible. More sophisticated people would say that it was the thought process of a small boy running to his mother when he is hurt. But I realize better than many how much of the little boy is in every man.

I wish you to know that Mr. H. Gregory Potter, the executive secretary of Senator Bottomly, has been most kind to me. In this area where

I was altogether unknown, I was altogether at a disadvantage in the present trouble and he furnished me from Washington a record of having decorations and rewards from the U.S. Maritime Commission. In an indirect manner, I feel that it had some influence toward leniency in my case.

Frank

Calvinville
March 5, 1956

Dr. Robert Straus,
Dear sir:

Thank you for your answer to my letter and the enclosure. There is nothing to be said or done that I know of. You speak of his good qualities. I can only say he has brought me grief for thirty years and will continue to do so. Where he is he will learn new tricks and if any one wished to give up liquor they would have to wish to. He will as all others like him go on (as he wishes to) taking advantage and doing as he pleases with no moral responsibility even tho he knows he will be arrested. He need not tell me that he did not give my address. Social Security is not giving as he infers.

. . . There is no use of writing to F. Just tell him that I've had all I can take. If he is sending mail thru you they will catch up with him as they did when he sent such abusive letters to me from Stonycreek. He abused me, stole my rings and then we must just forget because it is he. I conscientiously tried when he was at Heaven Hill. He even sent me a small sum, better had he kept it. The colossal nerve of appealing to a Senator. You may tell him.

I pray for him but it will do no good unless *he* cooperates.

Thanking you and wishing that I could write more cheerfully and legibly—my arm has never fully recovered. I feel that if there was any way of helping him you would have found it. He just speaks of his "case" and fools the lot. He told me one time he was afraid to go to sleep—*why?*

Roberta C. Greene

Sageville County Jail
March 5, 1956

Dear Bob:

I received the calculus a few days ago, & I am most grateful & appreciate the trouble & expense of getting it. Now here is a project that will keep me going a couple of years, providing I continue to have access to the book. Someone has said that fifteen minutes a day applied to some art or science, would make one a master. I doubt like hell that he was talking about this stuff. . . .

I received a letter from Doctor Cosgrove, the head of the mathematics department of the Institute of Advanced Study at Princeton, some time ago. It was a most informative & sincere letter & he pointed out that the information I requested would be found in the study of calculus, & specifically where I might find it. . . . There is no doubt that the higher a person's position in the realm of brains, the better person he is to deal with.

The pursuit of this study & the necessary expenditure of time, is a delightful surcease from the interminable "bitching" of communal life.

. . . . .

Sincerely,
Frank

Sageville County Jail
April 13, 1956

Dear Bob:

The vague unrest which stirred the Mongol hordes, the call of the flying cinders & box-cars, will remain unanswered, this spring, at least. There is a general idea regarding the hobo which is most fallacious. For instance, he is supposed to look forward to the unseen fields & hitherto unknown places. It is not the love of new places, but the hatred of the old. Some gifted pen-man will one day deal with this matter, & bury it in some unconsecrated ground, where it properly belongs. The tramp & the hobo move, not because they wish to move, but with the unerring instinct which leads rats to leave sinking ships. The allegorical ship which he leaves, is the ship of "civilization."

Joseph Conrad dispelled the love of a sailor for his ship. He ruled that the ship was the carrier of the hope & fortunes of the sailor, which accounted for that semblance of attachment. And so I would dispose of that unmitigated conglomeration of "crap" concerning the "song of the open road."

It has been your kind attitude to deplore that a particular vice might preclude a man from realizing the happiness of living. My own speculations have led me only so far as to consider what other type of s.o.b. I might have become, had I not consecrated myself to drink. I have concerned myself, necessarily, in finding compensations for the "fait accompli" . . . I say, "necessarily" because outside of my own poor efforts, negligible methods have been used. I am honestly inclined to forbear reproach, because I have been the first to consider that I have no money & in the absence of money, I possibly lack that personal merit & worth, which is sometimes just as necessary. . . . And so I will get on with my compensations, & believe me the experiences of this sort of life do have an extrinsic & intrinsic value. What have been referred to as "inner resources" gained thru such experience, might cause a man to walk with an upright step to the jaws of a problematical Hell. . . .

·   ·   ·   ·   ·

Frank

Sageville County Jail
April 21, 1956

Dear Bob:

·   ·   ·   ·

In regard to the letter from my mother, I wish that I might say that I felt relieved upon reading it. I wish I might say that I felt like Kipling's "man" who felt the desire to reach down & pick up his worn out tools to rebuild the things that are broken. The letter probably belongs in the archives of "alcohology" to substantiate the bitterness, recrimination, & condemnation of the inebriate by his "nearest & dearest." . . . I shall retain the letter; if you would like to have the letter, I will send it to you.[1] The actual sending of it touches some dormant chord of delicacy, as if there were something of a betrayal in the act. Then there arises the question: is there such a thing as betrayal of truth & fact, is there such a thing as betrayal in the exposure of fallacious thought & straight-jacket emotion—al mores? The unfortunate part of the whole thing is that I did wish to hear from her, & had expected something different. . . . I must console myself with that old whiskey-barrel aphorism: "What the hell, do you expect a medal because you drink?"

In its entirety & effect, her letter states:

Item One: "You analyze yourself & are egotistical as all alcoholics are."

Item Two: "You just have to have someone stand behind you & coddle you as all alcoholics do."

1. I did not request the letter.

Item Three: "If you have any regard for your grandfather & all he did for you, just don't talk about it, but pull yourself up by your bootstraps."
Item Four: "When your work folded up in New York, you could always manage to get the alcohol."
Item Five: "I am old & ill—you are to blame."
Item Six: "You are smooth & you have failed everyone, doctor included."
Item Seven: "You can get along without alcohol if you want to."
Item Eight: "You have had those who were good to you, your grandfather (reiteration here) whom you failed miserably, also your friend the doctor."
Item Nine: "I don't want any letters labeled 'jail' sent here."
Item Ten: "When it is time for you to come out, perhaps your friend the doctor will let me know."
Item Eleven: "I would not send a penny direct to you for alcohol."
Last Item: "I pray God to help you."

Dear Bob, I leave it to you, is not the lady gifted who can pack all of this on one page of ordinary stationery?

It is most noteworthy that this summation & evaluation of my character is based on the fact that I have not lived under her roof for one year altogether in the last 36 years.

If it were not for the sadness of the lady, it would be mentally hilarious that anyone should regard me as one of the "suave smooth fellows."

Yes, I certainly found money to drink. I think I have sold my blood in Riverpoint, Boston, New York, Philadelphia, Davenport, & Chicago. I would have gone back the next day, if there was a chance of "getting away with it." They look for needle marks.

Don't let her know when I am going to get out. I am not complaining but just to keep the books straight, let's dismiss this idea that I am being coddled. I haven't had a pair of socks on for two months (wore them out & washed them out), no shoelaces in my shoes, I do without underwear while my one suit is drying. I will be released in August in the battered rig I came in, without a dime. There is a hell of a lot of justice in this, but I'll be damned if I am being coddled.

Sincerely,
Frank

Sageville County Jail
May 31, 1956

Dear Bob:

. . . . .

Any fair minded person spending a good part of his life as I do, in jail, can not help but feel that I am a leech on the body politic, & wish that I might pursue a more useful life. But when you mention "useful life" to a given person, he means some endeavor that he would not tackle himself. . . . Rusty with repose, I will make my exit in the middle of August. When you consider I have had ample time to figure out what I am going to do, you will find me singularly devoid of all substantial notions. . . . I have considered "losing myself" in the Bowery, going to the Middle West & building a new life on foundations of air, etc. . . . If you will note the time element, 1st the Antabuse, then Heaven Hill & the present condition of servitude, the periods when I am sober are becoming longer (voluntary or involuntary, notwithstanding). Sobriety, per se, has not been a solution. I fear I will strike an incongruous note, the day of my release, hugging two texts of mathematics & three note books. It seems to me I have exhausted the possibilities of incarceration, & the field is narrowing as time marches on. Desiring so little in the material way, is it possible that I can only achieve that little in jail? I welcome constructive ideas & "positive" thinking.

Sincerely,
Frank

Sageville County Jail
June 9, 1956

Dear Bob:

Sometime ago I received a letter from my mother, most reproachful. And then in the past week, I have received another letter from her, a most contrite letter, setting forth her affection for me, acknowledging failure on the part of both of us, a letter that would wrench the heart of a devil. . . . if you think of it in your next letter, give me a brief resume of that Chinese philosophy of Yin & Yang (?) It seems that far back in my memory is some application of the situation that confronts me.

If it were in my power at this moment, I would write her that kind of a letter which her situation demands, a letter that would comfort her, & alleviate the bitterness which she feels toward life, & of course life has treated her shamefully. Any letter that I could write would have the opposite effect. Can I tell her how murderously handicapped I have been all my life by the re-iterated admonition of my grandfather: "when & if you get licked, don't let us know about it." This to her mind would be traitorous to the memory of my grandfather, to whom I owe any particle of common sense, I ever did possess. (In passing, I inquire in an abstract manner, if a man can not find sympathy & commiseration when he is "licked," wherever else in the world, would he find it, if *not* in the family circle?). . . . In all honesty I would feel constrained to inform her, that the inculcation of "self-reliance," as New Englanders understand it, is poor balm for any man who is occasionally a fool & all men who feel the need of "associated destiny."

When she inquires "why did things have to be this way," I could present a most logical exposition to the effect, that (1) the world is a rough place (2) only a small segment of men are engaged in pursuits which are congenial to their nature & ambition, (3) man's place in the world is strictly utilitarian, (4) man enjoys sufferance only in that he is useful to others, (5) about 99% of the world's courtesy & amenities are also utilitarian, (6) whatever real happiness a man will find in life, lies in his family circle, (7) that a man will endure cheerfully & willingly items (1–5) providing that (6) is a reality. However, such a letter would bring her pain. If you could, & feel inclined to write that sort of a letter that is best fitted to her needs, I will confer on you with my own hands a Doctorate of Humanity. It is something that I am absolutely unfitted to do, & I am presuming most heavily on your friendship.

To snap the somber thread—she mentions her fear that I will end up on a slab in the Bellevue morgues. Do you know, I have a sneaking hunch that some of those cadavers on the dissecting table are more useful in death than they ever were in life? "Many a son & daughter lies,

Far from home 'neath alien skies"—Keats.
Osteo-arthritis is infringing on the domains of Morpheus, subsequently I am smoking more tobacco. Will you send me the wherewithal.

Ever Demandingly
Frank

Sageville County Jail
July 14, 1956

Dear Bob:

The time draws near when I must put aside the determinants of linear homogeneous equations. I suppose the world is much as I left it October last, when the various citizenry were booting each others rumps, & loudly echoing that famous aphorism of Horace Greeley, "Root hog or die!" At first thought it might seem that I could draw some worthwhile summary of the past ten months, the turbulent days, the sheep awaiting the slaughter days, the simmon, the horse latitudes, & now, the expectant days. I will make my debut on August 10, which occurs on a Friday, & which in itself is a good excuse for not snatching a shovel from another man's hand. But human thinking like human aspirations is inconsistent & variable, we form opinions today & discard them tomorrow, otherwise what hope for fools?

On some happy occasion an accredited behaviorist will deal in a forthright, humorous, & revealing manner, the attitudes & postures of convicts & other persons in condition of servitude, as the time draws near when they shall be released. It is really quite weird. During my various junkets of the jails of this state I have never ceased to be fascinated by the sight of a man who will begin to shine his shoes about ten days ahead of time, & thereafter day by day to bring about a shine & lustre which would confound the professional boot-polisher, & who wangle the services of whatever prisoner possesses the skill to mend & press. Surely these fine birds with fine feathers have intentions contrary to work, or who would stoop to labor in such finery? There seems to be a general code that though one has no other intention than to get drunk, & move into another county jail, one must needs first get a hair cut before he is released. I think this is most peculiar, in that I have pursued those various behaviors such as to enhance my drinking. For instance, I have stopped eating a few days, & got twice the "kick" from my liquid refreshment. This I understand, & the hair business, I don't. If you could get a gander of these Beau Brummels, a few hours after the gaol doors swing open!!

During my long climb toward being a "gentleman of distinction," I have gathered various tid-bits of knowledge, & have passed them along gratis to my conferees. As for instance, down in New York, a ship's engineer insisted on buying a black serge suit, contrary to my pointing out that vomitus was especially noticeable on black. And so I digress re the frailty of my kind.

. . . . .

Frank

Central City
Sat. Afternoon
August 26, 1956

Dear Bob:

I have been here at the Men's Shelter for the past two weeks. The A.A. conduct weekly meetings here. As you know, there is a particular type of "drifter" who goes from city to city, affiliates with the A.A., for the purpose of the moment, & when he has "buncoed" them to the extent of cash & other material aid, moves on to new & greener pastures. Some dim ephemeral hope that I might make this program (A.A.) caused me to give one of these members your address in order that he might check, & learn all the awful facts from you, rather than have him conjecture as to whether I am trying to get my hands on somebody's pocketbook. During the past two meetings, I have been invited to meetings outside the center, but I am deathly afraid of arousing suspicion that I am the least sort of a "gate crasher," have social or sexual aspirations, etc. All of which is wrong, of course, but I would not be Moore if I did not feel this way about it. It would be damn nice to get acquainted, & to obtain job opportunity with the foreknowledge on somebody else's part, that I am an alcoholic. But the deathly fears & suspicions that will arise in that process, seems to me almost impossible. All of which thinking is caused by the fact that, being a s.o.b. myself, I credit other people with being the same (& I may not be wrong altogether about this). . . . I wish I might give you a good report on the center, here. Though there must be fifty inebriates here, only four go to the A.A. meetings. There is a very apparent hostility toward A.A. & naturally some of this tends to rub off on whosoever affiliates with it. My two weeks sobriety here, & my attendance at the meetings has aroused that intangible antipathy, unspoken but yet very apparent & real, by which I am most cognizant of the fact that I have not, as yet, been accepted as "one of the boys." The other phoney aspects, you are aware of: pool tables, library, reading lamps, chrome and leather chairs, etc. Drivers who draw fifty dollars per week plus

bonuses for extra rags and papers, broken down drunks who receive
one dollar a week & no bonuses. No one but a most expedient fool
would accuse these people of other than crassest commercialism, yet
a few waxed floors, and a decent well lit and clean dormitory will convince all you good people that there is a "soul" in this business.

Write to: Frank

[Post Card
Postmarked September 9, 1956
Staunton]

Will be here a couple of weeks. This is a "center" operated by a church
group. . . . A new phase in my investigation of how the dereliction
of man may rebound to the great profit of others.

Frank

Sacred Heights Home
September 25, 1956

Dear Bob:

Along with your impending move to Kentucky, I suppose I shall
soon prefix the address with "kernel." Shades of the blue grass & whiffs
of bourbon, who would have thought that the callow youth who mean-
dered out to James St., ablaze with that sport jacket would take root
in old Kaintuck?

None of the following to my mother: an excursion out of Staunton
then back into Staunton, a quick jump from a freight at 45 miles an
hour, striking my knees on a parallel railroad track, resulting in the
above address. . . . I was x-rayed at the hospital; a simple greenstick
fracture, & I would have been patched & relegated to the street, except for medical social service worker named Miss Hobson who called
up by phone (this place is 18 miles from Staunton) & obtained admission here for me in a convalescent status.

This sort of place is a religious parallel of Silver Hill, except that
most of the inmates are classified as medically "incurable." (Why not
me?) There are only three orderlies here & it would be a shabby trick
were I to entertain notions of muscling one of them out of a job. I
have been entertaining some hopes for such a job for duration of the
coming winter. I am able & willing to stay sober for such a length of
time. It is a tough job without written recommendations & no dough.
Any doctor or nurse could quiz me for five minutes & be assured that

I have that knowledge & experience needful for the care of the sick, but when I leave here a couple of weeks hence, I will be clean, well, decently dressed, & without funds. For only a couple of bucks I can establish an address and apply for such a job, sans albeit written certification of ability to do it. Don't you think I have given these "charitable" & "religious" outfits ample opportunity of "redeeming me"? For God's sake, don't say A.A. to me because I can't pay room rent with their pamphlets & you are welcome with them only so long as you can pay your own freight.

If you can send me a couple of dollars, I shan't ask you again. Calling on the adages of old, "the only way to find a lost arrow is to send another one in the same direction." Whether you believe in that old crap, I don't know, but the sooner I have the opportunity of getting away from here with a couple of bucks, the less time I'll waste, & I've sure as hell been wasting it.

Frank

1957

January–March	Riverpoint County Jail
April	Amsterdam County Jail
May–August	Roger's Retreat
October	Brief visit to Calvinville
October–November	Central City County Jail
November–December	Easton Heights Men's Shelter
December	Amsterdam County Jail

Frank's twelve letters for 1957 came from numerous institutions, which provided a total of forty weeks of custody. Features of these letters were his short-lived optimism (in Roger's Retreat); his intense awareness ("The most galling feature of this manner of living, is the popular assumption that the person most affected, is *unaware*") of society's hostile attitudes and fossilized approaches to his problems; and an assertion of the validity of his own experiences and opinions. In selected letters he discoursed cynically on the inadequacies, biases and the cash nexus on which both the legal and rehabilitation systems operated.

It is remarkable to me that millions of dollars are collected toward a purpose, and that the total benefit is derived by the administrators,

and that the persons for whom the money and time are expended, are so totally bereft of all benefits.
(December 8, 1957)

Amsterdam County Jail
April 14, 1957

Dear Bob:

The situation continues to deteriorate, disintegrate, etc. The advance of science has not yet reached the hinterlands. Fifteen days, public intoxication. Held for three days before trial, in order that the vast machinery of the law—teletype, fingerprints, photo, along with the attendant great expense—might possibly establish my connection with sundry unsolved murders, robberies, et al. . . .

Let us, by all means, permit the uninitiated to harbor their illusions of "fair & impartial trial," "speedy trial," "equality before the law," "inalienable rights of life, liberty, & the pursuit of happiness," but let us supplement these ideals with the words: *providing you have got a buck.* . . . The most galling feature of this manner of living, is the popular assumption that the person most affected, is *unaware.* Surely there is no person more aware, when the town policeman says to me "you don't belong around here anywhere, do you Moorey?" Let us discount paranoia & symptoms of persecution, & get down to the facts that none will be concerned with Moorey's arrest, that he will be prosecuted with zeal, & that he will be confined at public expense, however it might be contraindicated by experience which shows that no results are to be gained.

. . . . .

Frank

Roger's Retreat
Blue Mountains
May 1, 1957

Dear Bob:

At Sageville, you offered to send me Lillian Roth's "I'll Cry Tomorrow." I supposed it to be another recapitulation of alcoholic woes & so, envinced no interest. However, later & down in Amsterdam, I got the book in the paper-back cover. What struck me as the crux of matter, was the religious conversion.

So why didn't I try something like that? After all, it would not be the scientific method to reject something without having tried it.

So here I am in a religious colony. It is a non-denominational affair. There are about forty of us here.

Frank

This pencil is 1/2 inch long

Roger's Retreat
Blue Mountains
May 5, 1957

Dear Bob:

Religion is a method of thinking, & if it relieves me of my woes, it will be justified, however contrary it may be to other methods of thinking.

I would like to stay here for two years. It is hoped & is the vision of this place to send its graduates out to the skid-rows of the country on missionary work. I don't know whether I have the potential, but I do know my stay here is dependent on some small subsidy from some source or other.

In that we receive excellent food & housing, it is expected that we derive our razor blades, tobacco, stamps, etc. from other sources. As I told you, we are only permitted pipes, & to use them in restricted areas. I have the pipe & next week I will be out of tobacco. We are expected to be presentable at these meetings, & I am the shabbiest man here.

It would cost hundreds & possibly thousands of dollars to keep me in jail. Is there no way, Bob, that I can get these things which are so necessary to insure my staying here? This pencil (too) is only a stub, & so excuse the writing. It will be possible for you to visit here, when you next come up this way, & your sophisticated mind will sure receive the surprise of your life.

Sincerely,
Frank

Easton Heights Men's Center
Dec. 8, 1957

Dear Bob:

I received your letter & money while at Central City. Have been here for 10 days & expect to stay until it becomes warmer.

For the first four weeks, the new man is compelled to attend the

A.A. meeting once a week. I doubt if these visiting speakers are aware that they are talking to a "captive" audience, & know that the attendance is compulsory. I imagine they would feel most uncomfortable if they did know it. I feel little can be accomplished thru such a procedure.

Another compulsion is two religious meetings a week (on Sunday morning & Tuesday evening). The newcomer is positively devastated to receive $1 on a Saturday & have the collection plate passed to him on a Sunday.

The finances are run in the following manner: to stop the men from sinning, they keep all the money themselves, & what money they *do* give the men, they expect some of this also to come back. Needless to say, John Stuart Mill must be fluttering in his shroud at this equitable state of affairs.

At the present time, I am the only helper on a truck. The people who telephone & offer this furniture, clothing, etc. are altruists, who in all cases believe they are giving the "helping hand" & aiding a constructive program. The following case is a generality & not an exception. As I pointed out, there is a disparity of pay. The driver is guaranteed a salary of forty dollars a week plus a commission on what he brings in. The helper receives no commission, he receives one dollar the first week, two dollars the second week, etc. So you see, that the man who receives a fair salary is trying to drive hell out of a man who is not receiving anything for extra effort.

In every fair sized city, there are junk & salvage dealers. Not all the material donated to charity reaches its destination. If the junk or salvage yard is located off the "main drag," the truck pulls in & especially clothing and rags are sold. Last week my driver stopped on four different afternoons & sold rags & clothing, to which I attach an estimate of about $15 or $20. For my share (keeping my mouth shut), the driver bought me a pack of cigarettes on two occasions. He kept the rest himself. So we have here, not only a thief, but a selfish thief. (i.e.) I go into these houses, bring out these rags and clothing, place them tightly in bags, tie them up, & the driver reaps the whole profit. Possibly, if & when we might be apprehended, I will be answerable to the same degree that he is.

It is remarkable to me that millions of dollars are collected toward a purpose, & that the total benefit is derived by the administrators, & that the persons for whom the money & time are expended, are so totally bereft of all benefits. Owed you a letter & didn't put much time & thought into this one.

Frank

1958

January	Amsterdam County Jail, Broadmeadow County Jail
February	Elmtown County Jail
March	Wardhill State Hospital
April	City Infirmary, Anchorport; Anchorport County Jail; brief visit to Calvinville
May–December	Davenport State Infirmary

Frank's letters for 1958 are a chronicle of his moving in and out of six different institutions before settling down for fourteen months in the Davenport Infirmary. They recount the details of arrest (perhaps a favor, according to Frank) and incarceration; and the barely tolerable and demoralizing atmospheres of custody. From Davenport, Frank dwelt on the status of patient vs. employee and their interrelationship, the inefficiency and waste of physical and personal resources, and the incompetency and dishonesty of much of the staff he encountered, from professionals to those involved in general maintenance. Although he recognized that his view was not a detached one, he felt he was stating what every aware citizen and taxpayer should be stating.

Broadmeadow County Jail
January 19, 1958

Dear Bob:

I received your last letter & the enclosures, for which, many thanks. And so, from the above, you see that I continue my "Wanderjhar." One of the phenomena attached to this mode of living is the fact, that when released from durance vile, & in a strange city, & without employment, & without the means to support basic needs, it becomes most apparent that the pedestrians & motorists are all "going somewhere." So there you are, not going anywhere, & nobody giving a damn. Only the most liberal & detached persons could credit the general public of being "social minded." As, with strained faces & hurried steps they press on to their duties & appointments, in order to meet the next car or television payment (& other such worthy pursuits), I feel myself strangely isolated in the "agora," & must like Diogenes, take to "rolling my tub" up hill & down dale. And so I found myself on the road to Millbury not knowing anyone there, not giving a damn if I got there, & not entertaining hopeful expectations if I got there. I believe my plans paralleled those of a mouse, who gnaws a hole in the corner of a room trying to get to the other side, without knowing what in hell is on the other side, before he gets there. Perchance the rodent, too, is in search of the "Absolute," the "Eternal Truths" etc.

. . . I was arrested on the highway, light top-coat, no inner coat, no hat, three above zero, staggering, & five cents in my pocket. It probably occurred to the state policeman, *after* he had made the arrest, that he had done me a favor after all (what a damn cynic, I have become). Whenever I have about 20 sheets of note paper (full length), I hope to write you of the Blue Mountain experience "in extenso." It certainly merits a lengthy & deliberate critique. . . . I have twenty days to do, & tobacco, etc. are available if one has the coin of the realm. I hope soon to give you "Roger's" in toto.

F.

Wardhill State Hospital
March 9, 1958

Dear Bob:

Went to the Penguin Club (plastered) & was rejected. Mr. Carrey & one of his delegates (an angel who realizes his membership entitles him to a "pie card") suggested that I sleep on the river-bank for a night & then come back. They were poorly informed fools who did not realize that sleeping on the river bank was "old hat" to me. Having no desire to avail myself to the horrors of the jail which I conclude in passing compares favorably with the Newgate Prison of England of the 1600's, with the exception of some culprits' heads, fixed by pikes, on the surrounding walls.

And so Northward. State Police arrested me during the night & lodged me at their barracks; I was probably endangering traffic. Arrived in Anchorport, & stopped at the "Alanon Club." Met a guy that afternoon, there, who for two hours, told me all about Alcoholism. (Talk about carrying coal to Newcastle.) He told me the club would be open again at 7 that night. I went back at seven & hung around until eight & the club did not open.

I went out & got five pints of wine, to console myself, & slept in the YMCA that night (without pain).

The next morning, without money to continue drinking, & unwilling to avail myself to the tender mercies of these "help organizations," or to stomach the phoneys who always wangle their way in the best of organizations, I went to the police station, & told them that I was suffering withdrawal symptoms, & that I had experienced D.T.'s before. I expected that they would sentence me to a term in jail, until I was well, & then release me at some early date, to continue my aimless existence.

I have been out here since Friday. In view of what has gone before, this peck of pills & interminable hypodermic injections is rather pointless. This is one of those incongruous kinds of existence where they afford a television & then take away your eye glasses. For the past three days, I have been surrounded by a hundred periodicals, & unable to find an hour's surcease by reading. Many a cup of forbidden wine must be drunk to drown out the memory of my trust in mankind.

Frank

On March 11, 1958, I received from the superintendent of Wardhill State Hospital a form notice that "your friend, Frank Moore" was admitted on March 7 and a request to complete a questionnaire about him. I replied with a long letter but Frank's stay at Wardhill was too brief for any meaningful efforts to "treat" him.

Davenport State Infirmary
May 16, 1958

Dear Bob:

Too many things happen to a drunkard, for him to get everything down on paper. . . . It seems, that for anyone to stay at Wardhill for more than thirty days, called for a legal hocus pocus, which is called being "probated." They wanted me to stay, but it appeared that no doctors would sign the necessary papers, unless I was willing to stay. It was a fine place, with the "new look" psychiatry, and backed by proper financial appropriations.

Upon discharge, it was arranged for me to be admitted to the City Infirmary in Anchorport. The word for "infirmary" in some cities, is a euphemism for "alms house" or "poor house." I stayed there for three days—a bowl of oat meal for breakfast, & a bologna sandwich for supper. No one will believe me, but speaking with the authoritative voice of experience, jails & county penitentiaries feed their criminals better than their poor. It was quite a "come down" from the "bug-house."

Two days later, I was arrested on the highway, taken before some small town judge & sentenced to ten days. This jail in Anchorport county is brand new, modern plant, segregation of types, wonderful food, & the guards & overseers are anxious to build up a fine reputation for their jail. Smoking tobacco was issued, television every night, fine hygienic facilities, etc. It seems the jail is twice as big as needs be. More prisoners—more jobs for guards. Less prisoners—less jobs for guards. I envision that this particular calaboose, in years to come, & for years to come, will become a beloved sanctuary for the bottle gang.

In lieu of any plans at all, I hitch-hiked back to Calvinville in one day, arriving home about 10 P.M. Oh brother, & I had been worrying about this lonely old woman. She let me know that with her old age pension, she was very happy, & much concerned that I ruin the tranquility of her life. And so, out on the highway that night & up north. Hitch-hiked the next day. Caught a freight train for Harborville. The railroad yard employees are most gracious, telling me the time the freight comes thru, the best place to catch it, etc. Arrived in Harborville that night. Went to the Salvation Army for supper. I was told that I could stay that night, & shocked the clerk by saying that I preferred to sleep in the police station. He couldn't understand it. I didn't think he would grasp it if I went into a detailed exposition of conditioned reflexes & cited Pavlov's dogs.

Hitch-hiked the next day into Clarksville & up to Bancock. I had the entry fee to a saloon & ran into a heavy machinery operator who was on a spree. He wanted someone to listen to him, & so I listened (& had plenty to drink). The board bench, in the Bancock city jail, felt like a feather bed that night. Next morning, I spent my last 14 cents for a can of beans. Pushed a door-bell & asked the lady of that house to open them for me. Stepped into a side street & was eating the beans with a stick, under a tree, & a damn small dog raised such a barking, that all the women came out to see what he was barking at.

I have often wondered if these house pets, somehow, cultivate the outlook & mores of their owners. It was not a question of food or a place to sleep, but my shoe soles had worn thru to the skin, so the next day, I hitch-hiked down here to Davenport. It has been about seven years since I was here. There is a physical examination on admittance.

The examining doctor noted a lipoma, about as big as my fist on my left upper arm. He asked me if I didn't want it cut out, & told me that there was no need to be afraid because there was an excellent surgeon in attendance. Now you know a lipoma is only a fatty tumor & it had caused me no trouble, & I am sure the only concern was to keep the surgeon in practice & to improve his technique. I never would have had it cut out except for that statement that "I need not be afraid."

If I stick my hand in fire, it will burn. If I tie a rock around my neck & jump in the river, I will drown, but I don't know that I am afraid of anything. So I told them to hack away; & so a general anesthetic & ten stitches in my arm. I came out of the hospital today. About Monday, I will be assigned a job, & the endeavor will be, to get as much work out of me as possible. Tobacco is issued here *but* no cigarette papers, stamps, etc. Will be glad to hear from you.

Frank

Davenport State Infirmary
July 5, 1958

Dear Bob:

Meant to answer your letter sooner, but a kind of desuetude or enervation sets in after being in these kind of places for a short while. No man thru the effects of his lone mind could cause such a mass state of demoralization. Men leave here every day, without a plan of where they are going or what they are going to do. One thing, of which they are certain, is that no one here gives a damn, or is in any way concerned. Older buildings fall into disrepair, are abandoned, a new building goes up, the old fittings & equipment are left as they are, & a newer generation of indigents & incompetents are being cared for (corn meal mush for breakfast, bath once a week, & a bed to sleep in). A hundred years ago, this place was officially an alms house, the employees were drawn from the neighboring small towns, which had no industries. The older generation of employees has been buried, their sons, daughters, granddaughters have replaced them & notwithstanding that a forty-hour week has been in effect for a long while, more equitable pay, & in other places a general notion that the community at large has a definite duty toward its incompetents & misfits. I would swear on a stack of bibles a mile high, that patient-employees attitudes have not changed since 1840.

There are about 500 men here who would be employable, were they not alcoholic. Upon them devolves the assignment of all porter work, janitorial duties, kitchen help, laborers, et al. Under no consideration, do the paid employees ever perform these duties. Men have been appointed supervisors of attendants here, who have never offered their arm to an infirm person or picked one up. It is generally conceded, hoped for, that alcoholics will perform the arduous work, that they will always be available & are to be fully exploited. It seems quite logical to me, that these paid employees should feel quite enamored toward the urban alcoholic who finds his way here, but such is not the case, by word or action. It may be that thru ability, willingness, character, or temperament a patient might appear deserving of some recompense or altered attitude by the employee. Not so.

A couple of the attendants are appointed special police & cruise around in state owned vehicles on the back roads, consuming untold amounts of gasoline endeavoring to apprehend some patient with a fifty-cent bottle of wine. In the meantime no employee has been apprehended for larceny (ever), & I assure you they would count it a lost day, if they didn't bring a package to their car at quitting time. This is no picayune affair & must run into the thousands over the course of a year. I repeat that these acts are not of a group of individuals, but rather an accepted belief that anyone who works for a city, county or state institution is licensed to outfit their home with linen, foodstuffs, or anything that is portable.

Your interest while I was at Wardhill reflected greatly toward my benefit.

Sincerely,
Frank

Davenport State Infirmary
November 30, 1958

Dear Bob:

At my last writing, I told of impending changes at this institution & the first of the year will see a new dynasty & regime. This changeover is almost comparable to Darwin's fish which swam out to the shores of a beach & developed a lung, as it seems to me, it took damned near as long.

It is a sobering thought to walk in the paupers' graveyard here & to identify yourself with them. The separate grave system is used here, that is, side by side, with iron markers (numbers). When I was at Heaven Hill I saw the Potter's field there. I don't think it is anything like people generally conceive such things. There is an excavation made about the size of a factory cellar, & the wooden boxes are piled directly upon each other in a tier. So much for necrology.

The administration of this place in the past, would interest most any person that would pay 15 cents to see a two-headed calf. Up until the present time, the institution has been under a board of trustees, a shadowy form behind the scenes, whose presence one never sees, but which manifests itself in many patterns. There are 900 employees here whose sum output is equivalent to about 100 employees. If you see a man standing in one place raking leaves, in the same spot, there is only one answer: "He knows somebody."

Whether this policy will continue under the new regime is a matter of lively conjecture among the patients who are the least concerned about the change. It appears to be the "do nothing" & "pilfering" employee who is most worried. A word would not be amiss regarding the high professional type attracted to our institution. Two of the doctors were dismissed from probationary employment here this past summer because of an inability to pass state board examinations. Just before my return here in April, two doctors left under a shadow; their wives were apprehended on a shoplifting excursion in the nearest city & underwent the concomitant newspaper publicity (notoriety?).

It is most exasperating to us of the Cassius type, who have that lean & hungry look, to have, constantly, paraded before us the biggest assembly of middle aged ladies, who have long since passed a state of "en bon point" & fashionably stout, to a state of being frankly fat, & to realize that they are stealing the food, the money for which was appropriated for you, & for which you endure the opprobium of a bum. Yesterday, it was supposed to be meat loaf for dinner. There was 20% meat & 80% bread in the meat loaf. There would be no need to inquire what happened to the meat if you could view the buxom lassies behind the serving counter. At one time, I viewed a fat woman as gross or unesthetic, & now I am getting so I frankly hate their fat guts.

There is an idea that I would like to express, a kind of a hard-earned truth which I would never have reached under any circumstance except the circumstance in which I find myself.

What is the connotation of the word "bum"? It is *not* supposed that, in general, a successful or affluent criminal is called a "bum." I submit that the term is reserved for those who are strikingly unsuccessful in the acquisition of material goods. I believe a general enquiry will bear me out. For a moment consider the other fields of endeavor, the development of a moral capacity & the application & development of the mind. The first endeavor requires only an unwillingness to compromise with the palpably false, & the second is open to all, who need neither a natural talent or inordinate capacity; i.e. a knowledge of the arts & sciences is open to all, whatever their station in life. How great the progress & degree of knowledge depends altogether upon the application of the individual to a particular field. I suppose you to admit all this.

Now what do I find in general? Pursuing in an altogether *not* intent fashion, the sociology (practical) of my times, the two sciences of mathematics & physics, do I come in contact with people who have a sense of social responsibility, or the slightest glimmer of the sciences, outside of which, I call a "small cross section" knowledge? Of course I don't. The clergy have adopted expediency, & people of intellectual capacity have settled for "security." All of which has led me to a suspicion that the variety of "bums" is infinite, viz a man might be an intellectual bum, an esthetic bum, a moral bum, etc. each man making the choice of genus to which he aspires. Thus, a man who has, so far, avoided a drunkard's court, can not disclaim the title on all other counts . . . The bright beam which bends down to the muddy bottom where lurks this social carp (myself), consists of the fact that I have been able to apprehend to some extent, that he who chooses one thing above all others, must naturally forego the others, & still half the world is belly-aching because they do not have the possessions of others. If I have escaped this human bondage, to that extent, it may have been worthwhile being an inebriate. I hope I have not made my case so meritorious, as to cause you to go out and get "plastered."

Sincerely—

Frank

1959

January–July	Davenport State Infirmary; brief visit to Calvinville
July–August	Westville County Jail and House of Correction
August–October	Stonycreek Correctional Institution
November–December	Westville County Jail

Several of Frank's letters for 1959 dealt with a theme he had often touched on before—the exploitation of the alcoholic by those who pretend to help him. He denounced not only the lack of real efforts to effect rehabilitation for himself and others, but the multitude of ways in which others have actually profited from the maintenance of inefficient programs for the alcoholic, and the perpetuation of the revolving door.

Davenport State Infirmary
April 25, 1959

Dear Bob:

During the past three months, I have made an honest effort to assay the efforts of this institution toward the treatment of alcoholism, & what I "wind up" with is unpleasant. The usual reply to criticism is "What would you do?" So far, the only thing I have to offer is that a policy of honesty should be extended to the problem. In the first place, one does not place the intercontinental missile program into the hands of high school boys who have learned Galileo's law of acceleration for falling bodies. Along with this information, we should insist on a thorough instruction in Stokes Law showing that if raindrops *did* follow Galileo's law, we would likely be killed the first time we were caught in a rainstorm, & again, what would be the purpose of a parachute? This is not an isolated instance, but the general character of "physical laws" which science offers for man's guidance, that is, half-truths & generalizations. If this is true in regard to material things, how much more so when dealing with the complex human being? In so far as I am concerned, the glimpse of these half-truths, appears to have led so far, to a group of "know-it-alls" who have achieved a perfect technique for committing error, & the more the technique is practiced, the more adept they become. One might study for a lifetime the economic or the physiological aspects of alcoholism, & in the end, have a thorough understanding of these factors. On the other hand, suppose one turns to a moral study. I suppose ninety-nine men out of a hundred know (?) the difference between virtue & sinfulness, & the less experienced & less knowledgeable are always the most certain. These opinions are not abstract, but are the most powerful forces which will influence the decision of these judges, police, doctors, social workers, et al. Believe me, when I say the average man believes that his fellow traveler is either bad or good, & that he will reject any suggestion of the possibility of the duality of man's nature. These are men of whom he can conceive no sin (ask the average church communicant of his pastor) & men of whom he can conceive no virtue (ask the policeman on the corner of the drunkard).

I can not, in consideration of the narrow periphery in which I have lived, credit myself with being particularly discerning. I do not know what virtue is, but I recognize goodness when I see it, & I think other men are so fixed. I am too damned rational to be mystic or religious & so it goes for most of men. There is too much reverence in this world for things which are not deserving of reverence & so I suppose I am irreverent, & if there *is* a dividing line between me & the non-alcoholic, that must be it. And still again, this irreverence may be just a by-product engendered by the disregard of truth, which I see on every side. Imagine, as I am sure you can, the neophytes who will attend the summer course at New Haven.[2] Every damned mother's son who goes there, is *already* sure that he knows an alcoholic when he meets him. Tell him, if you will, along with Will James, "the sway of alcoholism over mankind is unquestionably due to its power to stimulate the mystical faculties of human nature, usually crushed to earth by the cold facts & dry criticism of the sober hour." In most cases, the listener will *rightly not* have attributed to the person to whom he thought was "alcoholic," the possession of "mystical faculties." And rightly so, because he did not know what an alcoholic was in the first place.

You wrote at one time that the prospect of living without the possibility of getting drunk would be frightening to an alcoholic. That is so. Would not the summer forum be better instructed if they were informed that their efforts (if directed toward true alcoholics) will be an endeavor to take away a man's escape from misery & his sole means of flight into the rapturous air of illusion. For the rest, who they have *thought* were alcoholics, they can go on treating like school boys who were over greedy with candy (as they have always treated all cases). The chances are that one out of a hundred of the students will look far enough & deep enough to learn anything of the subject. Ask them if you will, what they have to offer in place of alcohol. Would one exchange the inhabitation of fields of consciousness—wide, glorious, & delightful—for a Salvation Army dormitory? Like Aladdin, who rubs the magic lamp, the alcoholic has discovered a magic genie who lifts

2. Yale (now Rutgers) School of Alcohol Studies.

him up to the seventh heaven, & transports him over stellar spaces (sans gear of our scientific age), & who builds for him in half an hour's time, palaces of porphyry & jasper, fills his hands with gold, & breathes into his soul the sense & conviction of power. From melancholy, which must be aroused by sober reflection of a sensitive man, alcohol will lift to dazzling heights of happiness (like the magic carpet), like the magic ivory tube it will reveal all that he desires to see, & like the enchanted apple heals him of all illnesses.

. . . . .

Sincerely,
Frank

Davenport State Infirmary
June 7, 1959

Dear Bob:

. . . . .

The scientific writers which I have come in contact with in the field of sociology & in the field of study of alcoholism, appear to strive for a detachedness & objectivity employing such terms as "archtype" & "interaction." The drunkard in attempting to read his way out of his dilemma, feels the way a drowning person would feel if someone were to throw him a copy of Archimedes "Principle of Floating Bodies."

Despite the fact that, according to Robert Louis Stevenson, science writes with the "cold finger of a starfish," it has had, for me, its uproariously comical moments. Take for instance, the urging that "the full potentiality of alcoholics should be realized." This is mentioned in one of the scientific papers you sent me. Listen, while this old man tells you about the "birds & bees." For a hundred years & more, this place has operated as a dumping ground for indigent, crippled, & wholly incapacitated patients from other public & private hospitals. During that same time, the institution has been a haven for the destitute unemployable alcoholic. Admission has been gained on a voluntary basis. Discharge is gained in the same manner. The drunk is admitted because he will be useful (to others), & is discharged because there are so many coming in, who in turn will become useful (not to themselves of course). Anyone who writes of the "potentialities of the alcoholic," should apprehend that this is sure as hell one place where his potentialities *are* realized. Thus, upon arrival, the new drunkard is given a copy of "rules & regulations" of Davenport; paragraph one states that he will be given employment, & paragraph two, states what will happen if he does not conform to regulation one. The drunk is left in no doubt as to what is the purpose of admission. On the bulletin board at the present time, there is a notice to the effect that if anyone leaves without permission, he will be given a "Class A" work card on readmission. (Class A work card involves the hardest labor). As a matter of fifty-five years experience, I have long entertained the opinion that an exaggerated fixation on work is usually entertained by lazy persons, & only lazy people would regard work as punishment. But there we have it, above our beloved superintendent's signature. It is with some feeling of incongruity that I view the paid employees taking a half-hour coffee-break in the forenoon while one-armed & one-legged patients keep steadily at work, without pay & sans coffee break, & sans coffee. Most of the fat buttressed female paid employees have jobs sitting down, while a *80* year old female patient *stands* all day removing hot sheets from a mangle. I suppose in time, I will lose all true perspective, as most of these people drawing salaries apparently have. Friday afternoon is a slack time in the pressing department, & it is with a feeling of uneasiness, that one sees twenty paid employees spending the afternoon drinking tea & "setting" their hair while all this time unpaid patients are steadily at work. You sometimes get the idea that God is not in Heaven & all is not well below. I sometimes blame this on my sobriety & the awakening of critical faculties. You never would admit that sobriety has its disadvantages, would you? I believe it worth passing comment that convicted felons in our Commonwealth are paid 30¢ a day for their labors, while an alcoholic could go out of here after years of work in a bare-reared condition.

Dear Bob, all the abovementioned is preparatory to a sixty-four dollar question. As you and I know, efforts have been made by science, by the clergy, by the judiciary, to awaken public consciousness of the fact that something should be done for the alcoholic. Do you think it would be for the best interests of the people who administer an institution like this "to do something about alcoholism?" Would it not be like shooting a horse, & pulling the wagon yourself? If you can honestly answer this dual question, then you will have a proper guage of their so-called "programs."

· · · · ·

Sincerely,
Frank

Stonycreek Correctional Institution
October 30, 1959

Dear Bob:

I support the general opinion that vice, misconduct, & crime should not redound to anybody's profit.

All of which is a preamble to what I believe is a unique facet of alcoholism, known only to these parts. I don't recall reading in the scientific annals of any instance where getting drunk was profitable to anybody but the distillers. Hence the following.

I would estimate the average population here as consisting of about five hundred drunkards. They are transferred to this institution from the rock coast to the cow-spattered pastures of the Berkshire hills. In most cases they are conducted here by the police of their locality or "transportation offices," engendering the traveling back & forth of hundreds of miles, & in many cases by privately owned cars which, so far as I know, hold no franchise as common carriers, & provide no insurance for their human baggage. It is supposed that these officers have *one* pay day apart from their fees for trips to this Institution. The officers in the various communities take their "turns" conducting the prisoners to this place, & are paid car rental fees, mileage, meals, & "expenses." It is a general conception among the prisoners, that an officer would be allowed a comparatively small amount for transporting a drunkard from nearby while from a distant part of the state, the fee would be as much as "fifty dollars a head." It would be most interesting to know just how much of these thousands of dollars is "expense" and how much is profit. To summarize, in common business management, it would be most unsound to pay a man twice for performing his regular duties. If a community & the state supplies ambulances & police cars for public service, why has this "going business" of transporting prisoners in public owned vehicles been neglected? I submit that it is for the same reason that slavery flourished for hundreds of years, even in spite of the howling divines—i.e. because it is profitable. Referring to my first sentence of this letter, I would rather be brought here in a tumbrel than have anyone make a buck on the deal. Do you know that a professional writer is allowed a hundred pages to bring out a single idea, & I am allowed but this single page? Bear with me.

Frank

1960

January	Westville County Jail and House of Correction
February–mid-May	Westville County Jail (rearrest and resentence)
Mid-May	Visit to Calvinville, Alcoholic Clinic in Franklyn, wandering 150 miles westward
Mid-May–July	Riverpoint County Jail
July–August	Job as live-in kitchen helper in resort hotel, bender in Riverport, brief visit to Calvinville
August–September	Westville County Jail
September–mid-December	Stonycreek Correctional Institution
December	Westville County Jail

The first few letters from Frank in 1960 were introspective attempts to weigh his life as relatively harmless and honest when compared with those of a wide variety of "respectable crooks" in society. He also gave attention and merit to the experiences of the individual (himself), and pointed out that "do-gooders" have become so professional that they have lost sight of the worth of the individual they set out to help.

Frank's encounters with the law, its courts, and punitive and correctional houses during the year all added grist to his continuing analyses of their real purposes, their inefficiency, their lack of impartiality, and the law's insistence on defining "drunkenness as a crime."

While institutional dependency had long been a part of Frank's life, he gave increasing analytical attention to it as a problem, perhaps because he was making some tentative gestures toward returning to Calvinville. The whole problem of "Overdependency as Fostered by Repeated Institutionalization" (as he would entitle an exposition of his life) stimulated Frank to comment late in the year on the inadequacies of both treatment centers and students of the problem.

Westville County Jail
January 15, 1960

Dear Bob:

Received your letter of Jan. 11 & buck for which many thanks. I am at loss to understand why you did not receive my letter of Dec. 28.

The value (if any) of my communications to you lies in the fact that they present the views of the alcoholic himself, his understanding of the nature of his condition & possibly his lack of understanding. It may very well be, that a well integrated study of this social condition, embodying as it does, the moral, physical, & emotional responses of the individual to the society, of which he is a part, is incomplete when no provision is made for the views of the individual under consideration.

Surely one need not hide "the struggling pangs of conscious truth" for reason of social & economic necessity. It may be that this constitutes the one & only (intangible) luxury afforded by jails.

Jefferson wrote that "men are more disposed to suffer while evils are sufferable than to abolish the forms to which they are accustomed" & again, Hamlet states that "men are inclined to bear the ills they have than to fly to others, they know not of." Dealing as we are with a revolutionary concept toward alcoholism (& they are revolutionary as compared to the opinions entertained for thousands of years), it appears that one must, now & then, apply a wide board to the rump of some sacred cow. I never could understand why the people of India underwent famine when all these holy animals were available. Will be released on the 24th, & you will hear from me from some other monastic cell.

Regards,
Frank

Westville County Jail
March 23, 1960

Dear Bob:

. . . . .

. . . Do you know that sometimes I feel that I have lived at a time which saw the end of one era of philanthropy & the beginning of another. I can remember the days of the "settlement house" under the auspices of people who possessed a "sense of social obligation," & when a bum could expect to receive some money on the street, provided he possessed that particular kind of courage (?). The effort to help was pathetic & abortive in its results, & yet it warmed the heart of the giver & receiver. Such practices today have become as obsolescent as the trolley car. The spirit of philanthropy has now assumed a professionalism, with the paraphernalia of fund raising agencies &

disbursing centers. The new system operates with the idea that the funds are donated by people who possess what is known as "free social guilt" & that only these agencies possess the skill to determine whether the applicant receiver is "worthy." Whereas one judge has said that it were better for a hundred guilty persons to be set free than one innocent person should be convicted, these agencies, to my experience, believe it to be better that a hundred worthy persons should be denied rather than that one bum should receive the least assistance. I anticipate short shrift & lot more of "being in the hole." More anon—

Frank

Westville County Jail
April 25, 1960

Dear Bob:

I have received your letters & enclosures of April 13 & 19, for which I am deeply grateful. In regard to the paper of Mark Keller,[3] to clumsily paraphrase the writer, it is my opinion that this paper should be the "sine qua non" Chapter I of any authoritative treatise on Alcoholism. It may be considered an oasis midst the apocryphal dicta presented heretofore. This paper contains much "meat" & a happy choice of words, & I hope to present to you, in snatches, at future times, my reaction to it.

The inadequacy of medical dictionary's definition is apparent, if you stop to consider that verucca is defined therein as a wart, that canities signifies gray hair. Needless to say, that having a wart or gray hair, is not legally, morally, or socially significant, whereas "the inability to stop from drinking," if regarded as a disease, will justify the revision of legal, moral, & social codes, (at some long distant date), that is: the drunkard will no longer be considered a petty criminal; drunkenness (per se) will no longer be a sin; & a person weaving unsteadily down the street will no longer be considered a violator of the social contract.

It would be most interesting to be around when this redefinition finds acceptance, & the greatest spectacle of all will be the compromise effected between pseudo-moralists & the men of science. At the first acceptance, I envision many false starts in the wrong direction. In the

3. "Definition of Alcoholism," *Quarterly Journal of Studies on Alcohol,* 21: 125–34, 1960.

first place, as a "sociopathic personality disturbance," it may be deemed convenient to transfer (wholesale) these "sick" persons to insane asylums to share the same benefits afforded to gibbering idiots. Such a measure would satisfy the teetotaler who has a tough boss & nagging wife, but I imagine that there will be considerable opposition from the incumbent psychiatrists & hospital administrators.

That part of the paper which takes into consideration the "dependence on intoxication" appears to answer, in part, the choice of the words "ethanol, methanol, or other intoxicating substances." This "devil's work shop" idle mind deplores the fact that I may use only one sheet of paper. A salute to Mark Keller & regards.

Frank

Westville County Jail
May 12, 1960

Dear Bob:

One week hence, I shall face a jury of my peers. This trial will take place on the Lawrence Square opposite the site of the old High School, where I learned Portia's defense of Antonio in the "Merchant of Venice," in which, consider the line: "In the course of justice, none of us should see salvation." This court house is surrounded by a small park. In this small park & nearly sixty years ago, my father committed suicide with a pistol. Another case of history repeating itself. Please send me Two Dollars—

Regards,
Frank

Riverpoint County Jail
May 30, 1960

Dear Bob:

I suppose that I should paraphrase R.L.S. with some such opening as: "Home is the hunter," "Home is the sailer," etc. The only trouble with these homes is that they only last for 30 days. . . . By invoking amendments IV, VI, VII, VIII, I was able to be released at Calvinville. Went up to Franklyn to the alco-clinic, found them lavishly equipped for out-patient activities with clerks, sociologists, doctors, etc. who are certainly enjoying the benefits of a program, under which I was only eligible for a subcutaneous shot of vitamins in the "you know where." The smoking situation here can only be handled by mailing me Bull Durham Tobacco . . . can't be bought here. The situation is not acute, in fact, it is frantic.

Regards,

Frank

Westville County Jail

August 22, 1960

Dear Bob:

. . . The month of July saw me working in the Catskills, & believe me, if that is what is called a "meaningful" life & if that is called living decently & if that is called being useful to the community of which I am a part—I don't want it. They did want me & obstructed my quitting, offered me more money, said they could not get another man, etc. With that portion of the money that the employment agency & the federal government permitted me to keep, I went from there to Riverpoint & made everybody happy that I associated with, until the money was gone. The probation officer in Calvinville who interviews the prisoners before going to court asked me why I came back to Calvinville. Of course I couldn't give him anything definite but was tempted to remind him of the seals going back to the Pribiloffs, the salmon going back to the Columbia River, the eels going back to the Sargasso, etc. . . . I leave here the 7th of next month in the usual indigent condition having already attained one type of social security plus the four freedoms. Will be interested in knowing what goes on, on the other side of the tracks.

Sincere Regards—

Frank Moore

Westville County Jail

September 3, 1960

Dear Bob:

. . . I wish that sometime I could stay sober long enough, have paper enough, & be relieved of survival needs long enough to collate an exposition on "Overdependency as Fostered by Repeated Institutionalization." For a long time I have been associated with youthful offenders who are "grads" of reformatories & are en route to higher institutions. So you see, I also partake of other interests than alcoholism, or relate these interests to it.

Regards,

Frank

Stonycreek Correctional Institution
September 14, 1960

Dear Bob:

. . . However over dependent the alcoholic may be on the rest of organized society, he will not permit any one to be dependent on him. The capitalists among the drunkards hoard their money carefully in order that they may be able to get drunk, fall on their heads, & get back here again. I have often wondered what great truth is being demonstrated when a new man comes in here without funds, is compelled to roam the prison yards, pick up butts, shred out the tobacco, & roll it in toilet tissue. Surely there must be some grand socio-psychologico-penalogico lesson that I have failed thus far, to grasp.

Referring to your last publication on Myocardial Infarction,[4] let me especially commend that section where you state that all of us, thru our particular experience in life, develop blind spots & deaf spots, & are unable to see the things in front of our noses. This is royal prose, & particularly adaptable to those whose interests lie in alcoholic programming. The old Romans were a cynical & sophisticated lot. Whenever a new public works endeavor was under way, everybody asked, "Cui Bono?" which literally signifies, "For whose benefit is it." . . . I do get around as you know, & it seems the drunkard is going to be the last to benefit from these programmings, & believe me, we do have *some* programs. One fellow, with stenographer & elaborate office, said he could get me into a state hospital for forty days, or if I wished, he could send me to the county jail for ten days. Don't you think that I could get in jail or an insane asylum without his assistance? Why the office, the salary, his girl Friday? I shall not hear from anyone else & please write.

Frank Moore

Stonycreek Correctional Institution
October 4, 1960

Dear Bob:

Received your letter & remittance for tobacco, for which many thanks. It was an expensive day for you when I met you in New Haven & a lucky day for me.

To get on with the alcoholic critique: Harvard's Whitehead has accounted for the decline of religion (not of its panoply) as resulting from

4. Robert Straus, "Some Sociocultural Considerations on the Care of Patients with Myocardial Infarction," *Journal of Health and Human Behavior*, 1, 119–22, 1960.

the fact that every forward step of science has further limited the area of what our theologians call "sin." Nevertheless, I would not be compelled to go farther than the distance I could throw an empty wine bottle before encountering someone who would believe that I am "possessed by devils." Their opinion does not even compare favorably with that concept of the ancient Greeks, of the goddess Ate leading men on to ruin. (One supposes that she must have been beautiful, or who would have followed?) This line of thinking was occasioned by meeting a doctor, just a short time ago, who is in contact with a large number of inebriates & whose duty consists of making decisions regarding them. I was flabbergasted to learn from him, that the reason why I, and other persons, drank, was to be happy.

Did you ever stop to think of the farcical or tragic results, that are engendered by ascribing the wrong motives to the behavior of others.

You inquired about my sojourn in Sageville & Riverpoint. It is a Hogarthian picture & I will write you of it later. Again, many thanks.

Frank

Westville County Jail
December 16, 1960

Dear Bob:

Thirty days. In December 9 & out Jan. 8. Merry Christmas & a Happy New Year, etc. & etc., & so we continue the alcoholic treadmill. . . . The particular "bee in the bonnet" this fine winter's day, concerns the repeated "shibboletha" of scientific literature of alcoholism, thus: some months ago, I read an article by a lady connected with the Cornell School of Medicine. The terminology therein contained, assures me that she soars in the empyrean heights of the inner cabal. Conceding that this is a fair sample of the ideas relating to the subject, let us examine some of the word pictures set forth, viz (1) Acting a part, (2) Self-punishment & (3) Suspiciousness & Hostility.

In the order presented, I offer first, the case of men who return to their native towns after ten & twenty year absences, & longer, who no longer "fit" in industrial or commercial enterprises of that district, who find their playmates & school-boy friends fled or deceased, & who sit in the local bar rooms & drink for two days without recognizing a single person whom he knew in the long ago, & recalling his former attachments & loves. . . . The lady doctor states that he is "acting" the part of Enoch Arden, & solely on the basis that she, herself, has read the book. In nine cases out of ten, the poor slob has never heard of Enoch Arden. Why accuse the victim of "masquerade" when he doesn't know the libretto? May not the person be a veritable Enoch Arden, & without the implication of falsity? Her statement makes just about as much sense as if she said that Straus is "acting out" the part of Straus. It is possible to expound at great length on (1).

The choice of words in (2), self punishment, is really a "lu-lu." It evokes memory of the writing of Kraft-Ebbing, as if a man who fell asleep drunk in a snowdrift, were trying to achieve a sexual orgasm by setting a barn on fire or by being beaten with whips. Mayhap the gallant bum is one of the true ascetics in an age when even religion bows to realism & practicality. The connotation of "queerness" will not be helpful to the understanding of the subject in question. Has the lady been psycho-analyzed?

Number (3) is also a "dilly," which states that I (who am not a combat veteran), walk up to man who is, & start telling him about war & offer all that is known of it. In other words, I jump on his toes, & come away with the remarkable conclusion that he is "suspicious & hostile." Oh, my aching ivory towers! In addition to pulling your scientific leg, I really would like to hear from you. All my best feelings,

Frank

Westville County Jail
December 30, 1960

Dear Bob:

With the emergence of the second largest continent with its millions into an industrial & commercial field, with the complete restoration of war torn countries & their expansion in those same fields, racial integration, the replacement within the next ten years of all now existing machinery, automation, technological development, the utilization of nuclear power etc. will lead to new economic order & *without* the comparatively slow transitional periods which we have known in the past. Without usurping the role of a prophet of doom, it is safe to prognosticate that one half of the population will be able to produce what is necessary for the whole population. Whether one-half of this population is going to go about this willingly or whether they shall insist that all their less endowed fellow-humans be locked in jails & insane asylums, I don't know, but I expect the horses to run true to form. . . . The medical profession has long recognized the use of alcohol in smoothing the loneliness & disillusionments of old age. If, as it has been stated, that alcoholism is one of the top five health problems of today, I ask you what will happen under the economic order envisioned above? I don't foresee a change in our cultural anthropology which decrees that during this time that all men of brain or muscle will be "on the ball." The best that I can forecast, is one-half of the population hanging around a gin mill, which is, as Doctor Bacon so knowingly states: "a pretty well stigmatized field."

Regards,
Frank

1961

January	Westville County Jail and House of Correction
January–May	Liberty State Hospital
June–July	Bender
August	Liberty State Hospital
September–December	Wardhill State Hospital

Frank began 1961 in jail but spent most of the year in the Liberty and Wardhill mental hospitals. He wrote particularly on the characteristics of treatment and rehabilitation efforts as he had experienced them, on the differences between good and useless treatment, on the alcoholic as an individual, and on his own attitudes and feelings about himself, his condition, and what he might have become.

Liberty State Hospital
Jan. 21, 1961

Dear Bob:

I have been here about two weeks. Since it has been about nine years from my departure from this place, a commentary on the changes, evolution, or progress is indicated.

I forget whether it was you, or Dr. Bacon, who wrote that there was no other class of patient, other than little children, who was so quick to apprehend the interest, or lack of interest, of the doctor than the alcoholic. In the present instance, the eighty or more patients in this ward are aware that the present incumbent is such a "rara avis." . . .

It is most unfortunate, that after a short tenure in the present position, he will be transferred, by choice or necessity, to some unallied field. This is too often the case.

On meeting such rare people, I stifle my instinct to commiserate, lest I dull the edge of their crusader spirit. One informs them of the disappointments & pit-falls, with the same hesitancy as that employed when telling a small boy, that Santa Claus is an ideal rather than reality. I have already gathered that his colleagues regard the treatment of alcoholics as a disreputable practice & a stigmatized field. The alcoholic, himself, will enhance this opinion by repeated failures, his inability to preserve a common trust in the most trivial of matters, & his unlovable personality.

On the other hand, you will encounter a medical practice, which is considered as reputable. I offer to you hundreds of cases of arteriosclerotic insanity, senile dementia, & paresis (where organic change has taken place & irreparable damage has been done). Just exactly what can a doctor do other than sign a death certificate when the need arises? The amenities of civilization toward such patients are afforded in their entirety by nurses & attendants. I fail to understand why a doctor should believe it more respectable to deal with such patients, where there is no hope of recovery, rather than cases of alcoholism where there *is* an occasional recovery.

Send me money for tobacco & if I move on, your letter will be returned.

Regards,
Frank

Liberty State Hospital
March 8, 1961

Dear Bob:

. . . . .

Supposing that every man, whether he realizes it or not, has a "world idea" or philosophy in which he envisages his part in life, his aims, his relationships with others, his idea of the world as it is, or how it could be, or should be, the overwhelming tendency seems to be to choose the path of realism or idealism, without realizing that in the best possible life, that the two are interwoven. Most of us fail to weave this perfect fabric & go all overboard on one tack or the other.

It is quite possible to know one's short-comings without being able to do anything about it. The apparent choice of the two paths, mentioned above, if one looks for causes, appears to be a diathesis. Surely none of the Bourbons chose to be a hemophiliac, & exceptional people hate to be generalized.

I plead guilty to a frank admiration of Florence Nightingale, Pinel, & Fox, who were all regarded as crack-pots by the realists of their day, but this admiration has led me only in a path which is diametrically opposite to that of Carrie Nation, wherein I extol the virtues of alcoholics, & their worthiness, to such an extent that I deserve an annuity from the Brewers of America & the American Distilleries, Inc.

I am not surprised that you regard my promotion to eating in a small cafeteria as a "symbol." Every college has a campus except Harvard, which has a "yard," & so Yale is a place where everything is a "symbol." I was informing McCarthy at the clinic, out at Hillhouse,[5] of the disparity of my own financial & social status as compared to some of the other customers out at Hope Hollow (among whom—the secretary to a Mayor, an inventor, a Danish nobleman, & a magazine writer), & he brushed the whole thing off as "symbolism." One of the men who was discharged from here a few weeks ago, made a more accurate evaluation when he said: A man with a lot of money can get awful sick, but if he was financially broke, he would be twice as sick.

I profess a willingness to go along with this idea of symbols only provided that everybody is informed. For instance, the man who lets me out of the ward, in the morning, has a key. I do not have one. Now I know that the key is only a symbol but does he know it? Symbolism can be carried to some "wacky" extremes in an environment where even a white coat is a symbol. Yesterday there was a case here on the ward when there was a possibility a man needed to be catheterized. Employing asepsis & gentleness, imagine the trepidation of this patient had I attempted to catheterize him when, as far as he knew, I had been stacking dishes for the last month. On the other hand, if a trained baboon with a white coat & black bow tie had been brought in, the same patient would submit joyfully to appendectomy. As long as man can be hood-winked by symbols (forever), the word itself will only have significance to philosophers.

Further addenda to the Utopian alcoholic ward in the millenium. By the time an alcoholic has been confirmed as such, he has had many

5. Reference to Yale Plan Clinic in 1945.

unpleasant brushes with authority. This authority is of a various nature—familial, priestly, social, economic, judicial, et al. During that time
during which he is hospitalized, different kinds of authority will be
exerted toward him, according to the needs, as interpreted by those in
charge. There may be a wide divergence between what authority is
needful & that which is contrary to the purpose of hospitalization. As a
sop for those who advocate rigorous measures, it should be pointed
out that the world is not going to adjust itself to the alcoholic & that
sooner or later that he must return to that familiar world of various
authorities. In the meantime, that part of his life, which is spent in a
hospital, should not evoke memories such as would be evoked at
Molokai or Carrsville. Just as restraint must be exerted toward the alcoholic, so must restraint be exerted toward those who deal with him.
The answer seems to lie between a delinquent reformatory & a country
club for neurotic men.

Regards,
Frank

Liberty State Hospital
March 17, 1961

Dear Bob:

Sometimes, I suspect that what I write, has no more merit than the
grafitti found on the walls of public restrooms. Even to myself, it seems
that I become more articulate & vociferous, than the occasion demands.
This is a common error of our time. For instance, note the national
preoccupation with Bridget Bardotte & Marilyn Monroe—one would
almost come to believe that mammals have just been invented.

However, to the diligent searcher, there is an historical precedent for
any sort of writing. The Cro-magnon man, with his pictures of rein-
deer, in the caves of France, has an opposite number in the drunkard
who jots down his mental maunderings for posterity. Of a more recent
date, I give you George Herbert (circa 1630), who wrote: "I give to
thee who knowest all my wayes, My crooked winding wayes, wherein
I live."

If it were worth the trouble to collate the correspondence of the
past fifteen years, who could deny that mine have been crooked winding ways and as purposeful as that of a rat who gnaws a hole in the
corner without the least idea of what lies on the other side of the wall?
The preoccupation with the sordid & mean is only the reflection of the

media in which a man lives. Herbert would never have written those lines had he not engaged in skullduggery, possibly seduction, & broken faith. I presume the present day head-shrinkers would label Thoreau as a masochist, in that he went out to Walden Pond to find out if life was good & if it were not—to wring the last drop of rottenness out of it. I sometimes wonder what might have been written, had he been an alcoholic rather than a naturalist.

. . . . .

Frank

Liberty State Hospital
August 6, 1961

Dear Bob:

The following recapitulation is apropos. I commended to you, in January of this year, a Doctor Scariot who informed me & led me to believe, that if I remained sober over an extended length of time, it would be possible to regain my status as a regular employee at this institution. I completed four months & started the fifth month before I approached the employment manager. As is usual in such capacities, there are many supplicants. In his possible desire to expedite matters, he came from his office to inquire of the business with his office. I stated that the nature of my business was employment.

He informed me that he had received orders from the State House not to move up any more employees from a patient-employee status to a regular-employee status. It did not seem to me that the hallway was the proper place to state my qualifications, to cite the efforts which I made, & to refer him to all the persons with whom I had been in contact as a patient-employee.

I did not bother to return & tell the Doctor Scariot of this interview. It did not seem fair for him to pull my chestnuts out of the fire. I do not possess that small art to express my feelings of rejection & repudiation at this time. To express it, rather in the vernacular, "I blew my gasket," packed up and left, & embarked on a drunk to end all drunks.

I was re-admitted two days ago, & am back in the "untouchable" caste. One of the new doctors asked me why I came here, & believe me I am hard put for an answer.

Regards,
Frank

Wardhill State Hospital
Sept. 29, 1961

Dear Bob:

I received the Conference Report[6] a week later than your last letter. It was with a deep feeling of humility and gratitude that I noted the vast assemblage of "brains" gathered there & the efforts that are being extended toward my "kind."

I find it a remarkable coincidence, that, before receiving this reprint, I had written you a letter quoting Conrad, to the effect that "every man believes in efficacy of his own particular art." The multidisciplinary mode of thinking as contrasted to an interdisciplinary mode of thinking, was most refreshing. It has been necessary in all my experience to realistically recognize that I would be dealing with a judge at one time, a psychiatrist at another time, a sociologist at another & so on. It seems that I usually quit these various sessions with some such baleful & blasphemous thought such as: "Forgive them, Father, for they know not what they do."

Whatever else may be said of the respectability of dealing professionally with alcoholism, it most certainly leads to variant & divergent evaluations. Thus, to one group, I find myself a sinner; to another, a social criminal; to another, I am "sick" (with all that wide latitude of connotation), etc. etc. . . . How long will it be, Lord, before the limitations of one particular & specialized & narrow discipline, will be recognized?? . . .

. . . . .

I found it most provocative where you used the term "self-image" which the alcoholic has perpetuated when he has come for treatment & reported his own phaseology. It causes me to wonder, how objectively I have reported to you, & how much is self-image. Consider this, & in the words of Brutus: "Awake your senses that you may the better judge."

It seems to me that the "self-image" is fostered, in general, to reconcile self to existing patterns, & to extenuate one's behavior from the norm, & especially to solicit response & sympathy. In retrospect, it seems to me that I have never endeavored to be anything but a "bum" to the person, who by manner or speech, indicated his opinion in that

6. *Multidisciplinary Programming in Alcoholism Investigation.* Berkeley, California State Department of Public Health, 1960.

direction. Similarly, I have never endeavored to appear anything but stupid to a person, who by manner of speech, indicated that he thought I was stupid. In lieu of seeking compassion, it seems to me that I have been quite defiant &, in general, a pain in the neck to people who have dealt with me as an alcoholic. Instead of a joiner, I became a secessionist to the pretentions & falsity of accredited social, penal, & psychological method. When you mention "self-image" it implies to me, an inclination to jump on the bandwagon of "acceptability." Whereas, in truth, the alcoholic in penal or hospital institutionalization, becomes a "rebel without a cause," & an anomaly even among criminals or lunatics.

.   .   .   .   .

Seriously, I am proud of you—

Frank

Wardhill State Hospital
Dec. 1, 1961

Dear Bob:

Any man's "philosophy" might be composed of his conception of: (1) the universe, and (2) his position in relation to that universe. Following this idea, it pleases my fancy to consider what my position in relation to the universe, (a) should have been, and (b) could have been.

I lack the temerity to engage in the controversy provoked by (a) & rightly relegate this consideration to philosophers & the clergy. On the other hand, it seems that I have basis for the pursuance of (b).

This line of thought was evoked by an incident that happened a short time ago. An epileptic patient fell against a window & broke a finger (fracture of a distal phalange). A few hours later, he appeared back in the ward, with a board 4 inches wide, extending from his elbow (olecranon), beyond the length of his hand, with his arm, wrist, & complete hand swathed in bandage. He told me that a doctor had applied the splint.

Referring to (b) in the first paragraph of this letter, it is possible that I could have applied this dressing. At the age of 16, I had learned to apply the Barton bandage, the spica of the groin, the recurrent turn of the cranium, the gauntlet bandage, ascending and descending spirals, the figure of eight, & (that most complex of bandages) the Velpeau. Any bandage that I could have applied would have indicated the nature, or at least the extent, of the casualty.

At the age of twelve years, my uncle rewarded me with fifty cents for learning the names of the 206 bones in the human body. Likewise, a motivational reward (a year's paid membership to the Y.M.C.A. from my grandfather), prompted me to learn the circulation of the blood thru the heart, at the age of 13. In those years before a razor first touched my face, I became acquainted with the rudiments of materia medica, & the names of the twelve cranial nerves. In view of this precocity, (& had tangible gain been offered), it seems that I could have become a doctor of medicine.

It also appears to me, that in my late twenties, I would have failed in this profession. This failure could have been ascribed to my lack of adherence to the "ethics" of my profession. (I could never have cultivated a "bed-side" manner, the money grubbing, the hocus-pocus of my colleagues, & their reliance on the credulity & ignorance of the client).

This early frustration would probably have led me to the path of psychiatry. In consideration of my age, I would have escaped the history of the first 20 years of this profession. (Journeying to Europe to study under the great Kraeplin, learning how to classify, & to ignore any method of treatment).

It seems that I would have made my advent to this profession when treatments were first instituted. It follows then, that I would have practiced the psychotherapeutic fads of the ensuing years.

At first, I would have wrapped my patients in winding wet sheets or dunked them in tubs for such a length of time that the skin on their palms & soles became shriveled. The wet sheets, in the drying process, would constrict the bones & muscles, & the quietude of previously "active" patients would have assured me of the efficacy of this treatment.

In that particular time of the evolution of therapeutics, I would have induced hyperpyrexia (fever treatment). At this time I would have been a resident doctor at some public institution, & so this treatment would be imposed on patients of low resistance, vitality, & nutrition.

In the 1930's, I would have embraced the metrazol "boom." God only knows how many fractures, with their attendant pain, I might have caused.

Next, after this dunking, fever treatment, & metrazol craze had faded into the misty limbo of psychiatry, I would have embarked on the hypoglycemic shock therapy (insulin). The name of this treatment would have caused me to practice it, extraneous to the policy of the institution which advocated it.

Approaching the peaks (or the tinkling cymbals), of psychiatry, I would then have employed the indiscriminate use of shock therapy, with no thought of the injurious effects, or index for the selection of patients for this treatment.

In consideration of all that has been written above, it seems that I could have followed in the footsteps of the most brilliant & the most stupid of my time. In the final analysis of "what might have been," I arrive to the consideration of what my position in relation to the universe, could have been today.

As near as I can figure it out, I could have been in charge of a building where patients were crowded in sleeping dormitories, with such proximity to each other, as would not be tolerated by the health inspector of a Bowery flop-house. Hundreds of male & female patients of assorted classification would be assigned to my care & treatment. In addition to the patients, I could have had their hundreds of relatives, dependent on my God-like mission, & I would have employed a vast amount of time, assuaging their fears and stimulating their hopes.

Having reached the zenith of my profession, I would have foregone all the former pseudo-scientific devices of my calling, & would only employ the curative effects of cleaning pots & pans or raking leaves. I would detail an insurance salesman, with a manic-depressive psychosis, to unloading a car-load of flour. To anyone who cooperated with my work-therapy, I would offer an early release from custody, without consideration of what he might do when released to the community. In the event that my patients were not cooperative, I would have retaliated with all the congenital malice of a peasant, & would have prescribed indefinite confinement under conditions that are below par for most second-rate jails.

After many years of browsing thru dusty book shelves, & drinking of the wells of science, I could have become a combination of gaoler-employment manager.

In conclusion, & to offer a new "twist," permit me to offer thanks to Deity that I became a harmless old drunk.

Regards,
Frank

1962

January–February	Wardhill State Hospital
March–May	Liberty State Hospital
Mid-May	Wandering, visit to Calvinville
May–August	Stonycreek Correctional Institution
August–September	Anchorport City Jail (2 weeks), wandering, job as furniture mover, wandering Boston to River-point
October–December	Stonycreek Correctional Institution

Frank continued his observations in 1962 on forms of treatment and institutions, those holding out some hope and those he considered hopeless. The use of drugs, "involuntary servitude" of inmates, exhortations to Christian living, as well as the humane and decent treatment accorded patients at one institution were all considered. Frank asked why the waste of public moneys on ineffective treatment and institutional perpetuation was tolerated. And, even if treatment were to go through a metamorphosis as it appears it might in selected institutions, could the alcoholic, after a lifetime of experiences such as he has had, ever respond to resocialization of the most enlightened form? He continued to mince no words for the many misguided efforts to "study" alcoholism, misguided perhaps in part because he believed that hostile social attitudes toward and assumptions about the alcoholic had not changed, even on the part of "scientific" investigators.

Frank also showed that, in spite of his age, his constitution was still able to withstand physical hardships suffered on his infrequent journeys outside the walls of institutions. He was not without "stratagems of the drunk" to help cope with the vicissitudes of these occasional forays.

Wardhill State Hospital
Jan. 8, 1962

Dear Bob:

If you have tears, prepare to shed them now. . . . Frank Moore, man of distinction, has switched from bourbon to barbiturates.

Could it be that my doctor seeks the possibility of finding other drugs and substances which might satisfy needs presently satisfied by alcohol—& to do so in a way less harmful to the individual & society?

I am sure he has made a metabolic & a drug study that is necessary to find an adequate drug to aid in the treatment of alcoholism & of course he must possess all the data on the deleterious effects of the much used phenothiazines!

In that we have engaged in a "life history," or what I would call a longitudinal study, there comes a time when we must consider the denouement. It passes for current that when a soldier joins battle, the thought is always, that it is always the other fellow who is going to be shot, & not him. To the contrary, I have oft considered the probability that I shall die in one of these "laughing academies" or some second rate county jail.

In the olden days, one was bound to pay insurance lest he be tucked away in "potter's field." With the advent of social security, it is a case of "finder's keepers" among the undertakers. These body-snatchers can still make a few bucks profit after laying away the body in a rough pine box, & better still, they are guaranteed this payment by Social Security Administration. I would like to circumvent, if possible, anybody profiting by my death. With the connivance of a pathologist & the undertaker, there is still the possibility that the skin off my back might end up as a lamp shade in some ladies boudoir.

You asked about my work assignment. During time out between drunks, I committed the Declaration of Independence to memory, along with the Bill of Rights, & a working knowledge of the Constitution. I was probably trying to compensate for being an otherwise poor citizen. I never thought it would be useful.

The doctors here speak a sort of pidgeon English, along with being unfamiliar with the Western temperament. This fact necessitates a great reliance on the nurses & attendants. The doctors reciprocate by detailing to every patient this side of the graveside tasks—dirty, arduous, & necessary to the running of a state hospital.

Unfortunately, I am conversant with the 13th Amendment which states that involuntary servitude, except as punishment for crime, is prohibited within these United States. I write "unfortunately," because no one else seems to know the law. My doctor stipulates that he will consider my release if I contract to a few months labor without pay. Who would consider that the employment of this old drunk is so needful?

Regards,
Frank

Stonycreek Correctional Institution
May 29, 1962

Dear Bob:

Continuing the Wanderjahr: Arrived here about nine days ago. Have not been here for a year & a half. There is a continued trend away from the punitive & social reprisal. It is indeed a far cry from my first appearance here years ago. The most noteworthy advance, (it appears to me), is the changed attitudes & interpersonal relationships between the staff & inmates. More of this anon.

To get things chronologically straight: when I left Liberty I came to Calvinville. I knocked at the French door of the piazza of the old family manse, & learned that the house & property was sold, & that my mother was in the O'Laughlin Rest Home on Johns St. Of course, this is one of the best sort of those kind of places & located on one of those streets that have the "widows walk" atop the house. J. P. Marquand would have viewed with interest, the transition to Johns St.[7] of this aged lady. I only called her on the phone.

It has occurred to me that you might wish to implement my own viewpoints during the final dissolution, with information from people who have known me in these times. In such case, I offer Ralph Gordon, vice president of the Arbor Mfg. Co., who may be addressed at Fordham Lane, Midway. Ralph dressed me in a new suit & "pieced me off" with a couple of bucks for the sake of our boyhood together. . . . Also my only other surviving relative, Donald Kaiser, who has also reached the vice presidency of the leading emporium in Calvinville. He may be contacted at Forest St., Midway. All of the wealthy people move out of Calvinville to Midway for tax purposes. I "assessed" him for two bucks the last time I was in town. This second cousin was a "sissy" & we were never more acquainted than going to the same classes in school. I am sure he regards me in the same light as a dinosaur or pterodactyl. . . . After leaving I was arrested on successive days for drunkenness in four different towns & so the State Farm is logical.

Food, lights, books, hygiene, recreation, are adequately provided for. The one gnat in the ointment consists of only one pack of tobacco per week. Will you help me in this respect? I have been picking up butts for a week. Good thing I get a blood test so often in institutions.

Regards,
Frank

7. Upper-class residential area.

Stonycreek Correctional Institution
June 12, 1962

Dear Bob:

Received your letter Friday with enclosure, for which, many thanks. I thank whatever Deity it may be, who is concerned in the affairs of drunkards, that I have lived long enough to witness a metamorphosis. It is probable that no other place than my present abode affords a better comparison of "then & now."

Public enlightenment, committees on alcoholism, monetary grants, & the subsidization of cozy jobs dealing with alcoholism, in the present instance, must play second fiddle to the accomplishment of a single man with a modicum of intelligence & morality. The hundreds of men who were here with me many years ago & yet remain here, are most aware who is responsible for their betterment, improvement in a human living scale, & the awareness of human decency. . . .

This place is a prime example of the fact that if nothing can be done to cure alcoholism, it can at least be dealt with humanely & decently & without constituted authority itself being dragged down in the mud. It was not always this way.

When I arrived here years ago, we received a piece of cake every Sunday night for supper. This was the total pastry for the week. We thought of fruit juices as something that society people imbibed. It was assumed that a drunkard's guts were different than normal peoples'. Now in the course of a week, doughnuts, cookies, rolls, & fig squares make a regular appearance.

It was assumed at one time that if a drunk once got his hands on a match, that the whole damn place would be burned to the foundations. Everybody has been carrying matches for the past two years, & not a single holocaust yet!

In those days of yore, it was common practice for one guard to report another guard to his superiors for permitting a prisoner to smoke at his place of work. In retrospect, it seems to have been a hell of a way to make a living. We were sent to our dormitories at 6:30 P.M. & not permitted to smoke thereafter. Night guards with zeal, tennis shoes, & a rubber key would fling open the door without warning & apprehend a smoker. The guard received an 'A' on his efficiency report & the inmate was awarded a 30 days extension as a guest of the state. . . . Drunkenness was a terrible crime in those days.

An intangible but not less noteworthy change, is the general recog-

nition of the inmate himself, of his own inadequacy & his acknowledgement of the decency shown him & his unspoken appreciation. . . .
This is a skeleton of changes here. The other health problem in next
letter.

Frank

Stonycreek Correctional Institution
June 19, 1962

Dear Bob:

I promised a critique regarding the administration of barbiturates
& tranquilizers at Wardhill. An overall exposition of this subject must
refer to (a) the person prescribing; (b) the rationale of the treatment;
(c) the results obtained in a mass hospital population; & (d) my own
reaction to this chemotherapy. These doctors are informed of the different kinds of barbiturates & tranquilizers in stock at the hospital
pharmacy. Whatever he may know of hypnotics & cerebral depressants,
their dosage, physiological action, source, origin, forms of administration, & synergists, is limited by a number of drugs with which he is no
more familiar than the reading of a pharmacal brochure.

It is unthinkable that every patient shall not receive "treatment" &
to that end *every* mother's son is prescribed for. In this way every
relative or friend of the patient can be assured that he is "under treatment." . . . Once the patient has been prescribed for, it may be weeks
& months, & I mean literally *six* months before the doctor has the
opportunity to observe the effects of the barbiturates & tranquilizers.
The average length of time of a doctor in a single ward of a hundred
patients at Wardhill was usually about 15 minutes per day (signing
death reports, accident reports, examination of new arrivals, transfer
of patients, etc.). So much for paragraph (a).

Frank

Stonycreek Correctional Institution
June 26, 1962

Dear Bob:

Continuing the exposition of the use of barbiturates & tranquilizers
at Wardhill:

The school history-books tell us that Washington contracted pneumonia in 1799 after riding in the cold rain; rallied a few times & then
died. Just that. At your college of medicine, some students may be

curious to know which type of pneumonia, & conjecture as to his treatment. The medical records of that time show that the Father of his Country was bled to death by his attendant physicians, who like all their kind, of that time did not know a hell of a lot about blood. History will probably record that the doctors of today exhibit the same flocculent thinking in regard to barbiturates & tranquilizers.

So far as I know, even the most vociferous of miracle-mongers has not claimed that the use of this type of drug has "cured" a single case of psychosis, neurosis, alcoholism, et al. The manic type of patient in a state hospital can eat these kinds of drugs like candy, with no effect. To test the truth of this statement, make your way thru any state hospital grounds at this time of year when windows are open & the patients are confined on barred porches. They are still screaming & yelling as in the old time bughouses. The efficacy of these drugs (tranquilizers & barbiturates) is nil. To quiet this kind of patient, nothing is more efficacious (and after a few administrations, more deadly) than the old fashioned mixture of hyoscine, choral, & morphine.

The use of tranquilizers at Wardhill was a mass population administration. For ninety-nine percent of the population this was the sole treatment. The prescription of these drugs answered all questions regarding the treatment of a patient.

I would describe tranquilizers, (reserpine, thorazine, spyrin, etc) as drugs which lessen the relationships of the individual to reality. It is supposed that most of us, (in a state hospital or out of it), have a usual quota of shame, envy, hate, jealousy, shyness, embarrassment, pride, suspicion, anxiety, anguish, resentment. These are some of the needful equipment of life. Viewing long-term patients who had been subjected over the years to this treatment, one is struck by their docility, their willingness to work 365 days a year without pay, their reduction to the lowest common denominator, their institutional dependency, their lack of identification with the world at large. The closest approximation that I can think of, I have encountered in the pre-frontal lobotomy patients (the walking zombies who are the relicts of an outdated psychiatry). However, the results obtained, lead to a happy life for the hospital employee & staff. If the use of these drugs was discontinued, patients would clamor for release, attendants would have to go to work, & other terrible things of such nature would happen. Will continue. . . .

Frank

Stonycreek Correctional Institution
July 3, 1962

Dear Bob:

Received your letter of June 26 & enclosure, for which I am most grateful. In this modern Carcassonne, sufficient tobacco seems to be the only unfulfilled requirement.

I was most reassured by your statement regarding tranquilizers & the staffing of state hospitals. At some later date I shall inform you of my disposal of sedatives & tranquilizers while at the Wardhill hospital. My experiments on the effect of tranquilizers on sea-gulls may cause me to become a leading authority on the genus larus, their feeding habits, determination of sex, habit of habitat, eccentricity of flight, etc. I shall mention in passing, a most original & revolutionary concept for the use of tranquilizers & barbiturates in state hospitals, viz: If the doctors & attendants find that their association with noisy, disturbed, & disoriented persons & if they find the paroxysms of grand mal, too distressing or uncomfortable, then they can dose themselves with reserpine, spyrin, luminal, allonal, seconal, nembutal, etc. & etc. If the drugs are not injurious, why not?

. . . . .

I often feel it was a lucky day when we became acquainted in New Haven down on James Street.

Regards & thanks
Frank

Stonycreek Correctional Institution
July 10, 1962

Dear Bob:

Perhaps one of the disadvantages of pursuing a regular and steady job is that it leads to a limited & restricted view of life. And as it is with me, the perennial prisoner, presenting prison life as a microorganism of the whole social structure. . . . You might regard the following as an addendum or footnote to your forthcoming paper on Institutional Dependency. If you had informed me whether the victim is aware that he is dependent, (?) or whether he apparently enjoys the situation, (?) then the following would be significant.

Last week the Red Cross Bloodmobile arrived at this institution, & hundreds of these men (drunkards) volunteered as blood donors. The inducement was to be released five days earlier than their regular date of release. This seems to answer the second part of the question. And if the men, themselves, realized that they were institutionally dependent, it is sequitor reasoning that they will be released five days earlier in order to be arrested five days earlier, & this answers the first part of the question.

. . . . .

Admitting that these men have not given to society what society may have reasonably expected of them, has society given them what they might have reasonably expected?

Frank

Stonycreek Correctional Institution
July 31, 1962

Dear Bob:

I will be released from here on the 10th of August. It is ironical that I shall miss the Annual Fair which will take place in Calvinville during the first week of August. Returning there, as I do, periodically I become increasingly aware of the strange specie of Homo Sap incident to these queer New England towns.

It seems highly irregular that the pastor of the old South Church should turn his church into an enlistment office & so harangue his flock that 60 men jump out into the aisles on a Sunday & march thirty-six miles to Bunker Hill & commit treason to their lawful king & sovereign. And of course they could claim no precedent, in that they were the first organized unit (the Minute Men of Lexington were not an organized unit). It does not seem to me that these fowling-piece brawlers could have been composed of staid & stable elements, concerned by homes, wives, & property. I suspect that this first contingent was represented by a fair share of toss-pots & irresponsible elements. Considering that in the same war, twenty privateers were built & manned in Calvinville it would be naive to assume that all these crews were amateurs in piracy. One assumes that "lex gentes" only added legality to their natural proclivities.

To support my claim that an atavistic strain survives to this day, it is only necessary to offer that a salvage company purchased a World War II submarine & towed it to Calvinville docks. During that lengthy period before the acetylene torches got down to the water line, this submarine served as a nightly haven for the bottle gang & husbands in the dog-house. I swing abroad on a cable with the cry "Boarders

Away" just to keep my record intact, that I had slept everywhere, from a highway sand-box on top of picks & shovels to the battery room of a submarine. By the way, don't you do it; it is too damp. . . . I have no plans for the Tenth on. Do you have any suggestions? Any irregular procedure would be welcome. Spare me that common fate of being arrested by the same policeman, facing the same judge, & being remanded to the same jail. The stereotyped automatism of some of these lives about me, would have driven me to suicide long ago. . . .

Block Island is not new to me but I have yen to stick an iron into a good-sized sword-fish. . . .

Regards—

Frank

Stonycreek Correctional Institution

October 2, 1962

Dear Bob:

Since my last letter to you—I caught a 75-car freight at Anchorport. Only two unsealed box-cars & chose one with about four inches of wood-shavings. Very chic & immaculate & only one draw-back—a stray cigarette spark along with the wind could have sent me streaming over the New England landscape like Phaeton driving the Chariot of the Sun. Had some sort of a gauzy notion of getting off at Rutland, for no other reason than that the name sounded good. (Mayhap an overzealous Freudian would come up with a sexual connotation). Anyhow, the train was going too fast & I could not jump off there. Many Canadian National cars were hitched on, & I knew the immigration officials would give the cars a "going over" at some point farther north & so when the train slowed at a junction point, I hit the cinders with a couple of scratches, & found that the train was going to stop anyhow. One of the yard-men told me where to go in town. This cameraderie is mostly due to the fact that the genus hobo is now an anachronism in this part of the country & the average railroad employee looks upon him with the same respect as the sailor accords the albatross. . . . I walked to town & found the Gospel Mission, as directed. Would you have expected to find a mission in these latitudes? It seems that the Fishers of Men realize that there is gold in them thar hills. The installation has three double-decker beds & functions as a hostel to a provincial breed of tramp, indigenous to northern New England who follow an almost schedular route from county home & one night stands in the village lock-ups. The superintendent is a lay-man & receives the support of Community Funds, the council of churches, & I was unable to find out how much he was able to pry out of other civic bodies. Anyhow, business was so good (for him, that is), that he is determined to open another sanctum in a nearby town. It would be most interesting to make a recapitulation of the souls captured for Deity in that sort of place. Did you ever hear the following doggerel:

"Little we give & poor it is,
For that's the way we run the biz,*
On pies & cake, & chops & steak,
On these we dine for Jesus sake,
And Jesus (now don't rave or cuss),
Jesus means: simply "us",
While hungry bums just like you
Must flourish on salvation stew."

Will continue next week. Things static here. One pck. of tobacco a week. Luxury thru scarcity.

Regards,
Frank

(*Chaucer loused up things worse than this).

Stonycreek Correctional Institution
October 9, 1962

Dear Bob:

Continuing a resumé of the northern maneuvers: I arrived at that mission on Saturday night. There was only one service a week & that on Saturday night. However, a beach-wagon was sent every Sunday morning to the mission to convey its beneficiaries to the Baptist Evangelical Church.

. . . I remember, years ago, store windows displaying placards announcing that twenty-four Blackfoot Indians from the Dakotas would attend a particular church on a given date. Sitting in a park of a Sunday, I saw these men marching two by two, each wearing an unpinched black ten-gallon hat, each with a white shirt & black tie, & each with a missal under his right arm. It seemed to me at the time that the noble red man had struck his bottom (to borrow the terminology of A.A.). . . .

Anyhow, I am sure that my attendance, at the worship of Deity, dressed in a white sweat shirt & dungaree trousers insured the continued financial support of the mission by that church. Very few people heed the scriptural admonition of "not letting the right hand know what the left hand is doing."

I was instructed that I might stay as long as I wished, in return for whatever work I might do around the mission. There is a kinship between all organizations of this kind, in that all seem peculiarly blinded to the fact that the object of all work is gainfulness. In that the objects of this Christian endeavor are generally adjudged incapable of intellectual or spiritual gain, it should follow that material gain is to be afforded. However, we must recognize that organized religion supported peonage, slavery, & involuntary servitude for thousands of years.

I do not know of a more unhappy situation to confront an executive of this kind of institution than to have a number of good workers go out & earn their own living. The next day, Monday, I landed a job with an agent of a national furniture moving concern. Can you imagine me at 58 years of age, furniture moving? I had the occasion many times, in the ensuing week to recall those lines of Kipling: "if you can force your heart & nerve, & sinew to serve your turn, long after they are gone." Can you imagine the pitty-pats of your frail "ticker" after about thirty trips up and down stairs carrying assorted electric stoves, frigidaires, & davenports. One of my indictments against the supernal powers is based on the fact that the worst of people are blessed with physical invulnerability while the very best of people are most often damned to disability & early death.

After my first day at work, I returned to the mission with a box & a receipted grocery bill for $8. I thought the other two men would enjoy a diet that was supplementary to what the Lord (mission) afforded them. I continued staying at the mission that week because I hated missions & liked the kind of people who are compelled to go to them. Earned $79 that week at a gut-busting job that would have been play at one time in my life. The following Sunday (day before Labor Day), I was again exhibited at the evangelical church. The sermon title was: "The Reality of Hell." I believe that I could have "topped" the parson but my discourse would hardly have been homiletical. He exhorted the flock to use Labor Day by repairing to the church to do the necessary cleaning, painting, & other needful work, on that day & consecrate their united effort to the Lord. The three of us at the mission: one man with cardiac asthma, the other with the forepart of both feet amputated (frostbite), & myself would necessarily be called upon. I felt it would be better for the comfortable & the successful to care for their own consecrations & dedications rather than the crippled, aged & the unsuccessful.

(next episode—next week)

Regards—
Frank

Stonycreek Correctional Institution
October 24, 1962

Dear Bob:

. . . . .

You evinced an interest in my return from up north.

. . . After the Sunday exhortation to go to the church & labor for the Lord on Labor Day, I ate dinner & got out on the highway, outside of town. Got a ride with a priest as far down as Manchester. Does it not appear to you that Fate has cast "into my predestined plot of dust & soul," more than my fair share of the clergy? This guy was a kind of Friar Tuck—given to four letter Anglo-Saxon expletives, & was most refreshing compared with my recent experience with the quasi-Calvins. Did it ever occur to you, just how genuine & honest one can be if there is a certainty that you will never see that person again? I think the padre was refreshed too.

There are no legal liquor sales in N.H. on Sunday & so I went to the Marquis Club. Clubs have to make money whether you are a member or not. One drink always made a new man of me (but the new man always wanted another drink). Caught a bus to Boston & arrived about 9 p.m. Sought out the most notorious dive in the South End. Hadn't been there in 10 years. I have a weird theory that drunks go to this bistro & far famed "clip-joint," because their subconscious is flinging the gauntlet to the "Sharpshooters." Anyhow, I looked sufficiently dour & severe that I was able to stay 'til closing-up time, without having my trouser-pockets turned wrong-side out. Went to the bus station at 2 A.M. on Labor Day morning & bought a ticket to Riverpoint. My flight was influenced by endemic disease of these parts, called the State Farm Horrors. No bus was to leave until 8 o'clock, & so I slept sitting in the bus station. As you know, there are always police prowling the bus & railroad stations. To forestall an imminent arrest, I folded my topcoat with plaid lining, a Harris Tweed handwoven 100% wool, wrong-side out so that any minion of the law might read the label & know that he was in the presence of a gentleman of distinction & not just an ordinary drunk. Is there such a thing as an "ordinary" drunk? Sometimes I will write a monograph on the Strategems of a Drunk. Anyhow, I slept unmolested & got off to Riverpoint. More anon, write when you are not too busy.

Regards—
Frank

Stonycreek Correctional Institution
November 6, 1962

Dear Bob:

There is no doubt that people are ruled in a great measure by custom rather than by the light of history & of reason. Consider the ever ubiquitous chump who goes about yammering of his "natural rights." Of course we know that when any customary right has spread very widely & become deeply rooted in society, many fall into the error of calling it a "natural right." They believe the right is "established by nature" & therefore is not to be called into question. But in reality, there are no such rights. All true rights are rational—rights which can show good reason for their claims & justify their existence on the ground that they promote human welfare.

As it is with the individual, so it is with society. The long continued existence of a public institution should surely furnish strong evidence that it has ministered to social welfare. After almost twenty years, (in the aggregate), of almost continuous association with men whom Reformatories did not "reform," whom Penitentiaries did not make "penitent," whom Houses of Correction did not "correct," I have arrived at some conclusions which are surely not shared by the man on the street who pays for all of this. . . .

I could not write with sufficient mordancy of that ripest "hokum" ever inflicted upon the public—to wit, that large sums of public money is spent on the wrong doer himself. It is a human habit to tack a name on everything, & hence we refer to the criminal, the insane, as a "public charge." It would be most revealing to break down the expenditures of all public institutions & publish the figures showing what money is expended on employees, their salaries, housing & allowances, etc. & indicate just how much dribbles down to the incarcerated. In this way we might be able to properly apply the term of "public charge." I anticipate the insensate & inane argument that this personnel is needful for the supervision & security of the inmate. I look down my nose to those so poorly informed. I submit that for hundreds of men of my caliber, a chicken wire fence would be sufficient immurement. Why quit & leave these places upon which we have become so dependent? Like the majority of men in institutions do not need barber shop supervision, bathroom supervision, dining room supervision, & et cetera supervision. The kindest sort of a statement is to say that the public is being mulcted. . . . When I was a young person, I could recite the Declaration of Independence in its entirety. One of the indictments against George III states: "He has sent swarms of officers hither to harass our people & eat out their substance." Any future progress toward the millenium in the handling of drunkards, must take into consideration that the Commonwealth is not a branch of Job-Finders Inc. . . .

Frank

The following clipping from the Stonycreek institutional newspaper, was included with Frank's letter of November 6, 1962.

"REFLECTION"
By J.E.F.—Prison Department

You sit. Period.

You watch them—the veterans and the novices—the latter stridently trying to convince themselves: "I'll never be back!" The veterans, with glazed eyes and frozen, deep-etched masks, ignoring the words—so well-remembered as their own, when 20 or 30 or 40 years ago they too had stepped aboard treadmill to oblivion.

Time and blood have a similarity. They both flow—inexorably. To each of us, so little is allotted. And whether we are bled in droplets or in floods, each leeching, just that much, diminishes the total—irretrievably.

So sit and watch them, then. Watch them as the blood-rosiness of eager youth pales to the ash-grey of "los rotos"—the broken ones.

And know—that while you watch—you see—a mirror.

Stonycreek Correctional Institution
November 13, 1962

Dear Bob:

.   .   .   .   .

One of my confreres was so persistent in his claims of being "drained," that I made a special effort to adduce the basis of his belief that he dwelt in a rain-forest with leeches dropping on his body & sapping his life fluid. The more that he explained to me of his innumerable incarcerations, the effortless & remunerative life that he had afforded to other people, connected with his custody, & the great number of people who were collecting a great share of the material rewards of life, without either benefit to him, or the society they served, then his ideas had all the simplicity of a number of algebraic terms connected by a vinculum.

It would seem to me that all this "hemorrhaging" could find a more apt application. As you know, all public institutions go thru the clinical liturgy of a routine blood examination. In my time, I have lived thru the Wasserman, Noguchi, & Kahn tests. Having once entered a poorhouse, a hospital, or prison that would be the end of it. Not so, with the drunks. The men who come here three or four times a year, decade after decade, are tapped as regularly as a Vermont maple. If the actual examination were done here, I don't believe this scheme of things would exist. (Of course, that is my opinion). It is not to be expected that if the examination showed disease, that anyone would cavort about the courtyard hollering "I've got syphilis," but on the other hand, of the thousands of men that I have met here at different times, never have I heard of a case where any of these drunks had syphilis or was treated for it.

Consider the case of the sexagenarians, who, like myself, make up a large part of this jail's population. . . . An act of concupiscence might very well be fatal. The least that one could expect is that we might fall off and break a leg, unless rigged with a safety belt. Leave us to our drinking, & stop meddling with our median basilic & median cephalic veins. I must surely have more scar tissue on my veins, than you would expect to find on a prize-fighter's eyebrows. Write when you have time. How about the oldest boy? (School, etc).

Regards,

F.

Stonycreek Correctional Institution
November 20, 1962

Dear Bob:

Rarely, but once in awhile, a man arrives here for the first time. It is usually a younger person. No drunk in the Commonwealth reaches the age of gray hair, without having been introduced to the State

Farm. When I note a new man, it occasions me to look back twenty-five years & remember my first impressions on arrival. Before this debut, I had had some experience in communal living, had viewed the Southern Cross & was certified a Shell-Back. Nevertheless I was quite unprepared.

At the first meal-time, I sat in the building where the food formation is held, & viewed for the first time hundreds & hundreds of drunks seated on backless benches, back rubbing against back, haunch to haunch, elbow to elbow, & knee to knee. I was mystified by the pockets bulging with newspapers, books, towels & rags (handkerchiefs). I saw for the first time men with eyeglass cases & loose toothbrushes fastened to the front of their coats with safety pins beneath their left shoulder, as if they were wearing the Croix de Guerre. I learned that nothing was to be left in dormitories & that we carried all impedimenta on our person. Some of the more inventive & acquisitive had introduced an innovation called "thief pockets," which consisted of a towel secured by safety-pins in the inside of the loose-fitting gaol coat. Seated on the benches, it was always good policy to pull your saddle-bags close, lest they be sat upon. However, a man was ready at a second's notice to take a bath, or a shave, to read a book, go to bed, go to eat, etc. with no shilly-shallying. When I first read your "Concomitants of Alcoholism," I felt that you had missed a lot on account of not being familiar with this place. To my mind, the State Farm is the "sine qua non" for all who preach on the results of alcoholism.

. . . . .

The adaptability of this glorious animal, (of whom Hamlet said "in action, how like an angel" & "in apprehension, how like a god!"), is such that tho' the community rejects him from its society because he is a drunkard, it has never measured the thought that, in many cases, the drunk has the final say, &, that he will reject the community and accept jail as a way of life.

Regards,

F.

Stonycreek Correctional Institution
December 4, 1962

Dear Bob:

There was slight occasion to flutter when we learned from the newspapers, last week, that it had been recommended that alcoholism be referred from the Dept. of Correction to the Dept. of Public Health. The prison population were aroused, for an instant, from their apathy but quickly returned to their cowlike brousings in the meadows of uneventfulness.

. . . . .

Will James does not reject the possibility of there being some area of human endeavor wherein drunken thinking might be applicable. I allowed myself to imagine being placed on an advisory council made up of drunkards who would serve as a steering committee, & thus avoid the pitfalls into which the Dept. of Correction had staggered. The self-seekers would receive short shrift from our experienced souls. There is such a thing as being "fed up" to the Plumsoll Mark. No one would serve on such a committee who had not made the usual rounds of jails, seen his food pilfered, & his houses of meditation & prayer used as a trysting place for degenerates. However easy it may be to write the history of the Chartres Cathedral or of Yale, no one has ever written the true history of a penal institution. We are the history.

Frank

Stonycreek Correctional Institution
December 18, 1962
December in Jail

Dear Bob:

In the recital of the depressive effects of prison holidays, one must needs repress an inclination toward pathos or bathos. It may be sufficient, on Mother's Day, to recognize that alcoholics do have mothers (that they do not reproduce themselves by mitosis); that on Memorial Day, the grass does grow unattended on the graves of their forbearers, & that the drunkard released from the police lock-up with a big head, on Easter Morning, in New Haven, does hear the carillon on the Green.

And so the alcoholic, on Christmas, (with his sick mind), having long been a spectator to conventional piracy & legalized larceny, grins wryly at the platitude "good will toward men." Anyone who has viewed the compartmentalized behavior of his teetotaling fellow men, which permit them to go to church every Sunday & spend the rest of the week exploiting credulity, ignorance, & weakness, is unlikely to attach religious connotations to the day. I would say that an approximate evaluation of the spirit of Christmas in an institution, is of the nature of an indefinable embarrassment, of that same order as when you look into little children's eyes, & are struck by the thought that, on a percentile basis, they will mature to full-blown sons-a-bitches.

· · · · ·

Frank

Stonycreek Correctional Institution
December 26, 1962

Dear Bob:

Thru most of Charles Dickens' works runs the thread of prison & the criminal. When he was a small boy, he was often brought to visit his father in prison, & it was here he heard the cry, "Pray, remember the poor debtors." He did remember. . . .

Anent your question as to whether the majority of men at Stonycreek are ready for a dynamic approach aimed to resocialize them, I am inclined to the viewpoint that too much has already "happened to them." Most people would hesitate to admit their kinship to Pavlov's dog, but the fact is, when the patellar tendon is tapped with a rubber hammer to the accompaniment of a ringing bell, the foot will fly outward, after a thousand times, to the ringing of a bell & without the hammer. We do remember, despite ourselves. It is probably true that we here at Stonycreek shall continue to react in the same way to the same situations thru long habit. I know you will bear with my feeble echo of psychiatric & psychoanalytic thunder when I point out that repeated events in mens' lives do leave their impress.

Dynamic approach?? Do you believe that society will ever spend the same time, the same energy, & the same money to resocialize men, as it has toward "desocializing" them? Is it reasonable to expect that they should? Could a dynamic approach "balance" the intensity of the opposite measures that have been employed toward making them what they are?

Do you remember the ferocious commentary of Schopenhauer where he compares the intensity of the pain & suffering of an animal that is being devoured, with the intensity of the pleasure & joy of the animal that is doing the devouring?

It seems that I am "loaded" with questions today. Where shall we find enough Abou ben Adhems to administer such programs? Surely, we shall not let street-car conductors administer any part of a "dynamic approach" as we did in our prisons, or a meat & provision dealer as we did in one of our state hospitals. All too often the phrase "dynamic approach" spells out gracious living for somebody. The casual visitor to one of our bughouses (& I have been employed in four of them), who walks into the employees' dining room, & then compares their fare to the slop given the patients, must needs ask the question: "Is the institution created for the employee, or for the patient?" I quit each one of these jobs & went on a drunk, & feel no less a man because I did this. If I could only have "stuck it out" in these situations, I may have convinced myself that my guts were different from the patient's guts, & that their quality of coffee was not good enough for the people who cared for them. In the forthcoming letters I have a number of observations regarding the work attitudes of alcoholics who have become "institutionalized."

Regards,
Frank

8. Return of the Native, 1963-66

The four years from 1963 through 1966 represented a gradual return to Calvinville and "home" for Frank. This process was slow and uneven though calculated. The return and subsequent changes in his life-adaptation pattern were associated with his declining health and coincided with the death of his mother. There were repeated brief visits to Calvinville in both 1963 and 1964 in between commitments to various institutions. In 1965 a marked change in Frank's way of life became apparent, with only fifteen weeks out of the year spent in jail or prison as compared with forty-six weeks for the year before, and the rest of the year spent living in the Congress Hotel in Calvinville. The pattern extended into 1966, interrupted by two periods of incarceration, but culminating in three months of relative self-sufficiency while living in a rooming house. During this period, when Frank was not in jail he was in Calvinville exploring ways of meeting his basic needs in the community, with the help of local welfare resources. He also found a friend in the town postmaster, who developed an interest in him and provided occasional help. Of greatest significance, Frank had begun to avoid, rather than to seek, incarceration.

This new existence for extended periods outside the walls of institutions coincided with some changes in both the length of Frank's letters and their content, which he credited to the fact that they were no longer subject to censorship or institutional limitations on what or how much he wrote. Whatever the reasons, these letters represent a qualitative peak in his correspondence. In his letters he continued a trend, noted in Chapter 7, toward more generalized treatment of issues and more critical analyses of his own life experiences. He continued to deal with such familiar themes as rehabilitation of alcoholics, institutional dependency, the law, and the needs, rights, and status of the individual in society, and he found a new target in the community's welfare system.

A recurrent urgency, measured both in frequency and intensity, surfaces in this set of letters as Frank groped to establish respectability for himself in his own mind and in the eyes of the community. He expressed the wish that "this hoped for 'philosopher' will come to an understanding of himself" and his world (February 27, 1965) as he simultaneously struggled to assume a more active and less passive role in determining his future. In one instance, he actually managed his own defense in a trial (reported in detail in his letters for February 5, June 1, and June 8, 1965).

The very existence of this correspondence, combined with Frank's articulateness, provided him with an important vehicle for self-analysis and reconciliation with himself and the world about him. During this period, there were a few significant events which enabled Frank to express some satisfaction with life, and to look on himself as "no better or worse than most people."

1963

January–March	Stonycreek Correctional Institution
Mid-March	Brief visit to Calvinville
March–April	Westville County Jail and House of Correction
April–July	Stonycreek Correctional Institution
Mid-July	Brief visit to Calvinville
July–September	Westville County Jail
Mid-September	Brief visit to Calvinville
September–December	Stonycreek Correctional Institution

During 1963, although he spent fifty weeks in jail or prison, Frank managed to return to Calvinville three times. On each occasion he was arrested for intoxication and recommitted. He wrote prolifically during the year, thirty-seven letters in all. The letters warrant some division chronologically as they seem to cluster around certain themes.

January–February, 1963. Frank's letters during January discussed the rehabilitation of alcoholics and the perpetual loneliness of someone like himself. He rationalized his existence as a "libertarian" and "conditioned 'non-joiner'" (January 29, 1963). Noting the way he had been conditioned and beaten down to solitude and inadequacy, he rejected the view that "the real cause of alcoholism lies in a man's will" (February 19, 1963), for in someone like himself that will had been emasculated.

Stonycreek Correctional Institution
January 15, 1963

Dear Bob:

I met Curly Michaels for the first time in Philadelphia's tenderloin on Vine St. The next time I met Curly was twenty years later in the Riverpoint County Penitentiary. He had degenerated from a successful criminal, (having tripped just once to a stretch in the Eastern Penitentiary of Pennsylvania) to a chronic drunk. Already, at that time, I had amassed an extensive dossier of drunkenness, myself.

Just then, I had become enceinte with a scheme to solve the alcoholic problem of the city of Riverpoint. It seems that along the river bank, there were a number of shuttered warehouses, made of concrete (fireproof), which had been seized for non-payment of taxes. It was my intention to secure the use of one of these buildings & to solicit about fifty iron army cots, & bed clothing from the Red Cross, Salvation Army or other eleemosynary institution, & to institute a kind of a Farm for Drunkards. The condition for admission was drunkenness (past, present, & future), which I considered to be a new switch from the policy of other agencies. Further, I expected the cooperation of the police, who would dump their human cargo from prowl cars at all hours of the night. It was hoped that this shelter could be administered with a primitive ethic, making the provision that none were to be robbed, man-handled, or otherwise abused. I envisioned cooperation from the police, probation, & parole authorities, & if the place showed itself capable of operating along humane & unselfish lines, a small subsidy from the federations & councils of churches might be expected to set up simple, kitchen, bathing & laundry facilities. I was inclined to a Father Damien heroism, perhaps, because I even expected to put the "bite" on the Police Benevolent Association.

In this way, it would no longer be necessary for a turnkey to carry drinking water to a gang of howling prisoners in the city jail, all night long; the pantomime of justice would be eliminated; & the expense of confinement in the county jail would be reduced to nil.

I explained the whole idea to Curly & at much greater length than

I have outlined the plan to you. He was most patient & gave me a full hearing. I was most sincere in my belief that drunks would go to a place voluntarily, if they knew that they would be accepted, without phoney evangelism, insincere promises, etc.

Regards,
Frank

Stonycreek Correctional Institution
January 22, 1963

Dear Bob:

Those, who assault the fortress of status quo & the redoubts of self-interest, must needs be well-armed. Too often I find myself in the condition of a Roman legionary who has just sacked a winery. Out of the shambles I pass to you my blunted pilum. Are you in the mood for statistics?

Whenever a proponent of a plan to care for the casualties of the excessive use of alcohol, by other means than jail, has stated his case, his opponent will smirk comfortably with a triumphant gleam in his eye & say, "Where are you going to get the money?" Although it may savor of lese-majesty & presumptiveness, permit this Stonycreek stew-bum, for the nonce, to supply the answer.

In about 1792, the federal government originated the liquor tax to pay for wars, starting with the payment of the debt of the Revolutionary fracas. Every school-boy knows that Robert Morris handled the fiduciary affairs of the embattled colonists, but how many people are aware that the booze-hounds paid for the war?

There are 17 states in this country who are in the retail liquor business (state stores). The *federal* taxes on liquor & malt beverages average five times the cost of the production of that liquor & malt beverage. In this state alone, the liquor industry paid twenty-eight million dollars in taxes in the last fiscal year. The figures are culled from a newspaper report of proposed legislation to permit the liquor dealers to be compensated for the collection of taxes, which in the ultimate are paid by the boozer. The dealers stress their services as collection agencies for the state. If this proposed 2% compensation rate is passed thru the legislature, $565,000 will be diverted from the state treasury.

Where shall we get the money for alcoholic programs, indeed! Little does the liquor industry, the state & federal governments know, that I cast covetous eyes at their capital gains from this nefarious trade.

Unlike cerebral palsy, polio, diabetes, etc. which receive federal

ESCAPE FROM CUSTODY

subsidy, alcoholism is unique in that it is the only disease which could support itself. The man who pays gasoline taxes would hollar like hell if he did not have good highways. But as for liquor taxes, the alcoholic claimants of a piddling part of this revenue are only those who inhabit our bug-houses & jails, where in some cases staff salaries absorb 2/3 of the costs of operating these institutions (thus: one county in this state).

I apprehend that you are going to point out to me that the liquor industry have apportioned financial grants to the study of alcoholism. I'll bet the amounts they have donated are less proportionately than the shiney new dimes handed out by Rockefeller from his estimated fortune, at retirement, of one billion dollars.

The man who pays municipal taxes expects good schools for his children, police & fire protection, etc. By these standards the alcoholics are the most exploited, mulcted, & cheated persons on the face of the earth. Dear Bob, apply the squeeze to these Colossi of gainfulness. The drunks passing thru Stonycreek have left more bloody footprints on the snow in the skid-row streets than did Washington's troops at Valley Forge. You see, the cardboard slips away from that hole in the bottom of our shoes.

Regards,
Frank

Stonycreek Correctional Institution
January 29, 1963

Dear Bob:

It is unfashionable now-a-days to attack A.A., but stand back while this little David takes a side-swipe at Goliath.

Did it ever occur to you that there are such people: who are congenital or conditioned "non-joiners"? Like all Gaul, the ranks of alcoholics are divided into three parts (the good, bad, & indifferent), & to my mind, the best of the breed are the libertarians. I use the term to designate he who is not strait-jacketed by a profession, politics, or religion. He lacks the sodality of party, sect, or organization, since there never can be organized libertarians, but he is never to be found in the ranks of Black Shirts, Brown Shirts, lynch-mobs, & other "group-activities." Do you know that I would never waste sympathy on the boy who works his way thru college & is "deprived of the experience" of belonging to a Greek letter fraternity? Perhaps he might develop strength thru loneliness like George Bernard Shaw's "St. Joan."

Not for myself, but for these hundreds of others is there no hope beyond this bolus (horse-pill), Alcoholic Anonymous? or must we continue this sort of forced payment for the behavior pattern which was set for me & others, & made our views & activities inevitable? . . . I forgot to tell you of another attribute of the libertarian: He is often in jail.

Sincerely,
Frank

Stonycreek Correctional Institution
February 12, 1963

Dear Bob:

. . . . .

You have noted in your letter that it is eighteen years ago that we started this study. It has been a tremendous satisfaction to me that you have suffered, vicariously, my aches & pains. It is fashionable to think of alcoholism in terms of disintegration & deterioration, but do you know that one can actually develop an insouciance & confidence? When I consider the twenty years that I have spent in different kinds of jails, I am led to believe that, never again, can anyone place me in a narrower cell than which I have already been confined; feed me coarser or lesser food than has already been my lot; or cause me to be lonelier than I have always been.

Surprisingly, I have even caused a few judges, policemen, & jail guards to believe that I had deserved a better fate.

Ironically—
Frank

Stonycreek Correctional Institution
February 26, 1963

Dear Bob:

I will be released from here March 10. During the past five months, I have written to you nearly every week. Assuming the role of the drunkard's Boswell, I have derived all the benefits of the couch & of the confessional. Too many fools have given a complaisant account of their adventures & made their old age a laughing stock instead of a tranquil prelude to deserved oblivion. It must have seemed to you, at times, that I suffered a constipation of ideas & a diarrhea of words. I have striven for objectivity & achieved a melange. There is a good reason for this.

The liberal boasts in being able to see two sides of a question, but after twenty years of jail coupled with alcoholism, I have become afflicted with the capacity to see many sides of the questions which have been under discussion. Along the way I have lost my convictions & it is difficult for me to be a partisan of any principle.

At first sight, it appears a miserable plight not to "believe" in something or to "stand" for something, but I call your attention to the fact that the most staid & hallowed institutions in all ages have performed some remarkable somersaults & tergiversations (specifically, religion & politics). For the moment, review my long experience at the hands of the "law." It is of semantical interest that the law is one thing, & justice is another. I am sure that in the great multitude of laws, conventions, & social codes, there is always to be found, by the earnest seeker, some law that is the antidote to some other law. Why prate of "trespass" & "property rights" to a drunkard who flops in somebody else's car in a parking lot at night to keep from freezing to death? The itinerant boozehound becomes a veritable Blackstone of lex naturae.

Of course I apprehend that such reasoning will probably lead to my sitting cross-legged in some county jail & contemplating my navel (Yoga), but that is the way the cookie crumbles. On the other hand, it has been pointed out to me that I have another "choice." Almost any bright & enterprising social worker or member of A.A. would suggest that I get a job as plongeur (French, for dish-washer). They have somehow confused the idea of a professional with that of washing dishes in their own homes. At different times, I had two of these "dream jobs"—once in the Catskills & once on the boardwalk of Atlantic City. In the enumeration of the concomitants of the excessive use of alcohol, it was an oversight that caused me to overlook the fact that dishwashing is a tumorous excrescence on the derriere of alcoholism.

Nay, my most astute confidante, my late jail experience in a congregate system has absolutely conditioned me to one of two environments. Anybody who has been compelled to live for long under a gang system where the drone hangs on to the coat-tail of the worker, or slept for a long time in a dormitory listening to forty odd snorings, moanings, sighings & whimperings, (what an opportunity for a Freudian scholar), thru the long still watches, is fitted only to be a light-housekeeper on a rocky shoal, twenty miles off-shore, or for the quietude of a monastic cell in a county jail where men are locked up twenty-two hours a day without the opportunity to obtrude upon each other. Like Garbo, I wish to be alone, & like Byron's "Prisoner of Chillon," I would regain my freedom with a sigh (which I would shortly replace with hiccoughs). I have just received yours, (letter & enclosures), of the 21st. Will write once more before I am delivered out of Egypt.

Frank

Stonycreek Correctional Institution
February 19, 1963

Dear Bob:

. . . . .

I believe that among the best books I have ever read, is Dr. Hans Zinssner's Rats, Lice & History. He tells that the typhus plague was guarded against in Russian villages by yoking three widows to a plow & drawing a furrow around the whole community. (Ah, faith!).

This reminiscence was occasioned by looking at the Prison bulletin-board yesterday & finding thereon affixed, the following which I have copied verbatim. You will thus note that I am being exposed to the best minds:

Real Cause of Alcoholism

Dick Bascom, writing in the Temperance News, said, "Those who say that alcoholism is a disease confuse the effects of alcoholism with its causes. Of course the heavy drinker is sick. The point is however, the alcoholic does not drink because he is sick, he is sick because he drinks."

Mr. Bascom adds, "The disease theory of alcoholism is not sufficient, because man is morally responsible for his own deeds. No one can take a drink without his own permission. The real cause of alcoholism lies in a man's will."

Fulminating—
Frank

March–September, 1963. The next series of letters from Frank dealt principally with alcoholism and the law, and with the alcoholic as a criminal (compared to "the conventional non-drinker who raises an ordinary sort of hell in his home" [May 21, 1963]). These observations were related to Frank's ventures out of custodial care and trips back to Calvinville, where he encountered arrest, trial, jail, and the recurrent feeling that as an individual he did not count. "The law does not have time for little things" (May 14, 1963).

Frank also responded to an article I shared with him on the holistic approach to patient diagnosis and treatment. He projected this to mean that an individual alcoholic should be looked at and treated for the entire range of problems he suffers from, rather than being dumped into a class of incurables, as Frank felt he had been. He struck a note of optimism in response to another paper on the development of a social program in an alcoholic clinic in which the author recognized feelings that Frank had written about for years. He felt some satisfaction in this small but encouraging recognition by a professional of the "futility and insignificance of unrewarding sobriety" (June 26, 1963).

> Stonycreek Correctional Institution
> May 3, 1963

Dear Bob:

As I have remarked before, all the moral & physical forces of society are arrayed against the prisoner at the bar. The forces are symbolized by the national & state flags hanging over the justice in his black robe. Surrounded as he is by the hundreds of law tomes ranging the walls, the uniformed police & court officers with their sidearms, there is good reason for mere mortal to believe that he is vicarious Almighty sitting in the judgment of sin. To counter the brashness or kind of animal courage, the prisoner has been deprived of his belt (suicide), & comb. It is impossible to appear defiant while holding up the trousers with both hands, & having hair hang down over the eyes.

To begin with, the prisoner's name is called. The new-comer in the docket of the metropolitan court is always surprised, when he stands up to hear a clear ringing voice of a police officer softly shout, "That is the man, your honor."

This voice comes from the identifying officer. Now the strange thing about this procedure is the fact that the voice & the identifying officer are the same for all cases of drunkenness. These prisoners have been transferred from a half-a-dozen different police stations to the court building. In fact, the identifying officer has no recollection of ever seeing any of these men before in his life.

> Frank

> Stonycreek Correctional Institution
> May 7, 1963

Dear Bob:

I was released from here March 10 after serving five & one-half months. The present policy here, is to release the first offender (first commitment here), after 60 days.

In my own case, I preferred to stay because I had no clothing, no job, etc. & because of an increasing institutional dependency. With regard to the present sentence, I was sentenced on April 12 & could probably effect my release at the expiration of 75 days, if I could think of a decent reason to be "out there."

Regarding my last discharge & the interim period to my present sentence, I am afraid that my sins are monotonously repetitive & prosaic. The eels go back to the Sargasso, & the seals go back to the Pribiloffs, to breed. Inasmuch as I am too old to do any breeding, it would take a flight of imagination to figure why I go back to Calvinville. Some inkling might be supplied by the fact that while I was altogether absent from Calvinville for a period of ten years, in the military service, my grandfather mailed me, daily, the town newspaper. These newspapers were hand-addressed by him. Surely it was a labor of love, & he must have expected me to return to an honorable place in the community. I imagine that the "skull jockeys" could connect this last fact with my returning to Calvinville. . . . I slept in a hotel *one* night —the hostel yclept "Congress House" (Lord Edward Congress). Don't let the name misguide you. It is a rickety fire trap that would be outlawed in a large city. Torn between the desires for strong-drink & a warm place to sleep, I settled for the strong drink, & after two nights of sleeping in jacked-up cars along the wharf, I was arrested while staggering up Morton St. & minding my own business. This particular orgy was a lonesome foray during which I met no one that I knew or could remember. The policemen are the only ones who remember me. On the last day before arrest, I went up to the Emporium where my cousin Donald (grand-uncle branch), is the Vice President, & tried to "borrow" a dollar from him. Rejected. Gad, it must be nice to be respectable.

More anon—
Frank

Stonycreek Correctional Institution
May 14, 1963

Dear Bob:

Continuing my last letter, it passeth for current that the "drunk" does not know & can not remember what is happening to him. Let us see if this is so.

As stated in my last letter, I was arrested four days after my release from here on March 10. I was arraigned before the Hon. Isaac Chertok at the district court at Calvinville. I was brought from the cell-room about fifteen minutes before court was opened. I was the only one behind the prisoners' railing. The other malefactors (traffic cases) were roaming the hallways. In the silence of the empty courtroom, I had the time to contemplate the judge's dais, the witness docket, the counsel's railed cubicle, & the other expensive appurtenances that would dignify the process of sending me to jail.

I was dressed in a Marine overcoat (jail issue), which my physical self was damn glad to have. It is worth observing, however, the practice after every war, of dressing paupers, prisoners & lunatics in articles of military uniform. I noted this practice at Davenport, Wardhill, & Northway. It is doubtful whether this practice enhances the public's image of the honorable Profession of Arms.

In large cities, the trial for drunkenness is of the most perfunctory order. I can't remember the Latin aphorism to the effect that "the law does not have time for little things." Matters are much more deliberate in small cities. . . . The judge before whom I appeared is noted for the fact, that after all testimony is presented, his opinions are more lengthy than the whole of the trial, & have all the "weightiness" or ponderosity of Cardozo or O. W. Holmes.

Mine was the first case called. The charge is read by the clerk of the court; to which I plead guilty. Then the witness, (arresting officer) is called, who testified as follows:

"My name is Paul Marks. I am a police officer of the city of Calvinville. He had the strong odor of alcohol on his breath. The prisoner was very cooperative & gave me no trouble at all."

(This last statement was intended to be extenuating). If I was cooperative & not giving anybody any trouble, then why in hell pick me up?

Then the judge said to me: "Do you have anything to say." (There are two judges in the city & I find that they are interested in my blithe comments).

Now the actual court-room scene is much different than the television or movie counterpart. The accused had better damn sight be terse & (to use your favorite word), meaningful. As the bard has said: Each man in his time plays many parts, & I had my statement ready. The genuine old lag does not say: "Your Honor—." (Such salutation would show a habituality of court-room appearances).

I said: "Sir, I have completed twenty years of confinement for drunkenness." (The judge [de sotto] tragic!) I continued: "I have served twenty years confinement for drunkenness alone" (The judge [de sotto] pitiful!). Then I stood silent & (I hope) accusing.

The judge said: "This man is a human being. I must bear my share, along with my colleagues, for what has happened in this man's life. How long must we "put off" doing that which we must eventually do? I ask myself that question today"—

In the next letter I will conclude with this one instance of dealing with alcoholism at community level.

Frank

Stonycreek Correctional Institution
May 21, 1963

Dear Bob:

Continuing my last letter concerning the Public Intervention at Community Level in Cases of Alcoholism, we left the judge in the midst of commentary & opinionating. The trial continues:

Judge: "This man has violated the social codes & conventions & the public expects something to be done."

(In the meantime, I am still in the prisoners' docket, standing. A momentary pause in the judge's oral deliberations is my cue to render my own part of the libretto).

Moore: "As far as jail is concerned, I consider myself fairly well 'paid up.'" (Referring to the twenty years I have spent in jail for drunkenness).

Judge: "That is right. That is right." (continuing): "How much money do you have?"

Moore: "One dollar & seventy-two cents. I have no wish to present to the court a dilemma. If I am released, I shall leave town & walk out on the nearest highway." (Judge glances out the window. This March the Fifteenth is a somber, gray day; the dampness of the harbor permeates to the bones & the snow is falling as if the angels were furiously plucking geese in Heaven). Judge: "This is no kind of weather for anyone to be out on a highway."

(At this point, the City Marshal bobs up like a yo-yo. Calvinville does not have a Chief of Police; the job is delegated to a City Marshal).

City Marshal: "Moorey has been out in weather worse than this, your Honor."

Judge: "I don't doubt it, I don't doubt it."

Then the judge & the city marshal go into a dialogue, the result of which, it is decided that I shall be sentenced to Westville jail, & that during my incarceration the weather shall become more clement to the shorn sheep.

There is a verbatim account of Public Intervention & is probably parallel to the disposal of a hundred drunks on any given day. The essayist Emerson wrote: "Simplify! Simplify!" Our courts say: "Expediency! Expendiency!"

Calvinville is a small town, no worse or better than others, & everybody knows each other's business. Sitting behind the prisoners' railing in that court-room, many times I have ruminated about the local cases of adulterous husbands & unfaithful wives, bastardy, & unspeakable habits or unnatural vices. Never have I known these people to be before the bar of justice. The conventional non-drinker who raises an ordinary sort of hell in his home, & brings daily misery to wife & children, is never brought into court. The sober people who frequent crowded Washington St. in Boston during noon hour or who pile into the subway cars in New York City, transcend whatever unpleasantness I may occasion thru drunkenness.

Are these the social conventions & codes that I have affronted, & are these the persons who are crying for my scalp?

Frank

Stonycreek Correctional Institution
May 28, 1963

Dear Bob:

Received yours of the 16th with enclosures, for which, many thanks. There are so many things to write about, such as: Jurisprudence & its Sequelae in Cases of Alcoholism, answering your queries regarding my mother's status, your 'lecture' on interest & collateral, & a commentary of your latest papers in the Annals of the American Academy of Political & Social Science.[1] I shall deal with these subjects in a manner suggested by a lusty story concerning a particular Hollywood actress. She was 'on location' for the 'shooting' of a 'Western.' During the rest period, she stretched out on her back & fell asleep. A cow ambled over & stood astride her. The first thing she saw, when she awoke, were the udders of this Holstein. It is reputed that she yawned sleepily & said, "One at a time, boys. One at a time."

1. "Medicine and Society," Vol. 346, March, 1963.

In reference to the first paper: "Health, Society, & Social Science": I read with interest the emphasis upon the holistic approach to medical science & comprehensive health care. How long, oh, how long, Lord, before the holistic approach shall descend, penetrate, & permeate to persons of my social level? It has been a long time since the great Jan Smuts conceived of dealing with the whole organism rather than one part of it, but would you believe that ninety-five per cent of the employees in this progressive & modern institution (by the usual standards), consider that they are dealing with alcoholism, per se, without the least consideration of the variable nature of the subjects of their ministrations? Well, it is so. Genealogical factors, heredity, childhood training, tropism, occupational factors, lack of education, the aggregate of good & bad experience, economic factors—all of these mean nothing to people if they believe they are just dealing with alcoholism. I could go on ranting at great length, as could any person who has been summarily reduced to the lowest common denominator.

Frank

Stonycreek Correctional Institution
June 26, 1963

Dear Bob:

Received your letter of June 17th & enclosures, for which many thanks.

I wish to commend the author of the paper regarding the Development of a Social Program in an Alcoholism Clinic. There are many places beside a clinic to consider her statement that "during the pleasureable drinking days of alcoholics, they experience adventure as well as feelings of purposefulness & worthwhileness, in comparison to the futility & insignificance of unrewarding sobriety."

I suppose this shoddy type of sobriety is best exemplified by an A.A. group which sends an itinerant alcoholic to the Salvation Army to bale paper at the wages of a dollar a week with the admonition that "Easy does it . . ." This author must be a remarkable woman. Why couldn't I have met someone like her. I have been assured by voluminous writings that it was impossible for a woman not to personalize & relate everything to herself. Note that she also writes "alcoholics are sophisticated in that they have had years of life experience involving dramatic adventure & it cannot be expected of them that they will easily find purpose or pleasure in parlor games or crafts."

In Wardhill, I staged a one man revolt against this sort of thing. I

can be so unselfish to say that hundreds of poor devils in our state &
veterans hospitals are sand papering blocks of wood, cutting out paper
rabbits, & painting Easter lillies because of deathly fear that they
will never get out unless they "cooperate." A lady patient who kept
the records down there & with whom I dined, informed me confi-
dentially that the notation of "no progress" was marked weekly on
my index card. To paraphrase Winston Churchill, this was my finest
hour & to my mind, my most successful "failure."

Vincent VanGogh never sold a painting in his lifetime & I suppose
that never in mine shall I sell the idea that practically every institution
is fairly packed with "ham and eggers" with the pretensions of Clara
Barton & Nightingale.

Regards,
Frank

Stonycreek Correctional Institution
July 2, 1963

Dear Bob:

On the advent of my departure from this place of wrath & tears, it
is fitting that I should make some declaration of intentions. Such is not
to be. I am fairly overcome with what is known in jail circles as "discharge panic."

I intend going back to Calvinville. I have some sort of an idea, lying
down deep like a carp in muddy pond, that if I reiterate & persist in
presenting the same problem to the town fathers, I may be the means
of preventing another generation of drunks having to go thru the same
process. In the large city courts, the individual is lost in the shuffle &
shuttled off to jail like the stock cars that ply between beef country
& Chicago. The local authorities have given up hope that an act of
God or passing truck will solve the situation. Will write from river-
bank.

Frank

Westville Jail & House of Correction
July 19, 1963

Dear Bob:

After a three weeks interval we resume the meeting of the minds.
Once again I am in the toils of the law—that law that is all of one piece

in its imposed waitings, its slow evolutions of due process, and its calm impersonality of attitude. I had not been back in Calvinville two hours when, in the course of scouting the waterfront saloons, I encountered one of the town drunks of my own epoch, sitting at a table bewhiskered, dirty, bleeding from the rump thru his trousers & with legs in the pre-elephantiasis stage. After buying him two drinks, & with his permission, I went to the City Marshal, who summoned an ambulance, removed the drunk to the local hospital & the next day he was transferred to the Veterans Hospital where he was reported in bad condition.

I am not sure in my own mind, what in hell I was trying to prove, & mayhap others may be better able to judge. It may have been a quixotic challenge to the public conscience, a desire that under the same circumstances, I might be accorded the same consideration, or what seems more likely, a compensatory quirk in extenuation of the ensuing drunk. Thales said, "Know thyself," but I doubt that anyone does.

Nevertheless, fifteen hours later, I am arrested & brought before the local court. I pointed out, at that session, that whereas I had held on to the freezing railings of box cars during a number of winters, I wished to be at liberty during this clement weather. Hence I was given a suspended sentence of thirty days. Four days later, I was again arraigned before a different judge & sentenced to thirty days again, in addition to the thirty that had been suspended. Therefore, I shall be released about the middle of September to enjoy for a few days, I hope, the chemical alteration of foliage.

There is only one scientific observation in all of the above & so far as I know, it is being neglected in all the high-sounding literature of alcoholism. Which reminds me of that fragment of Kipling: (1) "Oh what the classic bent," (2) "And what the cultured word," (3) "Against the unvarnished incident," (4) "That actually occurred." This last judge questioned: "What are we going to do with this derelict? He will be brought right back when his sentence is completed." In view of the fact that I will be released from here without a job, without clothing, & altogether without money, I am led to question what else is expected of me.

This is about the only jail I have ever been in where sufficient tobacco, cigarette papers & matches are supplied gratis. I ascribe this to the fact that most prisoners are juvenile & are cared for by their relatives. I could not possibly express how much more I sympathize with the relatives than with the brats.

Regards.

Frank

October–December, 1963. Letters from Frank during October and November were appraisals of his and others' long experience with "communal life" in various institutions and the concomitants of institutionalization; e.g., "a strange relief in just being locked up again" (October 25, 1963); the "inexorable lowering of the critical and esthetic standards" (November 1, 1963); the social and moral leveling of inmates to the lowest common denominator, desocialization, spiritual emasculation and the destruction of individuality by institutionalization—all at a very high price to the taxpayer.

Frank turned to thoughts of Christmas by decrying what he saw as the insincerity, superficiality, and historically often violent bigotry of Christians at any season of the year.

Stonycreek Correctional Institution
October 25, 1963

Dear Bob:

I am inclined to comment on the book review which you sent to me of "The Unknown Citizen."

Tony Parker's yarn of "Charlie Smith"[2] who has served 26 years in jail, or roughly twice as much as a murderer, a dangerous traitor, or even a big time crook, has many a counterpart here at Stonycreek, & they, like Charles Smith, find a strange relief in just being locked up again. In Charlie's case, no matter how condign the punishment awarded he seems incapable of responding to it & mending his way. Please note that the word "condign" is usually misapplied. The dictionary meaning is "merited" & not "severe" as usually applied.

Who shall say that these men, now in their sixties, received a condign punishment, if in their thirties they were sent to jail so many times for being drunk that jail itself became a way of life? In Charlie's case a "Mr. Carter" took an interest & enlisted the help of counsel & the Appeal Court conditionally released him. These men have no such person

2. Frank's reference is to Tony Parker, *The Unknown Citizen* (London: Hutchinson and Co., 1963).

as "Mr. Carter" & I don't think I am going "out on a limb" too far
when I say they would not be interested in a "Mr. Carter's" efforts
toward de-jailing them. Whatever other virtues jail has inculcated, it
has taught them resignation—& not a dumb, unseeing resignation, but
of a conscious wide-eyed & awake sobriety. Perhaps I eulogize the
drunkards here who read the daily papers & grimace at the never
ending revelations of legal and illegal thievery in our political community.

The danger in Mr. Parker's book lies in that part where the question
arises "Is Charlie better off inside?" There will be too many convenient,
"yeas." I write convenient & give you a hint of a startling book which
will someday be written. Has anyone yet written of the tendency toward a monolithic structure of our state hospitals, jails, reformatories,
poor houses, with multiple staffs, pay increases, pensions, etc.?? The
parking space outside of any of our public institutions looks very much
like Henry Ford's Willow Run. A comparison of a patient's menu with
that of the employees gives rise to the question as whether the institution exists for the employee or the patient. The next time you go into
an institution of any kind, note the competing posters of different employee unions, & the absence of mention of inmate affairs.

Regards,
Frank

Stonycreek Correctional Institution
November 1, 1963

Dear Bob:

I received your letter and money for tobacco. My tobacco funds
were exhausted and I had watched the mailman with the same expec-
tancy of a nephew at the bedside of a dying and wealthy aunt. No
spoofing. I am grateful.

You asked whether I ever thought of comparing life at Stonycreek
with life in the Crystal Palace.[3] . . .

Rather than a crystal palace, I have used the fish-bowl metaphor in
my own case. I have lived the communal life over so long a period that
a transport to privacy, isolation, or a dependency on one's own self,
seems as remote to me as Paradise itself. You are most certainly right
in linking the more subtle forms of social organizations such as univer-

3. This reference is to Alan Harrington, *Life in the Crystal Palace* (New York:
Alfred A. Knopf, 1959).

sities and large factories with institutional dependency. (I.B.M. and G.E.??)

We have it from no less an authority than that archetype of all cracker-barrel philosophers (Ben Franklin), that a man's happiness or unhappiness is altogether dependent upon whether he forms the habit of always looking upon the bright and pleasant aspects of his circumstance or whether he is always prone to see the dark and miserable side. For instance, if we consider jail institutions and their impact on socialization and the fulfillment of life's needs, there is more than one viewpoint. If I were at the administrative or executive end of a correctional institution, I could probably produce a hundred pleasant reasons for promoting an institutional dependency. On the other hand, if I were a moronic inmate I could adduce a hundred kinds of data to prove that institutional dependency is itself, an end product which is worse than the social crimes for which he, the moron, has committed. Since I do not come under either category (I hope), I merely wind up as a lousy casuist, neither at peace with the administration or the inmates.

Tony Parker's "Mr. Carter" took an interest in "Charlie Smith," the *Unknown Citizen.* If you ever take an interest in a "Charlie Smith," for the love of all that is holy and sacred, don't ever invite him into your home. Even if he is sober, he will scorch your furniture with laid down cigarettes; he will splash water three feet high on the walls of your washroom; he will micturate on the floor beneath the urinal; and leave his excreta on the tops of a flush bowl. Despite these results of long confinement and inexorable lowering of the critical and esthetic standards, he will, all the time try to convince you that there isn't a damn thing wrong with him except that he takes too much to drink. . . . Believe me, there are other than economic concomitants of institutional dependency.

Regards,
Frank

Stonycreek Correctional Institution
November 8, 1963

Dear Bob:

I can remember one time when I was picked up for hitch-hiking down in Connecticut. On the way to jail this particular state cop said to me: "I used to be sorry for you fellows, but then I got smart. You guys have all the best of it and no responsibilities. You throw up your jobs whenever you like and take no crap from anybody. You travel wherever you like, and the worst thing that can happen to you is being arrested; and in that event you are fed and given a place to sleep."

You see that this fellow had all his own answers. In fact, it is a lousy life. If you are on the bum, you are always at the mercy of the weather, standing half a chance of getting either frozen to death or sunstroke on a clear deserted patch of highway halfway to nowhere, at the mercy of car drivers who you know have seen you and pretend not to; and if you don't have any money you spend most of your time being hungry and lightheaded which means you can't even enjoy the sights and the scenery and you have always to be on the watch for policemen who will pick you up for vagrancy and play games with you at the station-house if they happen to be bored.

Do you know that it is going to be the same way when we shall read the various treatises dealing with Institutional Dependency? It seems to me the most respected professor would whack the living daylights out of the phoney scholars in his department and eventually establish himself in an isolated and independent tree-top somewhere in the academic grove.

And now that I have the professors up their various trees, is this a vantage point to view the significance of Institutional Dependency? Are they not going to err in the sense that the aforementioned cop erred? Whence will come the detailed and intimate knowledge of institutions and their impact on socialization and the return of an inmate to a life outside of an institution?

D. H. Lawrence used to say that all of us are starved not so much of sex but of the societal instinct. He was talking about people on the outside of jails; how would he have talked of people in jails?

I would like to quote one of your favorite words, "gainfulness" in the sense that labor and effort should offer reward. Anyone who spends long periods of life in institutions faces the fact that someone rises betimes to cook his breakfast, someone else washes the dishes, someone else cuts his hair, someone else washes his clothes, and in short, he receives many services which are needful and mandatory. Now if someone else peels his potatoes, it behooves the inmate to perform some reciprocal service in the institution. Actually the man is living in a commune and should feel that he is upholding the dignity of labor and work and doing his share. Of such is the ideal inmate from an administrative viewpoint.

But the whole thing goes back to Garden of Eden, and man is "sentenced" to labor in the sense that it is punishment, and it certainly is not gainful or profitable in a money sense. The sine qua non in the consideration of institutional dependency is the realization that some men will work in jail and will not work outside.

More anon
Frank

Stonycreek
November 15, 1963

Dear Bob:

It seems to me that the social scientist, or the psychiatrist or the penologist who deals with the alcoholic must, inevitably, fall into one of the two errors. He might "intellectualize" which is the first mistake or he would reach a conclusion which is best illustrated by the following story, which I like to believe is true.

A gang of Viennese psychiatrists are discussing the case history of a particular patient and the dialogue is limited to psychoanalytical terms. At the end of the discussion, the great Sigmund Freud states: "When all is said & done we must remember that Herr So & So is a sonofabitch." (End of story).

Writing from a general experience of having lived in the army & navy, prison & jails, religious colonies & with gypsies, I have found the inebriate or the drunkard or the alcoholic (or whatever other euphemistic term) to be unclassifiable. It may be of interest for you to learn that the culprit himself, in the jail milieu, also classifies himself under an all embracing category in much the same manner as the above named professionals.

I don't think that I have ever been in a single jail yet (& you know I have been in a few) without listening to some prisoner saying of another: "He is a prisoner just the same as I am" or "He is no better than anyone else."

This is a concomitant of institutionalization and truly the philosophy of a bum who hopes to find, like water its own level in jail. This is what he hopes, what he generally believes & I'll admit that as far as clothes, food & lodging are concerned, he has a basis for that belief. I could just as well agree with a feeble-minded prostitute mother who says to her mongoloid son: "You are just as good as the other children."

After living with hundreds of drunks, in various kinds of jails, eating with them, working with them, sleeping in dormitories or in cells next to them, exposed to them day after day & month after month, I can assure you that all prisoners are not the "same" & that some are "better" than others. If we are blabbing & deserve no less than stabbing (which Sir Walter versifies of those who speak the truth) we might as well face the fact, in the consideration of institutionalization, that some inmates are a hell of a lot better than others. There are the workers & there are the drones. There are the clean & there are the filthy. There are those who must wake the consciousness of their guardians to the fact that they are worthy of a better fate, & those for whom an ordinary jail is too nice a place. If this is so, & I believe it is, then how do you explain the leveling process & the reduction to the lowest common denominator in all our jails, bug-houses & schools? I have reached the age where celibacy is a joke & I have always placed money in the proper perspective (by throwing it away), but this question "bugs" me "man."

Frank

Stonycreek Correctional Institution
November 22, 1963

Dear Bob:

Continuing to ride the nag institutions & their impact on socialization & the fulfillment of life's needs:

There is a widespread belief that if Adam had preserved his obedience to the Creator, he would have lived forever in a state of virgin purity, & that some harmless mode of vegetation might have peopled paradise with a race of innocent & immortal beings. It is consistent with the same principles to consider a state of celibacy as the nearest approach to the Divine perfection. With the exception of a couple of trashy magazines, I have never heard or read of any worthwhile exposition of the enforced celibacy of inmates in institutions. Is this subject tabu or verboten when we speak of socialization & the fulfillment of life's needs? If I were the son of a farmer, & had never been in jail, & had observed the behavior of a herd of cows which were long deprived of a bull, I might reach some general erroneous conclusion in regard to persons immured in various types of institutions. It is my belief that most people having to do with the perennially confined, indulge in poking their head under the sands to avoid the sirocco of Sex. Is it not paradoxical that the saint & the convict endure the same regimen of chastity? I can see nothing incongruous in the case of a man who had completed a long servitude in some jail or asylum, being hailed as a holy man. In the monastic cell, the loss of sensual pleasure is supposed to be supplied & compensated in spiritual pride.

In a way of speaking, the jailbirds long caged, do receive a kind of accolade from their fellows. For instance, I could never refuse to financially help out some bum that I met outside on the streets, whom I had served a jail sentence with, even if I had hated his guts every minute that I was in jail with him. The rationalization goes something like this, "He was one of us."

It may be supposed that the offender who is convicted of a misdemeanor would suffer no ill effects of celibacy over the short period indicated by the type of his crime. But if we recognize that there are thousands who actually serve more time (in the aggregate) for a misdemeanor than do our most desperate criminals, then we must recognize the effect on socialization. Certainly the out-going jail product is not to be regarded as some sort of a priest of the lower orders, or is it believed that during his periodical releases from confinement that he might backlog his libido? The Persian, Hafiz, assures us that courtship does improve the manners & carriage. You would have to live a short time with these men to apprehend the effect on manners & carriage. Some isolated article may lead you to believe that all these men practice the sin of onan, or homosexuality, or find a form of sublimation, when actually, they merely lapse to a eunochoid state.

Frank

Stonycreek Correctional Institution
November 29, 1963

Dear Bob:

I received your letter of November 18 & enclosure, for which many thanks. It might seem that I have been receiving an appanage from you, over such a length of time, that I may not seem to appreciate it. However, the men who arrive back here every day with no tobacco & no cigarette papers & nothing except a faceful of whiskers, is a constant reminder of how fortunate that I am. I note that on the left side of your envelope & after your address is the number 40506. You too???!!

It is fashionable to think of the pariahs & the "lesser breed without law" as a different entity from the rest of mankind. There are the rare occasions when the man on the streets suffers by comparison or is wanting. A case in point is the past weekend in a time of national catastrophe.[4]

Last week all the eyes in the institution were fixed on the two televisions. Just the same as my infrequent trips to the zoo in different cities, I find the reactions of men, women & children of more interest than the spectacle itself. It is surprising that among the sneerers & jeerers, the misfits & failures, the maladroit & inept, that I heard not one disparaging remark in memory of the leader of a social & economic system of which they are the rejected & unwanted, on the lowest steps of the ladder. During the memorial service on Sunday & later at screencast of the ceremonies at Arlington on Monday, the whole prison population watched the homage in the Capitol rotunda, the cortege, the widow and her children. Never before in the memory of a man did all these jaws quit flapping, & no event of the future will ever accord such silence. And yet to the "scientific eye," these men are supposed to be emotionally flattened & blunted.

The spoken reactions were pathetic. One man said, "With people like us, it probably won't make much difference who is president." And another, "He was doing so much for the unfortunate, I was hoping he might finally get down to us."

On the other hand, I give you the man on the street. While even jailbirds were mourning (in their own fashion), the Mr. John Q. Public was watching a prolate spheroid being kicked around. One spectacle drew 60,000 customers. Horseracing & hockey & basketball have well deserved a reservation to the financial & business pages of our future newspapers. If anyone ever doubted the ascendency of the dollar over the soul, here was the answer. Professional sports have stigmatized their name, the players & their customers. It will take more than their usual crumb to charity, to the disabled, to the poor, to offset the harm they have done to themselves.

To get back to our multons, how can you expect support & backing for your own projects in view of these slobs?

Frank

Stonycreek Correctional Institution
December 6, 1963

Dear Bob:

I have sometimes speculated as to whether, when a prophet is a

4. The assassination of President Kennedy.

participant in a catastrophe, he derives any measure of delight when he says, "I told you so." What has got me started off on this track is incident to a statement made by one of the highest ranking clergy of the most influential church of this sector. In a news interview, the Cardinal stated that reformatories do not reform & that penitentiaries do not make penitents. This statement should have a familiar ring to you, in that I wrote you of my same conclusion many years ago.

And again: many years ago, I wrote you that the men in Stonycreek are doing life sentences on the installment plan for drunkenness. Imagine my surprise when just last year I came across a brochure, under official imprimatur, telling of the intents & purposes of Stonycreek, & lo and behold, there is the typed word in all its pristine glory: "There are many men here serving life sentences on the installment plan for drunkenness." (Somebody has been stealing my thunder, said the medium sized bear). There are times here when some prisoner will complain & bellyache. I have admonished them to relax and enjoy themselves because it costs more to keep a man here for a year than it would cost to send him to Yale.

What I would like to know is whether I went wide of the truth. How much did your tuition cost at Yale? And what is the lowest possible cost of self maintenance in addition to the tuition? How does this tuition & cost compare to Harvard? Can you tell me anything of the costs & tuition of students in the more famous European universities such as the Sorbonne, Heidelberg, Universities of Paris & of Prague? Is there a basis for my believing that my kind of institutionalization has cost more money than the combined formal education at the world's greatest universities?

Frank

December 18, 1963

Christmas card mailed from Stonycreek from Frank to R.S.:

"Missing you at Christmas
Like a Christmas Tree needs Trimmings
Like a present needs a Bow
Like a Holly Wreath needs Berries
Like a Sleigh Ride needs some Snow
Like a Mantel needs a Stocking

> And a Stocking needs a Treat
> That's how much you're needed
> To make Christmas Day Complete."

to which Frank added:

> "I didn't pick this one."

Stonycreek Correctional Institution
December 20, 1963

Dear Bob:

A few days ago, I sent you a card. These cards were donated by some civic organization, one to a prisoner. The first card I was issued for transmission to you was covered with holly & emblazoned with the sentiment "Wish you were Here." Ingrate that I am, I applied for a substitute more appropriate, & can't seem to remember, whether or not you were sent a picture of some red nosed inebriate raffishly climbing out of a chimney. (?)

Without aforethought of the holidays, a week ago I had finished reading Gibbon's "Decline & Fall." I had devoted possibly three weeks to that section which covered the reigns of Hadrian thru Constantine & Theodosius. Before Gibbon really makes the point himself, I was impressed & struck with the fact that when the Christians attained ascendancy they out-murdered, out-burned, & out-expropriated & out-tortured any record that had been attained by the barbarians & the pagans. Truly this should be "required reading" for all seminaries & theological students. When the time comes to tell the child that there is no Santa Claus I suggest that the lazy parent provide an abridged edition of the "Decline & Fall of the Roman Empire." Though I had read excerpts before this time, I had not calculated such appropriate seasonal readings. Instead of shepherds watching their flocks, we have the edifying spectacles of auto-da-fe & the rock.

In reference to my last letter, I am reminded that the "Summing up" is one of the last of Maugham's works. Jail is a good place to sum up and recapitulate. You will remember that I hazarded a guess as to the relative expense of my frequent jailings & the expense of an education at the University of Bonn. In consideration of my wit & worth, character & personality traits, it seems that I might have emerged from one of these Rathskellars of knowledge with some impressive initials to

affix to my signature (& rotating in your own sphere where the Doc-
torates & Masters Degrees are commonplace, you will never know how
impressive they are to the laity).

To return to the "summing up," what have I to show for the great
sum which has been expended upon me? I have a doctorate of apocryphal value—Doctor of Jailology. My thesis has been the qualitative &
quantitative theory of alcohol absorption. I have drank in vain combat
against the inevitable hour of reckoning, reached & passed the satura-
tion point & finally arrived at that dismal outpost of intoxication (the
town lockup). I have lain on those wooden planks & seen the green
twilights where buffoons dance, where the dead are not dead, & one
can walk on water. And then there is the next day before court & justice which puts vague & tricky wonder in one's head. While the wheels
of equity declaim sonorous refrains of the town ordinances & criminal statutes, I have listened to the sound of construction being carried
on in my head, & knew that something big was being built. And then
at last I matriculate to various jails & learn all there is to know about
them. To what purpose? Oh, that this too solid flesh would melt!

Sincerely—

Frank

1964

January–February	Stonycreek Correctional Institution
February	Brief visit to Calvinville
March	Westville County Jail and House of Correction
April	Brief visit to Calvinville
April–July	Stonycreek Correctional Institution
August	Brief visit to Calvinville, Westville County Jail
September	Calvinville
October–December	Westville County Jail

Although forty-six weeks during 1964 were spent in jail or prison,
Frank made several more visits to Calvinville. Together with his several
brief visits in 1963 they marked a consistent and deliberate effort on his
part to identify with and return to his home town, although he was still
unable to sustain any living pattern outside of institutional walls.

During the year, I sent Frank several articles and studies on medical
ethics, the rights of the teaching patient in a medical-school hospital,
child abuse, the sociology of medical-student selection, and poverty and

the delivery of health care. He sent me nineteen letters, reflecting thoughtful response, especially with respect to modes of patient care, where he projected himself as the subject of the study.

Frank was also preoccupied with continuing his quest for respectability. He began a collection of memorabilia and testimonials to his "contributions to science," reflected on the positive aspects of his own personality, and on the respect he had already enjoyed from certain individuals such as the postmaster. He reflected, too, on a comparison of the adult career prospects for my children, given their background, with what he himself might have become or accomplished. But his life was symbolized, he felt, by a quote from Dante, "I did not die, yet nothing of life remained."

Frank's mother died on July 24. When he learned about her death in September he was moved to make several acid comments and to express an air of relief.

> Stonycreek Correctional Institution
> February 14, 1964

Dear Bob:

This will be my last letter of this term in jail. I shall be released on the 26th. My case paralells that of a brat who has been well-birched & is none the wiser. Would you believe that over fifteen hundred men have been admitted here since I entered? Most of them completed sixty to eighty days.

I know of the scholarly works produced mid the spires of Oxford, but cannot understand why the dons of Yale & Rutgers have not sent an expedition into these parts. Any serious preoccupation as regards alcoholism, without a survey of this institution, is like the consideration of a lion without its tail.

No other such opportunity exists in any part of the country (in the world?). Seven to eight hundred perennial drunks who will serve a large portion of their lifetime here. Indian, Negro & most ethnic groups are represented. There is no danger of opening up a case for study & then not have that individual return. If fifteen men out of the above-mentioned fifteen hundred have solved their drinking problems it would probably be an exaggerated optimism. There are times when a man disappears from here for a month or two months, but it will come to light that they have merely moved on to another jail as a respite from monotony.

There has been, over many years, a sporadic & most desultory effort to classify & categorize the alcoholics here. I think it is what might be called a "token" effort to quiet the muttering of a minority public. I would like to rile & agitate the dons by suggesting that they fear to take a professional prat-fall & they have become so "institutionalized" to the ivy covered walls & fake medieval towers that they dare not face the seven hundred men who will remain an economic & social zero for the rest of their natural lives solely because of booze.

You may be surprised to learn that the feeling of these men toward alcohol reform groups is mutual. You may be sure that if there is any activity which states that it is aimed toward sobriety, then ninety-five percent will turn toward cribbage or even Mickey Mouse on the television. Whether they are right in being suspicious or cynical toward people, who are making a damn good living by lecturing to them, is a moot question.

None would be here without the courts of justice, who alone of all the professionals, regard drunkenness as a crime (probably out of deference to people with a sixth grade education, which is the latest test for literacy). I wish that I had the money for a gravestone to be inscribed in my lifetime, "Frank Moore—An inebriate who was confined for twenty years for drunkenness alone." A pretty picture for posterity of law & justice of our day??? Too bad I couldn't be as nasty as Shakespeare in his "Measure for Measure":

> "But man, proud man
> Dressed in a little brief authority,
> Most ignorant of what he is most assured,
> His glassy essence, like an angry ape
> Plays such fantastic tricks before high heaven
> As make the angels weep."

Will write from Westville,
Frank

Calvinville
April 2, 1964

Dear Bob:

In arranging for a temporary address for the reception of mail, it came to the attention of the local postmaster that I was donating my eyes to the cornea clinic at the Eye & Ear Infirmary. The postmaster said he would feel honored to shake my hand. The usual reaction of people who know me is to sidestep me in a crab-wise fashion.

It is beginning to dawn on me that for too long I have failed to recognize the symbols to which other people ascribe importance.

Since meeting you over fifteen years ago & thru many years of correspondence while you were a research associate at Yale, a professor at Syracuse University, & your present position, you have expressed to me that I have contributed my widow's mite & materially aided the understanding of alcoholism.

At some early date, I wish you to draw up some form, in the manner of "This is to Certify" or "To Whom It May Concern" stating that I have striven to advance the knowledge & aided toward the understanding of alcoholics of my classification.

I have already reached that age where policemen no longer strike me over the head with a stick & there is no intrinsic value in the possession of the aforementioned document. I am not sure that I am not practicing an obscure form of snobbery toward my fellow alcoholic addicts by requesting such a document.

There is a time when some people do get away from individualized thinking & individualized behavior & do, episodically, indulge in racial & "advancement of the species" thinking. I claim a few such moments.

Shall I lay out manfully on a slab in some county morgue, a nonentity & an obscurity, or will you supply the necessary paper in order that, even in rigor mortis, I may indulge in risus sardonicus?

Sincerely,
Frank

Address: c/o Postmaster Parsons
       Calvinville

Stonycreek Correctional Institution
April 28, 1964

Dear Bob:

The statement was generous & there was no danger that I would exaggerate my importance. The only merits of such letters is that they are extremely self revelatory & I have not considered self-interest in those side swipes I have taken against different parts of the social structure, & venture that my muckraking has not endeared me to the constituted authorities to whom I have become so dependent.

You questioned me about my mother. I have reached that complex state where I do not consider the question but rather the reason for asking it. Perhaps you considered the possibility of a reconciliation in this, our dotage. Truly, never the twain shall meet. I have not seen her for a number of years. About two years ago, I called the nursing home by phone & she seemed rather excited & informed me that she couldn't see any visitors. Perhaps she was worried about my temperate state or the condition of my wardrobe. The Lord only knows what sort of an illusory background she has built up for herself & me in her new milieu. I am sure all the other old ladies feel sorry for her, & of course, that is what she wants. My own attitude? Well, I am still the kid in short pants who is pointed out as the boy whose father had committed suicide & whose mother had run off & left him as a baby. At least the Communists & Catholics agree on one thing. They say "Give me the person's mind for the first ten years of their life & we will not have to worry about other influences." I absolutely cringe to think of some of the procedures she adopted in later life to drive me to be a success (whatever that is)! Shakespeare must surely have known some such lady when he portrayed Lady Macbeth.

Frank

Stonycreek Correctional Institution
May 26, 1964

Dear Bob:

Let me collate the more vital matters. When I returned to Calvinville last September & was arrested, before I appeared in court, I was visited in my cell by the probation officer. I called his attention to the fact that it would not be too long a time before Calvinville would no longer be able to shunt me off to various jails & might in time have to face its financial responsibilities. Also, that as of the present time, I possessed enough of the necessary ills & infirmities to be admitted to the public health services at Davenport, with their attendant cost to Calvinville. I pointed out that as I grew older, I felt less sympathetic to the jail economy system.

The probation officer waited until I was sentenced & then mounted the dais, & asked the court to "continue" my case for a week until he had time to investigate my disabilities & the liability for the cost of treatment. I was released on my own recognizance but remember, for future reference, that my case was "continued."

I went to the head, then, of the Public Welfare & mentioned the possibility of my going to Davenport. He produced a check for twenty-five dollars & said to me (verbatim), "I am not telling you to leave town" (with a wise smirk) "but I am advising you to." This was the most money I had at one time in a year and I reasoned that he thought it inevitable that I would drink & get arrested. Beware of the Greeks bearing gifts.

Immediately, I left town, & was arrested two days later, & was sent here. At that time I wrote you of the court-room scene, the drunkards anteroom, etc.

When I arrived down here, or a few days later, I learned from a recent habitue of Davenport of the increasing costs of public health service. Two different sources revealed to me that such service was billed to the responsible towns at the rate of about fifty dollars a week.

Came the dawn & I began to understand the munificence of handing me twenty-five dollars. I have seen the time when I could damn near have traversed the continent on such amount.

I consummated my sentence here & was released on Feb. 26. On my return to Calvinville that night, while in a bona-fide coffee-shop with two of my bottle buddies, two uniformed munions of the law informed me that they had a "capias" for my arrest. Do you remember, the case that was "continued" at a time, six months previous?

The denouement & more later.

Frank

Stonycreek Correctional Institution
June 2, 1964

Dear Bob:

(Continuetur) I was at loss to account for the zeal of the person who presented the capias. Then, by discreet questioning, later, one of the guards at the Westville jail who supplements his income by serving subpoenas for the county court, informed me that an officer who serves a capias receives a monetary consideration. Of course, this is much better than in the old days of the Wild West when a sheriff's whole salary was contingent on a fee basis. In my own case, there was also the Three Dollar pay for "overtime," which is to say, appearing against me in court the next morning.

Believe me, there was no demoralized taciturn & uninspired Frank Moore in court on that morning. By prodigious waving of the flag in emulation of Daniel Webster, by calling the attention of the judge to the many drunks whom he had sent to jail & who were now making wassail in Valhalla, I out-Darrowed Clarence.

The case was filed & I was released. More is the pity, someone made money on the deal. Two days later, while still celebrating my release, I was arrested while sleeping on the ice pond at that public mall where my father had his "accident." It is curious to consider the connection of persons & places. All this between February 26 & Mar. 1. To be continued.

Frank

Stonycreek Correctional Institution
July 21, 1964

Dear Bob:

"Within limits of normality, every individual loves himself. In cases where he has a deformity or abnormality or develops it later, his own aesthetic sense revolts & he develops a sort of disgust toward himself. Though with time, he becomes reconciled to his deformities, it is only at the conscious level. His subconscious mind, which continues to bear the mark of the injury, brings about certain changes in his whole personality making him suspicious of society." (From a pamphlet on leprosy)

Anybody who has spent half their life in jail for drunkenness could aptly quote a line from Dante, "I did not die, yet nothing of life remained." Unfortunately, too many people say this in their own words which lose somewhat, the mellifluity of the quotation & take on the nature of caterwauling. I prefer to deal with drunkenness as a matter of personalities (see above).

The great Viennese who elucidated the "split personality" could never have intimately known an alcoholic. Instead of a dual nature, he would have come to recognize that some drunkards have a whole potful of personalities. This is best exemplified in the different manners in which a single person may go about getting drunk.

I do not write "getting drunk" in a disparaging manner, for this process is reserved for men to the exclusion of beasts, & can be elevated to a noble art.

Before continuing, it is best to interject that I will be discharged from here on July 31st which fact might be influencing the content of this letter. The epileptic experiences the "aura" & some kindred phenomena is experienced by my fellow jailbirds, long caged, before release.

About the noble art, I can remember a large moss-covered bone, in the woods, far from human habitation, & by squatting at the foot of a tree with a gallon of wine, studying the sponge-like cross section, enjoying a whole summer's day, with all the zest & imagination of an amateur paleontologist. I conjured visions of a primal struggle, law of claw & fang, & the elimination of old age. (Consider all the twaddle you have heard concerning "solitary drinking").

And then, there is the character in Calvinville who always looks me up when he is drunk because I can always supply the missing line from any quotation of Omar, which he happens to be maundering about at the moment. Surely, to him, I have not the personality of a bone-fancier. I believe I could go on, interminably, drawing pictures of what different people believe me to be. Of one thing I am sure, the people who don't drink agree that I am a son—.

I don't think I can usurp a conventional role, upon my release, which is to say, I am not looking forward to the possibility of seeing the four mop-headed Beatles. And as far as top-less bathing suits, has anybody come up with anything more sensational than "conical," "globular," "firm," & "pendulous"??? Within the past month, the newspapers report that an elderly man was repeatedly assaulted in an elevated train & none of the other passengers interfered; an elderly woman broke her leg walking along a highway & passing motorists chose not to see her. Nice people who "minded their own business." To hell with convention. Rationalizing before a drunk???

Frank

Westville Jail and House of Correction
December 1, 1964

Dear Bob:

Methinks I should caption this letter "The Passing of Lady Macbeth," but I would fall far short of the grandiloquent title when portraying the sordidness & grandeur of her demise.[5]

A chronological order sometimes makes for clarity, viz: I was released from Stonycreek on July 31; on August 3, I was arraigned in Calvinville for drunkenness. Having been arrested the night before, I slept on the board plank bed & was given a drink of water at daylight. It is fitting that I gratuitously offer the sage advice to any man of sixty years with a predilection to sleep on board beds that he drink to insensibility of those round top rivets that bore into the pelvic structure,

5. Reference to the death of his mother.

the scapula, etc. It is the custom to bring the prisoner into the docket enclosed by rails, about five minutes before the judge arrives in his black balloon robes, & as my conferes have stated "like a clown in mourning." The explanation of the time interval lies in the fact that drunken prisoners have been known to get physically sick during the most perfunctory disposition & short period of time allotted to such cases. On this occasion, I was the sole occupant to the place which is the "cynosure of all eyes"; all of the other malefactors charged with less heinous offense, such as speeding, being dispersed among the spectators, so that, until called before the bar, it is impossible to differentiate between the sheep & the goats.

The above explanation of those areas prescribed for occupancy by the personae dramatis of a small town court is designed to accentuate, what would to the casual observer, seem obscure. A few moments before the magistrate appeared, the probation officer left his allotted area, strode the width of the courtroom to the prisoner's docket & looked at me for a full minute. I have seen the same look in the eyes of a pitchman before his tripod on the boardwalk of Atlantic City, as if he wished to convey a message to me at the outskirts of a crowd.

He returned to his part of the arena, & left me with the impression of something unsaid, as if in common parlance he had something on his mind.

Anyhow, I was sentenced to thirty days down here in Westville, & only after the consummation of this sentence, & in the following month, & from an unforseen source of information, did I learn that my mother had died on July 24.

More anon—
Frank

Westville Jail and House of Correction
December 14, 1964

Dear Bob:

Your letter of December 7 & your paper delivered at the Fourth General Session of American Public Health, is at hand. Your paper has all the aspects of a twenty course meal—economics, ethics, sexology, education, politics, & all the history of human thought.

Consider the train of thoughts set in motion by a single paragraph (your reference to) The Fertility Rate of Bloody Harlan County: (1) a park bench acquaintance once instructed me that the quickest way to bring a flowering plant to bloom was to withdraw the water; (2) a snide joke about the State of Mainers is, that they have only two pursuits, fishing and bedroom athletics—and in the winter it is too cold to fish; (3) supposedly authentic accounts of genocide, portray the dead victims locked in sexual embrace when the freight cars & the gas chambers were opened; (4) there are at least two ethnic groups who believe that being fat is healthy. Do we have a parallel here of people who believe that fertility is a manifestation of manliness? And does it follow that the celibates of great religions are capons? (5) Plato's "Republic" foresaw the need of a high birth rate among the clods who perform the arduous work; (6) can I not just half remember reading a critic's review of a comical & libidinous stage play which was entitled "What a Way to Die"; (7) dear Bob, note the extent to which you have extolled the sympathy, support & affection of the women of Harlan County toward their unemployed husbands. To what degree has your own blessed state invoked the accolade? I love you for it, but there is in this innocent exhibition of female worship which induces a malaise in me & unfits me for dispassionate comment. You would be surprised at the number of men who have spent a lifetime without ever experiencing the aforesaid sympathy, support & affection; (8) how do you reconcile the biologists' dogma that race survival depends on female's selection of mates who can provide & support their children? Or haven't the ladies of Harlan County been told? etc. etc.

Frank

Westville Jail and House of Correction
December 28, 1964

Dear Bob:

Last month, I received a letter from a Professor of Anatomy at the Harvard Medical School, thanking me for contributing to medical science & education & leaving my body to the promotion of anatomical science. The legal papers have been cleared by the signature of two witnesses, my nearest of kin's signature, the vice president of the local department store (how's that for name calling?), the body to be delivered unembalmed; the modest cost of transportation by a licensed undertaker to be paid by Harvard Medical School, & after completion of studies, the body to be buried at no expense to the family in a cemetery maintained by the medical schools of Boston . . . imagine the relief to my cousin the V. P.! The poor guy doesn't know that my

obituary already filed with the local newspaper, states that I have no
near relatives & that there will be no services, & that I am more relieved than he is; a lifetime of rejection, & now acceptance.

I suppose the reason for doing this is a composite of many reasons.
A final nose-thumbing to convention? An answer to Waugh's "The
Dearly Beloved?" Thwarting the deathbed bandits, who could gain
even a small profit from Social Security provisions? A realization that,
like Socrates, I owe Aesculapius a rooster? Quien Sabe?

Frank

1965

January	Westville County Jail and House of Correc-tion (1 week)
January–mid-April	Congress Hotel, Calvinville
Mid-April–May	Westville County Jail
June	Congress Hotel (5 weeks)
July–August	Stonycreek Correctional Institution
September–December	Congress Hotel

Frank's first sustained correspondence from outside an institution was
initiated from the Congress Hotel, where he wrote ten of the twenty-one
letters for 1965. In most respects, his life in the hotel was actually more
difficult and conditions of living more desolate than in many of the institutions which had provided him with a home for so long, but, as
illustrated by events described in his letter of February 5, 1965, he had
begun to try to avoid rather than to seek incarceration with its relative
comforts and security and managed to spend all but fifteen weeks of the
year out of jail or prison.

Throughout the correspondence, Frank indicated his awareness that his
writing about his way of life and condition of living would be used in a
study of institutional dependency and alcoholism. His letters of 1965 included several deliberately written autobiographical sketches, including
both introspective ramblings and some fairly objective analyses.

Frank's search for self-assurance and respectability became even more
pronounced during this year. He undertook to serve as his own legal defense in a trial, his reminiscing tended to focus more on his "achieve-
ments," and he continued to collect mementos of his life record. There
seemed to be something urging him to a summation and recognition of his

life's record "of greatness and littleness, of virtue and vice, of nobility and baseness" (February 27, 1965).

Etiology & Materia Medica   Congress Hotel
                                                   February 2, 1965

Dear Bob:

Somewhere and at sometime I have read that there is nothing as boring as an old man's reminiscenses. Yet Socrates ascribes the soul to the recollection of former experiences. Insofar as they relate to the history of a disease, they may be excusable and interesting.

.   .   .   .   .

Thirty years ago at this time, I worked as a lumberjack for the Great Northern in Maine. . . .

Living accommodations were primitive and we slept on a straw-covered rack, very much looking like a litter of pigs. My partner informed me that when asleep, I wheezed like a running bear. His method of observation might have advantages over the most modern methods of auscultation. In retrospect, this was the first inkling to me to consider that it was possible that there might be something wrong with my respiratory apparatus.

It was about this time that I "discovered" drink. Here was a respite, here was the universal panacea for all the aches and pains, mental and physical, that infest the human soul. For twenty years, I did not attempt the relation of asthmatic condition with alcoholism, if there is a relation.

I have sometimes suspected that those who are accredited with knowing the secret and winding ways of the human mind, (Menninger, Freud, Jung, Adler) can only half understand the rationalizations and fantasies that we weave to account for what we do.

But with drink, I found a deliverance: I could forget discomfort and fatigue, I could slip off the burden and see clearly again; I could be the master of my own brain, my thoughts and my will. My dead self would stir in me and I could laugh with the crowd and joke with my companions. However low, socially, I could become a man again and master of my life. For many years, I was happy only when drunk and even then I was savage that the happiness would not last. I was angry with the boss, the policeman, the preacher, or any who would wreck this happiness.

It is a battle that has no end and it may be that there can be no end. At those times, when I attempted to quit temporarily, merely to walk down the street was to be put upon the rack. In every town there was surely a saloon on the corner, perhaps on all four corners; and some in the middle of the block as well; and each stretched forth a hand to me offering light, conversation, and music.

If I stayed in one city long enough, I found that each saloon had a personality of its own, an allurement unlike any other. At opening time and after dark, there was warmth and a glow, a friendly face, a jolly disposition.

In your home town, New Haven, I can remember Townie's Tavern, the sports pictures on the walls, the overstuffed leather cushions that were emplaced along the bar for elbow and leaning pads, that I have never seen elsewhere. I can sometimes understand the furniture fanatic, who goes into rapture because of Louis XIV furnishings—but only because I was an habitué of Townie's.

. . . . .

It is my belief that asthma might aptly be described as a "night disease." At least, that is when the victim is most concerned. In addition to the daylight relief from tension, worry, and Weltsmerz, I found an unbroken sleep whenever I could get drunk enough over all these years. However, others may have classified alcohol as a stimulant, excitant, et al, alcohol has had a narcotic effect to me.

. . . . .

"Narcotics are drugs which lessen the relationship between the individual and the outer world."

Don't you think that is neat, lucid, and for some individuals, is not alcohol a narcotic? Men work for this narcotic in order to escape for a while. Life may become only a struggle to get it. It gives them something to think about while they are working—they have the memories of their last drunk, and the hope of the time when they can become drunk again, and most especially when they are physically discommoded.

To get on with the evolution: In about 1950 when I was working for the Lackawanna Railroad in upper New York, in the fall of the year, I had been thru a drunk on the Bowery, passed thru the usual period of sickness, recovery of appetite, and found that I could not sleep at night because of difficulty of breathing. It was hard physical labor and there was the necessity for sleep.

At this time, I first knew that I had asthma. The environs were simply plastered with ragwood and goldenrod, and what had been a minor disability became a major one during the two months I stayed there. When I threw up the job, returned to the city, and got drunk, I was physically relieved. The necessity of finding another job, food, shelter, thrust asthma into the background.

Somewhere about this time, I took the Antabuse Treatment at the Liberty Hospital for alcoholism. I was questioned before treatment regarding a history of respiratory ailments and asthma. I was so anxious to take the treatment and so afraid that such a history would preclude my receiving the treatment, that I denied all history of malfunction.

The result was, that after massive dosage for a week, I was dressed in a bathrobe, given three shots of whiskey, each shot at twelve minute intervals, and damn near smothered to death.

I believe that, from the above, you may devise some commentary to answer Alcoholic Anonymous members when they say of others, "He probably did not have the honest and sincere desire to stop drinking."

About this time, or a year later, I went to Heaven Hill. It is well to remember that I had not, up to this time, been to a doctor for respiratory illness. Remember, I had the cure-all, the philosopher's stone, the magic fluid that makes kings out of paupers. From booze, I became footloose, ostracized, exiled, jailed, starved, broiled and frozen, and so asthma was secondary.

. . . . .

And so asthma and emphysema developed as the years sped on. The alcoholism remained static—neither better nor worse. . . .

A number of years ago, I began being sentenced to the State Farm at Stonycreek for drunkenness. Asthma, by now, has got quite a start. We sleep thirty or forty to a dormitory and rather than keep everyone else awake, I spent at least two hours every night in the toilet, coughing, wheezing, and smoking.

You may wonder why I did not seek medical aid. Bend your shell-like ear in this direction & I shall inform you.

Not everyone in jail gets the kind of work assignment that he would like. There are many ardous and unpleasant jobs. What better way to avoid such jobs than go on sick call every day and secure at least a *three hour* respite? The authorities have set up a defense mechanism to thwart these wheeler-dealers. In order to attend sick call, it is necessary the first thing in the morning upon leaving the dormitories, to stand in a single line, in an open yard, come rain, hail, sleet, gloom and the shadows, to give your name and prison number to a guard at the window of a warm and lighted room. After breakfast, and about an hour after the other prisoners have gone to work, the doctors arise and are ready for the "laying on of the hands." Prisoners who are going on sick call are summoned to the gate; and as his name and number is called, each prisoner steps thru the gate to form a double line waiting outside the gate. There is always one or two who can not be found and must be looked for in the barber shop or toilet, etc. Meanwhile, the others are waiting outside the gate, come rain, hail, sleet, etc. When there is the usual number (about a hundred), this process takes half an hour. The waiting and stalling are deliberate. The prisoners being waited for have said to themselves, "Why should I wait for somebody else; let someone else wait for me." Then the line marches to the hospital. Here again, each name and number is called again. Some have gone to sleep sitting on a bench, are deaf, or must be looked for. None can return to work or to the prison yard until every mother's son has been listened to, prescribed for, and received his allotted treatment. No prisoner is allowed to carry medicine, and therefore if a drug is prescribed three times a day, he can repeat the above process three times a day.

I hope I am making it clear to you why I never attended sick call at the State Farm after being sent there twelve times. I have attended the two compulsory attendances, each time, which are a physical examination (?) upon admission and discharge. The two appearances might well be enough for any man and left me no patience to attend daily sick calls.

. . . . .

Here is what the doctor down there thinks while he is going over my chest with a stethoscope. (One of them has seemed quite absorbed, tho' the ear pieces were not in his ears).

"No need to tell this guy that there is anything wrong with him. He wouldn't understand and it wouldn't do him any good to know. I have enough to do as it is, and so why make work for myself. This guy will kill himself drinking anyhow and so why be bothered with secondary pathology. This guy probably has not spent a dollar on a doctor for years and the only reason he is here now, is because it is compulsory and he doesn't have to pay anything. What a shame that I should waste time on such people who don't care whether they live or not, while thousands are spending hard-earned dollars in the search for good health, etc, etc, etc,"

Do you think I should go down to Duke University to attend E.S.P. sessions??? Like attracts like, even in jail, and a hundred of the more acute minds at Stonycreek agree with me in the substance of the above or at least they told me so. And don't forget your old master, Selden Bacon of Yale, informed you that drunkards and little children are quicker than a normal adult to apprehend sympathy or a lack of it.

. . . . .

About the first part of October, last year, I was sent to Westville Jail. I had not been beaten with alcohol, but I had been beaten with asthma. In contradistinction to Stonycreek, county jails may attract the latest and modern medical minds and because it is so "convenient" to attend sick call at county jail, the direct opposite of Stonycreek, I informed the doctor that I had asthma, emphysema and bronchitis.

He asked, "How do you know?" Most disparagingly, I answered, "Hitch up your apparatus and verify." He accommodated and prescribed Tederal. . . . Tederal, to me was a hypnotic, allowed me to obtain more sleep, relieved tension, caused me to be less concerned with my condition, was generally efficacious, a true palliative and alleviant.

I have already recounted to you that I obtained Tederal without prescription upon my release. However, a few days later, at the City Hall in Calvinville, I learned with surprise (and was not argumentive) that this drug could not be obtained without prescription. I bend with the wind like a willow and attend a doctor of my own choice. In so far as it is possible, I "squared" with the doctor; told him that I was not a veteran of the Army or Navy[6]; that I had served honorably my country in time of war in the Merchant Marine; and that the city of Calvinville was inclined to render me assistance as far as it was not related to booze. The doctor availed himself of the latest developments of pharmacology and prescribed Quiburon. This drug is a vaso-dilator and most efficacious; a capsule to be taken *tid* and if necessary, during an attack. It is possible to breathe freely fifteen minutes after administration and I suppose that is what most asthmatics seek for.

On a later visit to this same doctor, most indiscreetly, I mentioned

6. Actually, Frank was not an *honorably discharged* veteran and, therefore, not eligible for veterans' medical benefits.

that I did not hope or wish to live forever. It is remarkable how our spontaneous "wordiness" and "aboveboardness" can get a person involved. The next time I saw my social worker, she mentioned the possibility and necessity of psychiatric treatment. I don't know whether the doctor influenced the social worker or whether the social worker influenced the doctor. But there the matter stands, pro tem.

There may be good reason to believe that I am "nutty," but I only admit scientific and risky "nuttiness." For instance, I employ a special method of empyrics: if one capsule is good every four hours, perhaps two capsules are better. I have always suspected doctors of "underprescribing." Especially in the field of narcotics, it was better for a person to die in agony than that he might develop a "habit" as it is dealt with in the sensational press. A lethal dosage is by definition the smallest dosage which has been known to cause death. At one time, another man and I drank enough of a commercial alcohol containing Acetone to cause the death of four horses, that is, according to a table of lethal dosage. We emerged unscathed, tho' each drink tasted as tho' I had smoked a mentholated cigarette.

And so it has been with Quiburon, I have taken five capsules in one hour and it has resulted in one hell of a spasm across the transverse muscles of the gut. Anyone who wishes to commit hari-kari would best seek a less painful method. The ancient Pliney has told us that none has a better right to his own life than himself. The moderns shrink because suicide is a denial of the "life force" (instinct), and they are indignant because they are not certain that this instinct will not carry they, themselves, through.

Dear Bob, how can I reason, how can I admonish against the expense, how can I advise against the futility of psychiatric treatment in my case????

Remember the old verse: "A man convinced against his will, is of the same opinion still."

Do you think it would avail if I informed these authorities that I have already availed myself of the benefits of Psychoanalysis, the Yale Clinic, that I have been in private and public sanitariums, State Hospitals, jails, prison, the Antabuse Treatment, Emetine Treatment, Belladonna Treatment, that I have lived in Roger's Retreat, that I lived in a monastery, that I have been a chairman with the Alcoholics Anonymous?

For the love of God, or whatever powers may be, let me die privately in peace, drunk or sober, and let me not be a stooge selling propaganda, faith and ignorance.

Regards,
Frank

Frank Moore, Sea Lawyer
Congress Hotel
Calvinville
February 5, 1965

Dear Bob:

When I was arrested on October 8, 1964, I offered the plea of "guilty," and offered no statement. Nothing could be inflicted on me that I had not experienced before.

However, the presiding justice did not appreciate my passive mood. He said, in the open court, "I am tired of wasting my time with this bum." He further stated, "If I am not mistaken, that cap you have in your hand came from the Public Welfare Department. And I sentence you to State Farm at Stonycreek."

These remarks are particularly apropos to your Poverty Paper, in that they correspond with the stigma and shame of disease and "failure."

In a large municipal court, I could have shed these vapid mutterings like the proverbial duck. Something about living in a small town, having honorable ancestors, incited me to remember the motto of the Medicis: "No one harms me with impunity."

I appealed my sentence to the County Superior Court and there vegetated until the latter part of November. I had no ill will toward the County District Attorney and felt honor bound to sound a rattlesnake's warning. So, in the latter part of November, I wrote him a letter stating that I demanded a jury trial, that I wished to invoke the compulsory process for obtaining witnesses and records for my defense. I further requested that counsel be appointed to act in my behalf; and that, further, I did not wish a counsel to act "nominally"; but that I wished a counsel who would put in the time to benefit me with an "adequate" defense.

The District Attorney saw fit to ignore my letter, and it may have been as well as placed in a bottle and loosed on the Labrador Current.

About the 7th of January, 1965, I was brought to the Superior Court in Westville. I was the only prisoner, and handcuffed from the gaol to the courthouse. After a short wait in the ante-room, long enough for me to consider the enormity of my sins, the gyves were removed and two court officers each guiding me by seizure of arms, escorted me into the Hall of Justice. (All of this procedure is standard in the county for the crimes of hen-stealing to murder, inclusive.)

And there, my friend, you have Frank Moore surrounded with all the physical and moral forces of the community; the uniformed deputies; the senior court officer with an honest-to-god mace; the black-robed justice; the state and national flags flying horizontally; and the prisoner's box sixty feet from the podium as though the culprit would contaminate, by proximity.

This is a situation well calculated to cause a decent citizen to flinch, to curl up his toes, and start floating, belly-upward.

A suave, self-contained assistant district attorney approached my box and asked, "Are you ready for trial?"

I reminded him of a letter that I had written to his office and which the District Attorney had chosen to ignore. I tried to appear harmless, but he apparently saw warning lights. I have never been able to appear suave myself.

It is the usual procedure when a drunkenness sentence is appealed to Superior Court, to waive trial by jury; the court recognizes the time that has been spent waiting trial, and the case is placed "on file." But there is no certainty, that the case will be placed "on file." The judge in Superior Court can sentence a man to Stonycreek just as perfunctorily as a District Court Judge.

I had decided to give the District Court a lesson in "good manners"; to accept a plea of guilty without extraneous contempt for drunkards; and decided that, henceforth, when I was sentenced to Stonycreek, to run the full gamut of the courts; jury trial; witnesses; records; to exclude jurors by peremptory challenge; and for cause; and all the other expensive appurtenances which are constitutionally my right. In other words, I can be sent to Stonycreek, but who in Hell wants to spend a couple of thousand dollars to send me there?

The assistant district attorney approached the bench, and informed the judge of my intentions. The judge asked me if I wanted counsel.

I reiterated to him all the foregoing sarcasm regarding "nominal" counsel and "actual" counsel with as much contained venom as I could summon on behalf of the hundreds of men who have accepted this slapstick "nominal" counsel. He informed me that a counsel would be sent over to the jail to interview me.

I pointed out that I had already waited three months for trial (violation of 6th Amendment) and that I had spent three months in jail on the testimony "that I had the strong odor of alcohol on my breath." He stated that he did not care what testimony had been offered in District Court. I stated, "I only wished to point out that I had been confined in absence of $500 bond, which was excessive and a violation of the 8th Amendment."

Needless to say, the justice is getting rather "rattled" by this flaunting of a grammar school education. He asked me how much bail that I could procure. I informed him, in a most derogatory manner, that I couldn't even summon *five* dollars (to make $500 seem even more asinine).

I was returned to jail, and that afternoon, I was interviewed by the appointed counsel. This person was the exemplification of all that I despise in "nominal" counsel—a classic figurehead of "do-nothing," and "play ball" with court procedure in all its disregard of everything except that which pertains to arid statute, accustomed form, and eeny-meeney, miney-mo.

In restrained, but no uncertain terms, I informed him that I expected vigorous defense; that I desired every juror removed who had any alcoholism in their family; every workman or artisan who felt that they had been injured by alcoholism of their associates; every member of a religious sect, which proscribes all use of alcohol (such proscription in violation of the 21st Amendment). I demanded full representation of the Constitution, and that the jury be of my peers.

The defense counsel, also, is getting "rattled" at this time, and anxious to get rid of a "hot potato." I informed him that I wished to subpoena the Calvinville City Marshal to offer testimony regarding a local ordinance, forbidding the sale of alcohol to anyone convicted of being drunk, for a period of six months. I questioned the validity of a law which applied to 3 square miles of the United States; and I wished to adduce testimony from the City Marshal of the lucrative practice of transporting prisoners by private car to penal institutions, for drunkenness, etc., etc.

My counsel is now curling like fried bacon, and suggests that I could better defend myself. Of course, I laughed and told him, that I was certain. I did tell him that the only reason I had wanted him appointed was for the procurement of witnesses and records. He promised to notify the clerk of the Superior Court.

Back to court again, next morning, handcuffs, et al, seizure on both sides and you know how I so much love physical contact. Lo' and behold—twelve men and women, tried and true, waiting for me in the jury box, probably knowing less of the Constitution than I do of the encephalogram. The judge questions me, "Did you talk with your counsel?"

Statement by Moore, "I found him a most unwilling counsel, but he did state that he would notify the Clerk that I wished to subpoena records and witnesses." The court asked what these records would pertain to.

I stated to the court, that if the district attorney would stipulate that I could present the records of 3 different men from the State Farm of Stonycreek who had, in the aggregate, served twenty-five years in jail for drunkenness without even having committed any other offense, that I would waive the right to summon records.

Of course, the jury is "taking this in," and I interpolated that I myself had served about twenty years in jail for the same offense; the trial is not yet under way.

The judge affects to be dense, regarding the pertinence of such testimony.

I make sure the jury is listening. I point out that judges have long since become accustomed to such procedure, but that I doubt that juries could become so accustomed. Further, that a simple case of drunkenness in Washington, D.C. is going thru Appelate Courts and if necessary to the Supreme Court, for the same reasons, as I have cited above, defended by Civil Liberties Union, against violation of that clause in the 8th Amendment which pertains to "cruel and unusual punishment."

The judge then ordered that I be released in my own recognizance, without bail. So endeth the first jury hearing of drunkenness in the history of the county, so far as I have learned. Court officers said afterwards, "I don't know how you do it."

"Been out" since January 8. Write to above address.

Frank

Congress Hotel
February 15, 1965

Dear Bob:

. . . . .

You have noted that, for a full month, I have been a resident of the community, at large. Lest you be addled, and caused to believe that I have bettered myself, let us, as Al Smith said, "examine the record."

When I arrived, late in the day, back in Calvinville from Westville, I was unable to get in touch with the Public Assistance Administrator. That night, I went to the Night Captain in the police station, and showed him a statement signed by the deputy sheriff at Westville certifying that I had been administered the drug Tederal, three times a day, for a period of three months, for asthma, emphysema, and bronchitis. He called a drug store by phone and gave me a dollar out of his own pocket to pay for the medicine. He also endeavored to get in touch with the Public Assistance Administrator without avail. When I became disgusted and went down on the wharf to sleep on the sand and watch the ice cakes float by, he later sent a policeman down looking for me. He couldn't find me. I was sheltered by a building and some stone jetties. The instinct of self-preservation is truly a remarkable thing. Incidentally, the Night Captain shall be the new City Marshal within the next two years. He is the only one who has both brains and heart enough for the job. It is ironical that the community had paid so much money to keep me in jail and didn't give a damn what happened to me when I was released.

The next morning, Saturday, I did get in touch with the Assistance Administrator, and he arranged, by phone, to get me a meal ticket and a hotel room and an appointment for Monday.

Hearken, to how our President Johnson's "Great Society" operates, and check, if you will, in every detail.

Monday, I arrived at City Hall. The Public Assistance Administrator is a great guy, personally, but has been so greatly harmed by alcoholism in his own family, that it is impossible for him to be detached in his thinking (if he could think of such a thing). He refers me to a female senior social worker, beyond even my years, who has *also* experienced a terrific alcoholic problem in her family. I am thinking to myself, "Brother, brother, what a hard nut you have got to crack. All these people know is that you drink; that recourse to jail is the easiest way out for them; to hell with your asthma, emphysema, and bronchitis; and in a few days you will be back in jail again."

Contrary soul that I am, and unfortunate as they were in their lack of knowing my last obstructionist policy, I decided to play it cool and beat them at their own game.

Now, watch the workings of the Great Society: the first thing that is decided at City Hall, is that I can not have Tederal without a prescription. I pick a doctor at random at the City's expense at five dollars a call (and it was a good random choice). My night on the wharf did not help my condition as his stethoscope and thermometer verified. He questioned me as to whether the city would pay for an expensive prescription and I replied that I did not know any reason why they wouldn't. He prescribed Quiburon which costs ten times as much as Tederal. I am thinking, all the time of those opportunist's words: "if you can't lickem, then jine 'em." This Quiburon should cost about five dollars a week. Of course, it is part of the working of the Great Society that I make another appointment with the doctor at five dollars "a throw." Thus in the past month I have visited him five times. Twenty-five for him and twenty-five for the druggist, for an incurable progressive and hopeless disease. Where does my "rake-off" come in, in the Great Society?

Wait a minute, wait a minute, you haven't heard a thing yet. The senior social worker asks me if I could eat in a restaurant for one dollar a day. I reply that, of course I can, so long as I can stay drunk at the same time and that perhaps I could manage for less. It is decided that I shall have two five dollar meal tickets and the restaurant owner is happy, along with the druggist and the doctor. But wait!

You have noted my lodging is the Congress Hotel. Remember Lord Edward Congress? I don't think he is turning over in his grave—he really must be spinning. The weekly rate is seven dollars, and is managed by a native Levantine who has spent considerable time in the Gingerbread House. Way back in school days, we learned that a Greek could amass a fortune under the same circumstances that an acquisitive Hebrew would starve to death. This hotel should have been the locale for the writings of John Steinbeck—"Grapes of Wrath" and "Mice and Men." Thought of doing something like that myself, with a tentative title "The Zoo." I insist on two clean sheets and pillow cases a week, wash my own towel, make my own bed and clean my own room. In the other rooms, the beds are not made, or are the rooms cleaned. As far as I can see, the overhead consists of one twenty year old female delinquent who makes pretense of cleaning the lobby downstairs. The manager squats in front of the television all day, and watches for roomers, delinquent in their rent. The clientele is 90% alcoholic, including one female on my floor, suffering from some glandular defect with attendant gross obesity. Swears like a bos'n and screams like a sea gull. There appears to be three men who don't drink and strange as it may seem, they are the loudest of the lot. Next room to me is a man who chronically starves himself to death in order that he shall have more money for wine. Next to him, is a deaf and dumb man, but when I write "dumb," I mean nobody can understand him. He sure can roar like hell (but it may be that he has something to roar about). More about the "Zoo" later.

After I had been in town two weeks and gave no indication of going back to jail, my social worker said that she thought that my main trouble was alcoholism and that I should have psychiatric treatment. I wondered what particular bug-house she had in mind, and whether it was a scheme to get me off the city relief rolls. I paid a visit to my doctor and he assured me of my asthma, emphysema, etc., and he informed me that I didn't have to go to any institution, (I had informed him of my institutional background). He advised me to accept psychiatric treatment on an "outpatient" basis, so now some jolly headshrinker is going to make a thousand bucks—Great Society?

Listen, Bob, to this ungrateful soul. I have had to bum a dime from the restaurant owner today in order to buy some Bull Durham tobacco. The postmaster gave me this writing pad, and promised to pay postage for this letter. There is a well-rounded plot to preclude Frank Moore from procuring the price of a jug of wine. . . . I had all the tobacco I desired in Westville and at the State Farm you supplemented the one package a week they gave me there. I am at large, you say?

If you have tears, prepare to shed them now. About ten days ago, I went into the emporium and indicated to my cousin, the vice president, that I didn't have any socks. He said, "This is a sort of blackmail, you know. Why don't you ask the Public Assistance Administrator?" My cousin is a deacon of the ancient First Church of Calvinville. I recalled those biblical words from the 13th Chapter of Corinthians, learned at Roger's Retreat in New Jersey: "Tho' I speak with the tongues of men and of angels, and have not charity, I have become as sounding brass or a tinkling cymbal." So much for my last living relative. If anyone tells you that blood is thicker than water, then you may say: Not among New England Yankees.

F.

Congress Hotel
February 27, 1965

Dear Bob:

. . . . .

As far as mailing costs, while I am in this old town the postmaster says he will defray postage costs of letters written to you. He is your most ardent admirer.

I have reduced the intake of the drug Quiburon by two-thirds. There was a side effect to me—cerebral excitant. I made the obvious choice between breathing freely like a bellows, staying awake all night or to assure sleep with lung congestion and the early morning panic. Somewhere or other I have read that the coward dies a thousand deaths. The same thing might be said of emphysema and asthma. It is most strange, our preconceptions of death. Violence in death is rare. The end of life tends to become a matter of a slow leak rather than an explosion.

In the event that I am not further jailed, it will be noted that I have made a death preparation. On the closet door, at the head of my bed, where I might damn well strangle of some early morning, I have tacked an acknowledgement from the Boston Eye Bank for my support of sight restoration and eye research. Beside this, is tacked the blue-bordered Eye Donor Identification Card. Beneath these, is tacked your statement that I have chronicled, for nineteen years, by means of correspondence, a life experience that has aided the study of alcohol pathology. Beside this certification is tacked a legal form, properly witnessed, bequeathing my corpse to the Harvard Medical School, for contributing to science and medical education. Farther down on the closet door are tacked two authorization cards signed by the Maritime Commissioner, for the Atlantic War Zone Bar and the Victory Medal for service in the Merchant Marine in World War II. The replacement of these two ribbons is thirty cents apiece, so it is doubtful that I shall ever tack these on the door.

Besides these cards, is tacked the Presidential Testimonial Letter signed by Harry Truman, commending "courage, fortitude, resourcefulness, calm judgment," it also states that he looks to me "in time of peace for leadership and example" (before the war was over, and ever since, I have always been the first morning customer in any bar-room —so much for leadership).

Below these, is affixed a duplicate Certificate of Graduation from the Naval Hospital Corps Training School of Newport, R.I., awarded in 1920, by the Bureau of Medicine and Surgery, Navy Department, Washington, D.C.

Farther down on the door are tacked two discharges from the Maritime Service and Maritime Service Reserve, which attest to completion of course of gunnery, which I underwent before service in the Merchant Marine.

Beside these discharges is an honorable discharge (certificate in lieu of lost discharge) from the U.S. Navy issued by Bureau of Records, Kansas City, Mo.

Down on the bottom panel of the door, we have a letter from the U.S. Shipping Commissioner, Custom House, Boston, certifying that I had been issued Seaman's Identification Certificate, Statement of Service, Certificate of Lifeboatman, attesting to thirty-six hours actually spent in a lifeboat, that I had pulled an oar, was licensed to command any and all lifeboats, that I was familiar with the three dozen pieces of equipment, etc.

When I look back on the past thirty years, I remember other kudos which I have received: recommendations from employers; a statement from the Army Engineers commending my work with the Veteran's Conservation Corps; those two pieces of costume junk, the Victory Medal and Merchant Marine Emblem, which I shall never be able to tack on my door, because replacement will cost $1.70 prepaid, from the Department of Commerce, etc. and etcetera.

There is only one paper which I haven't been able to figure out how to procure. This paper, to my mind, will complement all the other documents and answer the purpose for which I have so lovingly nailed them on the door. This paper would be procured from the Department of Justice, Federal Bureau of Investigation, Washington, D.C.; it would attest to all my arrests in all the states, the nature of offense, the dates, and disposition (sentences). I have considered evoking the aid of the local chief of constabulary to that purpose, but as yet can think of no reason why he should apply to so high a source to supply me a document for a purpose which he is by temperament and profession, unable to understand.

Walter Mitty had his hour upon the screen and in the book. I wish to be a jot more practical. To wit: whether it be a day or years, when I answer the Last Post, when I stretch out in rigor mortis, when the siren of the ambulance sounds (instead of the riot car), when the police oversee the removal of my cadaver from this third rate flea-bitten enclave, I hope to awaken, in one, even in only one observer, a philosophical thought to be pursued and verified, that a wino is not just a wino, that all men are a hotch-potch of greatness and littleness, of virtue and vice, of nobility and baseness; that some men have more strength of character; or more opportunity; that some men give a freer play to their instincts; and that this hoped for "philosopher" will come to an understanding of himself, that he is no better or worse than most people, that if all our good and all our bad are tacked on closet doors, one will probably balance the other. I have long since become satisfied that this balance exists and am looking for converts.

Stranger thoughts than these abound in the lonely hotel rooms of the aged and sick. Thanks again for the money.

Regards,

F.

Westville Jail and House of Correction
April 26, 1965

Dear Bob:

Received your last letter at the hotel, over two weeks ago, & contents. On April 8th, I was removed from the liquor black list, having not been arrested since October 8th. A few days later I was given a summons to appear in court, last Thursday, on an assault charge. The futility of arresting me on a drunkenness complaint is becoming apparent to the local scene.

In brief the picture was this—while in the hotel (read zoo), one of the denizens took what is known in the vernacular, as a sucker punch at me in the hallway; it appeared that I was helpless & getting battered; one of the other roomers came out of his room & beat the hell out of the other guy. He swore out a warrant against both of us. It is not pertinent that this jackal is regularly employed, while drawing unemployment pay.

Sorry I could not be loose for your impending visit.

Frank

Calvinville
Congress Hotel
June 1, 1965

Dear Bob:

Sound off with Verdi's "Triumphant March" from "Aida"!!! I was brought to the Superior Court in Calvinville last Monday. Asked if I was ready for trial; I stated that I wished to subpoena four witnesses (one of these was in jail & so a habeas corpus was necessary); stated that I wished a jury trial. And so back to Westville poor wretch, twenty odd miles, shackled on both hands, going & coming except the few minutes from the ante-room to appear before the judge.

This to and fro junket, as above, is a kind of brainwashing or psy-

chological warfare calculated to cause the young or inexperienced offender to waive the right of trial by jury & to plead guilty (this is
known in jail argot as "copping a plea"). Sad, but is effective in most
instances.

And so back to Calvinville on Thursday, in gyves for trial; waited in
the ante-room for three hours with the court officers who told me how
anxious they were to get home; the district attorney instructed me that
they might not be able to summon twelve men (& women), tried &
true, that day & asked whether I still insisted on jury trial; I did.

Finally, I was brought in for trial at one P.M.; the judge tried his
damnedest to appoint a public defender & I was granite solid in deny-
ing that effort, & reiterating that I would be my own counsel. A public defender would have insured procedural guarantees, but I did not
care about that hanky-panky, & believed that I best could adduce the
facts (I was there, Charlie).

The reason I wished trial by jury was because a judge is, intrinsically,
a scholar & has been trained to form a certitude of opinion. I wished
to be tried by people like myself who have experienced different kinds
of lives & retain a fair modicum of doubts.

Instructed that I had the right to three peremptory challenges of
the jury, I glanced at the three women & wondered if all these belonged to the W.C.T.U. No way of knowing. I considered throwing
three men or women off, just out of vindictiveness, to cost the county
more time & money, to balance the hours that I had spent in handcuffs; refrained.

Trial got under way; complainant a lean & cadaverous Cassius;
stated that I had assaulted him & when he had fought me off, another
man attacked him with a knife; stated that he was glad that he was
not a "welfare bum." The trial lasted two hours; during the time that
I cross-examined him, & my witnesses, I kept myself under control,
except a few lapses when I waggled a handful of papers on which I
had written about five hundred questions.

I was partially able to adduce from the complainant that while he
had been working for weeks, contracting to cut wood lots, purchasing
a car, that during this time he was being paid Unemployment Compensation from federal funds, & that he was periodically registering as
being "unemployed." This was the first part of my cross examination
aimed at the "reliability" & "honesty" of the plaintiff. The judge tried
to shut me off this matter, as not being relevant to the assault. I an-

swered to him & the jury that it was relevant, not only to consider
the words of the testimony against me, but to consider the character
of the man who uttered that testimony. I think the jury was in accord
in assuming the plaintiff a petty thief. Subsequently, it seems that this
was a good mode of attack; when I was found not guilty, the plaintiff
moved out of the hotel that night & has been sleeping in his car ever
since, getting ready to fly, I imagine.

It is indeed a far cry from the academic walls to petty trials & so
I forbear too many details. In the final cross-examination of the plaintiff, I adduced that he had never been in the service (a responsibility
of citizenship); that he neither belonged to or contributed to the support of any church; belonged to no labor union or fraternal order; or
had any social connections which are symbolic of a staid citizen who
has the inalienable right to summon & jail the lesser breed without
the law.

Dear Bob, I know you will get a mental "kick" out of the way I
usurped the weapons that have been used against me for my own
defense.

One other highlight: plaintiff stated that he lived in the Congress
Hotel; I asked him whether it was a hotel in the usual sense of the
word, & asked whether beds were ever made, floors were ever swept
or mopped, etc. The judge interrupted, & said it could be assumed
that he lived in a rooming house. Then an attention calling silence, &
I addressed the court, stating that if I were permitted to pursue my
questioning, evidence would be given to show his honor & the jury,
that it was beyond their conception of either hotel or rooming house.
I brought out that the heat was not turned down but off during daylight hours in January, February and March; a cold water faucet with
the eccentricity of not running for half an hour at a time when one
cared for a drink or was midway in a shave; toilet bowls connected to
the same cold water piping, ergo, unflushable for thirty or forty minutes; locks that didn't work; windows that wouldn't open, etc. I
delineated to my prissy jury of New Englanders, the word picture of
the oldtime Bowery flophouse with shades of a sailors' rooming house
on the Barbary Coast before the fire of 1904.

Of my witnesses, one had died since I was jailed. I looked around
the court room & Yonder he was a 'moldering. This was the man who
slept in the next room; I told you of him, a retiree, who starved himself to death so that he would have more money to drink wine (which

he shared with his friends, of whom, I was one). The hotel manager gave me his poplin pajamas & bathrobe today; washed them this afternoon; do you think the ghost will walk! I would be glad to see him.

Another witness I had summoned, hid across the river, leaving me a message that he was mid-way in a week's drunk, & that he was afraid that he would do me more harm than good by appearing in that condition. Good old reliable alcoholics!

The other two testified that I was the one who was attacked, & that when my head struck the wall, I appeared dazed & helpless; then one of them interfered & beat hell out of the plaintiff. My rescuer was a sixty year old ex-prize fighter & never owned a knife in his life. He had already been charged with me in the lower court, pleaded "not guilty," and was found guilty; appealed his sentence; & after a few days in Westville had withdrew his appeal. Being locked up twenty-two hours a day in Westville jail does things to people, & he withdrew his appeal so that he could work on the penal farm and get more food.

I took the stand in my own defense, & pointed out to the jury that the guilty man & professional wrongdoer never takes the stand because he is liable to cross-examination by the district attorney & that his past record could be entered into the trial. I stated that in this case, I anticipated any derogatory questioning on the district attorney's part & that I welcomed the opportunity of laying my soul bare. At this time, the judge stated that he didn't believe the district attorney was going to ask me any questions regarding my character & past life. It seemed to me that he was "instructing" the district attorney, & this led to my intuition, for the first time, that I was going to be found "not guilty." I instructed the jury that I had been on "Public Welfare" since January 8; that the city allowed me a maximum of seven dollars a week (not cash) & that is why I resorted to such habitation; that I was disabled with emphysema & asthma; that my doctor was shocked when I told him that my social worker had expected me to eat at the rate of a dollar a day in a restaurant (not cash); that I had walked the streets for weeks at a time without a red cent in my pocket, & I drew a cozy picture of the welfare wastrel who plucks the pockets of the sanctimonious tax-payer.

I pointed out to the jury the man who interfered in my behalf; & drew the parallel of the injured motorist on the highway who signals his distress, & is ignored by people who do not wish to become involved; I presented to them the analogy of people attacked on the subways & elevated trains in the metropolitan cities & how the other passengers chose not to become involved, who chose to "mind their own business;" and how, in my own case, a man had chosen to become involved & how he had become penalized, found guilty of assault & jailed & how he withdrew his appeal because he had previously been arrested for drunkenness & jailed, & because of this record he had no confidence in the courts to hear his side. . . . When I was found not guilty, the jury swarmed about the judge wanting to know what they could do for this other man who aided me. Yesterday, I visited his son's house; found that he was welcome to live there; outlined a letter for the son to write to the chairman of the county commissioners to obtain his release. He has completed more than half his three months sentence.

In my final statement to the jury, I turned to the site of the old high school. I told them that I had not learned law. But that the earliest of written laws was the code of Hanmurabi in cuneiform writing baked on clay tablets. The teaching of law in that high school was fragmentary; I learned that the laws before the present courts descended from English Common Law & the Magna Carta. At that moment Perry Mason, Darrow, Earl Wilson, Abe Hummel & all the famous pleaders "possessed me." I stated that I remembered but one line of the Magna Carta: "To no man will we refuse justice." Not *except* the man who gets drunk; not *except* the man who has been in jail; not *except* the man who has a record; *but* to *no* man will we refuse justice.

The jury stayed out long enough to have a smoke, & found "not guilty." It seems to me that I waste a hell of a lot of time on lost causes, & a hell of a lot of energy on the smaller aspects of living.

Denouement

You will note by the preceding how I fought to be released. To what purpose??? Down to the City Hall at 4 P.M., from the courthouse; obtained a meal ticket; told to get a room; went to the four cheap places; no vacancies; everybody expects to be paid in excess of seven dollars; I think the city established these rates during the Hispano-American War; obtained three dollars cash for my meal ticket; did not drink 'til eight at night when it began raining & it became apparent I could not obtain even a room for the night. At nine at night, fatigued by my hectic day in court, I sighted an empty store entrance that was recessed from the rain; fire-proof; with no pedestrians on the sidewalks; raining hard; & masked from the street light; & I laid me down to sleep on the black asphalt. I forgot to mention that my clothing was pressed & clean when I sought the arms of Morpheus, guarding my old bones against the night's chill & dampness. You will note by the enclosed clipping, my sleep was not uninterrupted.

Up to the City Hall on Friday & welfare workers were all a-dither; it would so simplify their hum-drum life, if the court would send me to jail. Just too G.D. stupid to realize that jail is no solution, & that the same situation will recur a month or two months hence. I believe they can obtain state disability allowance for me, & get rid of the city's financial burden. So far, it has been easier to cast me in jail. . . . Obtained my old room here at the hotel. I have told you about the locks. The only thing I received back of my belongings was my razor. When Christ was crucified the Roman soldiers shot craps for his clothes. When I went to jail, my few belongings vanished into air, into thin air. The hotel manager is trying to make amends & today gave me a table lamp & an electric clock so I will always know my hour of doom, & some of the dead man's clothes. I have no money for soap or razor blades, because the social workers fear I will get drunk if I had as much as a dollar. I put my suit into the cleaners today & if I never have a dollar to get it out, I will have the vindictive satisfaction of knowing that no one can steal it from my room. Saw the postmaster this morning & he gave me this writing tablet & promised to stamp my mail to you (pay for it). He gave me a ball point pen in January but the vultures who cleaned out my room got that. Sometimes I think he is bewildered; he may or may not understand why a man of your status pays heed to me.

A somber Memorial Day for me. Visited my grandfather's grave; also my aunt's grave; died when I was 7; what a direction they gave my dust & soul!!

Sincerely,
Frank

Newspaper clipping accompanying Frank's letter of June 1, 1965:

Calvinville—Frank G. Moore, 61, who lists his address as a local hotel, is a real "in again, out again" case.

For much of yesterday, he was in Superior Court, where a jury and Judge Herbert Peters were hearing his appeal of a guilty District Court finding of assault and battery.

Moore refused counsel and insisted on defending himself. Eventually the jury found him not guilty.

But he had only about six hours of hard won freedom before he was in jail again. He was arrested by Patrolman Timothy Thomas at 10:50 p.m. for drunkenness.

Appearing before Special Justice Isaac Chertok in District Court this morning, Moore was found guilty. On the drunkenness complaint he was given a suspended sentence to Stonycreek Correctional Institution and was placed on probation for one year.

To which Frank appended the note: "Hard won? Yeh, Man!!"

Stonycreek Correctional Institution
August 3, 1965

Dear Bob:

One of the pleasures of old age is that one is afforded the opportunity of saying "I told you so." How it warms the cockles of my old heart, (when, after fifteen or twenty years) someone shall say to me, "Moorey, you were right in your evaluation of that person, or in the evaluation of this or that situation."

. . . . .

It may interest you to learn that my "rabid" thinking and writing of many years in regard to lack of legal counsel for indigent persons has reverberated from the Supreme Court to Calvinville District Court and that every drunk or vagrant is now offered the services of a lawyer, and where he refuses counsel, he must sign a waiver of such services. I wish to be among the first to indicate that representation by counsel in these cases is nominal and not factual. The counsel is appointed in the court and has no pre-trial knowledge of the case whatsoever. Let me think long enough and I shall develop a phantasy wherein this Supreme Court decision is designed to aid indigent attorneys-at-law, and not drunkards, vagrants, and petty criminals.

Frank

Stonycreek Correctional Institution
August 10, 1965

Dear Bob:

. . . . .

Like Rabelais' Pantagruel, I have consulted the magic bottle and prognosticate that Alcoholism with all its ramifications (your favorite word), will come under the domain of Public Health Service during 1975–1980. The main reason that I have come to this conclusion is that the federal government will administer the program and provide the funds. The cities, counties, and states' administrators, commissioners, and legislatures will never directly provide the funds for such a purpose, and the taxpayer will be compelled to pay to the federal government, what he would not willingly pay to the city, county, or state. Forcefully or otherwise, the general public will be compelled to acknowledge that, yea verily, they are their brother's keeper. You are going to be around to see this transition. It is not likely that I shall be. Appearing on history's scene too early, I have been a victim of a melancholy record of error, bumbling, and the evading of responsibility. I am most fortunate to have lived during the early stages of the transition and to experience the amelioration that science has so far effected.

F.

Congress Hotel
Calvinville
October 14, 1965

Dear Bob:

I received yours two weeks past, but procrastinated in answering because I hoped to give you some definite information in regard to my Disability Evaluation.

Last Friday, I met an appointment at the University Medical Center. The request form was checked for the following items: (1) Physical Evaluation (2) Probable length of disability (3) Drugs & Medicine required and (4) Patient's Needs.

Six interminable hours of blood tests, sputum tests, urinanalysis, percussion, auscultation, measurement of lung capacity, etc. And it was decided that I must come back tomorrow (Friday) to finish the examination, x-ray and God knows what.

On the forms that I brought back to the Calvinville City Hall giving notice of reappointment, the tentative diagnosis was a cardiac-pulmono failure, left sided; chronic emphysema; chronic bronchitis; & acute nocturnal dyspnea.

Whatever else they hope to find wrong with me tomorrow I can't imagine. However, it is interesting to note, that in the past two years when I was a Public Welfare recipient (at such times as I had not been placed in jail)—the welfare authorities pontificated that there was nothing wrong with me except that I drank, & if I stopped drinking there would be nothing wrong with me.

You can imagine, that in view of the latest finding, that I am tempted to go around town saying, "Ha, Ha, Ha, I told you so."

When this subject of Disability Assistance was broached to me at City Hall, I voiced my willingness to undergo the necessary examinations & procedure. So far, I get very ambiguous & indefinite information. The only thing for certain is that I will receive a check twice a month instead of the city paying hotel & grocery bills.

Whatever may be the enlightened social attitudes, it seems rather preposterous that I may achieve a kind of security after this long improvident history.

I have lived so damn long without money, & have walked the streets without money for weeks at a time, telling myself that I was lucky to have a full gut & a roof over my head. But what in hell does one do about a hair cut, broken shoelaces, & must I always "borrow" a needle & thread? The wiseacre who vouchsafed that "man wants little down here below" just didn't understand the number of exigencies that occur in ordinary existence.

It would be just my god-damn bad luck to die before receiving the aforesaid checks.

Hospital appointment tomorrow & I hope welcome news for you soon. The table is high, ergo lousy writing.

Frank

1966

January	Congress Hotel, Calvinville
February	Jail?
March–April	Congress Hotel, unaccounted for
May–September	Stonycreek Correctional Institution
October–December	Church Street rooming house, Calvinville

As 1966 began, Frank was still at the Congress Hotel awaiting word on his appeal for disability status, only to be rejected this time. Correspondence was sparse during the early part of the year although eventually he wrote eighteen letters. There are two periods, totaling ten weeks, which are unaccounted for. He probably served a jail sentence sometime between January and March, when he sent a brief message noting that he was "back in" the hotel and sick. By May, 1966, he was in Stonycreek. Discouraged and sick, he requested a maximum five-month period of custody.

In 1965 and again in the spring of 1966, I had written to Frank that I would try to visit him in connection with planned trips to the East. Both of my letters were unanswered, and at the time of my trips his whereabouts were unknown to me. However, an opportunity for a visit came again in late October, 1966, shortly after his release from Stonycreek. This time we made contact. My notes describing our visit on November 1, 1966 are presented with Frank's letters for this year.

The observations in Frank's letters for 1966 follow the themes of 1965, but the beginnings of a thinness and return to narrative detail are noticeable as he coped with the vicissitudes of illness, depression, and drunkenness, and struggled to avoid arrest and jail.

> Congress Hotel
> Calvinville
> Friday, January 14, 1966

Dear Bob:

I received your Christmas card & the enclosure. I am enclosing papers regarding rejection of my disability claim.

When I received the notification from the local Welfare Board—which incidentally was sent by letter even though I am compelled to go up there every Monday and Thursday for a grocery order (nobody in City Hall wanted to inform me, hence the letter)—I proceeded to the local doctor who had been treating me & showed him the grounds on which I had been denied (Not totally disabled). He remarked: "They mean you are still walking."

I appealed the decision. About a week or so later, I was given a hearing by a state referee. While I was cooling my heels, waiting for the hearing, I saw him being "briefed" in the Public Assistance Director's Office. I need not to have had paranoia to reach the conclusion that his mind was "made up" before I went in there. When I told my doctor that I was slated for this hearing, he told me to have the referee call him by phone. I followed his instructions, but the referee would not call him. So much for the "fair and impartial hearing."

Among other things, the referee asked me whether I believed that I had a drinking problem. Where would he get such an idea except from the "briefing" preliminary to the hearing? I informed him that in the past I had had a drinking problem & that I would often throw up a hundred dollars a week & get drunk, but at the present time I no longer had an alcoholic problem; that I was a sick old man, unemployable; that whatever drinking I had done in the last few years were purchased by gratuity by local people who had known me "when" & that the cash that the City Hall allowed me in the past year had amounted to the total of one dollar and a half which was given me on one occasion, that my hotel bill was paid by check from the city to the innkeeper & that my food needs were taken care of in the same fashion; that whatever drinking I had done in the past year was bought by people who felt "sorry" for me; that I existed in a modern society without five cents in my pockets for weeks at a time; & finally: "How the hell could I have an alcoholic problem?"

The referee's decision, the decision of the local welfare board, et al were predicated on the opinion of my dear social worker, aged 75, a long line of drunks in her family & whose present thinking is of circa 1920. You can surely wager that after working for the city for 30 or 40 years, her opinions have much weight. She is the same dear soul that told me my asthma & emphysema are due to my sinful past. I told the local doctor of it & he said: "Don't pay any attention to her." I replied: "Goddamit, she is the one who is making the decisions." She is the same dear heart who said, "I can eat good on five dollars a week." (She has what I would judge to be a 44 inch waistline, mine is 32). I imagine she could live off her hump like a camel for awhile on five dollars a week to her own betterment.

The crux of all the foregoing is that the city will not be relieved the burden of my bed, board, & an expensive drug which I take three times a day; that the city chooses to be saddled with this financial burden to please one of her moralists (???). Using the back of a book for a desk, excuse penmanship. More when I am not so furious.

Frank

Stonycreek Correctional Institution
July 13, 1966

Dear Bob:

"Since among all creatures that breathe on earth & crawl on it there is not anywhere a thing more dismal than man is." Homer's Iliad.

You inquired regarding my present status in Stonycreek. There is no definite sentence here for drunkenness. The term ranges from 60 days (minimum) to 5½ months (maximum). After the prisoner has been here from 5 to 6 weeks, he goes before a board consisting of a senior correction officer, a social worker & a psychiatrist, & it is determined at that time the date when the prisoner will be released.

It has been a matter of conjecture among the prisoner population, as to the process by which the board determines the date of release. Probably the physical condition, the age of the person & his employability are the determinants. Lively guesses are hazarded by the inmates as to whether the board "reads" the entrails of birds, resorts to pumpkin seeds, or has a "wheel of fortune."

I went before the "board" this afternoon & requested that I be given the maximum sentence. The maximum sentence is probably resorted to in one case out of a thousand admissions & by reason of gross misconduct. Without any desire to elaborate, I explained that there was nothing out there "on the street" that I was greatly concerned about. The board set my date for a 5 months sentence with the understanding that I could be released at a much earlier date if I changed my mind.

It is ironical that a few hundred of the oldsters look forward to the earliest possible date when they can again wrap their face around a wine bottle, get arrested, & come back to the sanctuary of Stonycreek, & another comparatively small group of younger men in their prime to whom this confinement is a real punishment. It may be that I am not a prototype or archetype, after all. I know that I have always hated like hell to be a rubber stamp or stereotype.

You were interested in the earlier part of the year, as concerned my comings & goings. Nothing ever happened to me sober & everything happened to me when drunk. Some of the single incidents of this year would comprise a whole letter.

Thanks,
Frank

Stonycreek Correctional Institution
July 26, 1966

Dear Bob:

Quoting from two excerpts of late news:

"A blow for the rights of alcoholics was struck last week in the United States Court of Appeals of the District of Columbia, when it was ruled that a proven chronic alcoholic could not be convicted of drunkenness because he was not responsible for his acts."

"The ruling was handed down in the case of DeWitt Easter, aged

59, who was tried in 1964 for public drunkenness & given a 90 day suspended sentence. It was the seventieth such conviction."

"The high court threw out the verdict on grounds that the trial judge erred in refusing to hear testimony that Easter was an alcoholic who had lost the power of self-control over consumption of alcoholic beverages."

"Such a defendant could not be punished under criminal law, the court found, because he had not the intent to commit crime."

"But there is a catch: the alcoholic needs a lawyer or an expert witness to prove that he is a chronic alcoholic. If he can not afford it, he will be sent to jail." (End of Excerpts.)

Many years ago when I went to Davenport on a number of occasions (along with thousands like myself), the doctors were anxious to make written record that I was a chronic alcoholic. Such diagnosis was a "down-grading" of the patient & was intended to be derogatory. This classification excluded the necessity of treatment, except primary sedation, & the alcoholic was then subjected to mop & broom therapy in addition to more arduous labors necessary to the maintenance of a hospital.

Does it not strike you as ironical that these people in Davenport with the intent to consign me to the nethermost regions with the appelation of "chronic alcoholism," would at some later day supply me with a defense testimony? If I went to a Superior Court on an appeal from District Court, I could subpoena my Davenport dossier.

Frank

Stonycreek Correctional Institution
August 16, 1966

Dear Bob:

It is the better part of intelligence to consider the advantages of one's position (whatever the situation may be). For instance, I can awake in the morning with the assurance that someone is already at work peeling potatoes & onions for my dinner, others are busy cooking my food; someone is ready to wash my dishes when I am thru eating, my bed will have been made sometime in the forenoon; in different departments men will be washing my clothes & bed linen; whenever my dusty brown locks become long the barber stands ready; the engineers department will be supplying hot water, heat, & light. The librarian stands ready to exchange books; the officers stand ready to turn the two television sets to two different stations in order that I have diverse entertainment. The toilet & shaving facilities are on the par with the Grand Central Station, Etc. To parody a First World War song: "How 'ya going to keep them out on the streets, after they've seen Stonycreek."

Such is institutional life—as Oscar Wilde has said "Pale Anguish keeps the gate, & the warder is Despair." Methinks I draw on an ideal cooperative picture. Should I enumerate the recreational facilities, then could I imagine the composite ghost of all the taxpayers rising up in just fury & wrath.

Truly, it is awesome, the amount of money which can be spent to vent the spleen, & to satisfy the retaliatory & vindictive desires of what we are assured, are the majority of the people. . . . Such expense is of a temporary nature, but unfortunately, getting in jail is a habit such as cocain sniffing. Behind the walls becomes a way of life, & over the course of years, one becomes inured as to rheumatism or a bald head.

. . . . .

Regards,
Frank

On November 1, 1966, I went to Calvinville and found Frank living in a rooming house on Church Street, which runs off one of the main business streets of the town, about three blocks from its center. I knocked on the front door and Frank came to greet me. He was dressed in a clean blue shirt, open at the collar, and a pair of very heavy wool work pants with cuffs sewn in heavy thread with large stitches which he had applied himself.

He had been anticipating my visit, and the first thing he said was that he had been hoping I would come that day. As we went up the stairs, past the bucket of suds he had been using to scrub the hallway, Frank said the other roomers didn't yet know what to make of him. They were apprehensive lest he bring trouble to their tranquility, and he was trying to reassure them by doing things like keeping the halls and stairs clean.

Frank's room was on the second floor facing the front of the house and was both light and airy. The room was very sparsely furnished (as were other rooms which I was able to see). An old metal-framed double bed with a thin mattress sat under an unshaded light bulb on a chain dangling from the ceiling. On a wooden bureau were several books borrowed from the Calvinville Public Library. One of these was James

Jones's *From Here to Eternity.* There was only one chair, a straight wooden one, on which I sat while he sat on the edge of the bed. There was a metal closet, empty except for some canned and packaged foods stacked in it. Frank said that his food allotment provided more than he could possibly eat, but his accommodations limited him to foods that did not require refrigeration.

Frank's general appearance had not changed much in the more than ten years since I had last seen him. However, his eyes and cheeks were hollow-looking. He alluded to this, and said that his chest, too, was hollow. He was having a good deal of trouble breathing, coughed quite a bit and wheezed. He smoked fairly constantly and said that the smoke forced him to cough and thus helped him keep from choking. He complained of a general weakness which was apparent later when we took a walk through the town.

First, we went to the library, which he said with pride had a very large collection for a small town. Frank felt accepted there and expressed a warm feeling toward the librarian. He explained that he spent several hours a day in the reading room. We then saw the YMCA, where he recalled that his grandfather once gave him a membership but later his stepfather would not let him join because he felt it was too "uppity."

A three-block walk brought us to a park occupying about the equivalent of three city blocks of uneven dimensions. The park contained a small pond, and several historical markers plus a couple of very old buildings. One of these was pointed out as a former jail. Some children were playing at the edge of the pond, and Frank mentioned that that was where his father had committed suicide.

We next walked to the post office and knocked at the door of the postmaster, Mr. Parsons, who had recently taken an interest in Frank and given him some help. Mr. Parsons was very gracious.

Next we walked up the street to the Congress Hotel, a forbidding brick structure about five stories high located a block from the main business section of Calvinville. Frank took me to the rear of the building and opened some trash cans to show me that they were full of empty liquor bottles. We then walked up a filthy rear staircase to the third floor. There we found a typical flophouse interior: rows of small rooms each with a cot and a chair and a naked light bulb. The corridor was filthy; the air was stale and permeated with the stench of alcohol, urine, excrement, and vomit. The public toilet and washroom were filthy, with torn bits of newspaper strewn around the floor. In several rooms, all of which seemed to be open, we saw men lying about in lethargy or drunkenness. We then went down the front stairs to a small lobby where several men whom Frank identified as permanent guests were sitting. He asked a man at the counter if any mail had come for him, and then (much to my relief) we went out to the street and fresh air.

On the way back to his rooming house Frank pointed out the prosperous-looking business of which his cousin was vice-president. We got into my car and drove back to a dry cleaner's, where I retrieved some of Frank's clothing that had been there for several months. He asked if I could help out with a haircut and I gave him the cash for it. I left him at the rooming house after he promised that he would write soon.

> 46 Church Street
> Calvinville
> December 1, 1966

Dear Bob:

Received yours, mailed Armistice Day, & enclosure for which, many thanks.

The first chapter of Pierre Louy's "Aphrodite" opens with Chrysis, a courtesan of ancient Alexandria, bewailing the fact that "the days are like each other."

And so it goes with the Hermit of the Shark-Tooth Shoals (my new self-inflicted nom-de-plume). It sure does beat hell how much a person may be isolated & a recluse in the center of a city of sixteen thousand.

But what is the beef? (I spent the great part of my life squawking that I lived in a gold fish bowl in the service & in jail). Privacy isn't half bad. Plenty of books, excellent library, plenty to eat, good room, heat & sanitary abode.

It is the infinitesimals that concern me most, such as the hair-cut you paid for, & it took two weeks to gain authorization for a pair of rubber heels (now I need a pair of those rubber patches which you can apply yourself with glue, to the soles of your shoes. The soles are so thin that I can stand on a dime & tell you whether it is head or tails.)

Oh, I haven't worn the suit up to City Hall. The appearance, de rigeur, of a public assistance recipient are dungarees, hair growing out of the ears, chin down & tail drooping. With that suit on, they would try to hand me a snow shovel.

Anent the hotel, you assured me that you had seen dives before, but certainly not in a small 'respectable' New England town. I am so glad to get out of that filthy joint, that in my present surroundings, I am the self-appointed & unpaid cleaner of the lavatory, hallway & stairway. Things could never again be clean enough after living in that rotten place.

It would be nice to stay out of jail, die in cleanliness & privacy, without making a hell of a lot of a commotion & being an inconvenience to others. I have seen more than one person die in county jails, laying in a cell with a blanket pulled up over their face for twenty-four hours with the occasional ghoulishly inclined prisoner peeking beneath the blanket to see what the "stiff" looked like.

What in hell is all this talk of dying? Sometimes, I thought I was going to die. Sometimes I was afraid I wouldn't & now I know I shall live forever.

Frank

9. "Mister Moore," 1967-72

From 1967 into 1970, Frank continued to improve his relationship to the outside world and was able to maintain himself in the community for significant periods of time with the help of public assistance. While his time spent in prison or jail totaled twenty-two weeks in 1966, this was reduced to only four weeks in 1967 and to just one week in 1968. During these periods, most of his time outside of institutional custody was spent living in rooming houses in Calvinville. There were occasional episodes of public intoxication leading to arrest. Although arrest meant displacement from the "homes" he had managed to arrange, on each occasion he was able to re-establish himself in the community with the help of the local welfare resources. From March, 1968, into the summer of 1969, Frank enjoyed an unusually long period of about seventeen consecutive months of freedom from institutional custody. However brief this period may seem in a lifetime, it was a time of personal triumph and satisfaction for Frank, who was so acutely aware of the depth and breadth of his lifelong problems.

During the years from 1967 into 1970, Frank enjoyed a relative stability, security, and touch of respectability that he had not known since childhood. This can perhaps best be explained by the turnaround in his motivation regarding custodial living. A consistent theme of Frank's letters and my several visits with him, from 1966 on, was his intense desire to avoid any further institutionalization. He was tired of institutions; he was tired of others making decisions for him; he just wanted to "die privately."

Frank was not able to maintain himself in the community entirely on his own. In many respects the welfare system met and sustained his dependency needs. But the most significant step for Frank was his ability to escape custodial living and thereby to exercise more initiative and self-care, and enjoy more privacy than he had had since he enlisted in the Navy in 1920 at the age of sixteen.

Even Frank's alcoholism, which helped meet some of his dependency needs and in the past had functioned often to place him back into custodial care, was "channeled" sufficiently to allow him to maintain himself in his "private" residence. When his rooming-house arrangements did break down it was because even in private the consequences of his drinking became unacceptable to a landlady or because his precautions against public exposure of his intoxication failed him. However, he was usually able to confine his drinking to his room.

After almost four years of this relatively stable pattern, Frank suffered a relapse in the summer of 1969, when an episode of public intoxication led to jail for several months. But, once again, he succeeded in reestablishing independent residence and avoiding custodial care. Finding all rooming houses in Calvinville full or closed to him, he settled in Westville, where I visited him in July, 1970, and where he had again collected a set of memorabilia, which seemed so important in his later years as a symbol of respectability and as evidence that his life had had some meaning.

In October, 1970, Frank's strength, initiative, and confidence were severely challenged by a vicious spiral of illness, drunkenness, eviction, injury, hospitalization, homelessness, arrest, a diagnosis of acute tuberculosis, and the onset of symptoms of angina pectoris. An earlier diagnosis of Parkinson's disease had been greeted by Frank lightly ("At last something respectable"), but the finding of TB ended, for a time at least, all hope that Frank could live by himself, no matter how strong his motivation. His disabilities of 1970 and thereafter made him wonder whether he would have adequate good health to maintain himself once again in a community even if he could shake off "my heredity, my early environment, my occupational habits, my life long experience."

In 1971 Frank spent more than half the year in and out of various hospitals, sanitariums, and sick wards of correctional institutions. During the last four months of the year Frank was released from hospital care but was unable to settle down again and entered an old pattern of wandering, intoxication, and jail. Ironically, he had difficulty reinstating his public-assistance checks, which had stopped during his hospitalization in a state institution. He needed the checks in order to establish a regular residence but was told that a residence was the prerequisite for reinstating his checks. Letters from me to his former social welfare worker in Westville may have helped resolve this problem and remove a major stumbling block to Frank's being able to establish community living once again.

Frank's correspondence during the period 1967 through 1969 dropped to only three or four communications per year, concomitant with his new-found security and independence of those years. These letters reflected his earlier style of narrative episodic accounts of personal experiences and feelings, with only occasional philosophical observations. His attacks on various social institutions mellowed noticeably and introspection thinned.

My visits with Frank during this period permitted me to see, hear about, and appreciate his new life pattern, which, with a dwindling correspondence, did not always come through graphically in his letters. These visits also served as a stimulus for Frank to comment in several later letters on what he considered to have been the significance of our correspondence to his own sanity and survival.

Beginning again in 1970 the correspondence picked up when illness and despair required a return to institutional living. It was almost as if the frustrations of institutional living tripped a repeat key as he renewed his attacks on institutional staff and professionals, whom he perceived to be just as "institutionalized" as the patients; on the futility of public health with its duplications, inefficiencies, and "phoney morality"; on women; on the inhumanity of man to man as he fails to recognize the existence and depth of feelings that even the most down-and-out derelicts have. He also reminisced about people who had expressed human concern and respect for him, and he made repeated inventories of his accomplishments. In this respect his letters became quite repetitious and his sharp memory for details from the distant past seemed to exceed his recall of recent events.

During the entire period of renewed instability and mounting physical problems (1970–72) I wrote several letters at Frank's request to varied institutional personnel encouraging them to take the calculated risks necessary to return Frank to community living, but the problems posed by his deteriorating health worked against him.

On several occasions in his letters Frank indicated the hope that his own demise would provide the final "escape from custody." His repeated references to "finishing up" and the "last chapter" reflected a despairing attitude and an impatience on his part with his continuing struggle.

Although convalescent-type care would seem qualitatively different from the incarceration he had experienced during so much of his life, he maintained his disdain, even fear, of having to spend his last days in any form of institutional setting. His mind, if not his body, was determined to avoid any and all types of custodial care.

Frank's yearning for a final taste of independence, self-respect, and a warm relationship with another human being was consummated when, after having been hospitalized off and on for almost a year and a half, he managed to establish himself in March, 1972, in a Harrison rooming house. Here, for six months, he was essentially on his own with the help of a kind landlady. Here, despite sporadic drunkenness, he was happy, respected, treated as a member of the family, and even loved. And, while he needed considerable attention to his physical needs from Mrs. Bourne, his landlady, he had succeeded in his own mind and in the spirit of the relationship with her family, to have escaped from custody.

Frank died September 24, 1972.

1967

January–August	Church Street rooming house, Calvinville
September	Jail (30 days)
October–December	Congress Hotel, Calvinville

For the first eight months of 1967, Frank continued to live in a rooming house in Calvinville. During this time, he finally won support from the welfare system. This was no mean accomplishment for such a dependent person, who was on his own in the outside world after almost a lifetime of institutional living. He also managed to work out a simple routine, which kept him out of trouble and out of jail.

In September Frank was arrested for drunkenness. He was given a thirty-day sentence, just long enough for him to lose his room on Church Street and all his possessions once again.

Upon his release he returned to the "flea-bitten enclave" of the Congress Hotel in Calvinville, from where he sent me the Christmas greeting: "Am back in the Congress Hotel, 'nuf sed'!"

46 Church Street
Calvinville
February 24, 1967

Dear Bob:

It seems that I have not written to you since the first part of December. In retrospect, it seems that I was complaining of being the "Hermit of Shark's Tooth Shoal," the feeling of loneliness in the holiday season, the winter of discontent, etc., etc.

In consideration of past life-wandering up and down the country, jumping into & out of box cars, physical exposure, being locked in a jail cell, three by six, for twenty-two hours out of twenty-four (Westville) for periods of thirty days, not being trusted with a match (State Hospitals), of being sick or injured in strange cities where no one cared or was concerned; of more times than I care to remember of subsisting for two or three days on a single can of beans or sardines & then tackling two jobs in steel mills, twice a lumberjack, innumerable times on the railroads & the same as a stationary fireman, etc.—it seems now, in truth, that I am sitting on the cock-eyed world, that no one, any longer, expects anything of me, that I have a security now that I have not previously known, & that writing to you in the vein mentioned above, was distinctly old-womanish. I remind myself of those superannuated old dogs that sleep in the sun, head on paws, that twitch in their members & that render muted mutterings as they dream away old age.

During your visit to C'ville I believe that I explained to you that when I returned to the Congress Hotel after four months in Stonycreek, all my clothing had been appropriated except the suit & overcoat which was in the cleaners, & which you redeemed for me. The suit will be appropriate for a shroud when fair Harvard gets thru sawing me up. Clothing is fairly easy to replace, but not a Navy discharge, a Testimonal Letter signed by the President, Merchant Marine Medal of W.W. II, the Atlantic War Zone Bar, cards of authorization for wearing these medals, discharges from the Maritime Service, a Certificate of Gunnery, Honorable Discharge Button, Merchant Marine W. W. II. Also your kudo under the imprint of U. of Kentucky that twenty years of correspondence & a life history had contributed to the understanding of alcohol pathology & institutionalization, etc. Also a Eye Donor's card & a certificate signed by the Dean of Anatomy, Harvard U., an authorization for payment of transportation costs for the shell of Frank Moore to Shattuck St., Boston. All these things were appropriated, destroyed, or otherwise disposed of when I was sent to Stonycreek.

It is doubtlessly incomprehensible to people not acquainted with the abyss of prejudice, bias, & ignorance which can be engendered by simple drunkenness. The only way that I can 'see it' is that people who have never done anything except for purely selfish motivations feel that it is inappropriate for an alcoholic (& a wino to boot) to possess any certificates or tokens of merit. I scarcely dare to go to sleep at night for fear that some god-damned undertaker is going to make money because I have not made proper provisions.

I would appreciate your sending a duplicate "To Whom It May Concern" in regard to my minuscule contribution to "alcohology."

Most sincerely,

Frank

46 Church Street
Calvinville
April 17, 1967

Dear Bob:

You will be glad to know that I have retrieved all my kudos & a few others that I had not previously thought of . . . certificate of gunnery, certificate of lifeboatman, etc. I don't know why I should have been so concerned, unless I was trying to account to myself, for the last 63 years.

You would never know how resentful a person could get, when he sees himself an "easy target." For example:

(1) A couple of months ago, I broke the ear piece on my reading glasses. I went to the optician & explained that I was 'on' Public Welfare; that I used the glasses only in my own room for reading; that I didn't care if the ear pieces matched for color; that I wanted the lowest possible estimate so that I could apply at the Public Welfare with an understanding of the costs. . . . When he heard the words "Public Welfare," he stated that I needed whole new frames. So I have not applied at the Public Welfare & I shall continue to read in my room with a loop of thread over one ear, attached to the frame. Of such is "Business."

(2) Three months ago, I reached the state where I could not walk two blocks because of the varicosity of my right leg. The doctor pre-

scribed an elastic stocking. The drug store notified the Public Welfare that they sold these stockings only in pairs. I don't need an elastic stocking on my left leg, anymore than I need a hole in the head. And this too, my friend, is also 'Business.'

Did you know that I have been out now over six months? Anno mirabilis, the year of miracles, etc. I attribute this fact to my new social worker. New, since October. She is at least as old as I am & has seen a lot of water flow under the bridge. She is kind, & I can't find anything wrong with her. Is this not the most supreme of accolade?

I continue to receive $14.75 grocery order each week, which is too damn much; my rent is paid by voucher; when I want a hair cut, the social worker telephones the barber shop; I feel like a small boy carrying a note to school; & have had to "borrow" a needle and thread from one of the junior typists to darn my socks. (The Welfare State)?

The farthest that I travel is to the Public Library. Very liberal policy & I may withdraw as many books at one time as I wish. Wade thru about six a week. When I can't sleep, I yank on the light, whatever hour, make some instant coffee (which will certainly preclude further sleep), and read, man read. Have quit reading for any serious purpose (if I ever did have one), & purely for pleasure. . . .

Frank

1968

January–February	Congress Hotel, Calvinville
March–October	King Street rooming house, Calvinville
November	Arrest, jail (10 days)
November–December	King Street rooming house, Calvinville

Aside from the Christmas card stating he was back at the Congress Hotel, I had not heard from Frank since August, 1967. In April, 1968, I wrote letters of inquiry to the manager of the Congress Hotel, the superintendent of the Calvinville Welfare Department, and Postmaster Parsons. My letter to the hotel manager was returned with an unexpected attached note from "a friend of Frank's, Bertie Brown." The note indicated that Frank was well and gave a new address for him in Calvinville. Two letters sent to Frank at this new address were also unanswered, and finally, on October 14, 1968, I went to Calvinville myself.

When Frank did not answer my knock at the address given me by

Bertie Brown, I left a note saying I would return later in the afternoon and then began a search through the town. I did not find Frank in town but incidentally acquired a first-hand view of the new image Frank had created in Calvinville. At the library, a friendly librarian said that she had not seen him yet that day, but implied that he was a regular and welcome patron. At the welfare department in city hall my inquiry prompted much sympathetic discussion among several social workers to the effect that they had seen "Mr. Moore" several times on the street, that he had not been drinking lately and that he looked fine, dressed very well, wore a bow tie, and had false teeth which improved his appearance. One clerk added that he usually carried a briefcase and she conjectured admiringly that he was writing a book.

I returned to the rooming-house address and this time my knock was answered by an elderly landlady, who inquired if I was the "doctor from the South" that Mr. Moore wanted to see. She then directed me to go right up to Frank's room, where I found Frank in bed, having slept off the effects of a bottle of muscatel wine.

In explanation for my earlier knocking's not being answered, Frank said he did not usually answer when people called to see if he was in his room. Some of his drinking "friends" had taken his clothes, food, even his medicine, and he thus tried to avoid having them come there. He also spoke of a reference of mine once to men who drank because they had nothing to protect. He said, "I have lots to protect now. I've never had it so good. I try to live hygienically, eat, walk, read, but I'm no longer useful economically or sexually." He said that his physician had advised sex as an antidote to drinking, to which he responded, "What's the purpose?" His room was simply furnished, but comfortable, personalized, and containing the basic necessities. One area of the wall was covered with the certificates and letters which Frank prized as representing significant events in his life, including my letter identifying him as the contributor of his life record.

When I mentioned the difficulty I had had in finding his new address, he pulled one of my unanswered letters from a dresser drawer and spoke of the correspondence I had had with his friend Bertie Brown. Bertie was identified as one of the drinking "friends" Frank tried to keep out of his room. He gave no reason for not replying himself but later made reference to the fact that I "had done so much" for him that he was embarrassed. It was also apparent that Frank had never recognized that his noninstitutionalized, nonalcoholic experiences would be just as interesting to me as his problems. In addition, the "wailing wall"—"confessional"—needs which I had met were certainly not needed in his current comfortable and satisfying situation.

Frank explained that his move from Church Street, where he had lived so long in 1967, was necessitated by his arrest on Labor Day, 1967. When he left jail in October, there was nothing left in his room on Church Street and he moved to the Congress Hotel. When the hotel was scheduled to be torn down in an urban-redevelopment project, other living arrangements were made for the residents, and he moved to King Street. The arrest on Labor Day, 1967, had been his last trouble with drinking, according to him. But he added that he now went on a "channeled drunk" about twice a month. He frequently used this term, which he said was mine, from a description of men who get drunk only periodically.

After visting in Frank's room for about an hour I suggested we go out while it was still light. Frank mentioned that he had recently walked to his grandfather's house and told the present owner about his family history there. He had been invited in with great courtesy and shown through the house. We then drove by the house, turned around, parked, and Frank got out of the car, walked up to the house, gazed at it for a few minutes, and returned to the car with moist eyes. He then commented that he made it a habit to deposit funds from his regular welfare check with the grocer, and never bought anything on credit, a trait he admired in his grandfather.

Back in the center of town, Frank asked me to park in front of the police station. We went in and he requested permission to see the marshal, who was sitting in a back office. After Frank introduced me, the marshal and I joked about the difficulty Frank had given arresting officers in the past. Frank told the marshal that he had seen him so often with his unrespectable friends he wanted him to meet me and to know that he had respectable friends, too. It was a polite ritual all around but here, too, I sensed a sympathy for this old man and his wasted life.

Frank's appearance was not only respectable but impressive: shirts were immaculate, trousers sharply creased, shoes well shined and in good repair. He said he did all his own washing and cleaned his room himself because he got pleasure out of maintaining his own environment. Most significant was the sense of dignity he had assumed and the sympathy and respect which I perceived for Frank among the people in the community. He, himself, said that now that none of his relatives were alive there was no longer any stigma.

A later visit with Frank in 1969 revealed that on November 1, 1968, he was arrested again. (He had not been imprisoned for over a year at that time.) He was sentenced to thirty days in jail, but he took the initiative to write a letter to the sheriff explaining that he would lose his room if he missed getting his check on the 15th of the month and could not pay his rent. He also mentioned the risk of losing library books, false teeth, clothing, certificates and papers, and his welfare status. As a result he was turned loose after ten days in jail and resumed his life as Mr. Moore of 34 King Street.

> 34 King Street
> Calvinville
> Dec. 8, 1968

Dear Bob:

My friend Bertie who informed you that I was "in the best of health," asked why I had not written to you for so long a period. I tried to explain to him, that in retrospect as far as you were concerned, I had always put my worst foot forward—how I was the Man Who Didn't Come to Dinner; how I called you by phone at three o'clock in the morning; how you secured for me the attention of the Yale Clinic; how you had secured for me admission to Hope Hollow; how you had sent me on to Heaven Hill; how you gave me a letter of introduction to the Social Service Center at Easton Heights; how you visited me at Wideway Hospital; how your mother visited me at the hospital in New Haven & got the book-keeping department "off my back" when I was more than half dead; how in countless places, while in confinement, you sent me money to buy tobacco; how in many places you had sent me text books of plane trigonometry, spherical trigonometry, calculus.

I explained to Bertie how very few alcoholics really desire sympathy, & how universally they crave understanding; how I had corresponded with you for over twenty years & how you had labored in the vineyard; that the practice of medicine for alcoholism is still not professionally respectable; that the courts yet regard this disease as a crime; that the hue & cry of the mob pressure the judiciary into sending these men to jail; that it is only the freshness of being jailed for the first time that is meaningful (your favorite word); that repetition dulls the senses; that it is impossible to react anew to a stimulus once before experienced; how the succeeding sensation produces less "shock" until a point is reached when the reaction, whether emotional or intellectual, too often repeated is imperceptible; how it is taken for granted & jail becomes a career; & lastly, how an alcoholic can not be hospitalized tho' half-dead.

Over the last couple of years I have gone for one period of eight months without being arrested, & lastly for one year before I fell by the wayside. Spent four months in Alcoholics Anonymous & spoke at a meeting. Was congratulated on all sides in such a whole-hearted manner, that it would have set a ordinary guy off on a speaking tour. I never thought I could speak publicly, but I suppose the secret lies in having something to say, & knowing your subject thoroughly.

I mention one curiosa in force in the local district court. For the past few years (two), a man arrested for drunkenness is asked if he desires a lawyer & signs a document if he waives that right. The ironical feature consists of the fact that I complained the loudest because a professional criminal had a lawyer appointed for him by the court, & that the drunkard was always unrepresented, & yet I have always waived that right. Viewing, as I have the litigation of others, with its costs to plaintiff & defendent & the rewards mostly to their legal counsels, I have become convinced that lawyers are friends to each other & enemies to the rest of mankind.

When I receive checks periodically, I spend the whole thing in one day—rent, groceries, cleaners, tobacco, hair cuts, clothing. In this way, I want for nothing & prevent a protracted spree. I have a low tolerance for alcohol now. About four pints of wine twice a month. I call it my "bi-menses."

Frank

34 King Street
Calvinville
Dec. 10, 1968

Dear Bob:

Three hours after mailing you a letter, I received your two pound box of Fanny Farmer fudge. I gorged myself (a pound at one sitting).

I pay twelve dollars a week (fifty three dollars a month) for rent. I could get myself a cheaper room, but I have lived too long like a pig. You must have noticed that I have a private bath and wash room, then a frigidaire, electric fan and iron; over the months to come I hope to save for a cheap record player—at my age I crave Sibelius, Brahms, and Rachmaninoff; to hell with this popular stuff—in short, I am a fancy guy huh???

I informed the Urban Renewal authorities at the time of my displacement, that after the stag atmosphere of the Congress Hotel, that I did not relish, under new lodgings, a nosy landlady prying about my room every day. I can't help but believe they must of so informed the landlady, in so much as that she has never ventured into my room. I wash my own sheets, towels, and pillow cases. During the past summer I took all my quilts and blankets to the laundromat.

I keep one bureau drawer filled with canned goods, have ample washing powder, scouring powder, toilet articles, razor blades and ran out of tobacco only once about three months ago. When I was a city welfare recipient, I applied for a hair cut slip every six weeks. Now that I receive checks, I get a hair cut once a month.

I have bought a winter hat, thermal underwear, socks, handkerchiefs, nylon broom, scatter rug, bath mat, gloves. I think you would be interested in my debts—I introduced you to Mr. Parsons, the postmaster; he died before I received my first check; I went to his brother and tried to give him the two dollars and he wouldn't take it. I tried to give an antique dealer, who had given me a stick, a dollar and he wouldn't take it.

These people were not going to let me inflate my ego, so I had to change my tactics. I began mailing money with an explanatory note, and I am enclosing a sample which was returned to me along with the dollar.

However, there are enough takers to keep me paying at the rate of five or six dollars a month for the next year and a half if Clotho and his sister Fates decree I totter on that long.

It may seem that I boast, but thereby hangs a tale. When I was on city welfare, I was allowed no cash allowance for fear that I would drink the money up and not properly care for myself. Now, that I am receiving cash, no one comes around to see how I am doing. Unrequited Virtue!! I live alone on this top floor and call myself: The Hermit of Shark-tooth Shoals. When I first came up here, I tried to befriend a few of my down and out friends, but was soon reminded— of Aesop's fable where the kindly man took a camel into his tent out of the storm.

Looking over what I have written, it would seem that I am floating on the euphoria of cloud nine.

Such is not the case. Over me dangles the sword of Damocles—which is the pattern of the years. One protracted drunk and I shall lose everything. One can be chained so long that he becomes too accustomed to the fetters.

In five months, my social status will change again. I shall be eligible for Old Age Assistance.

Whether it should be or not, public welfare is stigmatized. I think it is morally, at least, justified that the secure should by taxation support the sick, the old, the insane, and the inadequate. The squeaky axle gets the grease, and I have been awfully well taken care of. About two months ago I was fitted for glasses for the first time in my life. Previously I had been the recipient of unclaimed lost property of the police department. I needed these to keep from getting run over at street crossings. In regard to the false teeth, I am not so conscience-free. My guts were always made of copper and I could swallow anything whole (like a snake) and suffer no gastric disturbances. However, I have kow-towed to the opinion of people that I should have teeth.

In the coming holidays do not commiserate with me in the least. I never had it so good!

My sympathy goes out to those in nursing homes, who are unable to care for themselves, who are told when to get up, when to go to bed, what to eat, and when to eat. Remember the gunslinger of the old West who wanted to die with his boots on? Well, I want to die privately.

Frank

1969

| January–Summer | King Street rooming house, Calvinville |
| Summer–December | Westville County Jail and House of Correction |

In the first part of 1969, as in the year before, Frank was doing well. When I visited him in April, 1969, I found his health seemed better, his drinking was "channeled," he was on public assistance with a regular income, his living arrangements were comfortable and clean. Perhaps even more important, along with his new security he was continuing to enjoy respect from others. But both his security and status of freedom were temporarily interrupted in the summer of 1969 by a relapse into old company and drinking patterns.

The room in which he had been living on the top floor of a King Street rooming house became unbearably hot and be began going out at night because he could not sleep. His drinking friends increasingly came to him for money, a place to sleep, and companionship. Unfortunately, at this time he fell on the stairs and broke a rib, a very painful condition aggravated by his bronchial condition. He spent some time in a hospital but in addition switched from wine to whiskey for a little "self-medication," which was, Frank said, his undoing.

Sometime later in the summer he was arrested and sentenced to the Westville County Jail for the rest of the year. Frank's first letter of 1969 contained an especially descriptive review of his feelings about our association and correspondence over the years.

34 King Street
Calvinville
February 9, 1969

Dear Bob:

When I consider the recapitualization of my correspondence over the years under the variegated conditions of jails, mental hospitals, and etc., it seems that I must have been afflicted with cacoethes scribendi (I remember the expression but the spelling is from memory).

'Twas not ever thus. For instance, when I was in the military service I went for a period of two years without a single letter to my mother. She wrote the chaplain in the naval hospital where I was on duty in a surgical ward. He was a most tactful lout. He braced me in the presence of forty patients. He turned to them and said: "What do you fellows think of a man who wouldn't even write to his own mother?" I don't know what they thought, but they knew that I was carrying their urinals, emptying their crap, rubbing their backs, and giving them enemas. (The records of the last few wars cause me to be proud that I was once a corpsman.)

I might have forgiven her for hoarding her solicitude for me until such a time when I might have become productive, but never for shaming me in front of men, for a course which I believed to be right. Could I have said: "Hell, padre, that woman deserted me when I was two years old and came back ten years later after she had sown the female equivalent of wild oats, after ten years of what is generally regarded as the most formative years of my life"??? Could I have told him that she had ate her cake and wanted to have it too? Oh no! I promised him that I would write her a letter immediately. God, how she must have enjoyed her declining years in the role of a neglected mother, and how many people, who knew nothing about the case, must have sympathized with her.

I treasure your statement that I have contributed valuable insights to the study of alcohol pathology, but methinks I have received far more than I have contributed. My own evaluation of this correspondence is that it has been to me what the confessional box is to the Catholic, what the wailing wall is to the Hebrew, what the psychiatric couch is to the women in menopause—with the added advantage that God (abstract), you answer every time. I read, a few weeks ago, for the third time in my life Will Durant's "Story of Philosophy." I could not help being amazed again how Bacon, Neitzche, and Shapenhaur had anticipated Freud—the interrelation of intellect and instinct, conscious and unconscious, inhibition and catharsis. How much we owe these pessimistic, mad, unhappy, courageous philosophers of yesteryear!!!

My philosophizing (correspondence) came out of a veritable tub, like that of the humble Diogenes. In the jail correspondence, I chortled with Voltaire in the best of all possible worlds, where I watched the prison guards steal the prisoners' food, gasoline, silverware, soap, even toilet paper, and anything else that wasn't nailed down. In the hospital correspondence, I jeered at the patients eating oleomargarine while the employees ate the butter which was given to the hospital from government surplus for persons who could not afford that scale of rations.

Whatever this correspondence might have meant to you, it prevented me from laughing myself to death or murder. The correspondence was like the touchstone of alcohol to a man who had reached his Plimsoll Mark of sensibilities, or his particular peak of mental pain. How these letters must have puzzled the prison censors. I remember one particular prisoner, whom I had tabbed as never having done anything in his life that was unselfish. He asked me why I was writing letters to a college professor about jail. I answered in the only language comprehensible to him. I said that everytime I wrote a letter to this professor, he sent me a dollar for tobacco. (You don't talk Spanish to a Frenchman).

Another thing about this correspondence is that it has, to a small degree, learned me to talk. Books only taught me to think. In my halcyon years, I always had the idea, in my sincerest moments that I was orally implausible. Writing has helped me, in a large measure, to overcome this handicap. For instance, in one of my last court experiences for drunkenness, the judge asked me if I had anything to say after my guilty plea. I started to talk. The judge interrupted and said, "No speeches!" (One of his colleagues must have tipped him off that I aspired to a court-room manner)—I hesitated for a moment until I was (as the cliche puts it) the cynosure of all eyes. Then I started off again, in what I hoped was an unctuous voice, and in a tone so that the spectators had to listen to it. I pointed out to the good judge that men who stood behind the prisoner's rail as I did, accused as I was, having slept on a bare board in a jail cell, men who were physically sick, men who were morally demoralized, men who had become estranged from family and jobs, men who were inarticulate—had no training or inclination to make speeches. I hesitated a moment (a bit carried away by my own oratory). I had the little guy squirming in his black robe like he had ants in his pants. He absolutely blustered: "Get on with what you have to say." Oh, the denouement—he turned me loose—No further talk about speeches upon my subsequent appearances. Question—did I rebuke or admonish him? Ah, the secret victories of Frank Moore!

More anon,

F.

In mid-April I again visited with Frank in Calvinville. I found him still living at 34 King Street with a prominent sign "The Hermit of Shark Tooth Shoals" identifying his door. His room was immaculate, with the floor polished to a high gloss and a neatly arranged wall of his certificates and other memorabilia. Frank, too, was neatly dressed and well groomed.

After a visit in his room we again walked the streets of Calvinville while Frank told me of the town's history from the days of slave and rum trading through a period of prosperous manufacturing, to its current status of old rich families, commuter workers, and the down and out. I bought Frank a copy of Warner's *Yankee City* and suggested that he compare it with Calvinville. We visited the waterfront to see the abandoned cars and boats which provide shelter for drunks and to meet Bertie Brown. We met "Pete the cop," who was described as always good for a dollar from his own pocket to help a drunk. We again visited the Welfare Department, this time to meet a senior case worker who expressed a warm motherly attitude toward Frank and told me that Frank's mother had also been her "case."

We talked about our correspondence, and Frank emphasized again that his letters to me had helped keep him alive by letting him talk with someone and express his feelings. He also mentioned a local judge who had helped keep him alive by putting him in jail and protecting him from himself, the elements, and starvation.

As we walked through the town, Frank stressed that the entire community seemed to live on its past.

When we parted Frank promised to fill in some gaps in the life story if I would identify these. This I did in a letter of April 22, which elicited the following reply:

34 King St.
Sunday, April 27, 1969

Dear Bob:

Received yours of the 22nd. It was nice of you to visit the Hermit of Sharktooth Shoals. Nobody visits me unless they need a clean shirt or pair of socks.

Anent "Yankee City"—this is a stupendous work of social research. A man might well have spent a lifetime to produce such a noteworthy book. I believe you can well understand its honesty would be most unpalatable to many of the local minds in that town. For example, in the hierarchy of church membership, the book lists of the "upper-upper" affiliation with the Episcopalian sect. And of the "lower-lower" affiliation with the French Catholic or Roman Catholic churches. . . . I don't know of any field, except sex, where the emotions are more likely to becloud the intellect. Do you think that the social worker who assured you that she was a descendant of colonial stock is likely to have an objective and dispassionate view of the fact that she belongs to the sect of the "lower-lower"??? For no reason at all, I suspect that the collateral branch of her family immigrated here during the Irish potato famine of 1850. It has always seemed remarkable to me how the lower-lower, being mobile, once having advanced themselves, can out-snob the upper-upper.

As a sort of minor and insignificant addenda to Warner's "Yankee City" wherein he classifies attendance of the lower-lower to the Catholic churches, we in Calvinville have the sub-lower-lower who have no religious rites except for wedding and funeral. I cited the reasons that some people didn't go to church at all because they had no money to put in the collection boxes, but the unfortunate part seems to lie in the fact that these pariahs beyond the pale, do not appear to be deprived at all. There seems to be little moral difference between the clammer who poaches on restricted areas and the millionaire on Johns Street who hires a lawyer for tax-skullduggery. Of course, the guy who digs clams is more likely to be caught.

In answer to the questions in your letter:

(1) Did I ever maintain any contacts with my father's family? They were never spoken of. It is not that such conversation was taboo or verboten; early, I realized that I did not have a father as other boys did and that there was something shameful about my not having a father. My silence did not induce revelation and it became a habit. Navy papers show that he was born in Ogunquit, Maine, served on the *Deleware* in the Spanish-American War, and shared in the "prize money" (whatever the hell that was) for the "storming" of El Carney. Of longevity and heredity on his side, I know nothing. My mother was only reticent in this thing.

(2) In regard to enlistments in Maritime Service and Merchant Marine: The only purpose of the Maritime Service is that of a training organization for the Merchant Marine. Forty years ago the *Morro Castle* (passenger ship) burned; the biggest and blackest blot on the history of the Merchant Marine. An untrained crew of wharf rats were unable to swi 1g out and lower life boats. The survival qualities of rats are prove1 bial. Most of the crew saved themselves; most of the passengers roasted. In time of peace, it is necessary to have *three years* training at the U.S. Naval Academy or U.S. Coast Guard Academy including two training courses to be eligible for certification as lifeboatman. It will seem ridiculous to you that, like many others, I completed a course of training in 36 articles of signaling, survival, sailing equipment in four months, and received my Certificate of Lifeboatman, but there was a war on, man, there was a war on. Then I was discharged from the Maritime Service for service with the Merchant Marine. Looking back on it, the training was ten times as bad as the actual service. No damned wonder that I have emphysema and am varicosed.

(3) Dates of military service. I have a letter from the First Secretary of the Embassy at Santo Domingo stating that the Dominicans are unlikely to have such records as would serve my purpose. So we will "write off" service with Policia Dominicana Nacional and Gendarmerie de Haiti.

(4) The brief marriage: A civil ceremony at Biddeford, Maine, where there was the least waiting period (one day after application for license and not even a blood test). It was an obeisance to convention and spared her of publicity. Damn conventionalities!!! Publicity—I had already been arrested a number of times in Calvinville. She died two

years later as the result of an auto accident. My mother, who often told me of her eligibility to join the D.A.R. asked me why I had married this immigrant Irish lady. I said to my mother: "Because she was kind to me when no one else in the world was." And for once, that shut my mother up. . . . I can't remember anything about my wife except she was kind. I can't remember anything that was petty and mean. . . . As an index, she would read about some atrocious and heinous crime in the newspaper and she would say to me, "I wonder just why that man did that," as if she were trying to ameliorate or extenuate the acts of others. She was a good woman. I didn't know at the time when she died. Because of a marriage outside the Church, her relatives considered that we were "living in sin," and so they did not notify me. Is it a wonder that thenceforth when I went to Westville or Stonycreek and the forms were filled in upon admission, I always said "No religion." Some of those jail officials remonstrated, "You must be something." To which I answered, "I'll be damned if I am." Yet, there is no reason to catalogue me a soap-box atheist.

My grandfather died about the age of 72. He was a good man. When I see the personnel and material of the present-day sanitation department, I wonder if the incumbents realize what has gone before, how he worked toward procuring high standards, retirement pay, and sick benefits.

Say, I am getting graphospasm (medical name for writer's cramp) and your eyes are getting tired.

More anon,
Frank

Westville Jail and House of Correction
Censored
December 11, 1969

Dear Bob:

Over the last four months, I have received at least four letters from you which I have not answered. I can explain in a devious & perhaps incomprehensible way. . . . Twenty years ago I met a doctor at Davenport who had a private practice nearby. He arranged for me a private interview with a psychiatrist. No psychiatric couch, but I told this old man, with as much continuity as possible, the history of my boozing & inability to quit. After the 'story,' I remember I flippantly & brashly asked: "What is the prognosis, Doc?" How was I to know that this man was one of the most famous alienists of the last fifty years?? However,

I never forgot his answer: "All things are possible to the human mind." A simple statement & prognosis that served me as a ray of hope over many years. . . . In this institution & many other places, people have asked me how I got tangled up with Dr. Straus. . . . At a terrible price, this boozing, has led to the occasional acquaintance of persons far above my social & economic milieu. . . . I will score one more assist in explanation of my lack of correspondence—over 5 years ago I was out at Provincetown. The advantage of bathing trunks is that you can not tell the difference between a millionaire & a beach-bum. I came out of the water, had a drink with a perfect stranger to take the chill off; hence an acquaintance with Eugene O'Neil. We drank the length of the cape from Provincetown to New Bedford, over a week, making all the spas & carrying bottles in between. . . . When I was down at Providence, one of the doctors saw me reading *The Way of All Flesh*, Butler (?) & told me it was 'required reading' in his studies. I intimate that O'Neil's play 'The Iceman Cometh' should be a required study for anyone who hopes to understand alcoholism. Not a "respectable" character in the play. The central character is superficially an extrovert, a good spender, periodical boozer, & everyone is always waiting for him to come to town. Behind the facade of gayety & joviality until the last act when it is revealed that he has attempted to reform many times & always failed. His wife is ever forgiving & always without question to give him another chance. . . . Each of his failures become more poignant to him & in the last scene, in a saloon, & before he has been apprehended, he confesses to the saloon audience that he has shot this angelic woman to spare her further suffering. I am not going to shoot anybody, but I am trying to arrange with my social worker in Calvinville to enter a Seaman's Home, or permission to move to Boston, & to cut myself off from everything & everyone I ever knew. Can you understand?

Frank

1970

January–March	Westville County Jail and House of Correction
April	Diddle State Hospital (10 days)
April–September	Grant Street Rooming House, Westville
October–November	Eviction, roaming, hospitalization, Westville County Jail
December	Davenport State Hospital

Frank spent the entire fall of 1969 and first three months of 1970 in the Westville Jail as a result of his summer relapse. When he was finally released, he was almost immediately apprehended again and sent to the Diddle State Hospital, where he spent ten days in an alcoholic ward. On release in April he returned to Calvinville to find no room available and his belongings missing. He was able to have his welfare support reinstated by establishing residence in a rooming house in Westville, where I visited him in July, 1970. I found him glad to see me and happy once again to be living independently.

A few months after this visit, Frank began a cycle of events reminiscent of his earlier days of intoxication, eviction, injury, homelessness, arrest, hospitalization or incarceration in various but familiar combinations. His declining health may have been a precipitating factor in this relapse; certainly his inability to be the old "tough guy" of the past bothered him. He frequently mentioned in his correspondence his tremors (from Parkinson's disease), and the skimpy correspondence for 1970 lost some of the sharp humor and confidence that permeated his earlier letters. He summed up his situation: "I am the luckiest guy in the world to be able . . . to live without any sound reason for doing so. . . ." And, as throughout his past experiences, the frustration of the present backsliding and physical debilitation was heightened by the fact that he was too "damned AWARE" of everything happening around him and to him.

When a severely broken arm made it impossible for him to meet his own basic needs, he was scornful of my suggestion that he seek refuge at the Davenport Infirmary. Nevertheless, he did end the year 1970 at Davenport, where in addition to his broken bones there was a diagnosis of active tuberculosis, which ended for the foreseeable future his hopes to again "escape from custody."

35 Grant Street
Westville
May 1, 1970

Hi Bob:

About two years ago, I was told that I had Parkinson's Disease. I was elated that, at long last, I had developed something that was "respectable." However, when I began falling down (sober), I began to be concerned. Especially so, when the police began to offer me blankets, coffee & cigarettes. Whoever would have thought that being an ex-tough guy, would begin to "pay off."

I know that there is a great gap or hiatus since our last correspondence. A permanent tremor prevents a more lengthy correspondence.

I am the luckiest guy in the world to be able to live without relatives; without religion; to live without any sound reason for doing so; & especially without health. Shopenhaur really had something, when he wrote the *Will to Live*.

Do you suppose I will ever get to read *Escape from Custody*?? An awful sordid story.

Moorey

35 Grant Street
Westville
May 27, 1970

Dear Bob:

I recall in your latest letter, you reminded me the importance of a good diagnosis in Parkinson's Disease.

About the time you first visited me on Church St. in Calvinville, I believed that my leg trouble was due to varicose veins; easily fatigued & unsteadyness of gait. So thru Medicaid, I procured a pair of elastic stockings to the value of $13 & boasted to the ribald river rats of the riverside that my stockings were more expensive than any whore's in town. I failed to notice any difference in the condition of my legs & was advised that I must wear them for some time, before a difference would be noted. After a year, no change, & so phooey on the elastic stockings.

Next, after going four months without a single drink, I said to my friend, Bertie Brown, "Do you know that I have developed a permanent alcoholic tremor?" . . . I was upset because I over-turned the salt & pepper cellars & spilled sugar out the sugar spoon, but I accepted the fact, that my years of boozing were beginning to 'pay off.'

All of the above proves the old adage that only a fool is his own doctor. And then—I ran into a strange doctor who inquired about my 'shakes'! I casually answered "permanent alcoholic tremor." He said, "Why are you shaking in only one hand?" (At the time, it so happened). I hate to have a doctor talk 'down' to me & so I flippantly fabulated "it might be Jacksonian Epilepsy." He inquired, "What do you know of Jacksonian Epilepsy?" I began to simmer & told him that I had become a 1st class hospital apprentice at the age of 16; that I was a 3rd class pharmacist mate at 17, & that I had served on shores & stations where no doctor was assigned; that I had to do a hell of a lot of reading in order not to kill somebody thru ignorance; & finally that the epilepsy in question was a one-sided epilepsy; clonic & tonic convulsions on one side of the body.

And then I got 'told off.' He asked me if I knew what caused it. I had to reply "No." Then he informed me that the cause was a lesion on one side of the brain. I had always been interested in symptomology & not giving a damn for etiology. The doctor made me feel like Chic Sales "The specialist." Did you ever read the story? It is about a guy who constructed country crap-houses.

Finally, he had me walk up & down the room; said I had a typical Parkinson's "gait" & stated that I had Parkinson's Disease.

Every home for aged people has a few ladies tottering around & shaking; so I am satisfied with the diagnosis (the only thing in my life that was not attributed to alcohol).

The human spirit is indestructible, but it nigh well might not be so if it were not for the wonders of alcohol in times of stress & strain.

Frank

35 Grant Street
Westville
June 1, 1970

Dear Bob:

I wrote to my land-lady in Calvinville about two months ago requesting that she send me (collect) only the papers & documents that I had plastered on one wall of my room. Nothing else I desired. To date, I have received no reply. It may be that they were destroyed & again it may be that I was a good guy only as long as I was a source of income.

Bitter thoughts crowd the later years.

It took me a year to accumulate those papers & I am hard-headed enough to go thru the same weary process again.

I shall have to drive myself to resurrect those papers. In addition to postage I shall have to pay for the replacement of those ribbons & tin medals. It is going to be like Phoenix rising from the ashes.

Alas, no recording machine, no typist & only a shaking hand.

Frank

Early in July, 1970, I wrote Frank of my hope to visit him on July 15. When I arrived in Westville about 10:30 A.M. I found him waiting in the street, leaning on his cane, where he had been looking for me for about an hour and a half. He had been watching for fear I would drive into town, get confused on the one-way street and risk a traffic ticket. He had even inquired at the police station whether tickets were given to out-of-towners who happened to make a wrong turn.

Frank was dressed immaculately as in our previous visits. He wore a crisp white shirt, bow tie, white summer slacks, new black shoes, and professional-looking glasses. We sat and visited in his room for an hour or so; I was again impressed with the neatness and comfort Frank had achieved from simple surroundings.

Frank told me he was receiving three checks a month, one from the Railroad Retirement Fund and two from Old Age Assistance, which gave him a total of $160 per month in cash with payments for Medicare deducted. His money was quickly consumed by his rent, a deposit at the grocery store, laundry, and a few incidentals, leaving him little if anything for drinks, which in fact seemed to be his intention in quickly disposing of the cash. He had been able to acquire a few accouterments of comfort and style, including an inexpensive watch, a small used radio, a few books, and several sets of clothing. He also had new shoes, which he noted he hadn't really needed since his old shoes were still serviceable, but he had decided to invest his money just the same. He had also been sending out money in order to obtain again a collection of documents on his life experiences.

Frank referred back to the summer in the third-floor room in Calvinville several times and commented that it must have taken five years off his life. Thus far in Westville he had successfully stayed out of trouble by drinking on a "channeled basis." He was drinking only wine as he could not tolerate whiskey any longer.

We then began our usual walk. Frank particularly wanted me to see a favorite tombstone in the graveyard outside his window dated 1795 and reading: "Behold and see as you pass by, as you are now, so once was I. As I am now, so you must be, prepare for death and follow me." He wanted me to take a picture of him standing by the gravestone.

We visited two museums, where he had already picked out exactly what he wanted me to see. Then as we approached the business district I offered to buy Frank some fudge, which I knew he liked. He said he was no longer able to "tolerate" fudge and asked instead if I would be willing to replace a broken electric heating pot. When we arrived at the hardware store the proprietor indicated that, if the pot was not working, he would replace it. This was obviously a new kind of experience for Frank Moore, and I suggested to him that it was a response to the fact that in his immaculate clothing he looked quite distinguished.

We visited the Welfare Office so that, as in previous visits, I could be introduced. We then continued to his room, where we met his landlady, Mrs. Petrakis, who said that she read a good deal of philosophy and that she and Frank had something in common. She indicated that the social worker called occasionally to make sure that Frank was "behaving himself."

We were also able to replace Frank's cigarette-rolling machine. He said that on an ordinary day he made and smoked about thirty cigarettes, but when the weather was bad he might make as many as 90.

I noted on Frank's wall a copy of a letter to a local newspaper submitting the following obituary to appear upon his death.

Died—Frank Moore; born in Calvinville May 9, 1904. Served with the Abraham Lincoln Battalion of the International Brigade in the Spanish Civil War and in the United States Merchant Marine in World War II.
No near relatives. No services.

It was clear that Frank's military service in his own mind was his primary claim to respectability. This was the first and only reference by Frank to service in the Spanish Civil War and I did not discuss with him the discrepancy with his life history for that period. When we parted, Frank, as usual, promised to write soon.

While in an obvious state of inebriation, Frank wrote the following on the back of photocopies of several of his memorabilia, which had been torn from the wall of his room.

> Westville
> August 6, 1970
> Even my pen won't write

Hi Bob:
    I wished to acknowledge your visit . . . but like so many guys my road to hell is paved with good intentions.
    As I become more sober, I hope to rewrite more intelligibly. . . .
I *always* wished to be a "Lord Jim" but circumstances seemed to forbid anyhow I will write the letter and mail it. This god-damned thing begins to look like the Rosetta Stone, however, I will endeavor.
    It was a comfortable visit. I made special arrangements with the

Police Department in case you came up a one way street. I hope things get better as I write along. It is a real effort.

I am so proud (for you) Bob.

Because of James St.[1] and because you wanted to get me "special quarters" and because I am proud of myself.

(Despite your admonitions re controlled or channel drinking I bought straight whiskey.)

I am so proud of you because you are a Yale-man.

I (the eternal I) I "showed you off" to my social worker; she does not know the eternal hall-mark of a Yale-man; I got sort of acquainted with the mayor of Riverpoint, then I became sort of acquainted with Yale-men. They can listen, they do not look down their nose; they can learn. More power to Elihu!!!

I was glad to show you the museums. Of course, the thing is too tremendous to appreciate, as all Yankees are.

My handwriting is not getting any better . . . my mind(?) keeps getting two (2) steps in front of my mind (?).

I am so proud you did not accept the grant to South America. I know so much about South America that it is pitiful.

Dictatorships and perpetually controlled incompetence. I did not want (wish) you to become a part of these.

Christ, I am boring you. After all, the Archbishop thinks that I am a "good guy."

I am laughing when I think when they saw up my guts at Harvard (broad A's) that I have had cirrhosis, emphysema, malaria, demper & hemoroglabia??? (pissed black).

Did I write intelligibly enough. I pissed black and I guess that answers the question (what do you want, blood!!!)

Sincerely,
Moorey

Please send me one of your earliest publications "Merchant Seamen and Drunkenness." I would like to evaluate how wrong or how right you were. We are a special breed. Note: I got a kick out of your photographs. If there was a blown up picture, you would see a grin on my face.

This is a copy of a photostat letter on the back of which was written

1. This is a reference to the address of the Salvation Army in New Haven where Frank and I first met.

part of Frank's letter of August 6, 1970. To be noted are Frank's rationale for needing replacement of the items requested and his expression of pride.

35 Grant St.
Westville

Bureau of Medicine and Surgery
Navy Department
Washington, D.C.
Subject: A Statement of Service

1) A few years ago, your department sent me a letter under the seal of the Bureau of Medicine and Surgery, stating that I had graduated from the Naval Hospital Training School in 1920 and a 'fair-fax' slip with notation of H.A.-lc. The fair-fax slip has no civil significance.

2) Last winter, all my effects were destroyed in an apartment house fire in Calvinville.

3) Please send me a letter under the seal of the Bureau of Medicine and Surgery, stating that I had completed such a course of instruction at Newport, R.I. in 1920.

4) My reason for desiring this and similar papers is:

a) I have collaborated with Dr. R. M. Straus, University of Kentucky, in writing a life story. It may be significant that I was a First Class Hospital Apprentice at the age of 16 and a Third Class Pharmacist's Mate at age of 17.

b) The record of Corpsmen in the present fracas and all other wars, causes me to be proud to once have been a Corpsman.

Respectfully—Frank Moore

The instructors that I remember after 50 years are Lt. George Watts
. . .

Westville Jail and House of Correction
November 16, 1970

To: Mrs. Grace Rhoades, Senior Social Worker
Department of Public Welfare
Westville
Dear Mrs. Rhoades:

I have chosen this method of writing because it may be informative to you. . . . Will you please re-direct this letter to R. M. Straus, Ph.D., College of Medicine; University of Kentucky, Lexington, Kentucky.

Hi Bob: I fear that I am not destined to senile uneventfulness. . . .

More osteology. Broken humerus at junction with glanoid cavity . . .
Ab unito, the events occurred in following sequence. 1) Eviction; 2)
broken arm; 3) hospitalization for eight days; 4) prevented from occupying a room which had been arranged for me by a friend at the New
Crawford House here in Westville; 5) a cane that was useless in my
left hand; 6) falling down and arrested and slept on plank in police
station that night; 7) room arranged for by probation officer (Tuesday);
8) evicted on Saturday for groaning in sleep (not while awake!); 9) arrested and slept on plank again; 10) went to hospital to make sure that
bone in place; 11) doctor concerned, who made arrangements for me
to sleep in police station that night (plank again); 12) went to nearest
town to arrange for a room; 13) more falling down, robbed, arrested;
14) told judge that I was unable to tie my shoes or button my clothes;
suggested that he send me here to get me out of public sight.

Date of release—Dec. 3. Will you intercede with social worker, named
in heading, to request her to hold my old age assistance check which
is due today (Nov. 16). Otherwise, the check will be returned to government. When I am released on Dec. 3, I shall have to pay 7 or 8
dollars a day at a hotel until I secure a room. At present time owe $10
to Welfare.

I have bailed people out of this place, and payed other people's
fines, and yet I don't have a single smoke right now. Can't roll them;
cast from shoulder over hand. I can buy cigarettes here if I have
money. Picked cast from palm of right hand with thumb-nail of left
hand to write this. A real field study of pain and exhaustion.

Frank

In response to this letter, I told Frank that I had written to Mrs.
Rhoades, his social worker, requesting that she hold his check for him. I
also asked him whether a retreat to the Davenport State Infirmary might
provide him with an opportunity to recover his health as a prelude to re-
covering his independence.

Westville Jail and House of Correction
November 23, 1970

Hi Bob:

If you consider my long institutionalization in prison, countless jails,
various branches of military service, private sanitariums & three state
hospitals, it should be easy to understand why, at this late time, I wish
to die privately, whether it be a 'hole in the wall' or on Derby Wharf.

Davenport is that sort of an institution which receives government surplus foodstuffs for persons on marginal diet (butter, for instance: the employees eat the butter & the patients eat margarine). The employees eat the best of food at 30¢ a meal, the patients' subsistence is still marginal. My trouble, Bob, & all my damn life, is that I am damned AWARE. My Old Age Assistance checks & Railroad Retirement Pension would be taken for my maintenance & I would receive a cash allowance only for tobacco. . . . It can't happen because I will not endorse the checks.

The designation of Davenport has evolved over the years from Almshouse to State Infirmary & finally to State Hospital. Yet the breakfast is just the same—oat meal gruel, bread & margarine & institution (weak) coffee. . . . To paraphrase—a rose by any other color, stinks just the same. The probation officer brought me up to a Rest Home here in Westville & the first thing I was told was that there was no smoking on the premises; Quick Exit;

Rest Home, Convalescent Home, Nursing Home? As Scrooge would say—Bah!!! There must really be quite a profit in feeding these old bastards Jello & stewed prunes. Aforementioned, I am AWARE.

It was hinted by my social worker that my landlady on Grant St. would take me back, if I stopped drinking. Imagine—shaking off my heredity, my early environment, my occupational habits, my life long experience?? For her?? How presumptious can anyone get. As Santa Claus would say—Ho! Ho! Ho!

If you communicate with Mrs. Rhoades to justify her holding my check for Nov. 16 ($56), remind her that I will need 4 suits of thermal underwear at $2 a suit, replacement of eyeglasses, winter hat & gloves, etc. I will have to pay a hotel rate of $7 or $8 a day until I can find a regular room.

Thanks for cigarette money.

Frank

Westville Jail and House of Correction
December 1, 1970

Dear Bob:

My own general experience of the opposite sex is of a different order. Anyone engaged in husbandry knows that the sow, in her sloth & ignorance, often rolls over & crushes to death, her young. . . . Anyone who regards womanhood as the 'weaker sex' is deluded. . . . Witness a woman separated from her husband & already shacked-up with another man, prosecuting her husband for non-support. Practical, hard boiled, hard headed,—they always win. . . .

A long & perhaps interesting chapter of *Escape from Custody*, sub-titled 'Lushes & Landladies,' could be written of my many experiences with that prowling & nosey genus, accounting for the timeless appeal of the tale of Bluebeard. These tyrannous, despotic, creatures (remember, their choice) render a public service which arrogates the power of life & slow death to themselves, for those who come under their domination.

As you stated in your letter, my landlady has the right to place certain conditions. Lest you believe her to be a most injured party, may I remind you that she and her husband were most anxious to remove all my belongings early in the morning, including papers & certificates affixed to the back of my door. You would say "Emotionalism." However, being acquainted with her ethnic acquisitiveness, I'll bet that the room was already re-rented.

Previous to your visit, I had burned a hole, no larger than a dime in a scatter rug (bed-side rug) from an overloaded ash-tray. She said, "you have burned my rug." That same week I purchased a bigger & better rug ($5.15), and she told me herself (ipse dixit) that she had not expected reparations to that extent.

Months later, when I was evicted she told my social worker that I had burned her carpet (pyromaniac?). While I was in the hospital, I had made arrangements to stay in a cheap hotel. . . . The proprietor of the hotel thru inquiries with my social worker would not accept me. Both my landlady and my social worker (I introduced you) are sympatico, relicts of the dinosaur age, & vestigiae of the W.C.T.U. Weaker sex?? Bosh!

Frank

Davenport State Hospital
December 18, 1970

Dear Bob:

On Dec. 3, I found Mason Reeve, a native of Calvinville, who was stranded in Westville, and awaiting my emergence. We went up to see Mrs. Rhoades where I picked up one check. The check of Nov. 16 had been returned to the government to defray costs of moon missiles and boring of holes in the ocean bottom, and other such practical uses of money. We repaired to a bistro across the street from Mrs. Rhoades, where I reminded the owner to send two dollars to a long time customer, who was in durance vile. No libation for me at the time tho' my friend Mason needed a couple to shake off the chill from 'carrying the banner' of the night before.

From there I proceeded to the office of the County Commissioners and was interviewed and secured the release of another friend serving a month's sentence for drunkenness, on the grounds that he was receiving life-long disability compensation, was able to provide for himself, and that a county jail is not the proper milieu for cases of epilepsy. Then mailed two dollars to another friend at the county jail, because he asked me to (a clam pirate, fishing in a restricted area).

It would seem that all my intimates are goal birds and that I was following a Santa Claus script. . . . However, at this time I applied at four different rooming houses which were filled in three cases and the owner was absent in the fourth instance. I had assured you that I would be able to care for myself, but at this time I became less confident. The housing situation in Westville is really this serious, leading landladies to selectivity and tyranny.

Then again, I had my marooned friend from Calvinville on my hands. I introduced you to a friend last summer who was a cook. . . . I engaged him to drive me and Mason to Calvinville for twenty dollars. When it became time for him to pick us up in Westville he had a woman with him. To make a long story shorter, be abandoned us half way, carrying away my bag of remaining clothes and my cane.

The next day when I saw our "driver" in Calvinville and reproached him for leaving us in the shoals, his only lament was that "it was that god-damned woman." I forgot to mention my clothes to him and had bought another cane (the 4th in the last 2 years). Do you not think it remarkable that women have a way of screwing up my life (even when unsought, undesired and my antipathy).

Anyway, Mason bummed his way back to Calvinville and succeeded in getting arrested that night. I haven't the least idea of how I got back to Calvinville and it would only be explained by the eel's return to the Sargasso or the seals' return to the Pribilofs. To continue the Santa Claus role I appeared in the District Court of Calvinville on Dec. 4, before the Hon. Judge Kennedy as a spectator. When it came time for Mason to plead to the charge of drunk, I arose and asked permission to address the court. I suppose I appeared to be amicus curiae (friend of the court). It was indicated (by me) that Westville Jail would not solve Mason's problems, that altho' not wealthy, I was willing to pay his nominal fine ($15). The court commended my loyalty to friend and suspended sentence without costs. I imagine that I began to feel like a politician opening jail gates or an amateur Clarence Darrow. All the same, I regarded my insecurity too serious to enjoy my triumph over some kind of laws.

Mason and I made wassail that day but alas? the foxes have their holes but the son of man has no place to lay his head. Went to Boston alone on the last bus from Calvinville and slept on a park bench thru a damn cold night. In retrospect, laying on boards in jail in plaster cast for nearly a week, the previous month, causes me to feel somewhat sorry for myself and gather conjectures of the ultimate stress and strain (breaking point).

On the next day Dec. 5 (I remember, we are discussing how so much can happen in so little time) I met a friend (floater) who bought me a ticket to Carlyle and advised me to go to Davenport and give my arm a chance to heal. Arrived here the same afternoon. The admitting doctor, thru ascultation, detected advantageous sounds leading to about 30 x-ray pictures and 4 sputum tests.

I was transferred to this ward about 10 days ago. The head nurse has assured me that I have positive T.B. and I am to stay in this isolation room and away from other patients. Another nurse tells me I have a hole in my lung and that I am awaiting transfer to a tuberculosis hospital.

Despite what goes on in your medical center, the employees here do not spare you the least gruesome details.

The institution hasn't changed a bit since I was here 20 years ago. The head nurse here has been dealing for years with drunks, the friendless and the poor and adopts the attitude of a female bosun's mate.

Don't know how long I shall be here, if or when I shall be transferred etc. A young social worker, who must necessarily be under the thumb of his senior confreres has been kind to me and supplied stationery. He may be addressed as Mr. Ballaux, Social Worker at this address. Perhaps he can supply macabre details of which I am not cognizant.

Frank

1971

January	Westville Hospital
February–March	Middleway State Hospital
April	Westridge Sanitarium
May–June	The New Salem House (rooming house), Westville
July–August	Westridge Sanitarium
September–mid-October	Brief visits to Calvinville and Westville; roaming; Adams Hotel (one week), Westville; continued roaming; hospitalization (5 days)
Mid-October–December	Benton County Jail

The year 1971 was one of deteriorating health for Frank, complicated by active tuberculosis, a "heart attack," and accompanying despondency, perhaps stemming in part from his return to custodial care for the greater part of the year and acute disappointment that the weaknesses of the body were progressively frustrating his determination to make it on his own. Release from one hospital led almost inevitably to another, with interludes of wandering, vain search for rooms to rent, brief residence in cheap hotels, and the last two months and a half in jail as a "holding operation," awaiting re-entry to custody in the hospital ward of Stonycreek Correctional Institution.

At one point, Frank wrote of a plan to cause his own transfer to a violent and "vicious" ward where his heart would give out before he spent too much time in the institution. He ended one letter: "This would be a good ending for final 'Escape from Custody.'"

The triumph and satisfaction he had found in his earlier successful ventures at independence in rooming houses were slipping quickly away.

Westville Hospital
January 9, 1971

Dear Bob:

My transfer here occurred ten days ago because this hospital is licensed to care for my disease. My doctor assumes that I will be kept here rather than be sent to some other county's sanitarium. This county no longer maintains such a place.

However, I have cause to wonder, on account of what seems to me almost prohibitive costs, even when taking into consideration Medicare, Health Insurance, Federal, State and County subsidies.

Anybody would wonder what treatment to expect at the rate of a hundred dollars a day for extended care. However, a hospital is not adverse to great expense, when the bill can be collected.

In my own case, the expense entails private room; meals of choice; 18 medications daily of 3 varieties, daily injections of streptomyacin; daily temperature; twice daily blood pressure; x-rays too innumerable to remember; a social worker and library service on call because I am in an isolation room, cardiograms, tests of sputum, urinalysis, etc., etc. Already I can see you cogitating: "This bum never had it so good. . . ." It really does compare with Sick Officer's Quarters in Naval Hospitals.

And what have I ever done to merit such munificence?

I am guilty of the all too human frailty of blaming others. It can be pointed out that my present circumstance can be laid to booze and unhygienic life. However, need I point out to you, the long, long period of time (in the aggregate) that I have been compelled to live under the guidance of state, public, and community benevolence.

Ere this particular time, I have looked back at Bingham County Jail where I endured thirty days (one meal a day); the County Jail in Oldetown where we had coffee every morning except on Sunday when we had corn flakes (big deal); Moseley, N.J. where I was kept in the city lock-up for three days without any food whatsoever; to the myriad of county jails where the tenure of the sheriffs were so uncertain that they were compelled to steal as much and as quick as they could.

The records in Calvinville will show that I was being allowed $7.50 per week at the time I was granted Old Age Assistance in July of 1969. When it was found that I was eligible for Railroad Retirement Pension of $55 per month (unknown to me) that amount was deducted from my Old Age Assistance, lest I drink it all up (and I might add, eat it all up).

My fragmentary reading of "poverty levels" and "minimal subsistence" cause me to think that I have lived in such strata for a long, long time.

Then again, it can be pointed out that I had sufficient ability and intelligence to rise above this level. However, combined with my emotional capacities and combined life experiences; inadequate repartee. . . .

As the best excuse that I can think of, the faults, weaknesses, vices, failures, miscues of any man can be induced by a syndrome of thinking induced by heredity, early training, education opportunity, the pressure of a group of which he is a part at a particular time.

In the present instance, I assume the Public Welfare will withdraw all my Old Age Assistance wrongfully assuming that all my needs are cared for without considering minimal needs.

Monday, I purchased stamps, nail clippers, stationery, razor, shoe lacings, newspaper subscription which are not covered by hospital billing. I imagine that it is going to cost me plenty to get a barber into an isolation room (sterilization, etc.).

I expected Mrs. Rhoades and her confreres at Welfare to squeeze the $55 dollar railroad check from me.

Not a god-damned one of them will, for a moment, consider the difficulty that I shall encounter to obtain lodgings with a T.B. history. Nor will they consider my expenses if I arrive at an "arrested" stage of the disease or cost of rehabilitation (establishing myself outside of an institution).

Alas, the best laid plans of mice and men, and I thought I was going to live forever and there are still a few things I am curious of. . . . I have nothing else to do, but when you have time, write to

Frank

Davenport Hospital
January 20, 1971

Robert Straus, Ph.D.
College of Medicine
University of Kentucky   Re: Frank Moore
Lexington, Kentucky 40506

Dear Dr. Straus:

I was pleased and surprised to receive your letter of January 4 regarding our mutual friend, Frank Moore.

There isn't much that I can say as I only had occasion to enjoy his keen and critical observations during the few visits that I had with him. He was none too pleased about his brief stay at this hospital. He considered it a place for the poor, the drunks and the hopeless.

Mr. Moore was admitted to this facility on 12/5/70 and discharged to Westville Hospital on 12/30/70. There was question of active tuberculosis.

Sincerely,
Allan Ballaux
Social Worker

State Hospital
Middleway
February 14, 1971

I have many times spread
my lodging when the evening
has promised well, yet have
been forced to withdraw before
the day.—Dampier's Voyages

Hi Bob:

What better way to spend the anniversary of Chicago's St. Valentine's Day Massacre, than to write to my friend from the hinterlands.

To recapitulate, after a month's stay at the Westville Hospital, I was notified that I would be transferred to the County Sanatorium at Westridge. As you perhaps do not know, Westville County does not have such facilities.

I had hoped to be extended an afternoon's liberty for the afternoon to retrieve a check at Westville, get a hair-cut, procure the necessities for a sanitorium stay, viz: pajamas, bathrobe, slippers, etc.

When I mention this trivia, it would be best for you to remember the ancient adage concerning mighty oaks and little acorns, or in the words of P. G. Wodehouse, "wheels within wheels."

I was not granted the liberty, with the result that I arrived at Westridge using pajama bottoms for underwear sans slippers, sans bathrobe, sans everything. It seems to me that I arrived there in a state not becoming to my age and dignity, and a two month's growth of head-hair, I found to be uncomfortable. I think I managed for one night to stay there before going A.W.O.L. (or as the soldiers said, AWOLoose).

I had about twenty dollars at the time and called a cab to the front door of the Sanatorium. To reiterate my sincerity, I stopped for only one double rum before traveling half a block to the nearest barber-shop.

Mission accomplished, and then I was confronted with the problem of explaining my absence at the sanatorium. At the age of 67, one is not desirous or inclined to explain anything. My attitude for a long time toward general opinion might be summed up in the words "who in hell is trying to prove what"?

As you damned well know, I have one stock answer for all the unsoluble asininities of mankind. I procured a pint of that fluid that causes sailors to believe they are admirals and then proceeded forthwith by cab to sanatorium.

My problem posed no new problem to any such officialdom. On such circumstances, you merely drop the proverbial hot-potato in some one else's lap. I was transferred here the next day.

This place, I assume to be of the same standard of state institutions which is like saying that I don't know from one day to the next, whether I am to be transferred to a violent ward or turned loose on the general public tomorrow. "Loose as a Chinaman's slipper" is a better way of describing things.

This particular ward contains everything from congenital idiocy thru epilepsy to senile dementia. We are all on the same life raft as concerns being afflicted with Koch's Bacillus.

Sedentary senility? uneventful old age?? I had rather choose my later moments in the shower of sparks from a cheap Roman candle than the last sputtering spark from a hobo jungle fire.

"Escape from custody," how shall it be effected this time? Shall I pose as Father Damien among the lepers or Albert Schweitzer in Africa's jungles? There is opportunity here for martyrdom unless you write Charlie Kardwell, Social Services, this institution.

Sincerely,

Moore

Middleway State Hospital
February 23, 1971

R. M. Straus, Ph.D.
Chairman, Behavioral Science
College of Medicine
University of Kentucky
Lexington, Kentucky

Re: Frank Moore

Dear Dr. Straus:

I have recently had the opportunity to meet and converse with Mr.

Frank Moore. He is presently staying in the tubercular unit of our hospital. He is an exceptional man with exceptional ideas. He does not wish to remain here at Middleway State Hospital and it is my impression that he does not belong here.

I ask you for a letter of reference containing any pertinent information related to his present state of being, family history, early personal history, employment history, medical history and so on. Any information would be greatly appreciated.

Sincerely yours,
Charles Kardwell
Social worker

State Hospital
Middleway
February 21, 1971

Hi Bob:

Imagine anybody paying a hundred dollars for Mark Twain's signature!!

In retrospect, I must be the highest paid letter writer in history. Every time you write to me, you enclose two dollars. Over many years & in various places, that two dollars has seemed like twenty dollars.

In regard to my present situation I am, frankly, bored. . . . When you have been to one of these looney-houses, you have been to them all. Some are better or worse than others; the personnel are likewise better or worse.

I am glad you received a letter from Mr. Ballaux, my social worker, stating that he enjoyed my keen & critical observations. I would have been satisfied if he had just mentioned "realistic." Good God, how I hate sham.

My doctor may condone keeping me here because I might be in an active state of T.B. However, if I am declared non-psychotic other facilities are available for my transfer.

I thought I had everything "wrapped" up in the event of my demise but my coronary attack of December gives rise to the thought that I might shuffle off this mortal coil in this insane asylum. Will you write him concerning your opinion of my deviation from normalcy? (Whatever that may be).

Frank

State Hospital
Middleway
February 25, 1971

Finis to 25 years acquaintance and correspondence
Hi Bob:

One of my roommates has been here seven months and another for a period of years.

Like Coolidge, "I do not choose to run" or like a small boy "I will not play."

Within a few days, I expect to be transferred to a violent ward; tied up or tied down; in what I hope to be the most undesirable and vicious part of this hospital; force fed, etc. and etc.

This condition is brought about because of what is called "un-cooperative," which in other words means "kissing the chains of imprisonment."

My coronary state will not tolerate extreme conditions for long, and so I hope to evade long incarceration, emaciation, wasting away and other concomitants of T.B.

I wish you to grant one further request. I wish you to air-mail a letter to Mrs. Petrakis asking her to mail the check of Mar. 3 and *any other* further checks to you.

I hereby authorize you to endorse the checks with my name and apply this money to my financial obligations to you. I don't owe any other man a cent. Remember Socrates owing Esculapias a rooster.

At least I escape the harassments of religion and the promise of everlasting hell-fire and brimstone.

It is improbable that my wishes to donate my body to Harvard and my eyes to Boston Eye Bank will be complied with. I suppose I will be handed over to the first hick local undertaker so that he might share in his fair share of Social Security Burial Benefits.

This place is run as loose as a Chinaman's slipper and I suppose that is what will happen.

I know what I am doing and am neither despondent or down-hearted. This would be a good ending for final "Escape from Custody" and it is the way I would want it to be.

Frank

March 3, 1971

Dear Frank:

Your letter of February 25th has just arrived and I hasten to reply.

To quote a different literary and historical figure, "Don't give up the ship!!"

Last week I received a letter from Mr. Charles Kardwell in which he characterized you as an "exceptional man with exceptional ideas." I was quite pleased with his accurate perception. He recognizes that you do not wish to remain at the Middleway State Hospital and he asked for information which might help him consider other arrangements. As you had requested in your last letter, I sent Mr. Kardwell a brief summary of your situation and expressed the opinion that if someone could give enough attention to helping you get re-established in a community, you have demonstrated a capacity to maintain yourself. Another requirement would of course be the provision and administration of the necessary medications. I am in the blind, as I assume you are, regarding the severity of your tuberculosis and whether your present state is such that you could be maintained on an out-patient basis.

In any event, before taking the drastic measures implied in your letter of the 25th, be advised that you have not been lost in the mire of numbers; that there is someone on the staff there, who has recognized you as a unique individual and who is interested in you; and that there is someone here who is also interested in you as a remarkable human being.

There is another matter on which I hope I can put your mind at ease. You have no financial obligations whatsoever to me. Any and all funds which you have received from me over the years should be classified as tokens of friendship; or if you prefer, as business transactions in return for your contributions to science. Never has there been any intention that you were incurring a debt. You can therefore rest assured that you owe me nothing. On the matter of your checks, I would suggest that you write to Mrs. Petrakis asking her to either hold the checks for you until further direction, or send them to you, or, if you like, send them to me to hold for you. There is no way that I could endorse them or cash them for you without a legal power of attorney.

I am enclosing paper and two envelopes; one for your reply to me and the other for a letter to Mrs. Petrakis, should you want to write to her. I will write again to Mr. Kardwell.

Have heart,

Bob

March 3, 1971
Re: Frank Moore

Mr. Charles Kardwell
Social Worker
Middleway State Hospital

Dear Mr. Kardwell:

As a followup to my letter of February 25th, I thought I should tell you of a letter which I have just received from Mr. Frank Moore written by him on February 25.

The letter conveys a sense of futility and of giving up which is not characteristic of the man, although it may be quite characteristic of the disease from which he is currently suffering. I have written to him with a "don't give up the ship" type message and took the liberty of mentioning that I had heard from you and that you have expressed an interest in him.

Sincerely yours,
Robert Straus

March 10, 1971

Dear Frank:

In your last letter you mentioned your concern that the various documents willing your body to the Harvard Medical School and eyes to an Eye Bank were lost. Today I remembered that one of the letters which you sent me some time ago was written on the back of some Xerox copies of those documents.

We found the letter and have made fresh Xerox copies and I am sending these herewith. I know that this has been your intention for a long, long time, and I hope that it will be a comfort to you to have the documentary evidence again at hand.

With best wishes.

Sincerely yours,
Bob

Ward 2 E
Westridge Sanitorium
April 4, 1971

Dear Bob:

Your letters & the intercession of Charles Kardwell were instrumental in effecting my latest escape from custody.

Sometime when I am feeling particularly bitter, I must take into account the number of times when someone has endeavored to salt me away for life in various insane asylums.

The hopelessness of sickness in old age overwhelms me. . . . I lack illusions & look upon the whole damn thing in a terribly realistic manner.

If I didn't, I would be a traitor to intelligent thinking. I have watched too many people hang on when their minds & bodies are gone—clinging tenaciously to life of pain, helplessness, as if life itself had intrinsic worth.

I have had all the best of life, physically, & refuse to accept the consideration of a nursing home or a convalescent home.

Whenever anyone evinces the outward symptoms of doing what is best for me—I recognize restriction, confinement, & all the right names for their so-called good intention. My Old Age Assistance has been stopped on account of being here. . . . I shall experience the 'rags of life' to the end.

Frank

New Salem House
Westville
May 15, 1971

Dear Bob:

Discharged Westridge Sanatorium on April 4; disease is non-contagious as long as I continue daily control drugs; have received 60 streptomyacin shots, intensive chemotherapy; blood tests, a magnitude of X-rays, tests of sputum, electrocardiograms.

Hospitalized one day short of a month at Davenport; one day short of a month at Westville Hospital; after a few days at Westridge I went down town, got drunk & got a haircut (needed one after being two months in an isolation room in Davenport & Westville hospitals).

Woman doctor at Westridge thought I was crazy, despondent & depressed & had me transferred to Middleway State Hospital. Found non-psychotic & thru your influence & Mr. Kardwell's, they were glad to get rid of me after 45 days. It were better for them to deal with friendless, docile, cooperative patients who would mop, & sweep, & clean. In passing, I would strongly advise any mental patient never to touch a broom, & to be sarcastic & disagreeable as possible within the bounds of sanity, & altogether to act like that character in "The Man Who Came to Dinner." Thank God, I knew enough not to be friendly & pleasant. Things become nice & remunerative for employees of a state hospital as long as they can get rid of a bastard like me. "Bug-housing" has become an industry in this country & should no longer be regarded as a service employment, unless one means to the employee himself.

Of course, it was expected that I would continue treatment for T.B., especially as the X-rays indicated there was a strong possibility of carcinoma. I agreed & desired to go back to the sanatorium at Westridge, especially to confront that woman doctor who had sent me to Middleway. (You know, that word 'confrontation' is getting a hell of play "these days.")

One of the doctors at Middleway showed me the communication she wrote on my transfer here. "Despondent," "depressed," "didn't care to live," etc. The report that she wrote looked is if it had been copied verbatim from a medical textbook under the chapter of Melancholia.

Was I supposed to chirp & be happy that within 3 months time I had broken an arm, learned that I had tuberculosis, & had one heart attack (some form of angina)??

Did she know of the venomous conditions to which she had transferred me? Did she merely intend to ensure her continued professional comfort by transferring a patient who had the affrontery of going A.W.O.L., getting drunk & getting a hair cut? Whenever, after my return to Westridge, I discussed the affair with other patients & other doctors, they seemed to believe that she was the one who was demented.

In fairness to her, I do not believe she is crazy. She is only eccentric to the extent that, as a middle-aged woman, she wears dresses that nearly reach crotch level (In this, may be *I* am eccentric).

I do believe that she did have the normal (?) aversion of most women to a man who had rather get drunk than buy her a mink coat, & run himself into an early grave by directing all his energies, wealth, ambitions, & health to insure his fair share of the joys of bed-room athletics.

Biologically, it is necessary for her to feel this way, in order that she must bring forth & protect another generation to drop napthalm bombs, cross the seas & get the clap.

The dear ladies whose sensibilities are protected by statutory laws from viewing me drunk, have caused me to sleep on a hundred police station planks, to have been shunted to a dozen insane asylums, will be the death of me yet.

Not broken limbs & ribs, not heart disease, not T.B., not cancer, not malaria, dengue, not hemoglobinuria, not stab wound or broken head, will cause me to shuffle off this mortal coil, but the ladies, bless 'em, started working on me 67 years ago.

One thing I quickly learned of was reduplication & unnecessary repetition.

It took about (all the figures that I give you are correct) forty X-rays & six sputum tests at Davenport to insure the fact that I had T.B. I would have settled for one.

When I was transferred to Westville, I suppose some records must have been sent with me. Nevertheless, about thirty more X-rays & sputum tests, not counting blood pressure readings twice a day, & weekly cardiogram tests.

Then I arrived at Westridge as if I were a new patient without record; more X-rays in that sojourn.

Hence to Middleway & dozens of X-rays where the possible indication of cancer were shown.

Back again to Westridge, dozens of more X-rays & a dozen sputum tests.

The reason that I keep reiterating about the X-rays, it seems to me that the doctors could not believe what they saw the first time.

Anyone interested in the cost of public health (reduplication & repetition) should see me. . . . I am going to give you first crack at the records. They must be on file.

It appears that in the past five months that I have received the benefits of science & received many thousands of dollars worth of treatment which the ethic of present society believes reasonable, & that I should be duly grateful. Interested in hospital administration, as you must be, there are more factors than generally meet the eye.

Whenever any idealistic or altruistic program occurs to the fertile brain of man, the question arises of financing. Where is the money coming from & how is it going to be spent. Certainly, I am one guy who can tell you how some of it is spent.

For the past fiscal year, $3,829,000 was appropriated for the operation of the Westridge County Sanatorium for less than a *100* patients daily average. By simple arithmetic, if my primary school teachers are correct, this boils down to $38,290 per patient per year.

Eight doctors not in private practice, hordes of nurses of the three shifts, maintenance workers, maintenance of plant, occupational therapists, social workers, clerical workers, records clerks, waitresses, porters, attendants, etc. & etc. can not account for that money.

I haven't any way of knowing how things are at your Center but every damned place I have been is overstaffed. There is that old corny saying in A.A.: Live & let live. I don't mind how many parasites & paramedical people make a salary & living because of my disease. But when people talk of my medical costs & the money that is spent on me, I rightly observe, "Cui Bono?" (to whose benefit).

'There are more things under the sun than you and I know of, Horatio.' My old age assistance check while I was in Davenport was returned to the State. I would have gone without a cigarette on Christmas Day except the Lowell post of the American Legion gave all veterans of record $2. Incidentally, while at Westridge I joined & paid a years dues to the Veterans of Foreign Wars. I went down there every 3 weeks in order to fight the war over again & of course, to drink.

Then at the Westville Hospital my Old Age Assistance was returned because I was hospitalized.

The next day after I was transferred to Westridge, I received a letter which I think was probably sent with my records, from the Westville Office of the Public Welfare, notifying me that Old Age Assistance was indefinitely discontinued by reason that I no longer had a Westville address.

When I was notified that I was being transferred to Westridge Sanatorium, I understood that the general conception was: in that I received domicilary care (roof), food, the best of science,—that there were no further requirements.

There are always requirements. The admitting nurse formed no favorable opinion because I had no clothing except on my back (as tho' I had been picked up out of a life boat).

With your previous bout with heart disease & hospitalization, I suppose you (or someone else), thought of pajamas, bathrobe, & bedroom slippers, & the other amenities of a hospital stay. . . . As you know, I have slept on wharves, empty box cars, but I have always preserved an idea of what I conceived to be civilization. . . . I was ashamed, because of lack of material things which I had no respect for (but which other people did).

It was a most auspicious debut. . . . A man can become hard on the outside but not on the inside.

To insure not going on interminably, I was discharged on May 4 in the aforementioned arrested & non-contagious state. I tried to get advertised rooms in Hamilton & was unsuccessful. I really like Westville with its museums, & the relicts of piracy, privateers, near & actual criminals, my ancestry & heritage, which is so god-damned archaic & out of date. And so back to Westville.

You can imagine my reception—the bad penny come back, Lazarus resurrected, & the guy who will not die—at the Public Welfare & Old Age Assistance. "Enoch Arden" is wishy-washy stuff.

First, I was informed that I could not obtain assistance, however the need be obvious, unless I obtained a Westville address. Remember, I had a Westville address, when I left here—Westville Hospital.

I obtained a room & address, as above, to establish residence. The landlady has been informed that I will receive checks on the 1st of June, so she has taken me on trust.

A grocer to whom I had always paid advance credit, has agreed to keep me from starving to death until June 1. Lucky me!

Until June 1, walking death without the price of a newspaper. I have renewed my library connection.

I suppose my chief concern is the loss of my cane. I could navigate. I rationalize a side effect from two control drugs which bunch up the calves of my legs. I lost my last cane during the November debacle when I broke my arm. Tried Red Cross, Catholic Charities, & Physical Therapy at Westville Hospital for cane. No soap. Not available. Costs money. More than you would think.

Like to think that I am not amenable to fear, but dread the fact of Nursing Home, Convalescent Home, will be my lot if I can not get out to shop groceries, books. Fact is, I am only good for a mile. (& how, I wrote!)

Frank

May 29, 1971
New Salem House
Westville

Dear Bob:

Received yours of May 18. Was I certainly glad to hear?! Half of the $5 was expended on a 2nd class cane.

Don't these angels know that when I become un-ambulatory, when I can no longer attend to my shopping, to go to the public library, that I shall revert to expensive institutionalization? I suppose that simple arithmetic is not worthwhile.

Referring to question in regard to coronary heart disease—I believe

I wrote you that I went to Davenport to recuperate from a broken humerus. Happened on Oct. 18. The arm in a cast would not heal, due to my age, the inability to handle a cane in my right hand, to continually fall, to sleep overnight in three assorted police stations, to forego food, led to a condition where Davenport was indicated.

After 3 days with a routine examination that indicated that I had moderately advanced T.B., my treatment was held in abeyance. Legally, they were not going to diagnose T.B., to transfer me to some sanatorium where it would be determined that I did *not* have T.B., treatment was altogether withheld. From December 4 to December 29 at Davenport. On December 29, I insisted on release. I did not even have cigarette on Christmas Day. I was discharged, without any funds, whatsoever; Walked two miles & had the 'heart attack'. Some concerned lady called the ambulance from Davenport & had me returned there.

It has always been a mystery to me, of the kindness of people, who should not in the pragmatic sense be kind to me.

As far as I can remember, my 'heart attack' was related to a roaring respiration. I thought it was related to a change from a super-heated hospital atmosphere to a near zero temperature.

Anyhow, Davenport no longer wished any responsibility and transferred me to Westville Hospital, the place of my last address.

After a few days there, a doctor Pace (square shooter) informed me that the electrocardiogram indicated that I had suffered a heart attack. Some form of angina, & I remember it was not of the pectoral family. Since then, I have not been over-anxious to take off my shoes at night. More dangerous than Viet Nam or sleeping on the slopes of Vesuvius.

In regard to the carcinoma, when I was transferred to Middleway, the 'outside' doctors who were called in to read innumerable X-rays, discussed various shadings which indicated that I might have 'carcinoma.' These doctors discussed the affair in front of me, without understanding that I knew that 'carcinoma' was a medical sobrequet of 'cancer.'

When I returned to Westridge, the doctors told me that there were certain shadings of my X-ray pictures that called for further investigation. Grabbing the bull by the horns, in Moore's inveterate way, I said, "Yeah, I probably have cancer." They were shocked & hushed & in a remonstrated way replied, "We don't know."

Why in hell didn't they know, after a hundred X-rays at Davenport,

Westville, Westridge, Middleway?? It seems to me that I have had 10 thousand dollars worth of 'diagnostics' & ten dollars worth of treatment.

I am sure that you have faith in doctors & believe them to be infallible. Believe me, only a man in a generation comes along like William Dudley White (heart) who has the ears to hear what others can not. Only a man has the sense of touch like Osler to feel what others can not feel.

I served my apprenticeship among navy doctors whose treatment for the primary lesion of syphilis (chancre), varied from mild chloride of mercury (calomel); iodoform (which stinks); thymol iodide (aristol); 7% mercurochrome; & heroically surrounding the affected part with petrolatum (vaseline) & touching the affected part with fuming nitric acid.

In the light of modern treatment, they were floundering around like a shaman, or a voodoo doctor. And so it continues today. As we laugh at Galen, so will the future laugh at our "ham-and-eggers" of today who achieve a monetary fortune thru social legislation & policy.

Frank

Ward 2E
Westridge County Sanatorium
July 23, 1971

Dear Bob:

Received yours on Monday. Contents noted, & I am most grateful. While I am out here, I forfeit $160 per month, Old Age Assistance.

The zeal of social service & fiduciary departments, seems ridiculous, in collecting from me, & depriving me of this small amount, in that this amount of money collected from me each month would not pay the costs of a single x-ray picture (I have had at least a hundred of these pictures taken since last December).

Of course, you remember I was evicted years ago from the Congress Hotel in Calvinville on account of urban renewal. The apartment to which I moved did not meet the requirements of Resettlement authority & I forfeited free rental over a period of a year.

I chose to pay rent & forego free rental because of the accommodations on King St. (private bath, frigidaire, double electric plate, the use of appliances at no extra cost (radio, bread toaster, fan) & best of all my isolation by self on 3rd floor).

When I was discharged from Westridge on May 4, I arrived back in Westville in the middle of the afternoon (too late to go room-hunting), & so I secured accommodation at the New Salem House (hotel) at $17 per week. Rather expensive if you consider that I insisted on making my own bed & cleaning up my own room. I obtained this room at the New Salem House with the understanding that I would be evicted on July 3, (again, Urban Renewal).

My hotel life for the two months interim (May 4–July 3) might be summarized by sleeplessness, reading until 3 or 4 in the morning, sometimes watching the sun come up. My peripatetic activities consisted of shopping for groceries & trips to the public library. Once a day was enough to climb those stairs (god-damned stairs).

This reading is a far cry from my plodding years of plane & solid geometry, elementary & advanced algebra, plane & spherical trigonometry. When I had absorbed as much differential & integral calculus as was possible, without guidance, I felt like Gibbon when he concluded the Decline & Fall of the Roman Empire. It is tragic to know of something & because of milieu to have no one to converse with, regarding that 'something.'

During December, January & part of February & previous to December, I felt no pain whatsoever. In Westville, I was hospitalized for the whole month of January. Isolation, private room, television until the wee small hours, & then audio until daybreak, choice of food, dietician around daily for selection. I felt like a pampered brat. However, epicurean food—cauliflower, broccoli, brussels sprouts, steaks, chops, fowl—palls & does not compensate for restriction or confinement under the most luxurious conditions. A shot of whiskey, four times a day, would have seemed like Eden or the Elysian fields. However, it has been within my observation that spiritus fermenti has only been prescribed in terminal cases of cancer—when the poor bastard is too far gone to feel the benefit of it.

Paul de Kruif, the ballyhoo artist of the medical profession, has recorded the heroics of death-fighters. Actually, there is a crying need of 'pain-fighters': probably not in our time will the medical profession rid itself of phoney morality.

Pain is good; pain is beneficial; pain is moral! Phooey! How often have I seen a man reduced to a shadow of what he has been, crying, complaining, suffering, & behaving in a manner contrary to the history of his whole life.

In writing to you, hundreds of letters over the years, I have never been at loss for words (using the idiom, the argot & the metaphor). However, when you wished to know of my present condition, I resorted to Roget's Thesaurus (ref. 659—Deterioration). Good God, it covers two pages—some of which is as follows: Damnum (Latin); disintegration; moth & rust (Bible); decay; impairment; dissolution; decrepitude; ravages of time; immedicabile vulnus (Latin); wane, ebb & lapse; go down hill; run to waste, go to seed; fade, wither & shrivel; go farther and fare worse; have seen better days; dismasted; saprogenic & rusty.

It isn't necessary to cry. I can copy it out of a book.

What was the name of that Indian who complained that there was no one left to mourn for him?

I showed you the house where I was born & reared. Out of the parlor (!) of that house, I watched the burial caskets of my great-grandfather, great grandmother, uncles, aunts, cousins. That room saw more funerals than any public chapel. I console myself with the thought of an unknown Marine sergeant at Belleau Wood who shouted to his platoon: Come on you sons-of-bitches! Do you want to live forever!

> Characteristically,
> Frank

The following letter, postmarked in Westville, October 2, 1971, was written by Frank on the back of my letter of August 27, addressed to him at the Westridge County Sanitarium. Frank's letter was obviously written during a state of intoxication and was barely legible. It was, therefore, necessary to guess some of Frank's words in terms of their contextual meaning.

> [Postmark—October 2, 1971]
> Adams Hotel
> Westville

Dear Bob:

Reading in "Readers Digest" of prisoners in Viet Nam, my heart bleeds. Prisoners in this country endure much more.

See in the first chapter, the heart breaking ride. A drunk cannot feel anything.

You say honorable employment. I say, killing may seem to be honorable. Machine guns or pistol, national ethics.

Note in readers digest, inadequacies of toilet facilities. In Merrick Jail there are no toilet facilities.

There are no faculties of human imagination to visualize human degradation except to become filthy in habitat and seclusion.

There is no brutality except seclusion from water, use of toilet, seclusion from diet until I will be transferred to a county jail.

All these things await a drunkard. You wrote of it as "Concomitants of Excessive Drinking."

I write as empiric through experience and knowledge.

Don't get carried away by prisoners of war in Vietnam. Prisoners do worse in this country because we are tougher.

I am living on nitro-glycerin, because I can write to you later.

Sincerely,
Frank Moore

Write me often "as one who loves his fellowmen."

Benton County Jail and House
of Correction
October 12, 1971

Dear Bob:

Resumé of the past month—Discharged from sanatorium Sept. 7; went to Calvinville; unable to regain Old Age Assistance without an address; for two weeks I was unable to get room or address; went to Westville & ran into difficulty; finally about the 26th, the District Court at Westville called the Adams Hotel, & said they would be responsible for a week's room rent, until Oct. 4, when I would receive Railroad Pension, $61.50; of course it was understood the week's room rent $25 was to be repaid when I received my pension; the Public Assistance would extend no financial assistance except for a $5 grocery order which was to be deducted from my first Old Age Assistance check of $112 which I was to receive on Oct. 16th; it was pointed out to me that I would receive the Railroad money on Oct. 4; the hotel manager suggested that I give him $50 to cover two weeks until I received Old Age check; I don't believe he considered or cared that I owed $25 to the District Court; simple arithmetic indicates that if I gave him $50, then I would be eating on $5 a week until the 16th & I would still be in the hole $25 to the District Court; didn't get check forwarded from Westridge until the 5th; slept out on the 4th; went to Post Office & got check on the 5th, $61; got suit out of cleaners; didn't pay District Court $25; didn't pay hotel manager $50; bus to Boston, drunk, heart business; bus to Providence, drunk, heart business; bus to Fall Creek, stayed hotel one night & then heart business; Union hospital, Fall Creek, 5 days, bad heart condition; signed out of hospital yesterday; sent down here today for 30 days *or* until such time as sanitorium *might* take me back.

Frank

Benton County Jail
October 22, 1971

Dear Bob:
 Received your letter & $5 enclosure on Oct. 20.
> 'Those friends thou hast,
> And their adoption tried,
> Grapple them to thy soul
> With hoops of steel.'

Looking back over the past thirty years, I have been deeply grateful to you. The only times that I have been regretful are those periods when I have been financially burdensome.

As I become ancient, it becomes increasingly difficult to express myself without allusion to literature. For instance—the above preamble. Perhaps my stepfather was right, at the time when he said, he did not want me to become an educated god-damned fool. Latin, algebra & the Odyssey, forsooth!

Yet, literature & the recollection of literature, has been immeasurable solace to me, during my hurts, wounds, sickness, depressions & despondencies. I could not survive without my memory of those past artists, who have so much better expressed my own feeling.

At different times, I have recalled that noble writing of John Donne, which begins: 'No man is an island, entire of himself.'

Believe you me, before writing my last letter to you; during my childhood; when I was a sixteen year old kid serving in the navy with older men; when I was working on railroads & steel mills & in the woods; when I was unvisited in hospitals & jails; when alcohol became an addiction & I was unable to find oblivion & progressive loss of sensibilities experienced by my brother-drunkard; when I was confined in mental hospitals without the surcease of insanity; when I became old & all relatives had died; when I was unable to retain permanency of friendships; & as my human machine wears out; when I am unable to receive the full benefits of legal social legislation—then with these dark thoughts, I feel sure that I am an island entire of myself. Not bathos or pathos—only sincerity. Fortunately with these somber thoughts, the brain comes to the rescue.

For example, the court sent me here, not for wrong-doing, not because of false 'corrective' ideas; but because I was aged & sick, without means to preserve myself. The court was humane, & saw the larger framework of the picture rather than a questionable moralistic miniature.

Different people at different times have said that I write coherently, but only during the past ten years I have become orally articulate.

I don't know whether you know or remember the story, but in the last few years when I appear before the courts, I simulate the old war-horse who nibbled the green leaves of the vine attached to the bell of Atri.

Yesterday I received the bifocal eyeglasses from Dr. Berman, optometrist, Westville, & also thru your intercession. The huge quantities of anti-tubercular drugs, from 14 to 18 tablets a day, over a period of six months has affected my vision, necessitating change. No word from Mrs. Stont regarding a check due me on October 16. This money, if the Dept. of Welfare of Westville has the whole say about the matter, will revert to the coffers of the state.

Have they considered that I will be financially flat on my ass when I get out of here? That I will be in precisely the same condition when I get out of here, as at the time I entered?

Frank

1972

January–March	Hospital Annex, Stonycreek
March–September	Benjamin Street rooming house, Harrison
Mid-September	Hospital (1 week), death September 24, Harrison

---

Frank's first two and a half months of 1972 were spent in the hospital ward of Stonycreek, but he was sufficiently determined to shake off the pattern of the last year and a half's decline to leave the hospital against the doctor's advice and to settle into a rooming house in Harrison in mid-March: "I am glad to report a haven . . . a haven, in the real sense of the word." He was living, as a roomer, with a family of eight children and a landlady who devoted much time and concern to his personal well being.

During the next few months I heard very little from Frank—at times too sick to write, and at other times not motivated. Finally, I received a telegram from his landlady, Mrs. Bourne, informing me of his death on September 24.

I called Mrs. Bourne, at her request, immediately. It was evident from her interest, concern and appreciation of Frank Moore and the personal attention to his needs in his last months that he had found and enjoyed a loving home and, as he so desperately wished when hospitalized earlier in the year, had escaped from custody for his final days.

Mrs. Bourne offered to write a description of the last few months of Frank's life. Portions of her letter, which are included, provide a symbolic overview of the triumphs and the pathos of Frank's last few months.

> Hospital Annex
> Stonycreek Correctional Institution
> February 8, 1972

Dear Bob: I mailed you
a letter of Jan. 12 from this
institution acknowledging
receipt of previous letters.

Have received no reply.

It would be futile to write
extensively, if for some reason
or other, you do not receive my
letters

> Frank

> Hospital Annex
> Stonycreek Correctional Institution
> February 14, 1972

Dear Bob:

Wrote you on the 7th. At the time, I was concerned that you had not received mine of Jan. 12. However, I received a letter Feb. 9, so it appears I was not incommunicado (spelling?).

'Twas not ever thus. During the past year, sealed letters are permitted from penal establishments in this state (even directed to the press). This innovation has resulted in a plethora of published letters by the liberal (?) press.

Any reform leads to counter-balancing abuses. Any appeal for sympathy to convict causes ought to lead to a consideration of their victims.

The general public is only capable of unilateral thinking, whether it be politics, alcoholism, or foreign policy. Prevailing, latest & loudest voices hold sway, until time alone proves the asininity of human judgements.

The advent of law respecting the criminality of drunkenness & the unwillingness of district court judges to sentencing men to county jails, has aroused trepidation in the ranks of those who have adapted to jail life with its easy work-demands, food, clothing, shelter & sanitary facilities.

The intent & well-meaning of Half-way Houses is a anathema to the habitues of Stonycreek especially to those whose aggregate sentences have ranged from five to twenty years.

For instance, a large proportion of older inebriates have some sort of a pension (Disability, veterans', social security, railroad pensions etc.). If they elected to stay in a Half-Way House they would be reduced to a Tobacco Pension, sleep in dormitories, compulsive attendance to A.A. meetings, etc. In effect, Half-Way Houses have more restrictions than the present-day liberally operated jails.

As one grizzled seer has pointed out to me, a man is thrown out of a Half-Way House for getting drunk while the police will only throw a man out of the police station when he is half way sober or nearly competent.

In an obscure & individual way, I believe that I pioneered in enforcement of constitutional law in this state.

For the past few years, every mother's son haled before the district courts of this state for drunkenness, is asked if he desires legal counsel, & signs a form when he waives such counsel. I can remember the many times I ranted & raved that I was sent to jail because I had no lawyer, & that because I was poor I ended up in jail.

No one was exempt from my 'ear-banging'—the policeman on the beat, the turnkey of jail, the judge on the bench & whatever county or state official.

How often I pointed out, that I could have bailed myself out of jail in a few hours & got twice as drunk as I had been in the first place;

how if I had the money to pay a fine, I could have stepped out of the courtroom to the nearest saloon; how because I had no money, I was sent to jail (not because I was drunk).

Before I forget & go off on a tangent, I would like to point out a ridiculous concept by the general public who believe that any accused person has adequate counsel, whether or not he has funds.

Regards, & I hope that I will hear.

Frank Moore

Hospital Annex
Stonycreek Correctional Institution
February 25, 1972

Dear Bob:

I received your letter & enclosures yesterday which were most welcome. Our correspondence over the years has caused me to become one of the county jail & institutions' elite. By 'elite,' I mean one of those persons who has a source of tobacco & the creature comforts that money could buy.

This twenty-five cent wage has worked a profound influence in the courts. Perrenial inebriates ask to be sent here in order that in the course of two months, they shall have amassed (proper word?) as much as ten dollars. Whereas, a month in the county jail & there are no dollars, & in nearly every instance, the man is in no better financial position, than on the day sentenced.

Truly it has been said that one-half of the world doesn't know how the other half lives.

During the past ten years, the voluntary admission has been in effect here. Without being a part of it, I witnessed its advent & present day operation. It may appear to you & the uninitiated as a sensible procedure. In effect, the correction officers & the dyed-in-the-wool drunk who is committed by the courts has labeled these men who return ten or twenty times voluntarily with the appelation of "Door-knocker." The committed prisoner is jealous because the volunteers can be released in fifteen days, whereas he must stay sixty days or more.

The volunteers are sometimes bought down here by the A.A. (12th step work?) who find it cheaper to buy gasoline than risk the problematical benefit of spending the necessary amount to get any man out of the gutter.

Daily trips are part of Beacon's program (???) for alcoholics supplying the volunteers. As I have noted before, anyone must be well versed in Bumology in order to know where to apply & the restrictive hours of application. It is my well considered opinion that the perrenial & diurnal bum has a tremendous advantage over the casual & intermittent bum.

New York's bowery always demoralized me after a few days. The connivery of those derelicts overwhelmed me. They had well planned daily itineraries employing a time & map schedule of hospitals & parish houses & missions—the hours for the serving of soup; new underwear at such a street at such a time; new socks at such a place. Logistica is a military science of goods & personnel on the move. Those bums who could hold down the Bowery had a static science of their own.

As you & I have watched the change of opinion & public attitudes over the past thirty years, there is always the reservation that this change is restricted to a minority of intelligent people. Whether we like it or not, & despite the supposed advances in public education, only a minority is truly intelligent & probably could be bracketed among teachers, judges, lawyers, doctors, the clergy.

I would be damn mad if anything I wrote would seem plaintive. It has been so many years since I have been here & I will be released in such a short time (March 8) that I can be objective & disinterested. My myriad diseases, incarceration, & the rest, have found me unreconstructed, impervious & much like a brat that has been well-switched without knowing what in hell it was all about.

Your last letter mentioned a meeting (quote) "I will go without enthusiasm or expectation that it will be significant."

Buck up, do I see rust or a hole in your armor? Even I have moments of victory.

A dyspeptic judge in Calvinville a few years ago said for the benefit of the assembled spectators: "It is tragic of this man's life, & I and my confreres must share our part of the guilt."

Instances like this come only once in my lifetime, & are never experienced by my associates.

Back of the mind in every suicide is the hope that someone will be sorry.

This place now has a large number of drug addicts (20 to 30 year range). If all the cards were down I think a hell of a lot of these addicts (?) would hate to be discharged from here. Even prison & jail can be glamorous to a stupid bastard who never had anything & who will probably never have anything.

Loads of sunshine,
Frank

217 Benjamin St.
Harrison
March 29, 1972

Dear Bob:

Introspectively, & considering my insecure state of the past year & a half, entailing broken arm, diseases of the lungs & heart, & the 'thousand & natural shocks that the flesh is heir to',—I am glad to report a haven.

It is not a case of any old porch in a storm—but a haven, in the real sense of the word.

When I learned that rooms were available here at room rates within my projected income, I returned to the scene of my crime.

It was here that I lied about my age, eleven days after my sixteenth birthday & enlisted in the U.S. Navy.

And so, fifty odd (& I mean odd) years, here I am again.

The local Veterans of Foreign Wars Post (the oldest post in the state) telephoned to this address & rooms were available.

With eight small children & two dogs, I crowded my way into the landlady's heart.

It is not a measure of my worth, but the capacity of the body.

As usual, I was overt & above board. I explained my eligibility for hospitalization or other institutional care. I explained my projected income & my vehemence against nursing or convalescent homes. I explained my absence of need for personal care. I told her of my absence of debts.

Everything has been made wonderful here for me. This is what I desire (& how many men can say that??)

Young people live on the same floor with me, & ask me if there is anything that I need at the store.

I enjoy the greatest measure of personal freedom with a minimal dependence on others.

I have not achieved these things without difficulty.

Thanks, in part to your financial assistance, I was able to pay two weeks room rent in advance.

When I had established residency, I applied for restoration of Old Age Assistance, which I had forfeited because of hospitalization for over a year. This government subsidy amounting to $190 a month will be restored to me on the 1st & 4th of next month.

It is logical & acceptable to me that these pensions were withdrawn from me while I was being hospitalized at tremendous cost. However, upon my discharge, the 'waiting period' has been difficult and rugged until such pension shall be restored.

When I left the sanitorium I could only carry a shopping bag (with my cane). My interim in Fall Creek & Benton was experienced by total depletion of clothing.

In retrospect, when I consider the clothing that I have left in different cities of this planet, it must have been sufficient to outfit the refugees of Bangladesh.

The next month or so will be critical in a financial sense in reestablishing the hygienic situation regarding clothing & standards which have become a part of me.

I have incurred indebtedness for rent, which is pretty hard to achieve in these times. I shall buy clothing & walk straight even tho' I eat insufficiently.

I know that I have the opportunity to live within my own standards.

In the following matter, I am reluctant to have you 'pull my chestnuts out of the fire.'

When I was evicted by Mrs. Petrakis at Westville, my daily or future address was unpredictable & problematical. In the first twelve hours, I fell down & broke my arm.

Subsequently, I gave to Mrs. Stout, a social worker at the Westville Public Welfare, a number of personal papers, military, merchant marine, etc., which may or might be filed with my dossier in her city.

These papers no longer have significance to her department, or my records in her department.

I have in mind, Navy papers, Merchant Marine papers, & documents attesting to the donation of my body & my eyes, & the certification of my contribution to the understanding of alcohol pathology, my obituary, etc.

As stated, I have a reluctance to have you pull my chestnuts out of the fire. I doubt that a letter from me to Mrs. Stout would result in a response, even though a congressman of this state went thru the time & trouble of securing them for me.

It is unlikely that I shall go thru the time & trouble of securing these kudoes.

I continue with nitroglycerin & believe me, I am unafraid.

I forget the Shakespearean play & any of your undergraduates could tell me of the origin:

> "Every man owes one life, God wot! If death comes
> today, we are spared the fears of many tomorrows."

Regards,

Frank

These god-damned papers would be a solace to me. What have I accomplished??

217 Benjamin Street

Harrison

May 15, 1972

Dear Bob:

I have not meant to have neglected you, or to have seemed unappreciative.

I have been so damned sick for the past three weeks that I am just unable to write you the kind of letter you deserve.

Signed out of another hospital against the doctors' advice.

They call it coronary occlusion & they are trying to scare me to death.

It never did work, did it? Thank God, I don't have religion.

My landlady here has been most kind & understanding.

There is *talk* of a 20% increase in my living allowance; but hell, I have always lived, as the Puerto-Ricans say, "drapa la vita" (Rags of life).

More when I feel better.

Frank

September 7, 1972

The Proprietor
217 Benjamin Street
Harrison, Massachusetts
Dear Sir or Madam:

I am writing to ask if you can provide me with information concerning the current whereabouts of Mr. Frank Moore who, when I last heard from him in May of 1972, was living in your home.

As Mr. Moore may have told you, he has, for more than twenty-five years, maintained, through correspondence with me, a continuing record of his life history. This is a document which we hope will be of value to those who are concerned with the kinds of life problems with which Mr. Moore has struggled for many years.

I wrote to Mr. Moore in May, indicating that I would be out of the country for a few weeks and promised to try and contact him on my return. However, when I returned we had not heard from him and I have had no reply to my letters addressed to him in Harrison, the last sent on August 15th.

There have been occasional lapses in correspondence over the years and I would be less concerned but for the knowledge that Mr. Moore's health has recently been very precarious.

If you are able to furnish me with any information concerning his current whereabouts or where he was located when you last knew of him, I will be very appreciative. I am enclosing for your convenience, a self-addressed stamped envelope.

Sincerely yours,
Robert Straus

The following letter and telegram were received on the same day, September 25, 1972.

217 Benjamin St.
Harrison
September 23, 1972

Dear Mr. Straus:

In regard to your letter to me. Mr. Moore is in the Hope Hospital after being drunk and not eating for 2 wks. I have really got to know him very well. I do hope he will return here as we all love him very much. He still hasn't eaten anything. He went to the hospital Friday Sept. 16/72. He got your letters but I guess he didn't feel like writing. He has been pretty good except the last 4 wks. As you know I have eight children and am quite busy but I'll take time to let you know about Frank Moore.

Sincerely,
Andrea Bourne

P.S. He is a GREAT PERSON.

Harrison
Sept. 24, 1972

FRANK MOORE DIED THIS MORNING. PLEASE CALL OR WRITE.

Andrea Bourne

October 1972

Dear Mr. Straus:

Well, I really don't know how to begin but I guess I'll start with the day he came to our house.

It was kind of cold out and he came in and told me of his illness and about just getting out of the hospital. He had a black and gray overcoat, a brown cane, black shoes, brown pants and a shirt. Well, as you guessed that's all he had. I went to work and got some clothes from one of the friends I know. As the next few weeks passed he got his check and paid the rent. He stopped down stairs to see me quite often to say what he was doing. He would have me call a cab or call any of his business like welfare, S.S. He was always clean. This went on for quite some time.

The children grew to love him very much. Well, he took a liking to Tommy which is 7 yr. old. They used to talk for long times. He would always give Tommy money for ice cream or what ever he wanted. Well, he went over board drinking, and Tommy was hurt but he still would go up to his room to see him. He always would say how wonderful it was to see the children and how lucky I was to have them. When he was really drunk I would keep the children down stairs and I would talk to him for hours on end. He said what the doctors said, how it began and etc. I don't know the medical terms.

He would tell me of his mother, father and others in his family. He also made me promise not to send him to a rest home. Well, that I did keep. When he was low on money and didn't want to ask he would clean his room, mop all the floors and clean the stairs, polish his shoes, walk to the library and to the store. He was always clean except when he drank too much.

Well, I guess he stopped writing when he went to the hospital the first time. He was dehydrated and he had trouble urinating. They put a catheter in him. Well, he signed out of there, came home and was pretty good.

May came around and we had a wedding—my husband's daughter married. Mr. Moore helped the groom to get ready and when my husband's daughter went up in her wedding dress he cryed and wished her the best. He was always very tender hearted with this family. Well, he got drunk and stayed drunk for a week but I kept after him to clean up or out. He straightened out which was like 2 wks out of a month. He would have Susan, my daughter, sing church songs to him. He would give her a quarter of course. My 2 young boys Frederick (5) and Elliot (4) would go up and sit on his lap and hug and kiss him. He always gave them 10¢ or pennys. He said they all didn't know how lucky they were to have such a good mother. He said to me one day, which is worse to have nothing to do or too much, he'd say how the (Hell) could I stand it all day Maw this and Maw that.

Before he went to the hospital this last time he wanted me to write for him but would just cry and ask me how I put up with him drinking and being a slob. He was quite a problem when he drank. I would sit in his room until 3 AM or more so he wouldn't scream as he got the D.T.s.

He read a lot of books and he would tell me so much about life and drinking. He wanted to stop but couldn't. He made chair covers and hemmed table cloths. He sewed all his own cloths and was very sound minded. The end of his days here was hard on him. He drank too much and was dependent on me for the toilet and his needs. One night he fell into his closet and split his head on the floor. Had six stitches at the hospital. We had a tough time and he was delirious. He was swearing at the doctors & nurses and etc. I was the only one that could talk to him. The doctor said bring him back *sober*.

Well, he came back home, stayed in bed 3 days and just wanted to drink. I tried to stop him. I took his money so no one could buy drink for him. I'd give him a glass of wine to ease his pain. For one or two weeks before he died I sat with him all night. I tried to get him to eat. He wouldn't. Then I called the welfare office and tried to get some one to help him. It took five days for a nurse to come see him. Then they said they would put him in the hospital Friday, so Thursday I shaved him and washed him and etc. He thanked me for being so kind to him.

Friday I went upstairs to help him get ready. Well, he didn't want to take anything with him so he asked me to help him go to the bathroom. I did, and I got him to bed. He kissed my hand and said I was a wonderful woman. He always praised me. They came and took him to the hospital. It took 5 hours to find him a bed. They didn't want a drunk. They put him in a room (room 215). Then in the intensive care, then in a room (rm. 205). Well, that's where he died. He talked to me the second day in Rm. 215. Gave me his check and said to use it for the kids. I saw him in the intensive care and he knew me but was very sick. I saw him the day before he died. He just looked at me. I kissed him and asked God to be merciful to him as he was a great man. I and all my family plus my other tenants loved him and thought he was just Great.

Sincerely,
Andrea Bourne

10. The Meaning of Frank Moore's Life

Frank Moore made numerous efforts to salvage some sense of worth from his essentially wasted life. His collections of memorabilia from his military and maritime service and his preoccupation, especially in his last years, with the significance of his very brief service as a naval medical corpsman were very obvious attempts at building a sense of self-respect. Occasionally the fantasy so common to homeless men crept into these claims for immortality. For example, he prepared his own obituary notice identifying himself with the Abraham Lincoln Brigade in the Spanish Civil War. Actually, at the time of the Spanish conflict, he was in the beginning throes of the vicious circle of dependency, with transient live-in jobs, frequent intoxication, occasional arrests and incarceration.

Frank's striving to achieve some respectability was not limited to fantasy or reminiscences, however. During his last few years he tried against incredible odds to avoid the jails and public hospitals on which he had been almost totally dependent for at least twenty years. In addition, his more than three hundred letters recording his experiences and philosophical observations were a continuing medium through which he was able to carry on a search for some significance in his life. Finally, Frank not only contributed his life record but he also arranged to donate his body to "science."

One of the great values of the human life record is that, like the human cadaver, it can be subjected to a detailed examination of its structure, systems, pathways, and pathology. However, whereas the cadaver can be dissected only once and is then usually discarded, the life record can be examined again and again by countless different people and from many different perspectives. In the case of Frank Moore, it is hoped that students of the social and behavioral sciences can find his life record useful as a basis for testing theories and raising questions. It is often in the area of asking questions, rather than of answering them, that life-record documents can be most significant.

Although this chapter will consider some generalizations about patterns of behavior in Frank's life, it is essential to recognize and identify the uniqueness of every human personality. Frank Moore was a unique individual; he was very intelligent, highly motivated to maintain a life record, talented in expressing his thoughts and in relating the "stranger than fiction" events of his life. Also unusual was the fact that Frank outlived the majority of his contemporary homeless men. He was forty-one years old in 1945 when the prospective record of his life was initiated. Few persons who knew him then would have anticipated that he would live another twenty-seven years. Although death rates have never been calculated for the homeless-man population in general, Donald Bogue has reported a Chicago study indicating that "at most ages Skid Row inhabitants can expect to live less than one half the number of years remaining to men of the same age in the general population."[1] Frank experienced amply all the factors to which Bogue attributed his findings: inadequate food, rest, clothing, shelter, and medical care; prolonged heavy drinking; the necessity to work when ill; and excessive exposure to infectious diseases and accidents. Despite these and despite the physical impairments experienced by Frank in his sixties, his unusual combination of strong physique and motivation sustained him.

Otherwise, Frank's general pattern of living between roughly the first sixteen and the last six years of his life typifies that of thousands of other undersocialized, alcoholic, homeless, and dependent men. An examination of Frank's experiences, particularly as they pertain to institutional and alcohol dependency, will be the primary subject of this final chapter.

Institutional dependency has been described as a syndrome characteristic of individuals who have lived so long in situations in which their basic needs were provided, their expression of initiative prohibited, and engagement in normal socializing experiences of family, job, and community prevented that they have become unable to cope satisfactorily with independent living in the larger society. It has been suggested that, either prior to or at least as a result of institutional living, most institu-

1. Donald J. Bogue, *Skid Row in American Cities* (Chicago: Community and Family Studies Center, University of Chicago, 1963), p. 225.

tionally dependent persons have been deprived of opportunities for the development of personal and social traits necessary to meet with comfort some of the basic interpersonal and cultural expectations of society. Because of their undersocialization they feel inadequate to cope with even the most routine demands of community living, and they tend to seek out life-adjustment situations which protect them from anxiety provoked by such demands. It has also been noted that many institutionally dependent persons have found in alcohol-induced euphoria or oblivion a way of avoiding the intense discomfort which they experience when their dependency needs are not being met.

Like most of the hundreds of thousands of other men who have filled the live-in jobs and inhabited the skid rows, jails, mental hospitals, and public infirmaries of our country, Frank Moore had a background of early parental deprivation, disruption of normal family and community living, and undersocialization. He escaped into institutional living in the formative years of adolescence and, from that point on, had difficulty living outside of settings where his basic needs would be met. Frank Moore spent some forty years in the Navy, the Army, and the Maritime Service, the Civilian Conservation Corps, lumber camps, railroad labor camps, agriculture camps, resort-area live-in jobs, religious retreats, and numerous other institutions where he was able to find live-in employment. He frequented skid-row flophouses and work shelters, prisons and jails, and mental hospitals and public infirmaries. Between episodes of institutional living when his dependency needs were not being met, alcohol permitted him to escape from desperate feelings of despair, loneliness, and anxiety and, at the same time, served to assure access to institutional care and to provide a rationale for his way of life.

The combination of events, influences, and personality traits that produced Frank's particular pattern of life is complex. All human behavior involves the fundamental interaction of the biological nature of man; the physical environment into which he is born and in which he is nurtured; the individual's personality, including his intelligence, stress and anxiety thresholds, and characteristic ways of feeling, thinking, acting, relating to others, and evaluating self; man's basic social groups such as family, community, religion, and occupation and the particular activities and responsibilities which these groups assign to the individual; and the aggregate of customs, values, laws, expected ways of behavior, techniques, artifacts, and apparatus which characterize the culture of particular groups at a particular time.

Each of these basic components of behavior provides certain potentialities for and imposes certain limitations on individual behavior; each
contributes to the individual's relative vulnerability or resistability to outside stress. All of these components were important in Frank Moore's
life. Significant evidence pertaining to each will be presented as we seek
out those factors contributing to his undersocialization, his institutional
dependency, and his alcoholism.

Biological and Environmental Factors

There is evidence that both Frank's intelligence and his emotional instability were in part family traits. We know from her letters that his
mother was reasonably intelligent; and that she was ranked first in her
high school class. She characterized herself as "emotionally unstable" and
"of an extremely nervous temperament." We know, too, that his father
was "temperamental," had been discharged from the Navy for "neurasthenia," and committed suicide.

Frank was born and spent the first sixteen years of his life in the fairly
rugged climate of northern New England. He lived in a house in which the
upper rooms were unheated. Although some years in the military service
were spent in a tropical climate, he chose New England and upper New
York State in which to wander throughout most of his homeless life. During those years he was exposed repeatedly to extreme conditions of
cold and heat with no shelter, inadequate clothing, and little or no food,
and he was often sustained only by alcohol. Yet he survived. Perhaps
Frank's survival capacity, in spite of the odds, was partly due to his early
acclimation to stressful conditions. It is also worth noting that Frank's
mother lived to age seventy-eight, his maternal grandfather lived to
about the age of seventy-two, and his maternal grandmother, who died
in 1953, must have been in her mid-eighties, if not older.

In middle life, Frank was about five feet nine in height, of wiry build,
muscular, and remarkably strong. Despite his high caloric intake in the
form of alcohol, he never seemed to put on much fat. Physically, his
pulmonary system was the first to develop manifest signs of disease.
Frank was a chronic smoker, and it is possible that his intensive smoking,
which was relatively uninterrupted by his periods of incarceration, rather
than his drinking, which was chronically intensive but intermittent, was
a more significant cause of his death.

Frank's respiratory condition, particularly in its beginnings as an "allergy," seemed related to his nomadically changing environments. Although he had noted as early as 1935, while working in a lumber camp, that he "wheezed like a running bear" at night, the first inkling of serious impairment occurred in 1950 when he was living in a primitive railroad work camp, where "the environs were simply plastered with ragweed and goldenrod." He found he could not sleep at night because of the difficulty of breathing, and during the two months he stayed there, what had been a minor disability became a major one. "When I threw up the job, returned to the city, and got drunk," he wrote, "I was physically relieved."

It is also conceivable that Frank's alcoholism was related to biophysical as well as psychological and social factors. Frank mentioned getting violently sick on each occasion when he attempted to drink between the ages of seventeen and twenty-nine, suggesting a possible hypersensitivity to alcohol which will be discussed later in this chapter.

The Early Years of Undersocialization

Beyond his physical traits, much of the evidence available on Frank's heritage concerns the social, psychological, and cultural characteristics of the family and community setting into which he was born, and where he was nurtured for the first sixteen years of his life. During these early years, many of the conditions accountable for his undersocialization as he moved into adult life are evident.

Family. The circumstances surrounding Frank's birth are indeed bizarre. Frank's mother had married at sixteen after, and perhaps because, she had become pregnant—a considerable stigma in a small New England town at the turn of the century. Frank's grandmother's childbirth experiences had apparently been traumatic and she was determined that her daughter remain childless. She successfully encouraged Frank's mother to abort her first pregnancy and attempted to persuade her to abort this second one. Frank's mother refused but was "unhappy and disturbed" and bedridden throughout her pregnancy. The birth itself was difficult and accomplished only with "medical intervention," the details of which were withheld from his mother because "sometimes people thought things should not be done that way." It was in this atmosphere of extreme personal strife and tension, dominated by the hope that "perhaps it will die," that Frank came into the world. When he was only two weeks old, his father climaxed a feud with the grandmother by shooting himself. His mother was very ill and took seven months to recover from childbirth. Then she left Frank in the care of others while she sought "to make [her] life over" in another city where she trained for and practiced nursing, and eventually remarried.

Details about Frank's infancy and early childhood are sparse. His father's family had nothing to do with his mother's after the suicide, and his mother deserted him when he was an infant. His mother said that she had little love in her nature because it had been knocked out of her "from the beginning." She claimed Frank was cared for primarily by her sister. Of the maternal grandmother, we know only that she felt she married beneath her social class, worked outside of the home, and divorced Frank's grandfather while Frank was still an infant. Frank attributes his upbringing to a series of housekeepers, most of whom had only "artificial affection" for him. He said, "They all felt that I was just an obligation to them and nobody treated me as if I was their own." Frank never mentioned his grandmother. He made few references to any female relatives. His mother later wrote that during this period he had "everything he wanted," and there is no evidence of material deprivation.

Frank's grandfather is clearly identified as the only security figure in his childhood and youth. Frank characterized him as formal, hardhearted, reputable, honest, hard-working, clean-spoken, and of high moral standards. There appears to have been considerable affection but little overt display of warmth. Discipline was imposed by disapproval rather than physical punishment. Frank remembers his grandfather's frequent references to "walking the straight and narrow" and admonitions that when and if he "ever got licked" he was not to "come crying to him about it." Frank once said he had been "murderously handicapped" all his life by his grandfather's admonition that Frank must be "a winner." He remembers his grandfather acting "proud of me generally" and talking "as if he expected good things of me." The grandfather is remembered also as something of a social isolate caught up in a feud within his own family, without any close friends, and blackballed by fraternal groups in the community. Frank speaks of his grandfather as the only person for whom he ever felt any affection. Certainly for this orphaned child the grandfather was the only consistent parent figure, and many of his traits appear to have been reflected in Frank's own social isolation and moral philosophy. For Frank, too, was an isolate who rarely developed any close relationships with others. Even in the military, he reported few sustained friendships. In poker he chose the banker rather than the player role. His lifelong feud with his mother and other family members was perhaps an extension of his grandfather's example. One can conjecture also how much Frank's memory of his grandfather played a part in Frank's strong motivation to be a "winner" at the end of his life.

Other events in Frank's childhood undoubtedly also affected his later withdrawal and self-imposed isolation from society. As a child in the community, Frank lived with the stigma of his father's suicide and his mother's desertion. Of the suicide, he said that he never understood the real story except that there was some kind of disgrace connected with it which was hushed up and never talked about. He claimed his grandfather never mentioned either of his parents and that he never questioned him about them.

This stigma appears to have extended to Frank's associations with his childhood peers. He said that he knew all the time that something was wrong and he assumed it had something to do with his not having a father or mother. His playmates made fun of him in a way he didn't understand, running after him, yelling a diminutive form of his last name, and picking on him for reasons he associated with his parents. Frank's response was to avoid a confrontation whenever possible. In later life, Frank continued to be quite passive except when drunk and then, on occasion, he proved capable of committing violent physical assault on both persons and objects.

When Frank's mother remarried and returned to Calvinville, there was no change in atmosphere. In fact, Frank resented his stepfather as well as his mother's return. Obviously, he never gave the man a chance to fill a father's role. Frank described Mr. Greene as hard-working, a good provider, and successful, but uneducated. He said his stepfather looked upon him as an unwanted obligation. He characterized their relationship as an "armed truce," and expressed the feeling that, because Mr. Greene had had no advantages as a boy, he thought Frank was "having it too easy." Frank, in turn, held back and said, "I never took any questions or problems to him, never talked to him about my school work, never took any moral problems to him. I just knew he didn't understand me."

Clearly, Frank Moore looked upon himself as the victim of family deprivation. He wrote in 1963, "How long will it be before the social scientists, psychologists, psychiatrists, et al. begin to connect the family with the drunkard? If you could know of the complex, sordid, & insoluble problems that beset these men, you would arrive at the conclusion that they are better off in jail separated from their families. You may be able to tie this idea with your theory that if a man cannot find happiness in his own family circle, under modern conditions of life, then he is unlikely to find it anywhere."

Frank's mother. Much of the tragedy of Frank's story lies in the reciprocal intense ambivalence of mother and son toward each other. While mouthing what they perceived to be social expectation and convention in their condemnations of the other's attitudes and activities, as well as the feeling that blood should mean something, each actually sought from the other some affection to fill an almost total void in their lives. Both wanted more than either was capable of giving, and both seemed driven to impose on the other disappointment, hurt, and shame. Frank spent most of his life punishing his mother.

Frank's early feelings toward his mother were obviously partly acquired from and supported by other members of the family. He said, "As far back as I remember there was criticism about my mother because she wasn't there to look out for me." Of her leaving him, he recalled, "She must have thought I was a burden to her." "I'm not sure she was wrong, but at the same time she didn't play ball with what the world thinks. I suppose there's a parallel to the Hindu wife who is supposed to cast herself on her husband's funeral pyre." "My mother was a woman whose life was finished very young. She wouldn't stand for it . . . tried to make life over again . . . remarried and tried . . . to settle down with security." In his report of his early childhood, Frank passed lightly over the subject of his mother: "She led her own life and never bothered too much with me."

Frank resented his mother's desertion of him as an infant, and when she finally tried to assume the role of the "good mother" Frank resented it and thought she was motivated more by community approval than by genuine concern for his well-being. It was in this connection that he also resented her visiting his school classes. Details of his reaction to his mother's return are lacking, but there are references to his rebellion, stealing some books, stuttering, failing three courses in school, what his mother called "faulty reasoning," and his extravagance in spending the money he earned on his first job. When Frank joined the Navy at the age of sixteen, he had the opportunity to escape from home and pay back his mother for rejecting him as an infant. At the same time he emulated his father by joining the Navy, and his mother by running away from a tension-filled family setting to "seek a new life."

The Community. Although Frank Moore left Calvinville when he was sixteen and did not return until he was sixty, with the exception of occasional short and usually disastrous visits, the numerous references to his home town contained in his conversation and letters suggest that its culture and social structure as he had known it as a child continuously influenced his life pattern.

Calvinville's citizens traced themselves back to the very early settlers from England and were proud of their Yankee tradition. Relatively isolated from the mainstream of American life, the community was economically stale and culturally sterile. As novelist John Marquand described a comparable small city's rigidity, "There was a place for everything . . . and everything was in its place."[2] The population was approximately sixteen thousand, many of whom made it a point to know the business of the rest. As in so many similar communities, the behavior of people at all social levels seemed heavily influenced by fears of everyone's knowing and people's talking. The stigma of a family black sheep extended far and long and feuds were perpetuated from generation to generation.

In many respects the demographic characteristics of Calvinville are similar to those of the community "Yankee City," studied in the 1930's by W. Lloyd Warner and his associates.[3] When Frank was given the abridged copy of *Yankee City* in 1969 he seemed to delight in comparing that community with Calvinville. He also referred in several letters to the similarities between the social life of Calvinville and that of Clyde, the city described in some of Marquand's writings.[4]

Frank's family was Old Yankee and of relatively modest economic means. His grandfather owned his own home and, despite being something of a social isolate, appears to have commanded respect within his place in the community's social structure. Although Frank makes many references to his "middle-class" background, it seems more likely that his family was in what Warner characterized as the lower-middle social stratum. Some branches of the family had maintained their status and even achieved moderate upward mobility. A cousin was vice-president of a local busi-

2. John P. Marquand, *Point of No Return* (Boston: Little, Brown, 1949).
3. Especially relevant are W. Lloyd Warner and Paul S. Lunt, *The Social Life of a Modern Community* (New Haven: Yale University Press, 1941); Warner and Lunt, *The Status System of a Modern Community* (New Haven: Yale University Press, 1942); and Warner et al., *Yankee City*, one-volume abridged edition (New Haven: Yale University Press, 1963).
4. Particularly Marquand, *op. cit.*

ness establishment. Frank's maternal grandmother, on the other hand, believed that she had married beneath her status and his mother was downwardly mobile and died in an impoverished condition, her assets dissipated by the costs of severe illness and her care provided by public welfare. Frank was the last in the maternal line of his family and out-lived all of his close relatives.

Despite the many factors which combined to deprive Frank of a "nor-mal" home life during his childhood and despite the stigma which cast a constant shadow over his peer-group relations, Frank gives the impres-sion of having a fairly positive feeling for his early childhood associa-tions with Calvinville. His recollections of early school suggest a child who participated in the usual range of activities and had a sense of be-longing. There is a strong identification of the community's standards and customs with his grandfather. One senses that he associated some sense of security with both his grandfather and his grandfather's Calvinville. In 1963 he wrote: "It would take a flight of imagination to figure why I go back to Calvinville. Some inkling might be supplied by the fact that while I was altogether absent from Calvinville for a period of ten years . . . my grandfather mailed me daily the town newspaper. These news-papers were hand-addressed by him. Surely it was a labor of love & he must have expected me to return to an honorable place in the commu-nity. I imagine that the 'skull jockeys' could connect this last fact with my returning to Calvinville."

As he progressed through childhood, the mores and attitudes of the community both impinged on Frank's life and affected his own thinking. In describing his childhood, Frank depicted constant awareness of the community's disapproval and censure of something which he vaguely sensed was connected with his father's suicide and his mother's deser-tion. Frank's inability to accept his mother's quest for a life of her own was obviously supported by feelings in the community that "it just wasn't right." The estrangement which developed during the few years he was living with his mother and stepfather was the deciding factor in his join-ing the Navy at sixteen, but it was both family and community which he sought to escape.

It is difficult to estimate the true impact which Frank's stigmatization in the Calvinville community had on his life pattern or to separate family discord from community stigma and rejection. It is also impossible to separate the initial stigma associated with the circumstances of Frank's birth, and imposed on him by the actions of his parents, from the subse-

quent stigma he experienced as an adult associated with his imprisonment, drunkenness, and related behavior. Clearly, stigma played a for-
midable part in the vicious spiral of events and circumstances which
converged to prevent him from achieving a respectable place in society.
In this connection, Erving Goffman wrote:

By definition, of course, we believe the person with a stigma is not
quite human. On this assumption we exercise varieties of discrimina-
tion, through which we effectively, if often unthinkingly, reduce his
life chances. We construct a stigma-theory, an ideology to explain his
inferiority and account for the danger he represents. . . . We tend to
impute a wide range of imperfections on the basis of the original one.
. . . Further, we may perceive his defensive response to his situation as
a direct expression of his defect, and then see both defect and response
as justification for something he or his parents or his tribe did, and
hence a justification for the way we treat him.[5]

Certainly, Frank later included the stigma under which he lived as a
major justification for his inability to change his life's course and as a
rationalization for his continued drinking and dependency. Goffman calls
this the "secondary gains" of stigma; its use "as an excuse for ill success
that has come for . . . other reasons." He elaborates further: "In reviewing his own moral career, the stigmatized individual may single out and
retrospectively elaborate experiences which serve for him to account for
his coming to the beliefs and practices that he now has regarding his own
kind and normals. A life event can thus have double bearing on moral
career, first as immediate objective grounds for an actual turning point,
and later (and easier to demonstrate) as a means of accounting for
a position currently taken."[6]

Escape into Institutional Living—Frank's Military Experience. It has
been shown that parental deprivation and stigmatization within the community worked to isolate Frank from socializing forces and provide him
with a rationale for rejecting others. Compared to other young people of
his age, Frank was already undersocialized when he first left home. It
was probably for this reason that his initial reaction to military life was
quite positive. Frank noted that, although the usual conception of mili-

5. Erving Goffman, *Stigma, Notes on the Management of Spoiled Identity* (Engle-
wood Cliffs, N.J.: Prentice-Hall, 1963), pp. 5–6.
6. *Ibid.*, pp. 38–39.

tary life is discipline and restrictions, in his own case the restrictions which he associated with his mother and with Calvinville had been removed. He had joined the Navy for his "own selfish ends . . . to get out of an unpleasant situation and to start life over again."

Although he described his years in the military as marked by light-hearted freedom, there is evidence that even then he was not one of the boys. Men of the peacetime military services had three major forms of diversion: drinking, gambling, and sex. Frank's early experiments with drinking were unrewarding because he became violently ill. Gambling became a major activity, but he appears to have remained aloof from group enjoyment, preferring to play the role of organizer and entrepreneur. His experiments with sex were apparently not very satisfying and suggest that his early sexual orientations had profoundly inhibited his ability to experience really gratifying sexual activity. Frank's isolation from the society of the peacetime military was sealed when he became interested in literature and philosophy. He described this as a "sort of separation between the mental outlook and my environment."

Frank's sense of personal moral values did not carry over to respect for the law. When he was enlisted before reaching the legal age by a recruiting officer who suggested that he need merely lie about his age and birthplace, Frank noted, "That was my first experience that all rules and regulations are not to be followed literally. Later this brought me into conflict with powers that be." Quite early in his military career he became involved in some minor violations of military code but these were supported and respected by his peers, and the punishment was treated as a joke. He also found an opportunity to apply his intelligence and industry to learning the duties of a medical corpsman, and he advanced quickly in this role as far as his enlisted status would permit. Navy life was so supporting and need-fulfilling that he totally neglected family and home; when his term of enlistment expired, he re-enlisted routinely.

It is not possible to determine how much of Frank's later shift from Navy to Army and from medical corpsman to other duties was motivated by his search for new experience and challenge and how much was necessitated by disciplinary action. Eventually, however, his disregard for restrictions resulted in a serious violation and the five-year imprisonment which his mother disclosed but which he initially chose to omit from his own life story.

It is obvious that Frank did not "fit" very well even into the relatively institutionalized society of the military. He learned his specific duties well and performed them with sufficient competence to achieve promotions in rank, but he remained an isolate and was unable either to adapt satisfactorily to the extracurricular life of his fellow enlisted men or to accept the demands which military rules and restrictions placed upon him. Eight years of military life were followed by five years of confinement to a maximum-security prison, a period of Frank's life about which we know virtually nothing.

When Frank was released from Alcatraz and returned to Calvinville in 1933 at the age of twenty-nine, he had been away for thirteen years in military camps and prison. Although he had read widely some of the best literature in the English language, his formal and official education had stopped during the ninth grade. His work experience as a civilian was limited to a few weeks at the age of sixteen. His training as a Navy medical corpsman was not transferrable to employment of comparable responsibility or status in civilian life. To the small home town where everyone knew everyone else's business he brought the stigma of a prison record to add to that of his father's suicide and his mother's desertion. He had lived for thirteen years in an environment where his basic needs were provided for and his routine of daily living prescribed. His grandfather, who symbolized the only source of emotional support within his family, had died. And to complicate his return to community living, the nation was in the depths of a depression.

Frank's undersocialization was particularly evident in the estrangement he experienced upon returning home. Feelings of not belonging are common among people trying to make a transition to community living after prolonged periods of institutionalization. In Frank's case, he had missed an important period of normal socialization—the transition from adolescence to adulthood, when most people move from dependent living with parental family and school to establish their own home, find work, and become psychologically and socially independent. For thirteen years, while most of his age peers had married and either moved away or become engaged in the adult life of the community, all of Frank's basic needs had been met through institutional living. Of his return Frank said, "I suppose they tried to make me feel at home. I was very shy about meeting people. There was unemployment. My stepfather was working and I wasn't. I felt out of place. I had never realized the necessity of having a job. . . . It was a small town and I had lost the contacts with my schoolmates. I thought that people were overcurious about people they didn't recognize. I was dissatisfied and unhappy . . . there didn't seem to be any opportunity there." On another occasion Frank recalled, "Everything was all black or white there. When one goes back everyone asks 'Where have you been? What are you doing? What line are you in now?' I offer . . . the case of men who return to their native towns after ten- and twenty-year absences, and who no longer 'fit' in industrial or commercial enterprises of that district, who find their playmates and school-boy friends fled or deceased, and who sit in the local bar rooms and drink for two days without recognizing a single person whom he knew in the long ago, and recalling his former attachments and loves."

Alcoholism and Institutional Dependency

A Developing Relationship. When Frank returned to Calvinville after thirteen years of military and prison life, his personal and social inadequacies for re-establishing any satisfactory sort of relationships to his family or his community became quickly apparent. He soon departed for Boston, where he quite rapidly drifted into an alcoholic drinking pattern which served to help him live with his deep sense of personal inadequacy and to ensure his continued incapacity for anything other than a dependency pattern of existence.

It is significant that Frank's institutional dependency preceded his dependence on alcohol. Following his prison experiences, Frank set out to establish himself independently in a community, but the first job he was able to obtain was that of a live-in janitor. For several years thereafter, most of the jobs he sought and found included provisions for living-in. He frequently worked as an orderly or attendant in a hospital. He worked for a physician, living in the man's home. He worked in lumber camps. He enlisted several times in the Civilian Conservation Corps. He signed on as a railroad track laborer with companies which maintained camps to feed and house the men. He enlisted in the Maritime Service. His first serious drinking problems occurred in association with this pattern of work. In the mid-1930's when he was about thirty years of age, he began to be arrested occasionally for public intoxication or for fighting while drunk. Occasionally, too, he was injured in a drunken brawl and hospitalized. During this period, Frank's efforts to establish himself in a cheap hotel or rooming house met with repeated failure because he was totally unable to maintain sobriety under these circumstances. It was for this reason, Frank said, that he initially sought refuge in a Salvation Army Men's Work Shelter, where circumstances precluded most drinking except on weekends. By 1945, Frank's physical appearance and in some instances his reputation as a drunkard made employment increasingly difficult to obtain, and he began to depend more and more on custodial care.

Frank's letters from institutions, his self-styled "Memories from Custody," are replete with vivid descriptions of the brief periods of freedom from the walls of a jail or hospital during which he invariably sought to escape from the acute and unbearable stress of his freedom by retreating into an alcohol-induced euphoria. For example, early in 1948, when Frank had been released from the Northway Mental Hospital and had entrained for New York City, he wrote that he ". . . made a decision that it was a difficult task to begin anew at my age, with my limitations of earning power, and revolted at the forthcoming associations on what would become my social level. And so I disembarked at Riverpoint, purchased the ambrosia, that makes kings out of paupers, that dispels the fears and sorrows that infest the human soul."

Six months later, after discharge from the Wideway Hospital, Frank wrote that he had "lived the sober and frugal life" just long enough to "accumulate enough lucre to go on a bigger and more lurid binge." In September, 1948, he described the events between his discharge from Riverpoint County Jail on a Saturday noon and his rearrest on Sunday afternoon when he was "traipsing around with [his] own loneliness" until his "good intentions were becoming threadbare" and he began drinking once more. Released from Riverpoint, he found "sanctuary in Davenport" infirmary. Five months later, he wrote, "I left that station of travail . . . & purchased armloads of wine & staggered my sybaritic way to the banks of the beautiful Mercy River & camped alone on its sandy & silted banks for a week, leaving that sylvan dell only long enough to get to the liquor store & gather unto myself more armloads of that magic fluid. . . . After a week the police descended on my Eden, shrouded me in blankets & fed me warm soups & brought me back to this hard world of reality."

Beginning in 1948 and for the next sixteen years while he spent most of his life in hospitals or jails, drinking became the immediate response to life on the outside whenever he left an institution.

In 1956, he discussed an additional role of alcohol as a means of entry into custody: "Jail has become a sanctuary where the demands are few & token effort is rewarded. . . . Do you know that these places are loaded with people who have designated themselves as alcoholics, who come to jail 6 times a year, & during that time will not have consumed the equivalent of a gallon of whiskey in that year; that booze affords an alibi for being a loafer?"

For Frank, as for many homeless dependent men, alcohol was an integral part of the "revolving door" picture, both helping them to cope with life on the outside and assuring re-entry to the security of institutional living.

Total Institutional Dependency. As the years went on, it became more and more improbable that Frank could obtain even the menial types of work available to homeless men between periods of custodial living. He became more and more resigned to the inevitability of arrest, conviction, and incarceration. The table on page 349 clearly illustrates the pattern and magnitude of Frank's dependency on formal institutions—the revolving doors of hospitals and jails—as it developed over the years.

By the late 1950's Frank was referring to "60 days of assured and continued existence" in jail. He asked, "I wonder if you realize how increasingly inadequate I have become in following the mores and customs of the community? . . . It is quite certain that I shall be arrested." Describing another winter journey, he likened himself to "a mouse who gnaws a hole in the corner of a room trying to get to the other side without knowing what the hell is on the other side before he gets there." And of his arrest, "It probably occurred to the state policeman after he had made the arrest that he had done me a favor after all."

Many times it seemed as though circumstances conspired to discourage Frank from seeking work. In order to lighten their weekend staffing problems, many jails and hospitals schedule their discharges for a Friday afternoon or a Saturday morning. For the inmate or patient this means being thrown on the community at a time when opportunities for casual work are minimal and employment offices and many helping agencies are closed, thus imposing an insurmountable dilemma for a man without funds. Once in Calvinville, Frank told of being offered a job with the highway department which would require waiting a week for any pay. Since he had only two dollars and a hotel room cost three dollars, he rationalized spending his money for wine, slept in an empty house, and was back in jail the next day. On another occasion, contemplating discharge from jail, Frank sought suggestions from me regarding his next move. By this time (1962), jail had begun to lose some of its "attraction" and Frank pleaded, "Spare me that common fate of being arrested by the same policeman, facing the same judge, being remanded to the same jail." Yet life on the outside continued to be repelling: "It is a lousy life. If

LIFE-ADJUSTMENT PATTERN OF FRANK MOORE, 1945–1972

(by number of weeks per year and type of living arrangement)

Year	Prison or Jail	Hospital, Infirmary, or Rehabilitation Program	Shelter or Live-in Job	Hotel Room,* Bender, or Wandering	Sustained Residence in Rented Room	No Information
1945		1	43	8		
1946	2	12	33	5		
1947		26	9	15		
1948	10	38		2		2
1949	34	17		1		
1950	10	36	4	2*		
1951		51		1		
1952	6	1	9	9		27
1953	4	18				30
1954	16	34		2		
1955	48		1	3		
1956	33	6	2	1		10
1957	18	22	1	2*		9
1958	8	39		5		
1959	25	25		2		
1960	45		4	3*		
1961	1	42		1		8
1962	26	17		5*		4
1963	50			2*		
1964	46			6*		
1965	15				37	
1966	22				20	10
1967	4				48	
1968	1				51	
1969	20				32	
1970	16	6		1	29	
1971	4	26		4	8	10
1972†		9			29	

*Included a total of about 1 week in Calvinville in 1950, 1957, 1960, 1962; 2 weeks in 1963; and 6 weeks in 1964.
†Frank Moore died September 24.

you are on the bum, you are always at the mercy of the weather, standing half a chance of getting either frozen to death or sunstroke on a clear deserted patch of highway halfway to nowhere . . . and if you don't have any money you spend most of your time being hungry and lightheaded which means you can't even enjoy the sights and the scenery and you have always to be on the watch for policemen who will pick you up for vagrancy and play games with you at the station house if they happen to be bored." In response to a judge who asked, "What are we going to do with this derelict? He will be brought right back when his sentence is completed," Frank observed, "In view of the fact that I will be released from here without a job, without clothing, & altogether without money, I am led to question what else is expected of me."

This paradox is well illustrated in Frank's description of fellow derelicts awaiting court disposition: "The conversation runs on a consistent theme: What kind of a sentence they will get. Some wish to be released, although they would be hard put to give any reason except that they hope to crawl into a figurative cave and die a free beast. Some hope for a suspended sentence with the knowledge that they will be back in court in a short time. The most noteworthy group are those who have been jailed so often that they welcome the sanctuary that offers them a razor, a pair of socks, and a decent meal. The paradoxical part consists of the fact that they feel obliged to squawk like hell every minute in the sanctuary."

Although he often sought custody and on occasions sought the longest sentence possible, there were times when Frank also "squawked like hell" about being put in jail or retained in a jail or hospital when he wanted to get out. In 1948 he wrote, "I do not look forward with pleasure to the prospect of forever eating from battered tin cups, the constant and prolonged association with misfits, social casualties, and erratic personalities."

Yet Frank vacillated. In 1951, from Davenport, he wrote, "Come to think of it when I write to you, it usually happens that I am trying to wangle my way out of some psychotic sanctuary. Not so at the present time. Each licking is harder to take. Who knows but this may be the time that I bow gracefully to the fates." Nine months later, still from Davenport, Frank stressed that he could leave if he wanted to but was stayed by the realization that "I inevitably turn to booze sometime during the depressing struggle."

Perhaps Frank's best adjustment to life in an institution came in 1953 at Heaven Hill. There he was in a program that was designed to provide gradual and gentle rehabilitation through health care and resocialization. He wrote, "I have noticed that the men here who appear the best integrated, recognize the advantage of remaining here. . . . God grant that I have the native good sense, animal cunning, instinct of self preservation, to stay here & that thru the course of time I might rediscover beauty, intelligence & goodness and have the clear head to recognize them. . . . I am happier now than I have been for a long time." And then after Heaven Hill was closed and Frank and others turned away: "Is it inevitable that I return to periodic employment and a Baedeker tour of the country's jails?"

Quite typical of institutional dependency is a vacillation between seeking to gain and hold on to a dependency status and seeking to get out again. Frank experienced a particular dilemma because at the same time that he recognized his need for institutional living he could not become a member of the society within institutions or accept the values and norms of those whom he called the "common bums." He dreamed about a situation where he could be taken care of and work and live in relative isolation: "Is there no milieu for a person who is constitutionally, congenitally, temperamentally, etc., unsuited for this social interaction? Is there no place where a man might live and work alone to have the opportunity to collate his own experience in life, to avail himself of the legacy or history bequeathed by the men who lived before him? Hell, I desire nothing new. . . . Consider Moore's Utopia: a shack in the Adirondacks, Maine woods, in an island (geography is not important); plain subsistence, a token service where I would be custodian of a property, clearing land, improving the value of the property; a token salary (a dollar a day would suffice for clothes, tobacco, books) & the opportunity to investigate a single phase of human art & science." Significantly not mentioned by Frank was the presence or absence of alcohol.

Frank maintained a disdain both for the public who support custodial institutions and for the majority of men who inhabit them. He scoffed at the money spent on walls and guards, noting that "a chicken wire fence would be sufficient immurement. . . . Why quit and leave these places upon which we have become so dependent? . . . Are we to believe that this social parasite is possessed of such stamina, steadfastness, and singleness of purpose that he can circumvent the combined forces of society to change him? There is startling evidence that . . . these criminals, wrongdoers, and drunkards do not possess these qualities and are generally inadequate and incompetent." Frank laughed at the thought that "in many cases the drunk has the final say and that he will reject the community and accept jail as a way of life." He was skeptical over the capacities of most of these men (including himself) for rehabilitation: "I am inclined to the viewpoint that too much has already 'happened to them,'" and alluding to the Pavlov dog experiments: "It is probable that we here at Stonycreek shall continue to react in the same way to the same situations through long habit." And then he asked: "Do you believe that society will ever spend the same time, the same energy, & the same money to resocialize men, as it has toward 'desocializing' them?"

As Frank became more resigned to incarceration, he continued to resist parts of the system of institutions. His scathing attacks on the dishonesty of institutional staff were frequent, and he took pride in a rating of "no progress" in a hospital diversional therapy program, calling it "my finest hour and to my mind my most successful 'failure.'"

With aging and deteriorating health, Frank first clung more and more to custody. In 1964 he wrote of voluntarily remaining in Stonycreek for the maximum time allowed by law: "Do you know that each successive release becomes more perilous than pulling a man out of a fire or wrestling with a drowning person?"

In mid-1966, just before Frank was finally established in a rooming house for the first time by the Calvinville Welfare Department, he was writing some of his most vivid descriptions of institutional dependency: "God knows there is very little reason for tension here, no economic competition, no material want, no competition, everyone is reduced to the lowest common denominator, no good performance is expected." When he requested another maximum sentence: "I explained that there was nothing out there 'on the street' that I was greatly concerned about." Of advantages of institutional life:

> I can awake in the morning with the assurance that someone is already at work peeling potatoes & onions for my dinner, others are busy cooking my food; someone is ready to wash my dishes when I am thru eating, my bed will have been made sometime in the forenoon; in different departments men will be washing my clothes & bed linen; whenever my dusty brown locks become long the barber stands ready; the engineers department will be supplying hot water, heat, & light. The librarian stands ready to exchange books; the officers stand ready to turn the two television sets to two different stations in order that I have diverse entertainment. The toilet and shaving facilities are on the par with the Grand Central Station. . . . Getting in jail is a habit such as cocain sniffing. Behind the walls becomes a way of life, & over the course of years, one becomes inured as to rheumatism or a bald head.

Frank's resignation to institutional living illustrates what sociologist Robert K. Merton has called "retreatism."[7] Merton describes retreatism

---

7. Robert K. Merton, *Social Theory and Social Structure*, Revised Edition (New York: The Free Press of Glencoe, 1957).

as occurring in individuals who are shut off from legitimate and effective means of attaining socially acceptable goals. This results in defeatism, resignation, and escape mechanisms which lead to the desire to "escape" from societal expectations and requirements. When there is continuing failure to near goals by legitimate means and an inability to use illegitimate means because of internalized prohibitions, a conflict arises which is resolved by abandoning both the goals and the means. Merton also noted that persons characterized by retreatism experience an essential loneliness and isolation even though they may be continually relegated to environments (such as institutions) which are totally lacking in personal privacy. Frank's discussions of the advantages of institutionalization illustrate a process that sociologist Erving Goffman has called "colonization," in which inmates may build a "stable, relatively contented existence . . . out of the maximum satisfactions procurable within the institution."[8]

Neither Merton nor Goffman offers much optimism for the rehabilitation of the truly retreatist, colonized, institutionally dependent person. Yet Frank's period of greatest acceptance of and resignation to institutional living during the early 1960's just preceded a major change in his attitudes and behavior toward institutions and toward living on his own.

For the last few years of his life, although he was still economically dependent on society after years of institutional living, Frank Moore managed to establish a way of life in a community which utilized his capacities for self-care, reduced the manpower and economic burden to society, and enabled him to achieve at least a small degree of dignity and self-contentment. Frank's life experiences, while providing a devastating documentation of the destructive and oppressive aspects of institutional dependency, have provided as well a note of optimism regarding the potential which exists for breaking the vicious circle of institutional dependency, altering the course of the syndrome, and achieving a more satisfactory and less costly form of life adjustment.[9]

Despite his severely disrupted childhood, his long history of institutional dependency, and his continued problem drinking, Frank demonstrated that society can meet the dependency needs of an extremely incapaci-

8. Erving Goffman, *Asylums* (New York: Doubleday, 1961).

9. In 1969, I calculated roughly that the average per diem cost for maintaining inmates in two institutions which Frank had frequented (Westville and Stonycreek) was almost twice the per diem cost of maintaining Frank in the community. The latter per diem figure was calculated by adding to the monthly welfare payments Frank was receiving a day's salary of a social worker and dividing by thirty.

tated person without continuing to rely on expensive and ineffective jails and hospitals. By spending much of the last few years of his life in an arrangement whereby he prepared his own food, maintained his own wardrobe, set his own schedule of daily events, and even continued to find occasional oblivion through alcohol, Frank demonstrated that society could provide a more economical and humane way of caring for him, and succeeded in his own struggle to escape from institutional custody.

Alcoholism. While most theories about the causes of alcoholism assume that in most individuals there is a complex interaction of personality, sociocultural and biological factors, it is clear from our earlier discussion that undersocialization and dependency appear as the dominant factors in Frank's initial drinking and his rapid decline into alcoholism.

He was clearly ripe both psychologically and sociologically, irrespective of any possible contributing biological factors, to find in alcohol-induced intoxication a special meaning and an extra function. Like many alcoholics, Frank suffered from a deep-seated feeling of inferiority and inadequacy which can be appreciated in light of his early life experiences. He was unwanted, and he apparently sensed this at an early age. He was stigmatized and subject to ridicule from his age peers and the equally demoralizing patronizing pity of adults in the community. Although he credited his grandfather with providing care, love, and affection, he felt that his grandfather had set standards beyond his capacity of attainment and was far too insistent on his being a "winner." Frank also suffered for most of his life from diffuse anxiety, which he described as nervousness, a characteristic which apparently dominated his mother's personality as well. To people who suffer more than the normal degree of inadequacy and anxiety, alcohol can and often does have a special meaning, for it acts on the central nervous system in such a way that it depresses inhibitory factors, alleviates anxiety, and thus gives the drinker a temporary illusion of serenity and security.

It is probably significant that Frank's earliest attempts to drink whiskey were unsuccessful. He had his first drink in the Navy at age seventeen and reported that he became violently ill. Later he mentioned that drinking was almost a social compulsion but that he would get out of it if he could. In the Army, he said, "... drinking never became a habit. ... I had an occasional drink of corn whiskey, but it usually made me sick and then I wouldn't want any more for months afterwards."

But after going to Boston and obtaining a job as a live-in janitor,

Frank discovered the enticing atmosphere of a speakeasy, where he was able to drink beer. It is interesting that his initial ability to retain alcohol came with the consumption of beer, the beverage having the lowest alcohol content. After about two months, he began drinking Italian wine, still a relatively low-alcohol-content beverage. He said, "In a short period I seemed to develop a tolerance. I found I could drink a little more and a little more. This was when I really developed the drinking. I found that I could tolerate as much as some of the people who were drinking regularly. After a period of a few weeks I began to drink grain alcohol and ginger ale."

Frank's description of his anxiety the first time he found himself in trouble resulting from an injury he inflicted in a drunken fight which he did not remember is quite typical of most alcoholics' reaction to their initial experience of "blackout." But, within a few months, Frank was drinking in the morning, and he said he had realized even earlier that "the world could be a pretty dull place without something to drink."

Many forms of alcoholism develop over a period of ten or fifteen or even twenty years of exposure to large and increasing amounts of alcohol but Frank's rapid transition into a drinking pattern which had many of the common earmarks of alcoholism is not atypical of alcoholics who report an initial physical intolerance to alcohol. There are some people whose hypersensitivity to alcohol is associated with the rapid development of alcoholism if and when they ever acquire the ability to tolerate alcohol at all.

During the years between 1933 and 1948, Frank's drinking pattern was often dictated by the availability of alcohol or the period of pay from his various live-in jobs and enlistments in the CCC and Maritime Service. Frequently he left a job in order to drink or was discharged because of drinking or, on a few occasions, changed jobs in order to try to change his pattern of drinking. For example, he said that he left the Maritime Service on one occasion because he suspected that enforced periods of ten to twelve days without alcohol were causing him to go on big benders, and he reasoned that if he stayed on shore and drank steadily the effects would not be as devastating. While working in the CCC he was able to confine his heavy drinking to weekends so as not to interfere with his efficiency as a team leader. These efforts to avoid some of the worst effects of alcohol without giving it up, simply by shifting patterns of drinking, are quite common in the histories of alcoholics.

Also typical of many alcoholics, Frank initially held the fallacy that a man could get drunk and still maintain a moderate respectability. In connection with jobs in a Boston mental hospital and a V.A. hospital, he told of drinking a pint or more every day yet being able to maintain a façade of sobriety through a stiffly starched uniform and immaculate appearance.

The first serious effort to stop drinking, rather than just alter the pattern, occurred in 1938 when he was just thirty-four years old and had been drinking heavily for only five years. At that time, before the advent of Alcoholics Anonymous and community education programs on alcoholism effectively popularized some of the warning signs of alcoholism and influenced a trend toward earlier recognition of the problem, it was unusual for alcoholics to admit to themselves that they had a problem or to seek help after such a limited experience and duration of alcoholism.

Frank told of consulting a psychiatrist in Cambridge who allegedly reported that he had a bad prognosis and gave him a basis for assuming that he was "more or less psychologically predetermined to remain an alcoholic." Whatever the psychiatrist's findings may have been, Frank's reaction and interpretation typify a rationalization that many alcoholics assume in order to justify their continuing in an alcoholic pattern of drinking. A similar reaction followed his visit to a general practitioner in Calvinville who gave him a shot of vitamins. Frank rationalized: "That was the death of my hopes for treatment from a general practitioner. I didn't think I could go to a doctor to be treated for booze. I decided it was more or less impossible."

Frank's eventual shift in his later years from bender drinking to what he called "channeled drinking" was, in part, an adjustment to changes in his way of life which accompanied aging and the deteriorating of his general health and was, in part, perhaps, associated with changes in his body's ability to tolerate alcohol. In the later years of his life, he again became sick when he drank very much and he turned to using wine in preference to whiskey.

After Frank discovered that he could maintain himself in a rooming-house setting in 1965, he became highly motivated to stay out of jail and thus attempted to "channel" his drinking to twice a month, to drink in his room, and to avoid contact with former drinking companions. His perception of himself changed and in 1966 he wrote of informing a social worker, "I no longer had an alcoholic problem; I was a sick old man." But, despite his efforts to control and channel his drinking, Frank was unable to avoid drinking occasionally in inappropriate times or places, and he continued to get into trouble when intoxicated. The onset of active tuberculosis in late 1970 initiated a regression to former drinking patterns and attitudes. He sought leaves from his hospital refuges specifically in order to get drunk. For the last six months of his life, although he was living with a family who gave him loving care, alcohol use persisted and was associated with, if not a direct cause of, his final illnesses and his death.

The Meaning of Alcohol to Frank. Frank's descriptions of the meaning of alcohol to him may help us to understand how his patterns of drinking were integrally related to his personality, his social dependency, and his way of life. Many alcoholics will recognize in his fluency, expressions of their own feelings. He wrote that in 1965 he used alcohol to "escape from reality" and from "feelings of inferiority and worthlessness." His observation that "nothing ever happened to me sober and everything happened to me when drunk" had a double meaning.

> With drink, I found a deliverance: I could forget discomfort and fatigue, I could slip off the burden and see clearly again; I could be the master of my own brain, my thoughts and my will. My dead self would stir in me and I could laugh with the crowd and joke with my companions. However low, socially, I could become a man again and master of my life. For many years, I was happy only when drunk and even then I was savage that the happiness would not last. I was angry with the boss, the policeman, the preacher, or any who would wreck this happiness.
>
> It is a battle that has no end and it may be that there can be no end. At those times, when I attempted to quit temporarily, merely to walk down the street was to be put up on the rack. In every town there was surely a saloon on the corner, perhaps on all four corners; and some in the middle of the block as well; and each stretched forth a hand to me offering light, conversation, and music.
>
> If I stayed in one city long enough I found that each saloon had a personality of its own, an allurement unlike any other. At opening time and after dark, there was warmth and a glow, a friendly face, a jolly disposition.

Earlier, in 1959, he had written,

> 'The sway of alcoholism over mankind is unquestionably due to its

power to stimulate the mystical faculties of human nature, usually crushed to earth by the cold facts & dry criticism of the sober hour.' . . . Would one exchange the habitation of fields of consciousness—wide, glorious, & delightful—for a Salvation Army dormitory? Like Aladdin, who rubs the magic lamp, the alcoholic has discovered a magic genie who lifts him up to the seventh heaven, & transports him over stellar spaces . . . & who builds for him in half an hour's time, palaces of porphyry & jasper, fills his hands with gold, & breathes into his soul the sense & conviction of power. From melancholy, which must be aroused by sober reflection of a sensitive man, alcohol will lift to dazzling heights of happiness (like the magic carpet), like the magic ivory tube it will reveal all that he desires to see, & like the enchanted apple heals him of all illness.

The Later Years

Throughout the years of institutional dependency and alcoholism, there were two consistently prominent threads in Frank's life. One, a yearning to return to Calvinville, the other a continuing resentment toward his mother, which significantly influenced many of his actions and attitudes.

Return to Calvinville. In 1959 and 1960, Frank made several visits to Calvinville. Invariably, these were short; he became drunk, was arrested, and was shipped off to jail in Westville or to custody at Stony-creek.

Frank's nostalgic feelings for Calvinville had been evident from his discussions of his early childhood and from his strong identification of the community with his grandfather. Shortly after we met, he told me that he would return there if he thought he would be welcome. However, his mother's letters suggested that there would be no welcome and there were no opportunities for him in Calvinville. For many years, Frank followed his mother's admonition and stayed away. There was one visit in 1950 when he was taken in by his mother and stepfather, reclothed and fed. But their welcome vanished into despair and resentment when he stole from a crippled employer and was arrested for larceny. Following his brief visits between 1959 and 1963, all of which ended with drunkenness and arrest, he noted, "The policemen are the only ones who remember me." Yet Calvinville retained a hold on Frank, although the exact nature of this attraction seemed to puzzle him. Several times he explained his returns in deterministic terms—the swallows returning to Capistrano, the eels back to the Sargasso Sea.

As Frank grew older and less well physically, the attraction of Calvinville increased. During these years 1963 and 1964 he gravitated to Calvinville each time he was released from jail, and in 1964 his visits added up
to six weeks, made possible by the fact that he had obtained some support from the local welfare department and was living in the town's flop-
house "hotel" when he was not in jail.

Frank and His Mother. In many respects, there is great similarity between Frank's relationship with Calvinville and with his mother. There
is a yearning to belong and be loved, combined with deep hatred and a
need to hurt, punish, and seek revenge. Frank felt that the community,
like his mother, had a responsibility to care for him because it too had
contributed to his failure and had continually rejected him. Calvinville
also represented the greater society, full of injustices and inequities, permitting great crimes to go unpunished while using men like Frank as its
scapegoats. Eventually—after the death of his mother and his concerted
effort to remain free of jail and to be a permanent resident in Calvinville
—he qualified for welfare support, thus forcing the community to meet
his dependency needs. This support was also a kind of revenge on the
community, just as his earlier and consistently disastrous visits to Calvinville had been a punishment and revenge on his mother, when she was
alive.

Frank qualified his characterization of his mother by pointing out that
he had known her for only a short time and that they had never understood each other. His most scathing remarks referred to her preoccupation with security and material success. This, in Frank's view, was basic
to their misunderstanding and incompatibility. "A man can be a good
man without being a successful man. My mother believed that you've got
to have material things. She had no interest in honesty and fair play, just
in how much money you could make and what plans you had for security.
Women are twice as practical as men." This characterization of his
mother enabled Frank to rationalize some virtue in his own life's course
of materialistic failure and of causing discomfort to others, particularly
his mother. Of his mother's religious views he said: "My mother appears
to me to have been the most unorthodox of persons and yet a claimant of
all the conformist's awards. Her religious aims are toward comfort and
solace. And that is what, to my mind, religion of a decent, honorable kind
does not lead to. Great religious reformers always brought a hell of a
lot of discomfort to the social order of their time."

Despite his yearning for a mother whom he could love, Frank seemed
impelled to punish his mother and seek his revenge for her early aban-

donment and subsequent rejection of him. Although he could easily have given a false address when hospitalized or imprisoned and did so when it was to his advantage, he usually gave his mother's name and address. Thus she was plagued throughout Frank's adulthood with demands that she pay for his care and she was repeatedly embarrassed by newspaper accounts of his arrests.

It is almost impossible to review the correspondence about and between Frank and his mother without feeling great compassion for the needs each left unfilled and the disappointments each imposed on the other. The pathos increased as both became older and sicker. Mrs. Greene's letter of December 20, 1948, reviewing the main events in Frank's life, is a monument to human tragedy. Her writing expresses a combination of guilt and self-justification, frustration, anger, some compassion for Frank, and considerable pity for herself. The record is not clear as to just how many times after 1933 she and her second husband took Frank in and subjected themselves to his abuses, but it is clear that she never really escaped the shadow of his existence or the impact of his deeds.

After the episode in 1950 when Frank stole money from a cripple to go on a bender, Mrs. Greene launched an unsuccessful effort to have him permanently committed to a state hospital. Her compassion for Frank is clear: "Frank is sane enough to suffer" from forced association with "murderers and everything else" in prisons, but she feared that he might in the future commit a serious violent act while under the influence of alcohol or while seeking funds to obtain alcohol. Although these expressed concerns were for Frank himself and for others he might harm, it is evident that her motives were also based on the community sanctions she had long felt. She wrote to me, "I am not the only person with a son like this but would you believe it some of these *fools* in this city won't speak to me since it happened and the irony of it is that they have short memories of themselves and their sons."

By 1953, with the impact of the larceny episode somewhat dulled by time and with her own health deteriorating, Mrs. Greene expressed much more compassion for Frank: "I suppose he would be most unhappy in a hospital, but when I think of him night and morning, cold or wet, maybe hungry, it is heartbreaking. . . . Tell him I *do* love him and wish I could help him and that every night I pray for God to help him." And to Frank she wrote: "There is so much that was not right on both sides and as I near my end I see it very plainly. I failed you and you me. Forgive me." Two years later, when she had the impression that he was safely in residence at Heaven Hill, a warm correspondence began, and even after Frank was again back in jail, she wrote compassionately: "I love you dearly. You have made a misstep after doing so well. No one is perfect. . . . I shall continue to pray for your enlightenment, stability, and for the help you need so much. . . . Do not give up now. When you come out try again. . . . *Try,* dear son, *try.*"

But this feeling exploded in 1955 after a report of Frank's arrest for larceny appeared in the Calvinville newspaper giving Mrs. Greene's address as Frank's home. She wrote, "He is going from bad to worse and to my mind a menace and not responsible." At this point, as previously, Mrs. Greene tried to comfort herself by rationalizing that Frank's major problem stemmed from his experience in Alcatraz, where it was her impression that "he was not even allowed to speak." (Since Frank was released for "good behavior" after serving only five years of a seven-year sentence, it seems unlikely that he spent a great deal of time in solitary confinement.) Mrs. Greene totally rejected a reconciliatory letter from Frank and wrote to me: "I can only say that he has brought me grief for thirty years and he will continue to do so. . . . He will as all others like him go on (as he wishes to) taking advantage and doing as he pleases with no moral responsibility even tho he knows he will be arrested. . . . I pray for him but it will do no good unless *he* cooperates." After Frank was hospitalized in Staunton in 1956, he reported that his mother was "chagrined, incensed, embarrassed, etc., and I received a most condemning letter." When he visited Calvinville in 1958, he reported finding his mother "very happy, & much concerned that I ruin the tranquility of her life."

Frank's final epitaph for his mother was written in 1964, shortly before her death:

Truly, never the twain shall meet. I have not seen her for a number of years. About two years ago, I called the nursing home by phone & she seemed rather excited & informed me that she couldn't see any visitors. Perhaps she was worried about my temperate state or the condition of my wardrobe. The Lord only knows what sort of an illusory background she has built up for herself & me in her new milieu. I am sure all the other old ladies feel sorry for her, & of course, that is what she wants. My own attitude? Well, I am still the kid in short pants who is pointed out as the boy whose father committed suicide & whose

mother had run off and left him as a baby. At least the Communists
& Catholics agree on one thing. They say, 'Give me the person's mind
for the first ten years of their life & we will not have to worry about
other influences.' I absolutely cringe to think of some of the procedures
she adopted in later life to drive me to be a success (whatever that is)!
Shakespeare must surely have known some such lady when he portrayed
Lady Macbeth.

And then in reporting on her death, he added:

Methinks I should caption this letter "The Passing of Lady Mac-
Beth," but I would fall far short of the grandiloquent title when portraying the sordidness & grandeur of her demise.

It is interesting to speculate how much the death of Frank's mother contributed to his rehabilitation. With her gone he could no longer play the
role of the little boy protesting her failure as a mother. He could no
longer punish her effectively by playing on her guilt for the pitiful help
she could give him or by embarrassing her with his legal and moral transgressions. It is significant that the timing of Frank's mother's death coincided with his campaign to be cared for by the community of Calvinville.

Sexual Scars. Frank's relationship with his mother and his maternal
grandmother (who tried to prevent his birth and whom he rarely mentioned) may have contributed to what seemed a permanent scar on
Frank's sexuality and to his disdain and mistrust of women in general.

From Frank's mother's letters it is clear that he grew up in a household
in which human sexuality was considered bestial. He traces his sexual
education to the "smutty talk" of older boys at school which he began to
listen to at about the seventh grade. He speaks of gradually coming to
realize that boys were different from girls and of noticing girls developing breasts and thinking that this was "immodest and too early." Obviously, Frank's sex education was incomplete when he joined the Navy.
He told of not knowing what "the clap" was and of not knowing what
was expected and being unable to perform on his first visit to a prostitute. He described his naïveté and revulsion when first propositioned by
a homosexual. Later, it took Frank a month to get up his courage to have
his first sexual relations with a waitress. He said he found "you just can't
accept and have relations with any woman without affection. In later life,
for a woman to attract me sexually, I'd have to be in proximity to her

for a length of time and know her, like her, and all that." These conditions were, of course, precluded by Frank's way of life.

Frank described a nonsexual relationship with a "good" girl in Boston, ". . . the first decent girl I'd ever come into contact with," and said that when he realized she was serious he left town. It is perhaps significant that he reported never having visited a house of prostitution in New England. Other reflections of Frank's strong sexual inhibitions are found in his reference to a Freudian interpretation as "disgusting and ridiculous," his terming sex as "100 per cent biological," his noting that "women were always more or less setting a trap with their physical voluptuousness," and his comment in 1945: "You'd never marry either if you knew what I do about women." On several occasions, Frank mentioned avoiding or rejecting female ministrations when he was in a hospital: "There seems to be some connection between my being in bed and a woman wanting to boss me around." He expressed disdain for female employees of institutions, particularly stout ones: "At one time, I viewed a fat woman as gross or unesthetic, & now I am getting so I frankly hate their fat guts." Even Frank's brief marriage appears to have been an act of aggression toward a mother figure. His wife was twenty years his senior and he deserted her after only a few months.

As he grew older, Frank made numerous references to his loss of sexual prowess, and on one occasion stoutly denied the credibility of a newspaper report that sexual transgressions are rampant in jails and prisons because, in his opinion, a large segment of prisoners are neither interested nor capable.

References to sexual perversion were also fairly frequent in Frank's letters, yet they reflect a sort of detachment which characterizes his discussion of his own sexual experiences.

Some Personality Traits and Philosophical Views

Frank's identification with his grandfather seems to have influenced both his personality and his philosophy. It is difficult to determine to what extent Frank modeled himself after his grandfather or to what extent he tended to describe his grandfather in his (Frank's) own image. One of the strongest traits shared with his grandfather and noted earlier was that of being a loner, a trait he shared with most other homeless men as well. Rarely was Frank able to develop really close interpersonal relationships with anyone, male or female.

Frank made a virtue of being a loner and a nonjoiner. For years, he resisted Alcoholics Anonymous, in part because of its fellowship features. Speaking of A.A., he wrote,

Did it ever occur to you that there are such people who are congenital or conditioned "nonjoiners"? The ranks of the alcoholics are divided into three parts . . . and the best of the breed are the libertarians. I use the term to designate he who is not straightjacketed by a profession, politics, or religion. He lacks the sodality of party, sect, or organization, since there never can be organized libertarians, but he is never to be found in the ranks of the Black Shirts, lynch mobs, and other "group activities" . . . I forgot to tell you of another attribute of the libertarian; he is often in jail.

Frank revealingly wrote of once walking alone in a lightning storm: "What an absolute comfort to me to know . . . that a man, by himself, has nothing to fear! Only in contact with other men has he anything to fear!"

Frequently Frank referred to the repressive aspects of dormitory living: "Anybody who has been compelled to live for a long time under a gang system . . . or slept for a long time in a dormitory listening to forty-odd snorings, sighings, moanings, and whimperings . . . through the long still watches is fitted only to be a lighthouse keeper on a rock shoal, twenty miles offshore, or the quietude of a monastic cell in a county jail where men are locked up twenty-two hours a day without the opportunity to obtrude upon each other. Like Garbo, I wish to be alone." Only when drinking did Frank seek companions and even then his tendency to belligerence or violence made others avoid him.

But, even in the community, he was still a recluse. After settling down in Calvinville he noted the effect of the years: "I have been so penned up, immured, imprisoned . . . that I have lost touch with the man of the street." He began to refer to himself proudly as the "Hermit of Shark-Tooth Shoals" but added quite ironically that "it sure does beat hell how much a person may be isolated and a recluse in the center of a city of sixteen thousand."

Frank was an almost compulsive worker, and, significantly, he remembered his grandfather as being conscientious and industrious with a strong belief in the work ethic. When I first knew him in 1945 and 1946 at the Salvation Army Center, he rarely allowed an idle moment to pass without at least having a broom in his hand. Many of the letters we have about Frank from people who knew him in various rehabilitation programs or state hospitals refer to his contributions of hard work. When he became established in private rooming houses he took on floor-scrubbing responsibilities and other tasks related to house cleaning. Even during the last six months of his life, despite severely deteriorating health, he was described as helping with the housekeeping whenever he was not incapacitated by alcohol or illness. Except when he was drinking, Frank was equally compulsive about the cleanliness of his clothing and person.

In part, at least, Frank used work, neatness, and cleanliness as symbols of values which helped him to maintain an identity apart from his fellow man and to keep himself on a pinnacle from which he could isolate himself and look down on the "bums" around him. As Frank indicated when discussing his military life, a similar motivation was associated with his intensive reading. Later, when in prison, he relied on his study of mathematics, and finally he sought his identity through his great effort to turn his life around and become a respectable resident of Calvinville.

In the course of criticizing his mother for her materialism, Frank summarized his own ethical views (and probably those of his grandfather) nicely: "When a man seeks happiness he doesn't need money, property, social standing, leadership in public affairs. He can find it through work, fair labor for pay, honesty, assuming one's obligations, not tying oneself to any particular group or ideas of a particular group, self-sufficiency in an economic sense, congenial occupation, good health. A man can be a good man without being a successful man."

The elements of his philosophy which contradicted traits he attributed to his grandfather often were rationalizations of the debts he felt others owed him. His treatment of his mother—stealing her rings, abusing her hospitality, giving her name, knowing bills would be sent and embarrassment caused—was rationalized in terms of her debt to him. He often justified institutionally dependent life as retribution to the society which he held responsible for his personal failure, and for what he considered exploitation of many institutionalized groups, particularly alcoholics ("the most exploited, mulcted, and cheated persons on the face of the earth"). He could not take this society too seriously: "Any damn fool knows rules and regulations are not to be followed literally." When given three days in the brig in the Navy, he thought "the whole thing was a big joke." Of his gambling activities in the Army he wrote: "The whole code was not what you do but what you can get away with."

Throughout much of his life, Frank was in conflict regarding his grand-father's stress on self-determinism and individual responsibility for one's actions and his own deep-seated dependency. Frank rationalized his fail-ure to fulfill his responsibilities by projecting blame onto others—his mother, the people of Calvinville, the welfare system, the judicial system, his drinking buddies, institutional employees and administrators, and society-at-large. Frank's proclivity for projection helped him maintain some self-esteem in the face of a morass of institutional living, alcoholism, dependency, stigma, and the revolving door of failure. It also sustained a pattern of behavior that permitted many members of society to justify for themselves their rejection of Frank.

Throughout Frank's letters there is a pervasive cynicism and a pro-found sense of the ironic which is balanced by a delightful sense of humor. More often than not, Frank used his good humor and cynicism ef-fectively in both his observations on social settings and issues and in pro-viding some perspective on his own life's story. Thus there was always a point to his relating stories about the wives of physicians who had been caught shoplifting, of the police officers who took bribes, of the jailers who falsified expense accounts, and the institutional employees who be-came fat at the expense of the inmates. He not only enjoyed but purpose-fully recounted the moral transgressions, real or imaginary, of the more respectable members of his family. He also reveled in assuming that most respectable people conceal sinister motives and immoral acts behind a "phoney morality." Referring both to his financially and socially success-ful cousin who snubbed him and to the pious postmaster who befriended him, Frank said: "I am amused when I discover their defects and vices." He then wished that he had collected "an anthology of ministers who have seduced their choir singers." Frank used his tales of the mundane-ness, weakness, and vulnerability of others to put himself in a positive perspective, for out of these musings he was usually able to emerge with a favorable self-image.

Views of Death. It seems probable that Frank's capacity to rationalize his failures helped him maintain not only his self-esteem but life itself. He contemplated suicide at times but never actually brought himself to it. When we first met in 1945, in the context of relating his father's suicide Frank indicated that he had given some thought to taking his own life. The subject came up again in 1946 after a series of binges. Frank said his case was hopeless and spoke of suicide: "When I think about it I won-der if I've got the nerve. I don't own a gun. I don't think I could get one.

A knife is pretty messy because I'd be all over blood. There's a bridge down here in New Haven about thirty-five feet high, but I suppose if I jump off that I'd only break my leg. It all looks hopeless to me." On one occasion during this period, Frank did fall, jump, or get thrown off a bridge while drunk and recovered consciousness in the river.

With advancing age, Frank showed an increasing interest in preparing for his death. In 1954, Frank proposed that he carry my name and address on his person as someone to be informed of his death. He wrote: "So many people that I have known shuffled off this mortal coil in some back alley with an empty wine bottle in their pocket, it will inevitably happen to me." A few months later he described the suicide of a drunkard in his jail cell and noted: "I am quite sure that any man could effect his own demise with slight resourcefulness in spite of strictest precautions. Neck-stretching and tongue-protruding cyanosis seem quite unesthetic." More newspaper clippings reporting jail suicides followed from time to time.

In 1958, Frank told of earlier visits to Potter's Field at Heaven Hill and the cemetery at Davenport and mentioned that it was "sobering to walk in the paupers' graveyard and to identify yourself with them." A few years later Frank was actively planning to escape the fate of a pauper's funeral. Noting that he had "oft considered the probability that I shall die in one of these laughing academies or some second-rate county jail," he discussed his hope to bequeath his body to some medical school. He wanted to prevent anyone from profiting from his death or the possibility that the skin off his back "might end up as a lampshade in some lady's boudoir."

By 1964, Frank was so disabled with asthma that he predicted his own demise from an asthmatic attack with morbid detail: "If a man is not sober enough to wake up during asthma, he dies painlessly from what is generally considered agony." Soon he had made legal arrangements for his body to be delivered to the Harvard Medical School and his eyes to an eye bank.

Consistent with the isolation from society which had characterized his life, Frank expressed repeatedly the hope that he could die by himself: "For the love of God or whatever powers that be, let me die privately in peace, drunk or sober, and let me not be a stooge selling propaganda, faith, and ignorance." And later, "Remember the gunslinger of the old West who wanted to die with his boots on? Well, I want to die privately." At one time, Frank told me that I should derive some satisfaction from the knowledge that some day I would be mourned but, he added, "When I cross the River Styx I expect to bum a cigarette from Charon and do my own rowing."

In 1965, he wrote, "The end of life tends to become a matter of a slow leak rather than an explosion." His health was growing worse. His relatives had all died, leaving him the last of his line. In 1969, Frank wrote, "There is not much more for me to write to you," and in several of his letters during the last years of his life he indicated that the life record was closed and he was ready to die.

The Life Record: Its Value to Frank

In closing this interpretation of the life record of Frank Moore, it is logical to ask what role it played in Frank's life. What motivated him to provide his personal history in the first place and to maintain for so many years a faithful correspondence documenting what was for so long a continuing record of his failure?

In explaining the original life history, Frank wrote to me that I so "insinuated" myself into his "affection" that he "confided a personal history which would not be told to a close friend." My own interpretation is simply that I provided something which the average man in Frank's way of life rarely or never found: I listened to him, placed a value on what he said, and offered him respect rather than moral condemnation.

During the period immediately following our life-history recording sessions in 1945, and continuing through 1947, I saw Frank only irregularly, and our contacts were largely focused around my efforts to help him find some sources of help with his living and drinking problems. Several times I provided food, clothing, shelter, or transportation. It was clear that I had become the person to whom to turn when he "hit the bottom." It was not until early 1948, when the original life history was being prepared for publication, that we discussed specifically the idea of maintaining a continuing record. At that time Frank reasoned, "One must confide in somebody of course and I suppose that is reason enough for writing. You are my metaphorical Wailing Wall and Confessional." Through the ensuing years, Frank occasionally made further reference to his motivation for continuing the correspondence: "It would be of benefit to hear from you and to feel that someone, somewhere is concerned about me." "It is altogether probable that I derive as much benefit through writing these letters as a Romanist through the confessional or a neurasthenic woman through the highest paid psychoanalyst. Pent-up resentments are released and the patient recovers from self-induced toxemia"; ". . . nothing to read, nothing to do, unlimited time to recapitulate my past transgressions and resurrect my ancient grudges, afford the excuse of writing this letter"; ". . . my letters to you from various jails are a reflection of my own nature and the reaction of a drunkard to the measures that are employed toward his cure, his punishment. If it can be proved that my reactions are not unique, and that thousands of people feel the same damn way as I do, then surely here is a contribution to the understanding of alcoholism." "I am . . . a person who wishes to rid himself of his own thoughts by writing them down, which is to say 'to disembarrass myself.' . . . If never a word saw print or type, I have had my 'reward' . . . and best of all had the ear of someone who would listen to me."

As the years went by, it is clear that I became a status symbol for Frank. He mentioned that frequently people asked him why a "professor" or someone connected with the "vice-president's office" (my mailing address during the years of planning the University of Kentucky Medical Center) had any interest in him. He also took pleasure in the idea that he was contributing to science. In a note to the Calvinville Director of Welfare, Frank wrote, "Dr. Straus has been my confidant and amanuensis for over twenty years and, when I have shuffled off this crapulous existence, will publish a memorial designed to benefit those of my kind."

At some point, too, I believe I came to represent to Frank the man he might have been. He made numerous references to watching my career develop, predicting my success, and identifying with my "respectability." Despite the disparity in our ages, I also became something of a father figure, and he frequently alluded to my family life or identified with one of my sons. On several occasions Frank referred wistfully to my "normal family life" in a way which accentuated his own sense of deprivation: "Secretly, I have wondered about your children and wife. . . . I could not help but wonder what a different sort of life I might have lived." And later,

> In your own case your son will be a continuum of yourself, an image to cleave to your altruism. . . . What combination of circumstances shall decide his whole life? Surely he has what has been referred to as the good heritage. He need never be influenced by the smug busybodies who always speak of self-slaughter as if it were ipso facto a

shameful thing and . . . in recalling his father it need not present the implication of looking in Bluebeard's closet. If a boy begins feeling sorry for himself at the age of ten, he might never "get over it."

A marked change in the correspondence and in its meaning to Frank became obvious following our visit in the fall of 1966. At that time he was living "on his own" in a rooming house in Calvinville. While his basic needs were still being provided for by society through welfare benefits and his life continued to follow a fairly set routine, there was an immense contrast between his earlier institutionalized life and his living arrangements in the rooming house, with its freedom of movement and the demands placed on his initiative.

As Frank's community existence in Calvinville became more stable, his correspondence became less frequent. I asked him about this, and he said simply that there was not much more for him to write to me. He tried to explain that in the past when he had written I had always sent him one or two dollars and this "seemed as obvious as horse drippings in a garage." After our visit in the fall of 1968, he wrote reviewing some of the highlights of our relationship over the years and rationalized that because he had always let me down he had no further claim on my kindness.

Perhaps a more satisfactory explanation may lie in the fact that as Frank at last found a home in Calvinville he no longer had the need which our correspondence had helped him to fulfill. As he wrote on his 1968 Christmas card: "I never had it so good." It was not just that Frank no longer needed the material help of cash, clothing, and books, but he no longer needed to sound off about the injustices of the social system which he could not solve or his rejection by a family, all of whose members had predeceased him. Finally, although his various illnesses were under control in 1968, there was no doubt that Frank's urge to live was running down. He had arranged for his death by bequeathing his body to the Harvard Medical School, and he had filed his own obituary with the local newspaper. He had been carefully conserving the energy required for simply staying alive.

Significantly, in a 1968 reference to our correspondence, Frank spoke of it in the past tense: "I treasure your statement that I have contributed valuable insights to the study of alcohol pathology, but methinks I have received far more than I have contributed. My own evaluation of this correspondence is that it has been to me what the confessional box is to the Catholic, what the Wailing Wall is to the Hebrew, what the psychiatric couch is to the woman in menopause . . . with the added advantage . . . you answer every time. . . . Whatever this correspondence might have meant to you, it prevented me from laughing myself to death or murder. The correspondence was like the touchstone of alcohol to a man who had reached his particular peak of mental pain. . . . Another thing about this correspondence is that it has taught me to talk. Books only taught me to think."

Toward the end of 1970, when a series of mishaps, culminating with the diagnosis of tuberculosis and angina, forced Frank again back into institutional living, his correspondence resumed its former frequency and depth. This continued into early 1972, when he found a home in Harrison. Again, his life was in order and his motivation for writing diminished, while his health deteriorated.

Obviously, Frank's motivations for sharing his life record were as complex as his personality and his life itself. Through his letters, he could exhibit some of the content and product of his unusually intelligent mind. He could escape from the isolation which surrounded him in the society of the institutions as well as the society of the community. He could sound off. He could confess. He could protest. He could even obtain some of the meager material "rewards" I provided over the years, although in retrospect these were far less significant than my listening ear and my efforts to treat him as an intellectual peer. Basic to all these motives, however, was Frank's conviction that by contributing his life record (and his body) to science he had found a way of turning his life's failure into something that would be valued.

MAJOR EVENTS IN THE LIFE OF FRANK MOORE
1904–44

(Retrospective Record)

1904	Born May 9, father committed suicide May 24.
1905	Mother left town, grandmother obtained divorce and moved away.
1905–16	Lived in grandfather's home, attended primary and grammar schools.
1916	Mother returned to Calvinville with stepfather.
1917	Unhappy at home, spent free time at YMCA.
1918	Had influenza, began to stammer in school, failed three courses in 9th grade.
1919	Repeated 9th grade, lost interest in school, took job in neighboring town; continuing turmoil at home.
1920–24	Navy years: enlisted underage, trained as medical corpsman, reenlisted after two years, requested overseas assignment.
1924–28	Army years: trained as a gun mechanic in Coast Artillery, reenlisted after three years, committed serious offense and sentenced to seven years in federal penitentiary.
1928–33	Prisoner at Alcatraz. Grandfather died in 1932.
1933	Discharged from prison, returned to Calvinville, migrated to Boston, took job as a caretaker.
1934	Onset of alcoholic drinking pattern, high mobility, arrests, and hospitalization.
1934–39	Drank and wandered, relied on live-in jobs, recognized and sought treatment for alcoholism in 1938.
1940–43	Maritime Service on the Great Lakes, hospitalized for alcoholism in a mental institution.
1943	Returned to Calvinville, married a sixty-year-old widow, deserted her, signed on again with Merchant Marine.
1944	Hospitalized for "gastroenteritis," worked on labor gangs, continued heavy drinking.

MAJOR EVENTS IN THE LIFE OF FRANK MOORE
1945–72

(Prospective Record)

1945

January	Working as a freight handler in Fieldcrest and living in cheap hotel, drinking daily.
February–June	Salvation Army Men's Social Service Center in Fieldcrest.
July	Working as a freight handler in Fieldcrest, living at Salvation Army.
July–October	Salvation Army in New Haven.
October	Eight days hospitalization in New Haven.
October–December	Salvation Army in New Haven.

1946

January	Salvation Army in New Haven, working as laborer, bender, Yale Plan Clinic, Hope Hollow (A.A. rest farm.)
February–April	Yale Plan Clinic, working as laborer in New Haven, drinking, Fieldcrest County Jail for 5 days, Seamen's Church Institute and A.A. Club in New York City, live-in job on railroad labor gang, Fieldcrest County Jail for 10 days.
May–June	Salvation Army in New Haven.
July–October	Live-in job on railroad labor gang.
November–December	Davenport State Infirmary, first as a patient then as a live-in employee.

1947

January	Davenport State Infirmary.
January–March	Visit to New Haven, Seamen's Church Institute in New York City, working on railroad labor gang, bender, Bellevue Hospital, Yale Plan Clinic, bender.
April	Working in Fieldcrest, bender.
May–July	Rest home for alcoholics in Indigo.
August–September	Working as laborer.
October–December	Northway State Hospital.
December	Drinking and wandering, Bellevue Hospital, Wideway State Hospital.

1948

January–July	Wideway State Hospital.
September–October	Riverpoint County Jail, release and rearrest, resentenced.

| November | Riverpoint County Jail, cross-country trek. |
| November–December | Davenport State Infirmary. |

1949

January–April	Davenport State Infirmary.
May	Bender on the banks of the Mercy River.
May–December	Stonycreek Prison Farm.

1950

January	Released from Stonycreek to live-in job.
February	Hillhouse State Hospital.
March	Visit at mother's home in Calvinville, working as caretaker, bender.
April–May	Franklyn Jail, 60-day sentence for larceny.
May–December	Self-commitment to Liberty State Hospital.
December	Davenport State Infirmary.

1951

| January–November | Davenport State Infirmary. |
| December | Liberty State Hospital. |

1952

January–March	Liberty State Hospital as patient.
March–April	Liberty State Hospital, live-in employee, bender, Riverpoint Jail.
May–June	Hospitalized in New Jersey, New Jersey jail.
July	Visit to New Haven, live-in job in resort area.
Mid-August	Easton Heights Men's Center.
November	Indigo County Jail.

1953

January–June	Unaccounted for.
July	Chesterfield County Penitentiary.
September–December	Heaven Hill Rehabilitation Program.

1954

January–July	Heaven Hill Rehabilitation Program.
August–September	Riverpoint County Jail.
September–October	Oldtown County Jail.
October	Silver Hill Shelter (2 weeks).
October–December	Riverpoint County Jail (10 weeks).

1955

January	Riverpoint County Jail.
January–February	Sageville County Jail, wandering southeast 180 miles.
February–March	Anchorport County Jail, wandering northwest 150 miles.

March–May	Amsterdam County Jail.
May–mid-September	Riverpoint County Jail.
Mid-September–mid-October	Chippewa County Jail.
Mid-October	Westtown's Men's Service Center (1 week).
Mid-October–December	Sageville County Jail.

1956

January–August	Sageville County Jail.
August	Central City Men's Shelter.
September–October	Sacred Heights Home, Staunton.
October–December	Unaccounted for.

1957

January–March	Riverpoint County Jail.
April	Amsterdam County Jail.
May–August	Roger's Retreat, religious rehabilitation center.
October	Brief visit to Calvinville.
October–November	Central City County Jail.
Early December	Easton Heights Men's Center.
December	Amsterdam County Jail.

1958

January	Amsterdam County Jail, Broadmeadow County Jail.
February	Elmtown County Jail.
March	Wardhill State Hospital.
April	City Infirmary, Anchorport; Anchorport County Jail; brief visit to Calvinville.
May–December	Davenport State Infirmary.

1959

January–July	Davenport State Infirmary, brief visit to Calvinville.
July–August	Westville County Jail and House of Correction.
August–October	Stonycreek Correctional Institution.
November–December	Westville County Jail.

1960

January	Westville County Jail.
February–mid-May	Westville County Jail (rearrest and resentence).
Mid-May	Visit to Alcoholic Clinic in Franklyn, wandering 150 miles westward.
Mid-May–July	Riverpoint County Jail.
July–August	Job as live-in kitchen helper in resort hotel, bender in Riverpoint, brief visit to Calvinville.
August–September	Westville County Jail.
September–December	Stonycreek Correctional Institution.
December	Westville County Jail.

1961
January   Westville County Jail.
January–May   Liberty State Hospital.
June–July   Bender.
August   Liberty State Hospital.
September–December   Wardhill State Hospital.

1962
January–February   Wardhill State Hospital.
March–May   Liberty State Hospital.
May   Wandering, visit to Calvinville.
May–August   Stonycreek Correctional Institution.
August–September   Anchorport City Jail (2 weeks), wandering, job as furniture mover, wandering Boston to Riverpoint.
October–December   Stonycreek Correctional Institution.

1963
January–March   Stonycreek Correctional Institution.
Mid-March   Brief visit to Calvinville.
March–April   Westville County Jail.
April–July   Stonycreek Correctional Institution.
Mid-July   Brief visit to Calvinville.
July–September   Westville County Jail.
Mid-September   Brief visit to Calvinville.
September–December   Stonycreek Correctional Institution.

1964
January–February   Stonycreek Correctional Institution.
February   Brief visit to Calvinville.
March   Westville County Jail.
April   Brief visit to Calvinville.
April–July   Stonycreek Correctional Institution; Frank's mother died on July 24.
August   Brief visit to Calvinville, Westville County Jail.
September   Calvinville; Frank learned of his mother's death.
October–December   Westville County Jail.

1965
January   Westville County Jail (1 week).
January–mid-April   Congress Hotel, Calvinville.
Mid-April–May   Westville County Jail.
June   Congress Hotel, Calvinville.
July–August   Stonycreek Correctional Institution.
September–December   Congress Hotel, Calvinville.

1966
January   Congress Hotel, Calvinville.
February   Probably in jail.

March	Congress Hotel, Calvinville.
April	Unaccounted for.
May–September	Stonycreek Correctional Institution.
October–December	Rooming house in Calvinville.

1967

January–August	Church St. rooming house, Calvinville.
September	Jail, 30 days.
October–December	Congress Hotel, Calvinville.

1968

January–February	Congress Hotel, Calvinville.
March–October	King St. rooming house, Calvinville.
November	Arrest, Calvinville Jail, 10 days.
November–December	King St. rooming house, Calvinville.

1969

January–Summer	King St. rooming house, Calvinville.
Summer–December	Westville County Jail.

1970

January–March	Westville County Jail.
April	Diddle State Hospital, 10 days.
April–September	Grant St. rooming house, Westville.
October–November	Eviction, roaming, hospitalization, Westville County Jail.
December	Davenport State Hospital.

1971

January	Westville Hospital.
February–March	Middleway State Hospital.
April	Westridge Sanitarium.
May–June	New Salem House (rooming house), Westville.
July–August	Westridge Sanitarium.
September–mid-October	Brief visits to Calvinville and Westville, roaming, Adams Hotel, Westville (1 week), roaming, hospitalization (5 days); Benton County Jail.
Mid-October–December	Benton County Jail.

1972

January–February	Hospital Annex, Stonycreek Correctional Institution.
March–mid-September	Benjamin St. rooming house, Harrison.
Mid-September	Hospital (1 week), death September 24, Harrison.

LETTERS

A. Letters from Frank Moore to Robert Straus

	DATE	PLACE
1.	1946 January 31	Hope Hollow (rest farm for alcoholics)
2.	1946 April 18	Fieldcrest County Jail
3.	1947 December 3	Northway State Hospital
4.	1948 January 24	Wideway State Hospital
5.	1948 March 15	Wideway State Hospital
6.	1948 April 20	Wideway State Hospital
7.	1948 May 1	Wideway State Hospital
8.	1948 May 22	Wideway State Hospital
9.	1948 June 7	Wideway State Hospital
10.	1948 June 13	Wideway State Hospital
11.	1948 June 22	Wideway State Hospital
12.	1948 September 8	Riverpoint County Jail
13.	1948 November 2	Riverpoint County Jail
14.	1948 December 28	Davenport State Infirmary
15.	1949 May 19	Stonycreek State Farm
16.	1949 June 17	Stonycreek State Farm
17.	1949 August 24	Stonycreek State Farm
18.	1949 September 16	Stonycreek State Farm
19.	1949 October 11	Stonycreek State Farm
20.	1950 January 11	Oceanside (live-in job)
21.	1950 February 28	Calvinville (mother's home)
22.	1950 June 17	Liberty State Hospital
23.	1950 July 9	Liberty State Hospital
24.	1950 August 27	Liberty State Hospital
25.	1951 March 18	Davenport State Infirmary
26.	1951 December 8	Liberty State Hospital
27.	°1952 August	Easton Heights Men's Center
28.	1952 November 23	Indigo County Jail
29.	°1953 July	Chesterfield County Penitentiary
30.	1953 October 26	Heaven Hill (alcoholic rehabilitation center)
31.	°1953 December	Heaven Hill
32.	1954 September 1	Riverpoint County Jail
33.	1954 September 26	Oldtown County Jail
34.	1954 October 7	Silver Hill (domiciliary care center)
35.	1954 October 24	Riverpoint County Jail
36.	1954 November 5	Riverpoint County Jail
37.	1954 December 7	Riverpoint County Jail
38.	1955 January 25	Sageville County Jail

°Undated letters.

39.	1955 February 1	Sageville County Jail
40.	1955 February 6	Sageville County Jail
41.	1955 February 9	Sageville County Jail
42.	1955 February 20	Anchorport County Jail
43.	1955 March 6	Anchorport County Jail
44.	1955 March 13	Anchorport County Jail
45.	1955 March 27	Amsterdam County Jail
46.	1955 April 3	Amsterdam County Jail
47.	1955 April 10	Amsterdam County Jail
48.	1955 April 17	Amsterdam County Jail
49.	1955 April 24	Amsterdam County Jail
50.	1955 May 1	Amsterdam County Jail
51.	1955 May 8	Amsterdam County Jail
52.	1955 May 15	Riverpoint County Jail
53.	1955 May 23	Riverpoint County Jail
54.	1955 June 14	Riverpoint County Jail
55.	1955 July 3	Riverpoint County Jail
56.	1955 July 11	Riverpoint County Jail
57.	1955 July 25	Riverpoint County Jail
58.	1955 August 15	Riverpoint County Jail
59.	1955 September 16	Chippewa County Jail
60.	1955 September 21	Chippewa County Jail
61.	1955 October 24	Sageville County Jail
62.	1955 November 4	Sageville County Jail
63.	1955 November 14	Sageville County Jail
64.	1955 November 15	Sageville County Jail
65.	1955 November 23	Sageville County Jail
66.	1955 November 28	Sageville County Jail
67.	1955 December 11	Sageville County Jail
68.	1956 January 10	Sageville County Jail
69.	1956 January 27	Sageville County Jail
70.	1956 February 10	Sageville County Jail
71.	1956 February 11	Sageville County Jail
72.	1956 February 16	Sageville County Jail
73.	1956 February 29	Sageville County Jail
74.	1956 March 5	Sageville County Jail
75.	1956 March 21	Sageville County Jail
76.	1956 March 31	Sageville County Jail
77.	1956 April 7	Sageville County Jail
78.	1956 April 13	Sageville County Jail
79.	1956 April 21	Sageville County Jail
80.	1956 April 29	Sageville County Jail
81.	1956 May 10	Sageville County Jail
82.	1956 May 17	Sageville County Jail
83.	1956 May 18	Sageville County Jail
84.	1956 May 23	Sageville County Jail
85.	1956 May 29	Sageville County Jail

86.	1956 May 31	Sageville County Jail
87.	1956 June 9	Sageville County Jail
88.	1956 June 19	Sageville County Jail
89.	1956 June 23	Sageville County Jail
90.	1956 June 29	Sageville County Jail
91.	1956 July 14	Sageville County Jail
92.	1956 July 21	Sageville County Jail
93.	1956 August 1	Sageville County Jail
94.	1956 August 26	Central City Men's Shelter
95.	1956 September 9	Staunton (church-sponsored men's shelter)
96.	1956 September 25	Sacred Heights Home, Staunton
97.	1957 January 9	Riverpoint County Jail
98.	1957 February 21	Riverpoint County Jail
99.	1957 April 14	Amsterdam County Jail
100.	1957 May 1	Roger's Retreat, Blue Mountain
101.	1957 May 5	Roger's Retreat
102.	1957 May 14	Roger's Retreat
103.	1957 May 26	Roger's Retreat
104.	1957 July 1	Roger's Retreat
105.	1957 August 25	Roger's Retreat
106.	1957 October 30	Central City County Jail
107.	1957 December 8	Easton Heights Men's Center
108.	1957 December 29	Amsterdam County Jail
109.	1958 January 5	Amsterdam County Jail
110.	1958 January 19	Broadmeadow County Jail
111.	1958 January 26	Broadmeadow County Jail
112.	1958 February 17	Elmtown County Jail
113.	1958 March 9	Wardhill State Hospital
114.	1958 May 16	Davenport State Infirmary
115.	1958 July 5	Davenport State Infirmary
116.	1958 August 25	Davenport State Infirmary
117.	1958 October 5	Davenport State Infirmary
118.	1958 November 23	Davenport State Infirmary
119.	1958 November 30	Davenport State Infirmary
120.	1959 February 8	Davenport State Infirmary
121.	1959 April 25	Davenport State Infirmary
122.	1959 June 7	Davenport State Infirmary
123.	1959 July 28	Westville County Jail and House of Correction
124.	1959 August 29	Stonycreek Correctional Institution
125.	1959 September 15	Stonycreek Correctional Institution
126.	1959 September 26	Stonycreek Correctional Institution
127.	1959 October 2	Stonycreek Correctional Institution
128.	1959 October 14	Stonycreek Correctional Institution
129.	1959 October 30	Stonycreek Correctional Institution
130.	1959 December 3	Westville County Jail and House of Correction
131.	1960 January 6	Westville County Jail and House of Correction
132.	1960 January 15	Westville County Jail and House of Correction

133.	1960 February 11	Westville County Jail and House of Correction
134.	1960 March 23	Westville County Jail and House of Correction
135.	1960 March 30	Westville County Jail and House of Correction
136.	1960 April 15	Westville County Jail and House of Correction
137.	1960 April 25	Westville County Jail and House of Correction
138.	1960 May 3	Westville County Jail and House of Correction
139.	1960 May 12	Westville County Jail and House of Correction
140.	1960 May 30	Riverpoint County Jail
141.	1960 August 22	Westville County Jail and House of Correction
142.	1960 September 3	Westville County Jail and House of Correction
143.	1960 September 14	Stonycreek Correctional Institution
144.	1960 October 4	Stonycreek Correctional Institution
145.	1960 October 19	Stonycreek Correctional Institution
146.	1960 November 5	Stonycreek Correctional Institution
147.	1960 November 15	Stonycreek Correctional Institution
148.	1960 November 26	Stonycreek Correctional Institution
149.	1960 December 3	Stonycreek Correctional Institution
150.	1960 December 16	Westville County Jail and House of Correction
151.	1960 December 30	Westville County Jail and House of Correction
152.	1961 January 21	Liberty State Hospital
153.	1961 February 13	Liberty State Hospital
154.	1961 February 23	Liberty State Hospital
155.	1961 March 8	Liberty State Hospital
156.	1961 March 17	Liberty State Hospital
157.	1961 August 6	Liberty State Hospital
158.	1961 September 2	Wardhill State Hospital
159.	1961 September 11	Wardhill State Hospital
160.	1961 September 23	Wardhill State Hospital
161.	1961 September 29	Wardhill State Hospital
162.	1961 December 1	Wardhill State Hospital
163.	1961 December 13	Wardhill State Hospital
164.	1961 December 30	Wardhill State Hospital
165.	1962 January 8	Wardhill State Hospital
166.	1962 March 14	Liberty State Hospital
167.	1962 May 29	Stonycreek Correctional Institution
168.	1962 June 12	Stonycreek Correctional Institution
169.	1962 June 19	Stonycreek Correctional Institution
170.	1962 June 26	Stonycreek Correctional Institution
171.	1962 July 3	Stonycreek Correctional Institution
172.	1962 July 10	Stonycreek Correctional Institution
173.	1962 July 17	Stonycreek Correctional Institution
174.	1962 July 24	Stonycreek Correctional Institution
175.	1962 July 31	Stonycreek Correctional Institution
176.	1962 August 19	Anchorport City Jail
177.	1962 October 2	Stonycreek Correctional Institution
178.	1962 October 9	Stonycreek Correctional Institution
179.	1962 October 16	Stonycreek Correctional Institution

180.	1962 October 24	Stonycreek Correctional Institution
181.	1962 November 1	Stonycreek Correctional Institution
182.	1962 November 6	Stonycreek Correctional Institution
183.	1962 November 13	Stonycreek Correctional Institution
184.	1962 November 20	Stonycreek Correctional Institution
185.	1962 November 27	Stonycreek Correctional Institution
186.	1962 December 4	Stonycreek Correctional Institution
187.	1962 December 10	Stonycreek Correctional Institution
188.	1962 December 18	Stonycreek Correctional Institution
189.	1962 December 20	Stonycreek Correctional Institution (Christmas card)
190.	1962 December 26	Stonycreek Correctional Institution
191.	1963 January 1	Stonycreek Correctional Institution
192.	1963 January 8	Stonycreek Correctional Institution
193.	1963 January 15	Stonycreek Correctional Institution
194.	1963 January 22	Stonycreek Correctional Institution
195.	1963 January 29	Stonycreek Correctional Institution
196.	1963 February 5	Stonycreek Correctional Institution
197.	1963 February 6	Stonycreek Correctional Institution
198.	1963 February 12	Stonycreek Correctional Institution
199.	1963 February 19	Stonycreek Correctional Institution
200.	1963 February 26	Stonycreek Correctional Institution
201.	1963 April 24	Stonycreek Correctional Institution
202.	1963 May 3	Stonycreek Correctional Institution
203.	1963 May 7	Stonycreek Correctional Institution
204.	1963 May 14	Stonycreek Correctional Institution
205.	1963 May 21	Stonycreek Correctional Institution
206.	1963 May 28	Stonycreek Correctional Institution
207.	1963 June 4	Stonycreek Correctional Institution
208.	1963 June 15	Stonycreek Correctional Institution
209.	1963 June 18	Stonycreek Correctional Institution
210.	1963 June 26	Stonycreek Correctional Institution
211.	1963 July 2	Stonycreek Correctional Institution
212.	1963 July 19	Westville County Jail and House of Correction
213.	1963 September 20	Westville County Jail and House of Correction
214.	1963 October 5	Westville County Jail and House of Correction
215.	1963 October 10	Westville County Jail and House of Correction
216.	1963 October 18	Westville County Jail and House of Correction
217.	1963 October 25	Stonycreek Correctional Institution
218.	1963 November 1	Stonycreek Correctional Institution
219.	1963 November 8	Stonycreek Correctional Institution
220.	1963 November 8	Stonycreek Correctional Institution
221.	1963 November 15	Stonycreek Correctional Institution
222.	1963 November 22	Stonycreek Correctional Institution
223.	1963 November 29	Stonycreek Correctional Institution
224.	1963 December 6	Stonycreek Correctional Institution
225.	1963 December 13	Stonycreek Correctional Institution

226.	1963 December 20	Stonycreek Correctional Institution
227.	1963 December 27	Stonycreek Correctional Institution
228.	1964 January 10	Stonycreek Correctional Institution
229.	1964 January 17	Stonycreek Correctional Institution
230.	1964 January 31	Stonycreek Correctional Institution
231.	1964 February 7	Stonycreek Correctional Institution
232.	1964 February 14	Stonycreek Correctional Institution
233.	1964 April 2	Calvinville (c/o Postmaster)
234.	1964 April 14	Stonycreek Correctional Institution
235.	1964 April 28	Stonycreek Correctional Institution
236.	1964 May 26	Stonycreek Correctional Institution
237.	1964 June 2	Stonycreek Correctional Institution
238.	1964 June 16	Stonycreek Correctional Institution
239.	1964 June 22	Stonycréek Correctional Institution
240.	1964 July 8	Stonycreek Correctional Institution
241.	1964 July 14	Stonycreek Correctional Institution
242.	1964 July 21	Stonycreek Correctional Institution
243.	1964 December 1	Westville County Jail and House of Correction
244.	1964 December 14	Westville County Jail and House of Correction
245.	1964 December 21	Westville County Jail and House of Correction
246.	1964 December 28	Westville County Jail and House of Correction
247.	1965 January 4	Westville County Jail and House of Correction
248.	1965 February 2	Calvinville (Congress Hotel)
249.	1965 February 5	Calvinville (Congress Hotel)
250.	1965 February 15	Calvinville (Congress Hotel)
251.	1965 February 27	Calvinville (Congress Hotel)
252.	1965 March 17	Calvinville (Congress Hotel)
253.	1965 March 29	Calvinville (Congress Hotel)
254.	1965 April 26	Westville County Jail and House of Correction
255.	1965 May 11	Westville County Jail and House of Correction
256.	1965 May 18	Westville County Jail and House of Correction
257.	1965 May 25	Westville County Jail and House of Correction
258.	1965 June 1	Calvinville (Congress Hotel)
259.	1965 July 19	Stonycreek Correctional Institution
260.	1965 July 27	Stonycreek Correctional Institution
261.	1965 August 3	Stonycreek Correctional Institution
262.	1965 August 10	Stonycreek Correctional Institution
263.	1965 August 17	Stonycreek Correctional Institution
264.	1965 August 24	Stonycreek Correctional Institution
265.	1965 September 21	Calvinville (Congress Hotel)
266.	1965 October 14	Calvinville (Congress Hotel)
267.	1965 December 15	Calvinville (Congress Hotel)
268.	1966 January 14	Calvinville (Congress Hotel)
269.	1966 March 24	Calvinville (Congress Hotel)
270.	1966 June 9	Stonycreek Correctional Institution
271.	1966 June 21	Stonycreek Correctional Institution
272.	1966 June 29	Stonycreek Correctional Institution

273.	1966 July 13	Stonycreek Correctional Institution
274.	1966 July 19	Stonycreek Correctional Institution
275.	1966 July 26	Stonycreek Correctional Institution
276.	1966 August 9	Stonycreek Correctional Institution
277.	1966 August 16	Stonycreek Correctional Institution
278.	1966 August 22	Stonycreek Correctional Institution
279.	1966 August 30	Stonycreek Correctional Institution
280.	1966 September 6	Stonycreek Correctional Institution
281.	1966 September 13	Stonycreek Correctional Institution
282.	1966 September 20	Stonycreek Correctional Institution
283.	1966 September 27	Stonycreek Correctional Institution
284.	1966 October 17	Calvinville (46 Church Street)
285.	1966 December 1	Calvinville (46 Church Street)
286.	1967 February 24	Calvinville (46 Church Street)
287.	1967 April 17	Calvinville (46 Church Street)
288.	1967 August 24	Calvinville (46 Church Street)
289.	1967 December 14	Calvinville (Congress Hotel)
290.	1968 December 8	Calvinville (34 King Street)
291.	1968 December 10	Calvinville (34 King Street)
292.	1968 December 17	Calvinville (34 King Street)
293.	1969 February 9	Calvinville (34 King Street)
294.	1969 April 16	Calvinville (34 King Street)
295.	1969 April 27	Calvinville (34 King Street)
296.	1969 December 11	Westville County Jail and House of Correction
297.	1970 May 1	Westville (35 Grant St.)
298.	1970 May 27	Westville (35 Grant St.)
299.	1970 June 1	Westville (35 Grant St.)
300.	1970 August 6	Westville (35 Grant St.)
301.	1970 November 16	Westville County Jail and House of Correction
302.	1970 November 23	Westville County Jail and House of Correction
303.	1970 December 1	Westville County Jail and House of Correction
304.	1970 December 18	Davenport State Hospital
305.	1971 January 9	Westville Hospital
306.	1971 February 14	Middleway State Hospital
307.	1971 February 21	Middleway State Hospital
308.	1971 February 25	Middleway State Hospital
309.	1971 March 23	Middleway State Hospital
310.	1971 April 4	Westridge County Sanitarium
311.	1971 May 15	New Salem House, Westville
312.	1971 May 29	New Salem House, Westville
313.	1971 July 23	Westridge County Sanitarium
314.	1971 August 4	Westridge County Sanitarium
315.	1971 August 16	Westridge County Sanitarium
316.	1971 October 2	Adams Hotel, Westville
317.	1971 October 12	Benton County Jail
318.	1971 October 22	Benton County Jail
319.	1972 January 9	Stonycreek Correctional Institution

320.	1972 February 8	Stonycreek Correctional Institution
321.	1972 February 14	Stonycreek Correctional Institution
322.	1972 February 25	Stonycreek Correctional Institution
323.	1972 March 29	Harrison (217 Benjamin St.)
324.	1972 May 15	Harrison (217 Benjamin St.)
325.	1972 September 24	Telegram notice from landlady of 217 Benjamin St., Harrison, of Frank's death.

B. Letters from Roberta C. Greene to Robert Straus

1.	1948 December 13
2.	1948 December 20
3.	1949 January 4
4.	1950 February 25
5.	1950 March 9
6.	1950 March 15
7.	1950 April 28
8.	1952 November 28
9.	1953 May 11
10.	1954 November 6
11.	1955 November 3
12.	1956 March 5
13.	1956 August 10

C. Letters from Roberta C. Greene to Frank Moore

1.	1949 May 17
2.	1953 May 11
3.	1954 November 6

D. Letters from Frank Moore to Roberta C. Greene

1.	1947 December 9	Northway State Hospital
2.	1954 June 18	Heaven Hill
3.	1956 January 18	Sageville County Jail
4.	1956 June 23	Sageville County Jail
5.	1956 August 1	Sageville County Jail

Index

74 75 76 77 10 9 8 7 6 5 4 3 2 1